William Wordsworth

The Borders of Vision

The Source of the Arveyron, by Francis Towne (1781)

dumb cataracts and streams of ice—
A motionless array of mighty waves,
Five rivers broad and vast—
(1805 *Prelude*, vi. 458–60)

(By kind permission of Mr D. L. T. Oppé and Miss Armide Oppé.)

WILLIAM WORDSWORTH

The Borders of Vision

Jonathan Wordsworth

CLARENDON PRESS · OXFORD
1982

Oxford University Press, Walton Street, Oxford OX2 6DP
London Glasgow New York Toronto
Delhi Bombay Calcutta Madras Karachi
Kuala Lumpur Singapore Hong Kong Tokyo
Nairobi Dar es Salaam Cape Town
Melbourne Auckland

and associate companies in
Beirut Berlin Ibadan Mexico City

Published in the United States by
Oxford University Press, New York

British Library Cataloguing in Publication Data
Wordsworth, Jonathan
William Wordsworth: the borders of vision.
1. Wordsworth, William, 1770–1850—Criticism, and interpretation
I. Title
821'.7 PR5888
ISBN 0-19-812097-4

Library of Congress Cataloging in Publication Data
Wordsworth, Jonathan.
William Wordsworth: the borders of vision.
Bibliography: p.
Includes index.
1. Wordsworth, William, 1770–1850—Criticism and interpretation. I. Title.
PR5888.W65 821'.7 81-11327
ISBN 0-19-812097-4 AACR2

Set by Macmillan India Ltd.
and Printed in Great Britain
at the University Press, Oxford
by Eric Buckley
Printer to the University

In Memory of

Andrew Wordsworth

Preface

Not very surprisingly this book is intended to offer a way of thinking about Wordsworth's greatest poetry. In doing so it centres inevitably on the years of *Prelude* composition, 1798–1805, and I think of it as having rather the same shape as the full-length 1805 version of the poem. That is to say, it has a broadly chronological structure, but I have felt free at times, like the river of *The Prelude*, to turn and measure back my course. There are two reasons for this: first, that Wordsworth's poetry is backward-looking—it takes past experience for its subject, and judges itself by past achievement—and second, that my discussion is in fact sustained most of all by preoccupations (Wordsworth's and mine) that recur and interconnect. The book is not a collection of essays, but the individual chapters, like the different sections of *The Prelude*, can stand on their own and are deliberately varied in form and approach.

My concern has been to show what seems to me Wordsworth's amazingly consistent personal vision, in the context of his development and change. Some may feel that I emphasize too frequently the dates and facts of composition, but the circumstances in which the poetry was written altered very much during Wordsworth's most creative years, and only a sharp sense of chronology can enable one to isolate the qualities of mind and art that stay the same. The existence of three quite separate early versions of *The Prelude* (as well as numerous intervening drafts) offers a particularly interesting study of sameness and difference. Not only is more great poetry written for each—poetry that is in some ways characteristic, in others distinctively new—but passages from previous versions are switched about and used for different purposes. With an awareness of chronology one can see literary structures as counterpointed against the patterns of composition (the 'spots of time' sequence, for instance, has a new structural role in each successive version), and one can see how, and sometimes why, they cut across the patterns of actual experience. (The 'spots' *did* provide help in a particular situation in January 1799, but are *said* to have done so at two different much earlier periods as Wordsworth, in the years 1804–5, twice attempts to impose on his work structures deriving from Milton.)

Like the Glad Preamble of *Prelude*, Book I, with its self-defining allusions to *Paradise Lost*, and its mild creative internal breeze of imagination, Chapter One touches on much that will later be of central importance. It does not attempt to map things out, but suggests that Wordsworth's preoccupation with border vision and border states of mind, because it recurs over the years in so many forms and so many places, can provide a valuable way of looking at his poetry. Subsequent chapters return quite frequently to this preoccupation, noting its changing contexts and consistent motivation while presenting sometimes a critique of a single work (or portion of a work), sometimes a study of a mood, or mode, or moment of composition. Chapter Two examines Wordsworth's sense of election, and search for the origins of adult creativity, in Part I of the 1799 *Prelude* and related Goslar poetry. Chapter Three, though looking in detail at the Infant Babe, centrepiece of *1799*, Part II, does so in the wider context of Wordsworth's symbolic presentation of childhood. Chapters Four to Six look at the very different moods and achievements of three creative periods (the early months respectively of 1800, 1802, and 1804) that are at the centre of the book and of the poet's most productive years. Chapter Seven stands back to look at Wordsworth's seemingly very eccentric views of language, taking as its starting-point two passages from *Prelude*, Book V, and returning in conclusion once more to the Infant Babe. Chapter Eight discusses Wordsworth's successive and significantly unsuccessful attempts to introduce into *The Prelude* a personal Fall, and Nine examines Books VIII and VII (apparently so different, though written one after the other in the autumn of 1804) in the light of the poet's relationship to his fellow human beings. In Chapter Ten, the Climbing of Snowdon, taken out of its chronological sequence as it was by Wordsworth himself, is used to form a climax, and to pull together the recurring discussion of imagination. And in the Epilogue, the scheme for *The Recluse* (never completed by Wordsworth, and never adequately described by his critics) is taken as an opportunity to look back over the period already covered, and to range forward into the poet's middle and later years. Because of this final circling back, and because of its recurrent preoccupations, the book is to some extent repetitive. I would claim that it has to be so because that is the nature of the poet and poetry it seeks to describe.

Chapter One, and in a different sense the book as a whole, developed from my Chatterton Lecture of 1969, published in the *Proceedings of the British Academy*, lv (1969), and since reprinted in *English Romantic Poets*, ed. M. H. Abrams (2nd edn., 1975). Small parts of Chapter Two have appeared in the *Cornell Library Bulletin* (spring 1970) and *TLS* (11 November 1977), and an early version of Chapter Ten was published in *Bicentenary Wordsworth Studies* (1970). Chapters Six and Seven in their original form were lectures in honour respectively of Chester L. Shaver and M. H. Abrams; the first was printed privately at Oberlin College in 1974, the second appeared in *High Romantic Argument* (1981), ed. Lawrence Lipking. I should like to record my gratitude to my fellow Trustees of Dove Cottage for permission to quote from manuscript material at the Wordsworth Library. At different times I have been indebted to many scholars, and where I am conscious of the source of particular information I have acknowledged it in the Notes. I am afraid there will be cases where I have not been conscious: it wasn't until the book had been completed for months that I discovered, for instance, that its central view of the Wordsworthian borderer seems to recollect pages 201–2 of Geoffrey Hartman's *Wordsworth's Poetry, 1785–1815*. The Wordsworthian to whom I have been most and longest indebted is Mark Reed, who has been invariably generous with his material and never failed to answer questions by return of post however busy he might be. With Beth Darlington and James Butler I have had many useful discussions, and both have provided information that has been invaluable in establishing the texts in my Appendix. Michael Jaye has been most kind in answering questions about the chronology of *The Excursion*. Karen Green and Robert Osborn too have at different times given me details of the texts that they were preparing for the Cornell Wordsworth Series. Finally, I am fortunate to have been during the period when this book was written a Fellow of Exeter College, and to have had tolerant and expert help with my typing from Phyllis Boddington.

J. F. W

Contents

Note on Texts

In a book that lays stress on the original period and circumstances of composition, it is clearly important to quote Wordsworth's poetry in its earliest surviving versions. In all but a very few cases quotations are drawn from texts that I have published in the Norton Critical Edition of *The Prelude: 1799, 1805, 1850* (ed. with M. H. Abrams and Stephen Gill, 1979), or from those prepared for my forthcoming chronological edition of Wordsworth's poetry 1787–1807. Because they have been very extensively quoted in this book, and are still not available to the general reader of Wordsworth, three early texts—*The Pedlar*, the Prospectus to *The Recluse*, and *Home at Grasmere*—are presented as an Appendix. I have not thought it necessary to offer more than line-references to Wordsworth poems readily accessible in reprints of the early volumes (*Lyrical Ballads*, for instance). In other cases reference is made for the reader's convenience to editions of the admirable Cornell Wordsworth Series where they are in print, and, failing them, to the five-volume *Oxford Wordsworth* (ed. E. de Selincourt and Helen Darbishire, 1940–9); it should be emphasized, however, that my texts will differ frequently in accidentals, and on occasion in points of substance, from those that are cited.

Details of editions used for writers other than Wordsworth will be found in the Bibliography. In their principles these, of course, vary enormously. The texts in some are scrupulous almost to the point of facsimile, in others they have been modernized according to whatever principles are closest to the editor's heart. Yet all are in some sense of the word 'standard' editions. Myself I am largely in agreement with F. W. Bateson, who, as General Editor of the Longman Annotated English Poets, wrote 'whatever impedes the reader's sympathetic identification . . . whether of spelling, punctuation, or the use of initial capitals, must be regarded as undesirable.' Even readers who are aware that the use of initial capitals in the seventeenth and eighteenth centuries is sporadic (and quite as likely to belong to the printer as the writer concerned) cannot always prevent themselves reacting to it as a form of emphasis. And in a book where several authors may be quoted on a single page there is the further problem that as a result of the principles of their editions, Milton and Wordsworth may seem 'modern' beside Cowper and Coleridge. Or, again, the letters, or prose, of a single writer may seem 'old-fashioned' beside his verse. With these things in mind, I have taken the liberty of editing all quotations used in this book along the lines of my textual work on Wordsworth. In practice this has meant the removal of initial capitals (except for God, Nature, and personifications); the replacing of ampersands, and of apostrophes that occur in cases where a word would no longer be likely to be mispronounced; and a small amount of uncontroversial repunctuation (the removal, for instance, of excessive exclamation marks). Spelling has been left alone.

Italics in this book are mine unless (a) they are specifically attributed to the author who is being quoted, or (b) they occur in quotations from Coleridge and De Quincey.

Abbreviations

Bicentenary Studies	*Bicentenary Wordsworth Studies*, ed. Jonathan Wordsworth (Ithaca, N. Y., 1970).
BL	*Biographia Literaria*, ed. George Watson, Everyman's Library (1965).
BNYPL	*Bulletin of the New York Public Library.*
Butler	*William Wordsworth: 'The Ruined Cottage' and 'The Pedlar'*, ed. James Butler, Cornell Wordsworth Series (Ithaca, N. Y., 1979).
Casebook	*Wordsworth, 'The Prelude': A Casebook*, ed. W. J. Harvey and Richard Gravil (1972).
Chronology	Mark L. Reed, (i) *Wordsworth: The Chronology of the Early Years 1770–1799* (Cambridge, Mass., 1967); (ii) *Wordsworth: The Chronology of the Middle Years 1800–1815* (Cambridge, Mass., 1975).
CC	*Collected Coleridge*, Bollingen Series lxxv (Princeton, N. J.). i. *Lectures 1795 on Politics and Religion*, ed. Lewis Patton and Peter Mann (1971). ii. *The Watchman*, ed. Lewis Patton (1970). iii. *Essays on His Times*, ed. David V. Erdman (3 vols., 1978). iv. *The Friend*, ed. Barbara Rooke (2 vols., 1969). vi. *Lay Sermons*, ed. R. J. White (1972).
Darlington	*William Wordsworth: 'Home at Grasmere'*, ed. Beth Darlington, Cornell Wordsworth Series (Ithaca, N. Y., 1977).
D. C.	Dove Cottage.
EC	*Essays in Criticism.*

ELH	*English Literary History*.
Enquiry	Edmund Burke, *A Philosophical Enquiry into the Origin of our Ideas of the Sublime and Beautiful*, ed. J. T. Boulton (Oxford, 1958).
Erdman	*The Poetry and Prose of William Blake*, ed. David V. Erdman, Commentary by Harold Bloom (New York, 1965).
EY	*The Letters of William and Dorothy Wordsworth*, ed. E. de Selincourt, 2nd edn., *The Early Years, 1787–1805*, revised by Chester L. Shaver (Oxford, 1967).
Faulkner	Thomas Holcroft, *Anna St Ives*, ed. Peter Faulkner, Oxford English Novels (1970).
Gill	*William Wordsworth: 'The Salisbury Plain Poems'*, ed. Stephen Gill, Cornell Wordsworth Series (Ithaca, N. Y., 1975).
Griggs	*Collected Letters of Samuel Taylor Coleridge*, ed. E. L. Griggs (6 vols., Oxford, 1956–71).
Grosart	*The Prose Works of William Wordsworth*, ed. A. B. Grosart (3 vols., 1876).
Howe	Hazlitt, *Works*, ed. P. P. Howe (21 vols., 1930–4).
JEGP	*Journal of English and Germanic Philology*.
Jordan	*De Quincey as Critic*, ed. John E. Jordan (1973).
Ketcham	*The Letters of John Wordsworth*, ed. Carl H. Ketcham (Ithaca, N. Y., 1969).
Lefebvre	Georges Lefebvre, *The French Revolution from its Origins to 1793*, trans. Elizabeth Moss Evanson (1962).
LY	*The Letters of William and Dorothy Wordsworth*, ed. E. de Selincourt, 2nd edn., *The Later Years*, revised by Alan G. Hill, (i) *1821–28* (Oxford, 1978), (ii) *1829–34* (Oxford, 1979).
McCracken	William Godwin, *Caleb Williams*, ed. David McCracken, Oxford English Novels (1970).
Marrs	*The Letters of Charles and Mary Anne Lamb*, ed. Edwin W. Marrs, Jr. (3 vols., Ithaca, N. Y., 1975–8).
Masson	Thomas De Quincey, *Collected Writings*, ed. David Masson (14 vols., Edinburgh, 1889–90).

Mirror and the Lamp	M. H. Abrams, *The Mirror and the Lamp: Romantic Theory and the Critical Tradition* (Oxford, 1953).
Moorman	Mary Moorman, *William Wordsworth: A Biography*, (i) *The Early Years* (Oxford, 1957), (ii) *The Later Years* (Oxford, 1967).
Morley	*Henry Crabb Robinson on Books and their Writers*, ed. E. J. Morley (3 vols., 1938).
Music of Humanity	Jonathan Wordsworth, *The Music of Humanity* (1969).
MY	*The Letters of William and Dorothy Wordsworth*, ed. E. de Selincourt, 2nd edn., *The Middle Years*, (i) *1806–1811*, revised by Mary Moorman (Oxford, 1969), (ii) *1812–1820*, revised by Mary Moorman and Alan G. Hill (Oxford, 1970).
Natural Supernaturalism	M. H. Abrams, *Natural Supernaturalism* (New York, 1971).
New Perspectives	*New Perspectives on Coleridge and Wordsworth: Selected Papers from the English Institute*, ed. Geoffrey H. Hartman (New York, 1972).
NLH	*New Literary History*.
Norton *Prelude*	*William Wordsworth, 'The Prelude', 1799, 1805, 1850*, ed. Jonathan Wordsworth, M. H. Abrams, and Stephen Gill, Norton Critical Edition (New York, 1979).
Notebooks	*The Notebooks of Samuel Taylor Coleridge*, ed. Kathleen Coburn (6 vols., New York, 1957–73).
NQ	*Notes and Queries*.
Osborn	*William Wordsworth: 'The Borderers'*, ed. Robert Osborn, Cornell Wordsworth Series (Ithaca, N. Y., 1982).
Oxford *Prelude*	*William Wordsworth, 'The Prelude'*, ed. E. de Selincourt, 2nd edn. revised by H. Darbishire (Oxford, 1959).
Oxford Wordsworth	*The Poetical Works of William Wordsworth*, ed. E. de Selincourt and H. Darbishire (5 vols., Oxford, 1940–9).
Parrish	*William Wordsworth 'The Prelude', 1798–99*, ed. Stephen Parrish, Cornell Wordsworth Series (Ithaca, N. Y., 1977).

PJ	William Godwin, *An Enquiry concerning Political Justice*, (2 vols., 1793).
PL	*Paradise Lost, The Poems of John Milton*, ed. John Carey and Alastair Fowler, Longman Annotated Poets (1968).
PMLA	*Publications of the Modern Language Society of America*.
PQ	*Philological Quarterly*.
Prose Works	*Prose Works of William Wordsworth*, ed. W. J. B. Owen and Jane Worthington Smyser (3 vols., Oxford, 1974).
Raysor	*Coleridge's Shakespearean Criticism*, ed. Thomas Middleton Raysor (2 vols., 1930).
RES	*Review of English Studies*.
Sadler	*Diary, Reminiscences, and Correspondence of Henry Crabb Robinson*, ed. Thomas Sadler (3 vols., 1869).
SIB	*Studies in Bibliography*.
SIR	*Studies in Romanticism*.
TLS	*Times Literary Supplement*.
UTQ	*University of Toronto Quarterly*.
Vincent	*Letters of Dora Wordsworth*, ed. Howard P. Vincent (Chicago, 1944).
Ward	Thomas De Quincey, *Confessions of An English Opium-Eater and Other Writings*, ed. Aileen Ward, Signet Classics (New York, 1966).
WC	*Wordsworth Circle*.

Chapter 1

An Obscure Sense of Possible Sublimity

I seemed a being who had passed alone
Beyond the visible barriers of the world,
And travelled into things to come
(Wordsworth: *The Borderers*)

'One evening, walking in the public way', writes Wordsworth in spring 1804,

A peasant of the valley where I dwelt
Being my chance companion, he stopped short
And pointed to an object full in view
At a small distance. 'Twas a horse, that stood
Alone upon a little breast of ground
With a clear silver moonlight sky behind.
With one leg from the ground the creature stood,
Insensible and still; breath, motion gone,
Hairs, colour, all but shape and substance gone,
Mane, ears, and tail, as lifeless as the trunk
That had no stir of breath. We paused awhile
In pleasure of the sight, and left him there,
With all his functions silently sealed up,
Like an amphibious work of Nature's hand,
A borderer dwelling betwixt life and death,
A living statue or a statued life.

It is a very characteristic piece of work. No one else could have written it— perhaps no one else could have wished to write it. The faults (lame opening, final over-elaboration) are Wordsworth, and the virtues are Wordsworth. The draft in which it is found never became part of the 1805 *Prelude*, but was an attempt to provide sequels for the Climbing of Snowdon—further evidence that Nature can exert a power that 'moulds . . . endues, abstracts, combines' as does the human imagination.[1] In structure the passage is a 'spot of time', showing the expected progression from detailed and quite ordinary description, through the poet's heightened and heightening response, to a new, odder, and more general vision; the closest parallel in terms of form is probably the account of the blind London beggar in *1805*, Book VII.

Perhaps what one notices first about the poetry is its sense of wonderment:

> breath, motion gone,
> Hairs, colour, all but shape and substance gone,
> Mane, ears, and tail, as lifeless as the trunk
> That had no stir of breath . . .

The reiteration of 'gone' at the end of two consecutive lines, and the insistent return of the poet's mind to the absence of breath, convey a feeling almost of awe at the utter stillness of the animal. All the individually striking features and details—'hairs' is so much more impressive in this context than 'hair'—have been resolved into the essential facts of stillness, shape, and substance. It is an example if ever there was one of Wordsworth giving us eyes, enabling us to see what we might normally have missed, or passed; but one can overstress the ordinariness of what is happening. What the Grasmere peasant points out to the poet is a horse in the moonlight, sleeping as horses often do sleep, on three feet; what Wordsworth points out to us is something quite different. We are not, in this case at least, laid afresh on the cool flowery lap of earth, shown an object sparkling anew with the dewdrops of childhood. We are offered a strange, personal vision, child-like only in its intensity.

As 'an amphibious work of Nature's hand', the horse takes us back two years to the spring of 1802 and the most famous amphibian of Wordsworth's poetry, part sea-beast and part stone:

As a huge stone is sometimes seen to lie
Couched on the bald top of an eminence,
Wonder to all that do the same espy
By what means it could thither come, and whence,
So that it seems a thing endued with sense,
Like a sea-beast crawled forth, which on a shelf
Of rock or sand reposeth, there to sun itself—

Such seemed this man, not all alive nor dead,
Nor all asleep, in his extreme old age . . .

(*Leech Gatherer*, 64–72)

When first sighted the old man is exactly like the horse, just standing 'With all his functions silently sealed up'. The two of them inhabit a hinter-world, the Leech Gatherer 'not all alive nor dead,/Nor all asleep' and the horse specificially 'A borderer dwelling betwixt life and death'. One could, of course, say that Wordsworth was being whimsical, and really meant only that the man and horse were standing unusually still. Yet the Preface of 1815, though written long after the poetry it describes, suggests that at least the earlier of these two borderers was created with considerable care:

The stone is endowed with something of the power of life to approximate it to the sea-beast; and the sea-beast stripped of some of its vital qualities to assimilate it to the stone; which intermediate image is thus treated for the purpose of bringing the original image, that of the stone, to a nearer resemblance to the figure and condition of the aged man; who is divested of so much of the indications of life and motion as to bring him to the point where the two objects unite and coalesce in just comparison.

(*Prose Works*, iii. 33)

It could be that what we see here is Wordsworth the practical critic, rather than Wordsworth the poet recalling in detail the processes of creation; but there are many other examples in his poetry of this preoccupation with border-states. It is not very surprising to find old men singled out for their peacefulness, and horses asleep in the moonlight do have a certain numinous tranquillity, but the city of London in August 1802 turns out to have just the same attributes:

This city now doth like a garment wear
The beauty of the morning, silent, bare . . .

Ne'er saw I, never felt, a calm so deep—
The river glideth at his own sweet will—
Dear God, the very houses seem asleep,
And all that mighty heart is lying still.[2]
(*Upon Westminster Bridge*, 4–5, 11–14)

And a few months earlier the poet had addressed himself in still more surprising terms to a butterfly:

I've watched you now a full half-hour
Self-poized upon that yellow flower,
And little butterfly indeed
I know not if you sleep or feed.
How motionless! Not frozen seas
More motionless—and then,
What joy awaits you when the breeze
Shall find you out among the trees,
And call you forth again.
(*To a Butterfly*, 1–9)

'Not frozen seas/More motionless'—Coleridge might well have used the comparison in *Biographia Literaria* to exemplify '*mental* bombast', 'thoughts and images too great for the subject' (*BL* xxii. 258); yet this image of latent power, though ludicrous when applied to an insect, has interesting general implications. The butterfly makes it especially clear that these figures (London is human in Wordsworth's metaphor—wears clothes, and has a heart) are enviable not just for their peacefulness, but because in their extreme passivity they approach, or seem to approach, a boundary that is the entrance to another world. The analogy with Wordsworth himself is obvious. Clearly there is a sense in which the joy that awaits the butterfly among the trees is the same as the joy that enables the poet of *Tintern Abbey*, after being similarly 'laid asleep in body', to 'see into the life of things'. It is when his functions are 'silently sealed up', like those of the statue horse, that the poet is most aware of the song of the One Life:

in all things
I saw one life, and felt that it was joy;
One song they sang and it was audible—
Most audible then when the fleshly ear . . .
Forgot its functions and slept undisturbed.[3]

Kenneth Johnston has commented, 'In the realms of consciousness, Wordsworth is our first and greatest border poet.'[4] 'Greatest' is surely right, 'first' could perhaps be qualified a little.

It was Sir Thomas Browne who, in *Religio Medici* (1642) referred to man as 'the great *amphibium*', but his contemporary Marvell has in general far more striking affinities with Wordsworth. He too uses the image—the Unfortunate Lover is an '*amphibium* of life and death', the salmon-fishers of *Appleton House* become 'rational *amphibii*'—and like Wordsworth he is fascinated by human potential, by the overcoming of time and limitation.[5] In triumphant moments both poets are capable of

> Annihilating all that's made
> To a green thought in a green shade.
> (*Garden*, 47–8)

leaving the body's vest at the foot of the tree through an act of transcendent imagination. At other times they speculate about 'the soul, that drop, that ray/Of the clear fountain of eternal day', which, though responding differently to its new earth-bound situation, is capable in each of 'Remembering still its former height' (*On a Drop of Dew*, 19–22). More often they are both to be seen against a background of Nature asking questions about man. Marvell's fancy is anarchic ('And winnow from the chaff my head'), and his defensiveness rarely lets him confront a question directly:

> Thrice happy he who, not mistook,
> Hath read in Nature's mystick book.
> (*Appleton House*, 583–4)

But for all the differences of temperament, of date and wit and idiom, certain affinities remain. Marvell's salmon-fisher, shod in the canoe that is 'the dark *hemisphere*' of night, and death, is as surely a borderer as the Leech Gatherer, with his body 'bent double, feet and head/Coming together in their pilgrimage':

> But now the salmon-fishers moist
> Their leathern boats begin to hoist;
> And, like Antipodes in shoes,
> Have shod their heads in their canoos.
> How tortoise-like, but not so slow,

These rational *amphibii* go—
Let's in, for the dark hemisphere
Does now like one of them appear.
(*Appleton House*, 769–76)

That the seventeenth century should be especially rich in border poetry tells us much about the assumptions that underlie Romantic and later examples. Vaughan and Traherne seem more even than Marvell to anticipate the Wordsworth of *Intimations*,[6] and unexpectedly Herbert offers in the beautiful conclusion to *Prayer* something very close to the primary imagination:

Heaven in ordinarie, man well drest,
The milkie way, the bird of Paradise,
Church-bels beyond the starres heard, the souls bloud,
The land of spices; *something understood*.
(ll. 11–14)

Coleridge would have had no difficulty in thinking of prayer and imagination as synonymous—both equally 'the living power and prime agent of all human perception . . . a repetition in the finite mind of the eternal act of creation' (*BL* xiii. 167).[7] For the Christian, border vision is an act of faith: for those with less, or no, belief it is an imaginative compensation in the face of mortality and affronting human littleness. Keats, though he envies stout Cortez, 'Silent, upon a peak in Darien', and the Bright Star 'watching, with eternal lids apart',

Or gazing on the new soft-fallen mask
Of snow upon the mountains and the moors . . .
(ll. 3, 7–8)

is for the most part too uncompromising, too aware of being betrayed by the symbols that should be standing for hope. The Nightingale may offer permanence to his verse, but it does nothing to stop the man who writes it from being trodden down by hungry generations; the Urn will unfeelingly befriend the future when the poet's own generation has been wasted by old age. The border impulse seems at some level to be more optimistic, implying that the poetic spirit, and not just the poetry, may be transcendent. It is exemplified in the Shelley of *Alastor*, and *Mont Blanc:*

My own, my human mind, which passively
Now renders and receives fast influencings,
Holding an unremitting interchange
With the clear universe of things . . .

(ll. 37–40)

In different shapes and forms, it appears in Arnold's *Scholar Gypsy*, in Clough's 'luminous large intuition', and the 'moment, one and infinite' of Browning.[8] And among examples in this century, all looking back a little enviously to the uncomplicatedness of the Romantic border impulse, are the wish of Yeats in *Sailing to Byzantium* to be 'gathered' 'into the artifice of eternity', and Stevens's frequent reaching out for 'ghostlier demarcations, keener sounds':

Perhaps there are moments of awakening,
Extreme, fortuitous, personal, in which

We more than awaken, sit on the edge of sleep,
As on an elevation, and behold
The academies like structures in a mist.[9]

Wordsworth's borderers, border conditions, states of mind, implications, words, are so numerous and so ramified that they amount to a way of looking at his poetry as a whole. Or not quite as a whole: the poetry of suffering stands a little to one side. Looked at dispassionately, as the opposite to action which must necessarily be transient, suffering may seem to have all the border attributes. As Rivers puts it in *The Borderers:*

Action is transitory—a step, a blow,
The motion of a muscle this way or that,
'Tis done—and in the after-vacancy
We wonder at ourselves like men betrayed:
Suffering is permanent, obscure and dark,
And has the nature of infinity.

(III. v. 60–5)

There is some danger in reading these famous lines outside the two contexts in which Wordsworth himself presented them,[10] but even if their most general implications are allowed, they cannot apply to the great poetry of personal identification—*The Ruined Cottage*, *The Brothers*, *Michael*—where the poet suffers with, and within, his characters. Pain, for Wordsworth, however nobly borne and long-endured, is always of the moment, never loses its sharpness. The grandeur in the strength of Margaret's and Leonard's and Michael's love is no less impressive than the imaginative permanence that consists in loss of self, but it is essentially distinct. Suffering is dark because it cannot be comprehended, and because the universe that condones it cannot be comprehended, not because it is felt to contain the wisdom that is so often associated with obscurity. In a narrative of survival, the Female Vagrant may come out on the far side of pain, turn borderer on shipboard after the horrors of war are passed:

> And oft robbed of my perfect mind I thought
> At last my feet a resting-place had found;
> 'Here will I weep in peace' (so fancy wrought),
> 'Roaming the illimitable waters round . . .'[11]
>
> (*Female Vagrant*, 172–5)

For Margaret and Michael, however, endurance will last till death; there can be no comparable relief. 'I have slept/Weeping', says Margaret,

> 'and weeping have I waked. My tears
> Have flowed as if my body were not such
> As others are, and I could never die.'
>
> (*Ruined Cottage*, 354–7)

But her body *is* such as others are, and she will die in undiminished pain, 'one torturing hope . . . Fast rooted at her heart' (ll. 489–90). Only in retrospect, when the sharpness has gone, can she be seen as a borderer, and then significantly it is not within the narrative itself, but as a response to the needs of the teller. The Margaret who 'sleeps in the calm earth' at the end of the poem is euphemism, a needful consolation; not so the recurrent fantasy that the Pedlar has on his walks, of

> one
> By sorrow laid asleep or borne away,
> A human being destined to awake
> To human life, or something very near
> To human life, when he shall come again
> For whom she suffered.
>
> (ll. 370–5)

Robert will not come again, and Margaret would not wake if he could; but the urgency of Wordsworth's border compulsion consigns her to a limbo where love is stronger than time, and stronger than death. The Pedlar's fantasy belongs possibly to summer 1797, more probably to spring 1798; either way, like the Female Vagrant, 'Roaming the illimitable waters round', it is a very early example of border vision, and shows both how characteristic it is, and in what unexpected circumstances it may be found. The borderers of different periods vary according to the preoccupations of the moment, but the vision they reflect is very little changed. To know Wordsworth for the great poet he is, is to be sharply aware of change and development within his work, yet aware too of a strength that lies in sameness.

The point can be quickly made by placing the Old Man Travelling of May 1797 beside the blind London beggar of November 1804:

> He travels on, and in his face, his step,
> His gait, is one expression; every limb,
> His look and bending figure, all bespeak
> A man who does not move with pain, but moves
> With thought. He is insensibly subdued
> To settled quiet: he is one by whom
> All effort seems forgotten, one to whom
> Long patience has such mild composure given
> That patience now doth seem a thing of which
> He hath no need. He is by nature led
> To peace so perfect that the young behold
> With envy what the old man hardly feels.
>
> (*Old Man Travelling*, 3–14)

Pain has gone, effort has gone, patience—the most passive of virtues—is no longer needed; and in the last enigmatic lines it seems that even the peace, so enviable to others, is hardly felt by the man himself. And yet, despite this whittling away, what remains is a human being, not a symbol. The poet, one feels, is emotionally concerned; and the poem seeks to understand, not merely to define, the old man's state of mind. By 1804 all this is changed. Silent, propped, and blind, the London beggar is completely an object, save that a label attached to his chest claims for him human attributes—a story and a name:

lost
Amid the moving pageant, 'twas my chance
Abruptly to be smitten with the view
Of a blind beggar, who, with upright face,
Stood propped against a wall, upon his chest
Wearing a written paper, to explain
The story of the man, and who he was.
(*1805*, vii. 609–15)

The beggar exists not for himself, but for his impact on the poet. 'My mind', Wordsworth writes, 'did at this spectacle turn round/ As with the might of waters' (vii. 616–17).[12] We are back in the world where butterflies can be compared to frozen seas, where sleeping horses become 'amphibious work[s] of Nature's hand', or where—to use the case of '*mental* bombast' that did irritate Coleridge especially—a child can be the 'best philosopher', a 'mighty prophet, seer blest' (*Intimations*, 110, 114). And yet, if one looks more closely, the poet's border instincts are unchanged. It doesn't seem likely that many young people of the late 1790s envied the composure of elderly beggars; but Wordsworth did. Not that he wanted to be similarly peaceful himself—he was temperamentally more inclined to 'wish the winds might rage/ When they were silent' (*Pedlar*, 190–1)—but that the beggar has come out on the far side of pain, been led in life by nature (or Nature) to the perfect peace associated normally with death. As a state of mind, 'animal tranquillity and decay' offers the gentlest of border-crossings; and despite the lessening of human faculties involved, it can in its way be seen as an achievement.

Wordsworth gazes on the London beggar and his label 'as if admonished from another world' (*1805*, vii. 623), the Leech Gatherer appears 'like a man from some far region sent/To give [him] human strength and strong admonishment' (ll. 125–6), and even the most silent of the borderers act as an admonition.[13] Often, as Carroll and Beerbohm noticed (though not before Wordsworth himself), the poet is represented as compulsively asking them questions.[14] But of course there can be no answers. The borderers possess a symbolic, not an actual, wisdom: their existence is in itself a guarantee for the imagination of the possibility that truth may be attained. In February 1798, six months after *Old Man Travelling*, Wordsworth composed *The*

Discharged Soldier.[15] The poem's incorporation in *1805*, Book IV disguises both its many new border characteristics and the fact that it is the first of the 'spots of time', earlier by eight months than those of the 1799 *Prelude*. It begins, as does the 1804 account of the horse, with the poet walking by moonlight in 'the public way'; on this occasion, however, he is quite alone. The road has taken on the utter night-time stillness which London assumes in *Westminster Bridge*, and which is possible only in places normally frequented:

I love to walk
Along the public way when for the night,
Deserted in its silence, it assumes
A character of deeper quietness
Than pathless solitudes.

(ll. 1–5)

Responsive to its surroundings, the poet's body draws in a tranquil restoration—

Thus did I steal along that silent road,
My body from the stillness drinking in
A restoration like the calm of sleep
But sweeter far . . .

(ll. 21–4)

—and his mind turns inward, producing from the far region of its own inner depths a corresponding harmony:

What beauteous pictures now
Rose in harmonious imagery—they rose
As from some distant region of my soul
And came along like dreams, yet such as left
Obscurely mingled with their passing forms
A consciousness of animal delight,
A self-possession felt in every pause
And every gentle movement of my frame.

(ll. 28–35)

This is not just Wordsworth's earliest account of a mood of his own mind, it is exceptionally thoughtful poetry that has never received its due. Solipsism, so often 'self-closed, all repelling' (as in Blake's Urizen), is here open and creative. Reverie comes as the reward of total receptiveness, and never extinguishes the bodily awareness that is a vital part of this. The final self-possession is of a mind wholly sufficient, a body whose movements give delight even when suspended. The blanking-out of experience caused by darkness, solitude, stillness, has led to a refinement of the faculties, not to a restriction. The poet is '*sensibly* subdued to settled quiet'. In this mood, turning a sudden symbolic corner in the road, he comes upon a curious version of himself:

> a man cut off
> From all his kind, and more than half detached
> From his own nature.
>
> (ll. 58–60)

Reduction of the faculties has in this case led not to greater intensity, but to something that is disquietingly close to death:

> While thus I wandered step by step led on,
> It chanced a sudden turning of the road
> Presented to my view an uncouth shape
> So near that, stepping back into the shade
> Of a thick hawthorn, I could mark him well,
> Myself unseen. He was in stature tall,
> A foot above man's common measure tall,
> And lank, and upright. There was in his form
> A meagre stiffness. You might almost think
> That his bones wounded him. His legs were long,
> So long and shapeless that I looked at them
> Forgetful of the body they sustained.
> His arms were long and lean; his hands were bare;
> His visage, wasted though it seemed, was large
> In feature; his cheeks sunken; and his mouth
> Shewed ghastly in the moonlight. From behind
> A milestone propped him, and his figure seemed
> Half sitting and half standing. I could mark
> That he was clad in military garb,
> Though faded yet entire. His face was turned
> Towards the road, yet not as if he sought
> For any living thing. He appeared
> Forlorn and desolate, a man cut off

From all his kind, and more than half detached
From his own nature.

He was alone,
Had no attendant, neither dog, nor staff,
Nor knapsack—in his very dress appeared
A desolation, a simplicity,
That appertained to solitude. I think
If but a glove had dangled in his hand
It would have made him more akin to man.
Long time I scanned him with a mingled sense
Of fear and sorrow. From his lips meanwhile
There issued murmuring sounds as if of pain
Or of uneasy thought; yet still his form
Kept the same fearful steadiness. His shadow
Lay at his feet and moved not.[16]

(ll. 36–72)

One is almost surprised that the Soldier possesses a shadow. At the back of his mind Wordsworth has not only his own early description of an actual ghost in *The Vale of Esthwaite*, but also Milton's account of an uncouth shape whom Satan met at the gates of Hell, and whose name proved to be Death.[17] The poet's vision is awed; the details he recalls—the Soldier's unnatural height, meagre stiffness, ghastly mouth—have taken on an obsessional quality. The faded uniform is noticed as 'entire', but Wordsworth's sense of the man as 'more than half detached/ From his own nature' is reflected in a dislocation of his parts and faculties. His legs seem not related to the body they sustain, his bones may actually be wounding him, sounds issue from his lips over which he has apparently no control. So desolate is his solitude, that the poet in a vividly imaginative detail feels the wish to add something to him to make him seem more human:

I think
If but a glove had dangled in his hand
It would have made him more akin to man.

(ll. 64–6)

The Old Man Travelling had been subdued to an enviable composure, the Discharged Soldier is reduced to frightening inhumanity. Like the London beggar he is propped, has become in his fearful steadiness an object. The poet scans him in mingled fear and sorrow, but fear at this stage predominates.

Fear, however, can be over-emphasized.[18] To the poet in his creative reverie this seems a traveller who has returned from Hamlet's 'undiscovered country'—he is a ghost, or, as the Milton echo implies, a type of death. And yet he is also one who has approached (and not yet crossed) the border, by virtue of his extreme suffering. As such, he may be expected to have a wisdom to offer. The poet's awe never goes completely—

He appeared
To travel without pain, and I beheld
With ill-suppressed astonishment his tall
And ghostly figure moving at my side.

(ll. 121–4)

—but it is overcome by the border compulsion to ask questions:

While thus we travelled on *I did not fail*
To question him of what he had endured . . .

(ll. 136–7)

Finally the poet becomes over-confident, takes the Soldier's 'strange half absence' for feebleness, and is firmly put in his place:

[I] told him feeble as he was 'twere fit
He asked relief or alms. At this reproof
With the same ghastly mildness in his look
He said, 'My trust is in the God of heaven,
And in the eye of him that passes me'.

(ll. 160–4)

Like the child-borderers of *Lyrical Ballads* (Edward of *Anecdote for Fathers*, the nameless girl of *We are Seven*), the Soldier is shown to possess in imaginative terms more understanding than the poet who is bullying him. Which is to say that already in February 1798 Wordsworth himself understands the nature, even to some extent perhaps the cause, of his compulsive questioning. He describes the reproof administered in youthful arrogance to an old and suffering man, because the ghastly mildness of his countering rebuke holds out the possibility that questions may indeed be answered, wisdom attained.[19]

Wordsworth is of course perfectly clear that the Soldier does not himself possess such wisdom—or rather that he possesses it solely in the eye of the beholder. Though valuing, and taking comfort in, the thought of the man's faculties as being refined and not reduced, he states very precisely his actual limitations:

> solemn and sublime
> He might have seemed, but that in all he said
> There was a strange half-absence and a tone
> Of weakness and indifference, as of one
> Remembering the importance of his theme,
> But feeling it no longer.
>
> (ll. 140–5)

At the end of the poem the Soldier becomes 'the poor unhappy man', and here he is shown as prematurely aged, scarcely more alert than the Old Cumberland Beggar, who draws his scraps one by one from a bag and scans them 'with a fixed and serious look/ Of idle computation' (ll. 11–12). And yet there is the curious suggestion that but for his abstractedness he might have seemed 'solemn and sublime'. Again Wordsworth is echoing *Paradise Lost*, but this time the connection is with the Archangel Michael, who (rather less surprisingly) is 'solemn and sublime' when he descends to talk with the fallen Adam, 'Not in his shape celestial, but as man/Clad to meet man' (*PL* xi. 236–40). The Soldier's decrepitude, and his 'military garb,/Though faded, yet entire', have a ludicrous pathos beside Michael's full armour, his 'military vest of purple', and the 'starry helm' that he wears unbuckled to show his prime of angelic manhood; but if the link was a conscious one it is unlikely that it seemed incongruous to Wordsworth. Sublimity was an ideal that he did not invoke for nothing. The passage quoted connects *The Discharged Soldier* also to the highly important fragment, *In storm and tempest*, written at the same moment about the Pedlar who tells the story of *The Ruined Cottage*:

> there would he stand
> Beneath some rock listening to sounds that are
> The ghostly language of the ancient earth,
> Or make their dim abode in distant winds;
> Thence did he drink the visionary power.
> I deem not profitless these fleeting moods

Of shadowy exaltation: not for this,
That they are kindred to our purer mind
And intellectual life; but that the soul,
Remembering how she felt, but what she felt
Remembering not, retains an obscure sense
Of possible sublimity, at which
With growing faculties she doth aspire,
With faculties still growing, feeling still
That whatsoever point they gain, there still
Is something to pursue.[20]

The opening of *The Discharged Soldier* offers Wordsworth's first portrayal of reverie: *In storm and tempest* presents the first of those more exalted moods which, though in fact rare, have come to seem typical of his poetry. It becomes clear that what Wordsworth values above all is not achievement, but aspiration. The Soldier could not *be* solemn and sublime, because though remembering the importance of his theme he could no longer feel it. He is thus at the opposite pole from the Pedlar—or, one could say, from Wordsworth himself—who retains 'an obscure sense/ Of possible sublimity' by virtue of the fact that feeling has survived the loss of detailed memory. Feeling in this sense is for Wordsworth nothing less than the power of imaginative re-entry into past experience—the power that links past and present in the creative process described in the Preface to *Lyrical Ballads*, and forms as well the basis of future aspirations.[21] Through lack of such feeling the Soldier is constricted; its presence in the poet himself will guarantee him during his great creative years the principle of growth, expansion of the faculties.

In storm and tempest shows Wordsworth writing Wordsworthian philosophical poetry as if he had been writing it for years. Especially remarkable in his handling of the new idiom are the casualness with which the Pedlar is introduced standing under 'some rock' (any old rock) yet listening to 'The ghostly language of the ancient earth', and the control of tone that enables this act of communion then to be glossed as a mood of shadowy exaltation. One is left with an impression that great claims have been made, and yet no certainty as to what they amount to. In what sense are the sounds ghostly (spiritual)? How do they constitute a language? How are they related to Coleridge's Berkeleyan views of the symbol-language of God:

> all that meets the bodily sense I deem
> Symbolical, one mighty alphabet
> For infant minds . . .[22]
>
> (*Destiny of Nations*, 18–20)

No questions are answered, or can be answered, because Wordsworth is writing a poetry of deliberate imprecision. He sets up numinous suggestions, half undercuts them—just how reductive are the adjectives 'fleeting' and 'shadowy'?—and leaves them to work in the mind. His concern is with imminence, with the *possible* sublimity that will always lead on, because it will never be realized. Certain words and states in his poetry alert one at once to this border potential. Solitude and silence are almost invariable preconditions, together with that kind of stillness that is opposed to fixity (which in Blake and Wordsworth alike is the universe of imaginative death). Waiting and wandering both often suggest the urgency of the borderer's quest:

> In my mind's eye I seemed to see him pace
> About the weary moors continually,
> Wandering about alone and silently . . .
>
> (*Leech Gatherer*, 143–5)

Another group of words gives expression to the poet's own vital unease: from the same passage of *The Leech Gatherer*, 'the lonely place/The old man's shape, and speech, all *troubled* me'; or in *Tintern Abbey*, 'I have felt/A presence that *disturbs* me with the joy/ Of elevated thoughts' (ll. 94–6). Sourcelessness, the fact of having no apparent origin, becomes oddly important: the sounds of the earth's ghostly language 'make their *dim abode* in *distant* winds', the cuckoo's is a wandering voice, on Snowdon there is 'the *homeless* voice of waters' (*1805*, xiii. 63), the mist of imagination comes athwart the poet 'Like an *unfathered* vapour' (vi. 527), the smoke in *Tintern Abbey* is sent up 'With some *uncertain* notice' (l. 20). Incomprehensibility, or difficulty of perception, is closely related: the songs of the Danish Boy and the Solitary Reaper are in foreign tongues; the 'obscure sense' is valued partly *for* its obscurity,

> Suffering is permanent, *obscure and dark*,
> And has the nature of infinity.

The Wordsworthian double negative, though often tedious, can be very effective in its border implications: '*Not without the voice*/Of mountain echoes did my boat move on' (*1799*, i. 91–2),

the distant hills
Into the tumult sent an alien sound
Of melancholy, *not unnoticed* . . . [23]

(*1799*, i. 165–7)

Such imprecision implies, or allows, the sense of 'something evermore *about to be*', that is essential to Wordsworth's vision, and is so frequently to be found at the centre of his greatest poetry.[24]

No Wordsworth poem more skilfully uses the border language, or more beautifully evokes the yearnings, than *Stepping Westward.* In September 1803, the poet and Dorothy, walking at sunset on the shore of Loch Ketterine, were greeted by the strange half-question, 'What, you are stepping westward?'. Almost two years later, in June 1805, when Dorothy was copying her *Recollections* of the Scottish tour, Wordsworth turned the memory into a poem full of tender numinous suggestion:

'What, you are stepping westward?' 'Yea.'
—'Twould be a wildish destiny
If we, who thus together roam
In a strange land and far from home,
Were in this place the guests of chance;
Yet who would stop, or fear to advance,
Though home or shelter he had none,
With such a sky to lead him on?

The dewy ground was dark and cold,
Behind all gloomy to behold,
And stepping westward seemed to be
A kind of *heavenly* destiny.
I liked the greeting: 'twas a sound
Of something without place or bound,
And seemed to give me spiritual right
To travel through that region bright.

The voice was soft, and she who spake
Was walking by her native lake;
The salutation had to me
The very sound of courtesy.

Its power was felt; and while my eye
Was fixed upon the glowing sky
The echo of the voice enwrought
A human sweetness with the thought
Of travelling through the world that lay
Before me in my endless way.

In completing *The Prelude*, only a fortnight before, Wordsworth had spoken of the mind of man as 'A thousand times more beautiful than the earth/On which he dwells' (*1805* xiii. 447–8), but now he seems to be taking time off from the big assertions. Despite the recent death of his brother,[25] he is for a moment relaxed, and pleased, and happy to share his pleasure: "I liked the greeting . . .'

Even though the italics are Wordsworth's, it would be a mistake in *Stepping Westward* to read too much significance into '*heavenly* destiny', or to see in the glowing beauty of the sky a promise of the Christian afterlife. Associations of the west and sunset with finality—Henry King's 'west of life' (*The Exequy*)—are qualified by Wordsworth's sense of the endlessness of the present participle. Stepping westward has become a guarantee of never-reaching, and therefore of never sinking into stasis and death—never *needing* rebirth. Taking on a life of the mind, the woman's greeting is released not merely from space and time, but from the limitations of language as well:

'twas a sound
Of something without place or bound,
And seemed to give me spiritual right
To travel through that region bright.

Dorothy, and the terrestrial journal that she and the poet were making, have disappeared. The greeting has become pure sound, the perfect evocation of boundlessness. It confers the right to travel not in, but *through*, a 'region bright' of childlike wonderment, untrammeled imagination. The poetry, it seems, has floated free of constriction. Fixed on the sunset, the eye has been made quiet, lost its dominance; the senses are laid asleep. And yet the echo of the woman's voice, as it comes back within the mind, brings alongside its intimation of immortality a return of the merely human:

> and while my eye
> Was fixed upon the glowing sky
> The echo of the voice enwrought
> A human sweetness with the thought
> Of travelling through the world that lay
> Before me in my endless way.

The image, if one thinks about it, seems to work in two quite different ways, so that human sweetness may be either cause or effect of the poet's final imaginative response.[26] With such intermingling, perhaps it is safer to say that it is both. Aspiration and the wish for permanence—the world as an 'endless way'—spring from the value that Wordsworth sets on transient human joy; and the joy in its turn is exalted by his feeling that we are greater than we know.

Wordsworth is not of course entirely idiosyncratic in his methods and preoccupations. Coleridge, in the Shakespeare Lectures of 1811–12, identifies 'a middle state of mind more strictly appropriate to the imagination than any other, when it is, as it were, hovering between images'. 'As soon as it is fixed on one image', he continues, 'it becomes understanding; but while it is unfixed and wavering between them, attaching itself permanently to none, it is imagination.' The relevance to Wordsworth's border imagery is obvious, but the poet whom Coleridge goes on to quote is Milton. Whether by chance or otherwise, his thoughts turn to the description of Death that lies behind *The Discharged Soldier*: 'The other shape,/ If shape it might be called . . . '. 'The grandest efforts of poetry', he concludes,

> are where the imagination is called forth, not to produce a distinct form, but a strong working of the mind, still offering what is still repelled, and again creating what is again rejected; the result being what the poet wishes to impress, namely, the substitution of a sublime feeling of the unimaginable for a mere image.
>
> (Raysor, ii. 138)

The passage could stand as an account of Wordsworth at his greatest—'a strong working of the mind, still offering what is still repelled, and again creating what is again rejected'—but its thinking is referred by the editor to Richter, Schiller, and Kant;[27] and behind these distinguished figures (whom Wordsworth could not have known) must lie the dominant English late-eighteenth-century influence of Burke. The *Philosophical Enquiry into the Origin of our Ideas of the Sublime and Beautiful* (1757) had been so widely read, quoted, plagiarized, that it would be difficult to prove a direct connection, but it is interesting that Burke should single out Milton as having known better than any 'the secret of heightening, or of setting terrible things . . . in their strongest light *by the force of judicious obscurity*', and more so that he should happen to quote in this context the very same passage from *Paradise Lost*:

it is astonishing with what a gloomy pomp, with what a significant and expressive uncertainty of strokes and colouring he has finished the portrait of the king of terrors.

> The other shape
> If shape it might be called that shape had none
> Distinguishable, in member, joint, or limb . . .

In this description all is dark, uncertain, confused, terrible, and sublime to the last degree.[28]

The Burkean stress on terror as the source of the sublime would have appealed to Wordsworth only in certain moods—at other times he would surely have preferred Blair's emphasis on power[29]—but there is no doubt that he would have sided with Burke against his critics on the virtues of obscurity in language:

hardly any thing can strike the mind with its greatness, which does not make some sort of approach towards infinity; which nothing can do whilst we are able to perceive its bounds; but to see an object distinctly, and to perceive its bounds, is one and the same thing. A clear idea is therefore another name for a little idea.[30]

Wordsworth's poetry of aspiration is above all a refusal of littleness, an approach to infinity. As Burke put it elsewhere, 'the imagination is entertained with the promise of something more, and does not acquiesce in the present object of the sense' (*Enquiry*, 77).

Three times in his life Wordsworth seems for a short period actually to have lived on the level of his aspirations. The first of these occasions, known to us only through retrospect in *The Prelude*, was during his commitment in 1792 to the then peaceful and prospering French Revolution:

> Bliss was it in that dawn to be alive,
> But to be young was very heaven . . .
>
> earth was then
> To me what an inheritance new-fallen
> Seems, when the first time visited . . .[31]
>
> (*1805*, x. 692–3, 728–30)

The *last* of these periods of lived aspiration belongs to early 1800. To the poet, newly established with Dorothy at Dove Cottage, it seemed for a moment that all his hopes had been achieved, and paradise regained:

> surpassing grace
> To me hath been voutchsafed. Among the bowers
> Of blissful Eden this was neither given,
> Nor could be given—possession of the good
> Which had been sighed for, antient thought fulfilled,
> And dear imaginations realized
> Up to their highest measure . . .[32]
>
> (*Home at Grasmere*, 122–8)

But neither of these periods, important as they were, had such lasting significance for Wordsworth's poetry as the spring of 1798, which he and Dorothy spent at Alfoxden to be near Coleridge. The three moments have in common personal relationships of unusual intensity, and moods of buoyant optimism that were not very likely to be sustained. It was through Michel Beaupuy (and in some measure, no doubt, Annette Vallon) that Wordsworth became a patriot in 1792; in 1800 it was Dorothy's presence that made life at Grasmere seem 'A promise and an earnest' of future millennial happiness; and the acceptance of pantheism in spring '98 came as a result not of rigorous philosophical enquiry, but of the excitement of being and working with Coleridge. Pantheism was almost an expression of the mood of the moment. Wordsworth could write of the Pedlar 'in all things/He saw one life, and felt that it was joy' (ll. 217–18), because he himself had joy to spare. Coleridge's Unitarianism—he had very nearly become a minister in January—was taken over not as a form of Christian doctrine or worship, but as a confirmation of

Wordsworth's own intuitions. He may well already have believed, as many did in the 1790s, that 'There [was] an active principle alive/In all things',[33] and under Coleridge's influence he went on from this quite ordinary position to assert a universe of blessedness and love, based on the assumption that the individual could perceive as well as share 'the life of things'. To put it in Berkeleyan terms, as Coleridge did at exactly this time in *Frost at Midnight*, the individual could interpret the symbols of Nature,

> see and hear
> The lovely shapes and sounds intelligible
> Of that eternal language, which . . . God
> Utters, who from eternity doth teach
> Himself in all, and all things in himself.
>
> (ll. 58–62)

It was a moment not just of private exaltation, but of certainty lived and shared. On 6 March Wordsworth announced his scheme for *The Recluse*, the great never-completed philosophical work that was to be written for the betterment of man (*EY* 212). And four days later Coleridge, quoting Wordsworth, shows how pantheism—had the belief persisted—could have become the millenarian vision that *The Recluse* was designed to convey:

> Not useless do I deem
> These shadowy sympathies with things that hold
> An inarticulate language: for the man
> Once taught to love such objects, as excite
> No morbid passions, no disquietude,
> No vengeance and no hatred, needs must feel
> The joy of that pure principle of love
> So deeply, that, unsatisfied with aught
> Less pure and exquisite, he cannot chuse
> But seek for objects of a kindred love
> In fellow-natures . . .[34]
>
> (Griggs, i. 397–8)

But the belief did not persist—or at least it seems never again to have had quite the same compelling force. Coleridge's retreat from the One Life began rather later, and took the form of a theological debate that left him Trinitarian in theory, Unitarian still at heart.[35] Wordsworth's retreat from what had amounted to his personal version of Unitarianism seems to have begun almost as soon as he left Alfoxden and Coleridge's inspiring companionship; but at no stage can he be pinned down to a precise philosophical position, and he is capable not only of incorporating old pantheist material in later poems, but also at times of writing new.[36] Looking back, he seems not to have thought of his views as having changed, and such is the consistency of his intuition that there is an important sense in which they hadn't. The exalted belief of spring 1798, though, he never again achieved. Even in *Tintern Abbey*, written only four months after *The Pedlar*, and containing the grandest of all Wordsworth's pantheist affirmations ('And I have felt/A presence . . . '), there is some doubt as to whether the elegiac voice does not imply a sense of lessening conviction:

> That time is past,
> And all its aching joys are now no more,
> And all its dizzy raptures. Not for this
> Faint I, nor mourn, nor murmur: other gifts
> Have followed, for such loss, I would believe,
> Abundant recompense.
>
> (ll. 84–9)

One would expect *Tintern Abbey* as a revisit-poem to be nostalgic about the past, and no one can ever have felt more deeply than Wordsworth the loss of early, unthinking, uncomplicated response to Nature, but it remains an astonishing context in which to claim the ability to perceive and embody the presence of God. There is no doubt that that is what Wordsworth *is* claiming, and that he takes the claim seriously:

> And I have felt
> A presence that disturbs me with the joy
> Of elevated thoughts, a sense sublime
> Of something far more deeply interfused,
> Whose dwelling is the light of setting suns,
> And the round ocean, and the living air,
> And the blue sky, and in the mind of man—
> A motion and a spirit that impels

All thinking things, all objects of all thought,
And rolls through all things.

(ll. 94–103)

'*Therefore*', the passage continues, 'am I still/A lover of the meadows and the woods . . . '. Wordsworth is resting his continued love of the natural world firmly on the presence of the One Life. It is because the One Life can be perceived through the human senses that he can find, or claim to find, in Nature

The anchor of my purest thoughts, the nurse,
The guide, the guardian of my heart, and soul
Of all my moral being.

(ll. 110–12)

Yet for all this, the regret in *Tintern Abbey* is so strong that it comes near to undermining the affirmation: 'for such loss, *I would believe*,/Abundant recompence'. One is left remembering the earlier juxtaposition in the poem, when the beautiful and compelling enactment of mystical experience—the moment where if anywhere in his poetry Wordsworth carries us with him to the borders of vision, creating in his rhythms a sense of what it might be like to lose one's bodily awareness, see into the life of things—is qualified by a sudden paltry taking into account of other people's views:

that blessed mood,
In which the burthen of the mystery,
In which the heavy and the weary weight
Of all this unintelligible world
Is lightened—that serene and blessed mood,
In which the affections gently lead us on,
Until, the breath of this corporeal frame,
And even the motion of our human blood
Almost suspended, we are laid asleep
In body, and become a living soul;
While, with an eye made quiet by the power
Of harmony, and the deep power of joy,
We see into the life of things.

If this
Be but a vain belief . . .

(ll. 38–51)

In the fervour of spring '98 there had been no room for such a possibility, just as there had been no feeling that the shared joy of the One Life could be second best to earlier, dizzier raptures. Perhaps the belief itself was still the same in July, but the quality had surely changed.

By the end of the year, with the poet and his sister now at Goslar, there is an entirely new Wordsworth, the Wordsworth of the Lucy Poems and Part I of the 1799 *Prelude*. Pantheism in any full sense of the word has almost disappeared from his writing, and with it the 'chearful faith that all which we behold/Is full of blessings' (*Tintern Abbey*, 134–5). There are no more trances, moments of exaltation in which the individual enters into direct contact with the principle of being; but the border vision—in abeyance as one would expect while the poet felt himself to be a borderer—has returned in a vividly imaginative form:

> A slumber did my spirit seal,
> I had no human fears:
> She seemed a thing that could not feel
> The touch of earthly years.
>
> No motion has she now, no force,
> She neither hears nor sees,
> Rolled round in earth's diurnal course
> With rocks and stones and trees.

The poem suffers from being so famous that it is difficult to think about; but it shows clearly the change that has taken place. As David Ferry puts it, the Lucy Poems symbolize Wordsworth's relation to the eternal,[37] and this move into a world of symbols is very important. *A slumber* in fact opens with an actual loss of bodily awareness, but the poem then goes on to present what is, or can be seen as, a re-enactment of the process in symbolic terms. In her death Lucy achieves the harmony to which the poet himself had recently attained.[38] Or perhaps one should say she achieves a state which is essentially like his in one respect, essentially distinct in another. To claim that Wordsworth's insight is now into a world of death would be too literal-minded—death had after all been the central metaphor of *Tintern Abbey* ('laid asleep/In body, and become a living soul')—but the poem has lost its immediate relevance to life. The

Wordsworth of *Tintern Abbey* had been, or assumed himself to be, firmly anchored in the ordinary world. His seeing 'into the life of things' had been '*that* serene and blessed mood', a mood which others would know about too, and from which he had returned with a message of optimism applicable to all. Now, by contrast, he has moved very obviously into the realm of wish-fulfilment.

It is the same with the companion-poem, *Three years she grew*, though in this case Lucy is an active rather than a passive borderer—or, to be more precise, she crosses the border into an active rather than a passive harmony. She dies into a life that she could perfectly well have lived:

> 'She shall be sportive as the fawn,
> That wild with glee across the lawn
> Or up the mountain springs,
> And hers shall be the breathing balm,
> And hers the silence and the calm
> Of mute insensate things.
>
> . . .
>
> And vital feelings of delight
> Shall rear her form to stately height,
> Her virgin bosom swell—
> Such thoughts to Lucy I will give
> While she and I together live
> Here in this happy dell.'
>
> (ll. 13–18, 31–6)

It is not, of course, a lover with whom Lucy will share 'this happy dell', but Nature, in effect death:

> Thus Nature spake—the work was done—
> How soon my Lucy's race was run!
> She died, and left to me
> This heath, this calm and quiet scene,
> The memory of what has been,
> And never more will be.
>
> (ll. 37–42)

What put it into Wordsworth's head to write these beautiful, elegiac love-poems we shall never know.[39] Love is no doubt part of the answer—Coleridge associated *A slumber did my spirit seal* with a morbid fantasy that Dorothy might die (Griggs, i. 479)—but just as Hopkins's Margaret grieves for herself not Goldengrove, so one feels that there is a sense in which Wordsworth is the subject of his own lament. Less than a year before he had believed passionately in a harmony accessible to all: now he could envisage it only in a private other-world of abstraction. He had known what it was to share, or to believe he shared, 'the breathing balm . . . the silence and the calm/Of mute insensate things', and was now left with 'The memory of what [had] been/And never more [would] be'. Yet there is a danger of overstressing the sense of personal loss. More remarkable as one reads is the delicacy of the imaginative harmony that has replaced the actualities of Alfoxden. Wordsworth's beliefs have changed, or certainly are no longer felt with the same immediacy, but the sense of possible sublimity is as strong as before. The border vision is merely finding new symbolic forms.

If one moves across to the blank verse of the Goslar period, and the beginnings of *The Prelude*—Part I of *1799*, *Nutting*, *There was a boy*—it is to find a very similar process taking place. Wordsworth is not creating symbol-worlds, but trying to see his own past as evidence of total harmony and personal election. His concern is suddenly with the phase dismissed in *Tintern Abbey* as 'The coarser pleasures of my boyish days /And their glad animal movements' (ll. 74–5)—the phase before Nature became all in all, and the sounding cataract began to haunt him like a passion. Only once at this period does he portray responsiveness in any ordinary sense, and then it is unconscious:

And when it chanced
That pauses of deep silence mocked his skill,
Then sometimes in that silence, while he hung
Listening, a gentle shock of mild surprize
Has carried far into his heart the voice
Of mountain torrents; or the visible scene
Would enter unawares into his mind
With all its solemn imagery, its rocks,
Its woods, and that uncertain heaven, received
Into the bosom of the steady lake.

(*There was a boy*, 16–25)

In this most perfect of the early portrayals of a border-state, the lake takes on humanity (receiving the moving cloudscape into its reassuringly steady bosom, just as the boy captures a mental image of the landscape as a whole), and the voice of torrents—similarly human—is carried far into a heart that has assumed the vastness of exterior space. De Quincey's response was absolutely right:

> This very expression, 'far', by which space and its infinities are attributed to the human heart, and to its capacities of re-echoing the sublimities of Nature, has always struck me as with a flash of sublime revelation.[40]

The tones and quality of the poetry are so impressive that we do read it very much in terms of 'sublime revelation', and yet 'the sublimities of Nature' (De Quincey was presumably not conscious of opposing the two phrases) amount in this case to a background noise of streams, and a perfectly ordinary Cumbrian landscape.[41] Transcendental possibilities are touched in very lightly by 'that uncertain heaven'—'heaven is not the same as 'sky'; and uncertainty, here as elsewhere, is a border condition—but this is a world animated only through metaphor. Nature and man interchange, coalesce, as do the stone and sea-beast of *The Leech Gatherer*, and not in a pantheist sharing. The internalized landscape that the boy receives is of infinite value, but there is no reason to think that mid the din of towns and cities it will provide the basis of future mystical experience.

The pantheism that does appear at Goslar, in *1799*, Part I, and in *Nutting*—

> Then, dearest maiden, move along these shades
> In gentleness of heart, with gentle hand
> Touch, for there is a spirit in the woods.
>
> (ll. 53–5)

—has a strangely sub-classical air. In place of the pervasive life-force of *The Pedlar* and *Tintern Abbey* there are tutelary spirits, 'a godkin or goddessling', in Coleridge's later phrase (Griggs, ii. 865). To some extent perhaps these may have stood for the One Life in the poet's mind, but even when the spirit-world is used in Part I to convey his sense of having had a favoured childhood, it is too literary to be taken very seriously:

> Ye powers of earth, ye genii of the springs,
> And ye that have your voices in the clouds,
> And ye that are familiars of the lakes
> And of the standing pools, I may not think

A vulgar hope was yours when ye employed
Such ministry . . .

(*1799*, i. 186–91)

The supernatural machinery provides Wordsworth with a means of grouping recollections that seem to him of particular importance,[42] and it noticeably disappears in the second half of Part I when, *c.* January 1799, he arrives at his theory of memory as nourishment and inspiration:

There are in our existence spots of time
Which with distinct preeminence retain
A fructifying virtue, whence, depressed
By trivial occupations and the round
Of ordinary intercourse, our minds—
Especially the imaginative power—
Are nourished and invisibly repaired;
Such moments chiefly seem to have their date
In our first childhood.

(*1799*, i. 288–96)

In *Tintern Abbey* passing responses had similarly been held to contain potential for the future, but then the poet's memories had been of a landscape beautiful in itself and permeated by the One Life. Now it seems that not only pleasant, but also painful experiences can be fruitful,[43] and even those which at the time seem to hold no significance at all. In returning over the years to a specific moment, the mind both establishes it in the memory and guarantees its future importance. Wordsworth is in effect re-writing *Tintern Abbey* in untranscendental terms. As before, it is the memory that lightens

the heavy and the weary weight
Of all this unintelligible world . . .

(*Tintern Abbey*, 40–1)

but the process has been secularized. The pantheist claims have gone, and there has been no attempt to replace them. Wordsworth asserts that his early memories have a restorative power, but was perhaps less well placed than his readers to see why this should have been so. Though varying in mood from the tranquillity achieved in *There was a boy* and the skating lines, to the guilty apprehension of 'unknown modes of being' or the sense of 'visionary dreariness' (the boat-stealing episode, and that of the Woman on the Hill), the 'spots of time' have the power to strengthen and reassure because they stand in the poet's mind for the ability of the individual to transcend the limits of ordinary experience. As a child he himself had been a borderer, approached unknowingly the verge of the sublime: as an adult he derives from this early experience a strength that enables him consciously to aspire towards sublimity.

The impressive assurance of this Goslar poetry carries forward into the work of the following year. The Infant Babe of *1799*, Part II becomes the ultimate child-borderer as the poet goes back yet further in his search for origins, asking questions about the very earliest sources of adult security and power.[44] Spring 1800 has a quality of its own: day-to-day living achieves the intensity of visionary experience, and the poetry (*Home at Grasmere*) exists to an unusual degree to celebrate the present and the actual. It is the work of 1802 and 1804 that shows how much border vision comes to be associated with re-entry to the pantheist world of Alfoxden. Looking backwards Wordsworth now sees childhood and early 1798 as two golden ages of his past, and a merging of the two takes place in *Intimations*, in which childhood—relatively unimportant at the time of *Tintern Abbey*—becomes symbolic of the promise that the One Life had briefly seemed to hold.[45] In addition to childhood there is a proliferation of border images of every kind as Wordsworth, as this last and greatest of his creative periods, seeks imaginatively for the peace and certainty that elude his conscious mind. 'Me this unchartered freedom tires . . . I long for a repose which ever is the same', he writes in February 1804 (*Ode to Duty*, 37–40); yet within a matter of weeks he had written, or was to write, the last two-thirds of *Intimations*, the Quixote dream of *1805*, Book V, the Climbing of Snowdon, the description of a horse with which this chapter began, the Book VI lines on imagination, and the Simplon Pass—all of them unrestful border poetry. One way to show how far he had come, yet how much he craves the earlier certitude, is to put beside the Simplon Pass the Pedlar's 'high hour/Of visitation from the living God' (February 1798):

> The ocean and the earth beneath him lay
> In gladness and deep joy. The clouds were touched,

And in their silent faces did he read
Unutterable love. Sound needed none,
Nor any voice of joy: his spirit drank
The spectacle. Sensation, soul, and form,
All melted into him; they swallowed up
His animal being. In them did he live,
And by them did he live—they were his life.
In such access of mind, in such high hour
Of visitation from the living God,
He did not feel the God, he felt his works.
Thought was not; in enjoyment it expired.
Such hour by prayer or praise was unprofaned;
He neither prayed, nor offered thanks or praise;
His mind was a thanksgiving to the power
That made him. It was blessedness and love.

(*Pedlar*, 98–114)

The immeasurable height
Of woods decaying, never to be decayed,
The stationary blasts of waterfalls,
And everywhere along the hollow rent
Winds thwarting winds, bewildered and forlorn,
The torrents shooting from the clear blue sky,
The rocks that muttered close upon our ears—
Black drizzling crags that spake by the wayside
As if a voice were in them—the sick sight
And giddy prospect of the raving stream,
The unfettered clouds and region of the heavens,
Tumult and peace, the darkness and the light,
Were all like workings of one mind, the features
Of the same face, blossoms upon one tree,
Characters of the great apocalypse,
The types and symbols of eternity,
Of first, and last, and midst, and without end.

(*1805*, vi. 556–72)

Certainty has been replaced by the border condition of imminence seen in the 'stationary blasts of waterfalls', seen in the conjunction of tumult and peace, darkness and light, seen at its most bizarre in the speaking crags. Though the days of his own pantheist conviction were long past, the Wordsworth of 1804 would have agreed with Coleridge's letter to Sotheby of 10 September 1802:

> Nature has her proper interest; and he will know what it is, who believes and feels, that every thing has a life of it's own, and that we are all *one life*. A poet's *heart and intellect* should be *combined, intimately* combined *and unified*, with the great appearances in Nature—and not merely held in solution and loose mixture with them, in the shape of formal similies.
>
> (Griggs, ii. 864)

The power of the Simplon Pass derives from Wordsworth's need to feel again the intimate combination and unity with Nature that he had known in *The Pedlar*. Similes in this case refuse to be formal, and catch magnificently both the craving for total harmony and the distance from achieving it—'Were all *like* workings of one mind, the features/Of the same face, blossoms . . . '. Wordsworth's unsupported implication that it is the eternal mind, the face of God, that reconciles the warring features of the landscape is vastly more impressive than the Pedlar's laborious communion.[46]

Such compulsive seeking for repose could not go long unsatisfied. *Intimations* speaks already of 'the faith that looks through death', 'years that bring the philosophic mind' (ll. 178–9), and the border poetry of this period is itself on a verge of too comfortable belief. No doubt it was the death of his favourite brother, John, in February 1805 that carried the poet over into acceptance, but the signs had all been there the previous year. The *Prelude* treatment of imagination tells the story most clearly. In the famous lines of Book VI, written just before the Simplon Pass, Wordsworth is seen—not for the first time—restating the central experience of *Tintern Abbey*:

> In such strength
> Of usurpation, in such visitings
> Of awful promise, when the light of sense
> Goes out in flashes that have shewn to us
> The invisible world, doth greatness make abode,
> There harbours whether we be young or old.
> Our destiny, our nature, and our home
> Is with infinitude—and only there;

With hope it is, hope that can never die,
Effort, and expectation, and desire,
And something evermore about to be.
(*1805*, vi. 532–42)

'The invisible world', 'destiny', 'infinitude', 'hope', 'expectation', the poet's language cries out for a transcendental interpretation, but for the moment he has none to offer. The lines that follow make it clear that in this border state, the mind is 'blest in thoughts/That are their own perfection and reward' (vi. 545–6), that the sense of 'something evermore about to be' is infinitely valuable, but not a religious experience. A year later, as he brings the thirteen-Book *Prelude* rather hastily to a conclusion after John's death, Wordsworth permits himself a new optimism. Imagination, now seen in far more expansive terms ('absolute strength', 'clearest insight', 'amplitude of mind', 'reason in her most exalted mood'), has been at once the subject and the guide of his 'long labour', and leads directly, and without hesitation, to a Christian immortality:

And lastly, from its progress have we drawn
The feeling of life endless, the one thought
By which we live, infinity and God.[47]
(*1805*, xiii. 182–4)

Wordsworth's preoccupations do not suddenly change when he accepts the doctrine of an afterlife. After *The Solitary Reaper* (November 1805), *Peele Castle* and *The Waggoner* (1806), there is as everybody knows a falling-off in his poetry, and this must surely be associated with slackening tension. Yet the baptized imagination[48] has its triumphs—the cloudscape New Jerusalem in *Excursion*, Book II (1810), *The Vernal Ode* (1817), *The Power of Sound* (1828), to name only the most obvious. The angel who in *The Vernal Ode* lands upon 'a rock of summit bare', 'Beneath the concave of an April sky', and sings his song of Nature's divinely appointed cyclical power is as much a borderer as the Danish Boy of 1799, and as surely present to the poet's eye as the Leech Gatherer himself. Perhaps there is little in the later Wordsworth that is at once distinguished and distinctively new, but at all times the poet is capable of thinking himself back into his earlier modes: in the London vision of 1808, for instance, where, pacing 'a length of street/Laid open in its morning quietness', the poet suddenly perceives

> The huge majestic temple of St Paul
> In awful sequestration through a veil,
> Through its own sacred veil, of falling snow.[49]

or, nearly thirty years later, in the inspired sequel to *A Night Piece* (1798), *Airey Force Valley*, with its 'soft eye-music of slow-waving boughs' (l. 14). The 'clinging to the palpable' of which Coleridge complained is often a saving grace of this later Christian poetry. The urgency of Wordsworth's quest has gone, but though he may speak of 'faith's transcendant dower' he is never content to rest his belief upon passive acceptance of revelation. The aspiring human mind continues to be of more importance to him personally than the faith it may achieve. The sense of possible sublimity is valued because it *is* a sense, and not a certainty:

> We men, who in our morn of youth defied
> The elements, must vanish—be it so;
> Enough, if something from our hands have power
> To live, and act, and serve the future hour;
> And if, as toward the silent tomb we go,
> Through love, through hope, and faith's transcendant
> dower,
> *We feel that we are greater than we know.*[50]

Chapter 2

Spots of Time and Sources of Power

> And then it started like a guilty thing
> Upon a fearful summons.
> (Shakespeare: *Hamlet*)

Wordsworth began work on the two-Part *Prelude* soon after his arrival in Goslar on 6 October 1798, but can have had no idea that that was what he was doing. Turning to the end of a notebook later used by Dorothy for one of her *Journals*, he began to write, working backwards and forwards in an irregular progression of two or three leaves at a time, sometimes across the page, and sometimes along, as the fancy took him.[1] His opening lines consist of a series of self-reproachful questions that start not just *in medias res* but in mid-sentence:

was it for this
That one, the fairest of all rivers, loved
To blend his murmurs with my nurse's song . . .?

For this didst thou
O Derwent, travelling over the green plains
Near my 'sweet birthplace', didst thou, beauteous stream,
Make ceaseless music through the night and day . . .?
Beloved Derwent, fairest of all streams,
Was it for this that I, a four years' child,
A naked boy among thy silent pools,
Made one long bathing of a summer's day . . .?
(*1799*, i. 1–3, 6–9, 16–19)

The reiterated 'was it for this?' takes us straight to the centre of a personal problem, but despite appearances the writing is very deliberate. For a time Wordsworth seems to have intended to compose some introductory lines that would explain what it was that 'this' referred to,[2] but to have done so would have been to spoil the impact of a rhetorical pattern which had been used in succession by Milton, Pope, and Thomson, and which had clearly an established tradition.[3] Though the Pope and Thomson examples occur in poems elsewhere drawn upon in *1799*, Milton's lines are especially important. Manoah in *Samson Agonistes*, shocked at the condition of his son, 'Eyeless in Gaza at the mill with slaves', reproaches God because it appears no longer possible that Samson can fulfil his appointed task:

> *For this* did the angel twice descend? *for this*
> Ordained thy nurture holy, as of a plant;
> Select, and sacred . . . ?
>
> (ll. 361–3)

Like Samson, with whom Milton of course identifies, Wordsworth has a mission—the writing of the prophetic and redemptive *Recluse*—and he too is failing to fulfil it, despite a childhood in which nurse and Nature had combined to create a '*nurture* holy, as of a plant;/Select, and sacred'.[4]

If ever there was a case of the anxiety of influence it must be this. We can't know whether the *Samson* echo was conscious, but it beautifully catches the sense of Milton's presence looking over the ephebe's shoulder as he writes.[5] *The Recluse* had been designed to supersede *Paradise Lost*, yet here was Wordsworth unable to make even a start, and addressing to himself guilt-laden questions that cast doubt on his very calling as a poet.[6] As one follows his inspired crabwise progress at the end of *MS JJ*, however, one sees a remarkable change in mood. With each sidelong draft it becomes clearer that though he is not making the poem he ought to be making, he is writing something of considerable scope. After 94 lines, that include both the bird's-nesting and woodcock-snaring episodes, he pauses, reckons his total, and sets off again with evident confidence: 'Nor while, though doubting yet not lost, I tread/The mazes of this argument . . .'.[7] This time the reference is to *Paradise Lost*. The poet it seems is measuring up to his precursor, and he refuses to be placed with the fallen angels, 'in wandering mazes lost', as they reason 'Of providence, foreknowledge, will and fate' (*PL* ii. 558–61).[8] Though obviously he does so in more personal terms, these are the subjects about which Wordsworth too is reasoning. Geoffrey Hartman has written of his 'Puritan quest for evidences of election',[9] and already in these earliest drafts Wordsworth is asking, as he does throughout the different versions and revisions of *The Prelude*, how he can justify his peculiarly strong sense of vocation. It can hardly fail to be significant that his mind should turn at this moment to fallen angels, that he should feel at this point a need to assert that his new poem is not a maze of error. Could his inability to go ahead with *The Recluse* mean that he was indeed not among the elect? Confidence, however, had increased as the poetry began to flow, and as the memories with which he was preoccupied showed themselves to be a valuable source of material. After its initial unease, the two-Part *Prelude* in fact becomes a remarkably *un*anxious poem.[10] Wordsworth is seen writing at the top of his powers, and for the moment subject neither to the sense of loss that had permeated *Tintern Abbey*, nor to his later fears about declining vision. In 1804 he was to write, 'the hiding-places of my power/Seem open, I approach, and then they close', and this was to be very much the mood in which the full-length *Prelude* was completed the following year. In *1799*—and perhaps nowhere else—Wordsworth looks back with assurance that the hiding-places *are* open, and will remain so as he searches.

It comes as a surprise to see in *MS JJ* that the connecting-links of the first half of Part I were written at the same moment as the intervening 'spots of time'. Their literary polytheism ('Ye powers of earth, ye genii of the springs') contrasts oddly with the naturalistic detail of the child's experiences, and they have very much the air of supernatural machinery added later like the sylphs of *The Rape of the Lock*.[11] The context, however, is not one in which a spirit-world can be dismissed. Wordsworth was wholly serious in his wish to portray himself as a chosen son, and if he claims to be guided in his education by 'beings of the hills', 'powers of earth', 'familiars of the lakes', we have to take them as seriously as we can. *MS JJ* in fact shows that the pantheism of his original drafts was of two distinct kinds. The tutelary spirits were there from the first, serving to link the bird's-nesting and woodcock-snaring episodes; but when Wordsworth returned to his draft at line 95, intent upon defining (or defending) his own position against Milton's, he did so in terms of a world-soul that was very close to the single 'motion and spirit' of *Tintern Abbey*:

> Nor while, though doubting yet not lost, I tread
> The mazes of this argument . . .
>   may I well
> Forget what might demand a loftier song,
> How oft the eternal spirit—he that has
> His life in unimaginable things . . .

Though cut almost at once, the passage is of great importance, and concludes in a direct address to a Platonic 'Soul of things':

>   oh bounteous power,
> In childhood, in rememberable days,
> How often did thy love renew for me
> Those naked feelings which when thou wouldst form
> A living thing thou sendest like a breeze
> Into its infant being. Soul of things
> How often did thy love . . .[12]

For a moment, apparently, the One Life did seem to Wordsworth a possible basis for his poem. The lines form a sort of pantheist Creation-myth to set beside Genesis and the waking of Adam in *Paradise Lost*. They have evident power and conviction; and yet for some reason they are discarded. Perhaps in October 1798 Wordsworth did indeed regard first principles as appropriate to *The Recluse*—the 'loftier song'—rather than the autobiographical poem he seemed by mistake to be writing. More probably he decided that his early memories couldn't really be fitted into a pattern of this kind. They had an extraordinary power, and were associated in his mind with the feeling that his childhood had been unusually favoured, but that did not mean that they could be portrayed as renewals of the initial gift of life.

The crucial episodes of *1799*, Part I, fall into two groups of three, separated by the section of 'home amusements', written largely in the manner of Cowper, and remarkable only for the skating lines. The first group, consisting of the woodcock-snaring, bird's-nesting and boat-stealing episodes, belongs to October-November 1798; the second (the Drowned Man of Esthwaite, the Woman on the Hill, and the Waiting for the Horses) was written after Christmas. The rationale of the second group is the doctrinal passage, 'There are in our existence spots of time', here seen in its original position; that of the early sequence is a passage drafted in *MS JJ* as a replacement for the pantheist lines quoted above. It is not by any means clear how this last piece of poetry should be read:

> The mind of man is fashioned and built up
> Even as a strain of music. I believe
> That there are spirits which, when they would form
> A favored being, from his very dawn
> Of infancy do open out the clouds
> As at the touch of lightning, seeking him
> With gentle visitation—quiet powers,
> Retired, and seldom recognized, yet kind,
> And to the very meanest not unknown—
> With me, though rarely, in my boyish days
> They communed. Others too there are, who use,
> Yet haply aiming at the self-same end,
> Severer interventions, ministry
> More palpable—and of their school was I.
>
> (*1799*, i. 67–80)

Wordsworth's sense of election is now seen to rest on a belief in tutelary spirits rather than the One Life. But, would he have made such a distinction himself? Coleridge had speculated in *Religious Musings* in 1796 that the 'contemplant spirits' might be monads, or particles, of the infinite mind;[13] and in 1802 he condemns Greek religious poems as 'poor stuff', fancy not imagination, on the grounds that they 'address always the *numina loci*, the genii, the dryads, the naiads, etc. etc.', whereas 'In the Hebrew poets each thing has a life of it's own, and yet they are all one life' (Griggs, ii. 865–6). The trouble about Wordsworth's spirits is that they are so evidently fanciful. They may be intended as a way of talking about the One Life, but despite the solemnity of the poet's 'I believe' they remain, because of their sub-classical associations, hard to take very seriously.[14] It is difficult not to think that in his revisions of *MS JJ* Wordsworth was aware of removing a vital pantheism in favour of something more literary. There are, however, ways in which the new artificiality proves useful. The spirits have something of the force of metaphor, allowing Wordsworth to imply his sense of election without stating that his upbringing (like Samson's) had been ordained by God, and enabling him at the same time to distinguish between conventionally happy childhood influences and the moments of troubled joy, guilt, terror, sublimity, that seemed in his own case to have been more formative.

It is interesting that though Wordsworth later switched the bird's-nesting and woodcock-snaring (presumably in order to present the more striking incident first), the episodes of group one in their original sequence got increasingly uncomfortable: first the unspecific threat,

> While on the perilous ridge I hung alone,
> With what strange utterance did the loud dry wind
> Blow through my ears; the sky seemed not a sky
> Of earth, and with what motion moved the clouds!
>
> (*1799*, i. 63–6)

then the menacing retributive pursuit,

> and when the deed was done
> I heard among the solitary hills
> Low breathings coming after me, and sounds
> Of undistinguishable motion, steps
> Almost as silent as the turf they trod.
>
> (*1799*, i. 45–9)

and finally the 'huge cliff,/As if with voluntary power instinct', that pursues the child not just across the lake, but into his mind, troubling his dreams and displacing all comfort and reassurance in his waking thoughts. The poetry is dependent on a double awareness. We respond to the low breathings of the Woodcock-snaring, the huge and mighty forms of the Boat-stealing, both as child and as adult—at once vividly aware *with* the child of the presence of the supernatural, and conscious that *in* the child this awareness is the product of guilt. But this is to ignore the poet's underlying preoccupation. It is finally the vision of the child that we are left with, because the child as borderer is the guarantee of his creator's adult strength. In the Bird's-nesting it is almost a sleight of hand that brings us to the borderline. Loneliness and danger give to the loud dry wind—the three heavy beats are curiously important—a strangeness of utterance that allows unspoken suggestion to dominate. Though no transcendental claims are being made, the force of the poetry persuades one to read the final line more as a question than an exclamation, as if it were implying that the sky was indeed not a sky of earth, that the clouds might truly be moved by some other-worldly power. One recalls that for De Quincey in *Suspiria De Profundis*, wind was the 'sole audible symbol of eternity' (Ward, 131).

In the Woodcock-snaring these hints of the supernatural are developed, and the relationships of reader, poet, and child become more deeply interfused. The child initially seems quite in harmony with his surroundings—

> 'twas my joy
> To wander half the night among the cliffs
> And the smooth hollows where the woodcocks ran
> Along the moonlight turf.

—but then one discovers that he is acting out a fantasy of violence:

> In thought and wish
> That time, my shoulder all with springes hung,
> I was a fell destroyer.
>
> (*1799*, i. 30–5)

The mocking adjective 'fell' and comically exaggerated 'destroyer' are held back for greater effect, though the child's posturing has already been revealed by the reference to his impotent 'wish'. At this point the text of *1799* differs in significant ways from that of *1805*:

> *Gentle powers,*
> *Who give us happiness and call it peace,*
> When scudding on from snare to snare I plied
> My anxious visitation, hurrying on,
> Still hurrying, hurrying onward, *how my heart*
> *Panted; among the scattered yew-trees and the crags*
> *That looked upon me, how my bosom*
> *Beat with expectation.*[15]
>
> (*1799*, i. 35–42)

At first it seems that the gentle powers (omitted in *1805*) have conferred happiness upon the child despite his would-be violence and their own equation of happiness and peace. But in the onomatopoeic anxiety of the rhythms that follow, it becomes clear that he is terrified, no longer wandering harmoniously amid a scene of natural beauty and calm, but hasting between snares like a boat or a cloud with the wind at its back. Nature too has changed, smooth hollows giving place to scattered yew-trees, with their dark foliage and dismal associations, and cliffs to accusing crags that 'look upon' the child in anticipation of the Boat-stealing. With so much going on, the juxtaposition of 'heart' and 'panted' probably goes unnoticed, but it is more than just a characteristic Wordsworth transferred epithet. Though perhaps unconscious, the pun on 'hart', and tacit reference to the psalm,[16] suggest that despite his predatory wishes, the child himself is the hunted animal. But one shouldn't overstress this aspect. It becomes dominant at the end of the passage, and is the theme of the *1805* revision—

> Moon and stars
> Were shining o'er my head; I was alone,
> And seemed to be a trouble to the peace
> That was among them.
>
> (*1805*, i. 321–4)

—but the child's emotions in *1799* are conflicting: his bosom, for all the anxiety, can beat with expectation that the next snare will have caught a woodcock.

After treating his former self at first with neutral seriousness, then with distancing mockery and indulgence, the poet is drawn into identification with the vividness of the child's reactions. The episode is building up to a climax in which intense but ordinary emotions will give place to the something more that above all he seeks and values:

> Sometimes strong desire
> Resistless overpowered me, and the bird
> Which was the captive of another's toils
> Became my prey; and when the deed was done
> I heard among the solitary hills
> Low breathings coming after me, and sounds
> Of undistinguishable motion, steps
> Almost as silent as the turf they trod.
>
> (*1799*, i. 42–9)

On a surface-level the child falls for temptation (the too Miltonic 'strong desire / Resistless'), steals a bird from someone else's snare, and is chased from the scene by outraged moral avengers who are the product of his guilt. This makes perfectly good sense—woodcock were worth a surprising amount at the time[17]—and insofar as the episode is based on fact, it may be a good deal like what actually happened. But it has little to do with the power of the poetry. The child thinks of his fairly trivial act as an evil deed, creating for himself terrors of retribution: the adult, though capable to an extraordinary extent of reliving the terror, turns out to be envious. Among the solitary hills the child had approached that borderline of human experience at which sounds of undistinguishable motion can be heard and the supernatural apprehended—whether it is present or not. In this case presumably it isn't. Wordsworth's concluding line has a curious double effect, 'Almost' having at first the impressiveness of an attempt to be accurate—'Thoughts that do lie *almost* too deep for tears'—but acting finally as a reminder that these particular steps were quite as silent as the turf they trod.

Though the last part of the boat-stealing episode will offer an account of after-effects within the mind that is an entirely new departure, the first two-thirds follows the same basic pattern as the Woodcock-snaring. As before, the child's mood is one of superficial confidence and underlying guilt; and as before, his vision is treated first with adult indulgence, then with unexpected seriousness:

> I went alone into a shepherd's boat,
> A skiff, that to a willow-tree was tied
> Within a rocky cave, its usual home.
> The moon was up, the lake was shining clear
> Among the hoary mountains; from the shore
> I pushed, and struck the oars, and struck again
> In cadence, and my little boat moved on
> Just like a man who walks with stately step
> Though bent on speed. It was an act of stealth
> And troubled pleasure. Not without the voice
> Of mountain echoes did my boat move on,
> Leaving behind her still on either side
> Small circles glittering idly in the moon,

Until they melted all into one track
Of sparkling light. A rocky steep uprose
Above the cavern of the willow-tree,
And now, as suited one who proudly rowed
With his best skill, I fixed a steady view
Upon the top of that same craggy ridge,
The bound of the horizon—for behind
Was nothing but the stars and the grey sky.
She was an elfin pinnace; twenty times
I dipped my oars into the silent lake,
And as I rose upon the stroke my boat
Went heaving through the water like a swan—
When from behind that rocky steep, till then
The bound of the horizon, a huge cliff,
As if with voluntary power instinct,
Upreared its head. I struck, and struck again,
And, growing still in stature, the huge cliff
Rose up between me and the stars, and still,
With measured motion, like a living thing
Strode after me.

(*1799*, i. 82–114)

The posturing hunter of the Woodcock-snaring becomes the proud oarsman, whose fantasy is mocked in the diction of 'elfin pinnace' as it had been before in 'fell destroyer'. In this more fully developed 'spot', however, there is new scope for anticipation and interconnection. It is the child's acting of the part that in this case renders him vulnerable: fixing his ridiculously 'steady view' on the top of the lower ridge, 'as suited one who proudly rowed / With his best skill'—the mockery of the 10-year-old is affectionate but unmistakable—he creates the situation in which the sudden uprearing of the larger crag will have its maximum effect. It is perhaps less often noticed how the poetry has prepared its explanation for the living motion of the peak. The final quoted sentence, 'I struck, and struck again . . .', refers one back to the opening lines:

from the shore
I pushed, and struck the oars, and struck again
In cadence . . .

The boat's movement at this early stage had been evoked in stilted iambic rhythms and an incongruous image:

> Just like a man who walks with stately step
> Though bent on speed.

Behind the lines one hears another simile, equally dominant in its different rhythm, and standing out equally from its context:

> Like one, that on a lonely road
>   Doth walk in fear and dread,
> And having once turned round walks on
>   And turns no more his head,
> Because he knows a frightful fiend
>   Doth close behind him tread.
> (*Ancient Mariner*, 451–6)

The link with Coleridge is confirmed within a few lines when the 'track/Of sparkling light' recalls (and rhymes with) the 'tracks of shining white' made by the water-snakes (*Ancient Mariner*, 266). It could well be unconscious, but serves to emphasize a connection between stateliness and fear:

>   my little boat moved on
> Just like a man who walks with stately step
> Though bent on speed. It was an act of stealth
> And troubled pleasure. Not without the voice
> Of mountain echoes did my boat move on . . .

Intent upon suppressing his anxieties, the child sees his boat as 'elfin', magical, heaving through the water with the beauty and power of a swan. But the anxieties cannot be suppressed. They are enacted in the movement of the boat; and it is of course the boat that imparts the movement to the cliff, enabling it to stride 'With measured motion, like a living thing'. At this stage one should recall the 'voice of mountain echoes', the first sign in the passage that the child would empower Nature to punish his act of stealth and troubled pleasure. The crags that had before merely 'looked upon' his intrusions are beginning to take an active part.

As with the Bird's-nesting and Woodcock-snaring, no supernatural events have taken place: it is a fact of geography, or geometry, that larger more distant crags become visible above smaller and nearer ones as a boat moves out from the shore and alters the angles. Wordsworth's concern is with mental process. And yet the episode begins with a categorical statement that in taking the boat he had been guided by the spirits who used on his behalf 'severer interventions'. We may not take this with full seriousness, but here as elsewhere it is the sense of *possible* sublimity that gives the poetry its strange additional strength:

> With trembling hands I turned,
> And through the silent water stole my way
> Back to the cavern of the willow-tree.
> There in her mooring-place I left my bark,
> And through the meadows homeward went with grave
> And serious thoughts; and after I had seen
> That spectacle, for many days my brain
> Worked with a dim and undetermined sense
> Of unknown modes of being. In my thoughts
> There was a darkness—call it solitude,
> Or blank desertion—no familiar shapes
> Of hourly objects, images of trees,
> Of sea or sky, no colours of green fields,
> But huge and mighty forms that do not live
> Like living men moved slowly through my mind
> By day, and were the trouble of my dreams.
>
> (*1799*, i. 114–29)

It is very important that in this last stage of the episode we stay within the mind of the child, within the brain that had 'worked'—like the compulsive swell of the sea—'with a dim and undetermined sense / Of unknown modes of being'. If one pauses to think about it, this last magnificent phrase says very little: it is so vague, so heavy with border negatives. And yet it is highly impressive because in it we respond to the urgency and appropriate *un*success of a struggle to define the child's experience as it was felt at the time. No adult wisdom is offered, and none would be acceptable. Similarly, the 'huge and mighty forms' have an absolute rightness. The child, tortured by the slowness of their measured motion, is forced by their striding through his head to think of them in human terms; and yet mountains they remain. And so we get the vividly imaginative compromise, powerful above all in its inadequacy: 'that do not live/Like living men'.

Written immediately after the first group of Part I episodes (and thus probably eight or ten weeks before the second) are three oddly disparate 'spots of time', *There was a boy*, *Nutting*, and the skating lines.[18] To judge from *MS JJ*, the original first-person drafts of *There was a boy* followed the Boat-stealing by a matter of hours, or days at most. It is a warning of the difficulties of generalizing about Wordsworth's mood that lines of such perfect composure should be so close to an incident of 'stealth and troubled joy'. *Nutting* is not found in *MS. JJ*, but the guardian-spirits who in the earliest texts of the poem appear as the poet's guides confirm that it too was originally part of *1799*.[19] The time-gap since *There was a boy* is probably very small, but the mood has changed again, and now we have a cautionary tale about violence. Wordsworth portrays, and on this level is evidently conscious of portraying, a rape of Nature:

Among the woods,
And o'er the pathless rocks, I forced my way
Until at length I came to one dear nook
Unvisited, where not a broken bough
Drooped with its withered leaves—ungracious sign
Of devastation—but the hazels rose
Tall and erect, with milk-white clusters hung,
A virgin scene! A little while I stood,
Breathing with such suppression of the heart
As joy delights in, and with wise restraint
Voluptuous, fearless of a rival, eyed
The banquet; or beneath the trees I sate
Among the flowers, and with the flowers I played . . . .
Perhaps it was a bower beneath whose leaves
The violets of five seasons reappear
And fade, unseen by any human eye . . . .
Then up I rose,
And dragged to earth both branch and bough, with crash
And merciless ravage; and the shady nook
Of hazels, and the green and mossy bower,
Deformed and sullied, patiently gave up
Their quiet being: and unless I now

Confound my present feelings with the past,
Even then, when from the bower I turned away,
Exulting, rich beyond the wealth of kings,
I felt a sense of pain when I beheld
The silent trees and the intruding sky.[20]

(ll. 13–25, 29–31, 42–52)

The description is oddly painful, oddly shocking. Nature passive and brutalized has so much more sexuality than the wanton enticing of Spenser's Bower of Bliss, or Marvell's *Garden*. To a very surprising extent Wordsworth enters into the *pleasure* of rape—restraint is wise because (like the line-ending) it delays and enhances the voluptuous—but there is no possibility of reading this as a titillating poem. Nor, on the other hand, is it in any conventional sense a moral one. The final lines pretend such a moral might exist, or might be appropriate—

Then, dearest maiden, move along these shades
In gentleness of heart, with gentle hand
Touch, for there is a spirit in the woods.

(ll. 53–5)

—but, though moving in its sudden tenderness, the conclusion seems strangely out of place. It is not just that Dorothy was gentle anyway, or that the polytheism appears incongruous, but that the sources of the poetry, and of its power to disturb, are felt to go far deeper.[21] It is almost as if Wordsworth were turning to Dorothy—the younger self who in *Tintern Abbey* can smooth the future—to ask for reassurance: if she can make the future unthreatening, can she perhaps assuage the guilts of the past? It is on this level that the *Paradise Lost* echoes of the passage seem to be working. The 'wise restraint / Voluptuous' is Miltonic not only in structure, but in its tacit reference to the 'sweet reluctant amorous delay' of Eve (*PL* iv. 311). But Wordsworth the voluptuary is not Adam; he is Satan, landed for the first time in Paradise, 'where the unpierced shade / Embrowned the noontide bowers' (*PL* iv. 245–6):

Beneath him with new wonder now he views
To all delight of human sense exposed
In narrow room Nature's whole wealth, yea more . . .

(*PL* iv. 205–7)

To read *Nutting* after the Milton lines is to become aware of countless minor echoes, but more important is the way the moods of the earlier passage—the sensuality of its description, the feelings of exclusion, the mingled admiration, envy, and wish to brutalize—have all been carried over.

The skating lines were not inserted in Part I until Wordsworth's revisions of late 1799, and though they may have been written at first to exemplify the 'gentle visitations' and then for some reason set aside, it seems quite as likely that they were separate in origin, called into being (in Dorothy's phrase) by Goslar skating scenes in this coldest winter of the century. Apart from its Hawkshead setting, what the episode has chiefly in common with the poetry of 'severer interventions' is the profusion of border images:

All shod with steel
We hissed along the polished ice in games
Confederate. . . .
With the din,
Meanwhile, the precipices rang aloud;
The leafless trees and every icy crag
Tinkled like iron; while the distant hills
Into the tumult sent an alien sound
Of melancholy, not unnoticed—while the stars,
Eastward, were sparkling clear, and in the west
The orange sky of evening died away.
(*1799*, i. 156–8, 162–9)

The distant hills, the sunset, the melancholy, the double negative 'not unnoticed', all in themselves have a border quality; but it is the 'alien sound' that above all establishes the tone of the passage. It is, of course, alien to the tumult and the camaraderie, not to the poet; but it cannot help being also slightly threatening. Nature is not rising against him, but she is singling him out, reminding him of other moods, perhaps of other responsibilities. The conjunction in the sky—day, and the lingering orange of the sun to the west: to the east, night, and the earliest stars—catches perfectly a border moment. And at the centre, on the border, at the still point (as it will later appear), is the boy.

As if conscious that for him 'glad animal movements' are not enough, that 'Our noisy years [are] moments in the being/Of the eternal silence' (*Intimations*, 152–3), he accepts the call to solitude:

> Not seldom from the uproar I retired
> Into a silent bay, or sportively
> Glanced sideway, leaving the tumultuous throng,
> To cut across the shadow of a star
> That gleamed upon the ice. And oftentimes
> When we had given our bodies to the wind,
> And all the shadowy banks on either side
> Came sweeping through the darkness, spinning still
> The rapid line of motion, then at once
> Have I, reclining back upon my heels
> Stopped short—yet still the solitary cliffs
> Wheeled by me, even as if the earth had rolled
> With visible motion her diurnal round.
> Behind me did they stretch in solemn train,
> Feebler and feebler, and I stood and watched
> Till all was tranquil as a summer sea.
>
> (*1799*, i. 170–85)

First the ordinary withdrawal into silence, then the display of individuality, finally a moment at which the boy imposes himself fully upon his surroundings. Giving their bodies to the wind—yielding, that is, to a consistent border influence—the skaters impart motion to the cliffs, and receive it back again in a sense-impression of the shadowy sweeping banks. The boy, however, stops; and, ceasing to co-operate bodily, creates the motion still within the mind. On a banal reading, he is dizzy;[22] but for Wordsworth this is a dying into life. The echo (or anticipation) of *A slumber did my spirit seal* can easily be misread. The boy is not Lucy, 'Rolled round in earth's diurnal course/With rocks and stones and trees'; he is the poet whose entering into the life of things her death so powerfully enacts.[23]

Though Skating and the first group of Part I 'spots' imply through Wordsworth's early memories his mature preoccupation with border states of mind, they make no connections between past and present, suggest no continuities. Primal experience is used to justify the poet's sense of election, and not—at least in any very considered way—to examine the sources of his power. The second group, written two to three months later, attempts to define how such experience is intensified within the mind, becomes a link in the chain of development, a portion of the child's, and of the adult's, consciousness. These later 'spots' show in their original context a progression that may be assumed to be deliberate. Wordsworth starts with the episode of the Drowned Man, which is highly important in its effect upon the sequence as a whole, but in itself very simple. The poet as a child of 9, newly arrived at Hawkshead Grammar School, is exploring Esthwaite Water—

> thy paths, thy shores
> And brooks, were like a dream of novelty
> To my half-infant mind . . .

—and sees across the water a pile of clothes:

> Twilight was coming on, yet through the gloom
> I saw distinctly on the opposite shore,
> Beneath a tree and close by the lake side,
> A heap of garments, as if left by one
> Who there was bathing. Half an hour I watched
> And no one owned them; meanwhile the calm lake
> Grew dark with all the shadows on its breast,
> And now and then a leaping fish disturbed
> The breathless stillness. The succeeding day
> There came a company, and in their boat
> Sounded with iron hooks and with long poles.
> At length the dead man, mid that beauteous scene
> Of trees and hills and water, bolt upright
> Rose with his ghastly face.

(*1799*, i. 261–3, 266–79)

Fantasy (the 'dream of novelty'), twilight (etymologically the moment *between* the lights of night and day), breathless stillness and watching, induce a border mood of expectation. All that happens happens in the last two and a half lines, but the narrative is so pared down, so beautifully controlled, that these need to be looked at almost word by word. It is the syntax, and especially the poet's delaying of the verb 'Rose', that is chiefly responsible for the effect. 'At length' (more waiting, more watching) is followed by confirmation that the owner of the clothes has indeed been drowned; but then comes the all-important delay with its emphasis on harmony and calm: 'mid that beauteous scene/Of trees and hills and water'. What is taking place has an inappropriate horror that is increased in the shocking force of 'bolt upright'—dead men should lie down. This one won't, and at last, past the final pause of the line-ending, we get the active verb that shows his refusal. This is no corpse, caught by the hair and pulled to the surface. More clearly even than the Discharged Soldier, whose 'mouth/Shewed ghastly in the moonlight', and whose disturbing uprightness he recalls, he is the traveller who did return, who crossed to the unknown bourne and yet came back.

So much for the actual description, plain, beautifully visualized, making no claims for itself. In *1805*, when exiled to the fifth (and most obviously hodge-podge) Book of the longer poem, the passage is followed by some fairly unconvincing assertions designed to tie it into the theme of education—the child is apparently not frightened, because he has read about such things in fairy-tales (v. 473–81).[24] In *1799*, however, there is a bridge-passage of great importance that links the episode through into the discussion of 'spots of time': 'I might advert' it begins, rather pompously,

> To numerous accidents in flood or field,
> Quarry or moor, or mid the winter snows,
> Distresses and disasters, tragic facts
> Of rural history, that impressed my mind
> With images to which in following years
> Far other feelings were attached—with forms
> That yet exist with independent life,
> And, like their archetypes, know no decay.
>
> There are in our existence spots of time . . .
>
> (*1799*, i. 279–88)

Thus in the two-Part *Prelude* one moves from the Drowned Man (whose ghastly face is allowed to be disquieting) through a discussion of the imaginative process that stamps such 'tragic facts' upon the mind to the fully worked-out 'spots' that reinforce it. It is not too much to say that the Drowned Man exerts his influence on the whole sequence, setting up an expectation of the sort of memories that are to be talked about, and preparing for the mood of 'visionary dreariness' that is to be evoked. In itself, however, the episode is limited. What happens is vividly seen, vividly described, but still on the level of an event—something that could be experienced by others, though most impressive to the poet because of his 'more than usual organic sensibility', and because of the solitary intensity of his waiting. The incident prepares the way for Wordsworth's definitions, and these in turn prepare for the 'spots' in which experience becomes fully imaginative, takes on an independent life within the mind, and, in that context, achieves an archetypal permanence.

As it stands in Book XI of *1805*, the assertion 'There are in our existence spots of time . . . ', though of course highly impressive, is removed a very long way from the poetry of Book I with which it had originally been connected, and has to take a structural weight that it cannot easily bear.[25] In *1799*, by contrast, it is at the centre of Wordsworth's thinking—a support alike for his faith in the value of primal experience, and for the further definitions of Part II as he goes on to explore more fully the role of imagination.[26] In its early form the passage is brief and to the point:

> There are in our existence spots of time
> Which with distinct preeminence retain
> A fructifying virtue, whence, depressed
> By trivial occupations and the round
> Of ordinary intercourse, our minds—
> Especially the imaginative power—
> Are nourished and invisibly repaired;
> Such moments chiefly seem to have their date
> In our first childhood.
>
> (*1799*, i. 288–96)

Wordsworth is concerned, as he had been six months earlier in *Tintern Abbey*, with moods in which 'the heavy and the weary weight/Of all this unintelligible world/Is lightened', and lightened not by a present event, but by memories of the past. One can go further, and say that in both *Tintern Abbey* and *1799* the memories as well as being restorative imply an imaginative creation, and that they are abnormally non-nostalgic. And, in terms of function, one can add that the poetry in both cases demonstrates, and exists to justify, the prevailing optimism of

Wordsworth's view of life. Here the resemblances cease. In *Tintern Abbey* the restorative memories are of landscape, whereas the 'spots of time', if they are about Nature at all, are about it in a far less obvious sense. But the main difference, of course, is that in the lines from Part I the pantheism of July 1798 has been replaced. Wordsworth, who six months before had derived his love of Nature, and his belief in her restorative influence, from 'A motion and a spirit, that impels/All thinking things, all objects of all thought', is now seen taking up a purely humanist position.

The first episode is a little slow in getting under way, partly because Wordsworth has added in revision a two-line parenthesis:

> I remember well
> ('Tis of an early season that I speak,
> The twilight of rememberable life),
> While I was yet an urchin, one who scarce
> Could hold a bridle, with ambitious hopes
> I mounted, and we rode towards the hills.
> We were a pair of horsemen: honest James
> Was with me, my encourager and guide.
>
> (*1799*, i. 296–303)

In the previous incident the poet had looked back to a child (whose mind was noticeably 'half-infant') wandering in an actual dusk; now 'twilight' reappears to characterize the borders of memory. The addition halts the movement of the verse, but suggests the extent to which already in 1799 Wordsworth thought of the child as father to the man, nearer to the sources of vision. On a different plane he also thought of him—as he had thought of the 'fell destroyer', and the proud oarsman of the 'elfin pinnace'—with a good deal of indulgence. The urchin on this occasion sees himself as a knight setting out on a quest with his trusty squire, honest James, who was in truth his grandparents' servant at Penrith. His fantasies are quietly sent up in the poet's mock-heroic tones: 'I mounted, and we rode towards the hills' (meaning, presumably, that he was helped into the saddle and taken up the slope behind the house). His probable age was 5.

The lines that follow provide one of the few cases in which the text of *1799* is better than *1805* in ways that really matter. To read the two passages side by side is to remind oneself that

Wordsworth's revisions usually took the form of elaboration, and that, even at the height of his creative period, they were normally for the worse.[27] It is in the account of the murderer's gibbet that they differ. The original version reads:

> We had not travelled long ere some mischance
> Disjoined me from my comrade, and, through fear
> Dismounting, down the rough and stony moor
> I led my horse, and stumbling on, at length
> Came to a bottom where in former times
> A man, the murderer of his wife, was hung
> In irons. Mouldered was the gibbet-mast;
> The bones were gone, the iron and the wood;
> Only a long green ridge of turf remained
> Whose shape was like a grave. I left the spot,
> And reascending the bare slope I saw
> A naked pool that lay beneath the hills,
> The beacon on the summit, and more near
> A girl who bore a pitcher on her head
> And seemed with difficult steps to force her way
> Against the blowing wind.
>
> (*1799*, i. 304–19)

In *1805* the opening is the same —as is the description of the woman on the hill, for which in either text the earlier lines are really preparation—but the middle of the passage quoted has been greatly expanded:

> The gibbet-mast was mouldered down, the bones
> And iron case were gone, but on the turf
> Hard by, soon after that fell deed was wrought,
> Some unknown hand had carved the murderer's name.
> The monumental writing was engraven
> In times long past, and still from year to year
> By superstition of the neighbourhood
> The grass is cleared away; and to this hour
> The letters are all fresh and visible.
> Faltering, and ignorant where I was, at length
> I chanced to espy those characters inscribed
> On the green sod: forthwith I left the spot . . .
>
> (*1805*, xi. 290–301)

'The monumental writing was engraven/In times long past'—Thomas Nicholson, the murderer in question, had been hanged for killing a local butcher in August 1767, only two and a half years before the urchin's birth. The letters, even if carved *very* 'soon after that fell deed was wrought', were at most seven or eight years old; the gibbet, unless made of remarkably inferior wood, would not even have fallen, much less 'mouldered down'. For all the circumstantial detail, we are dealing not with fact, but with poetry of the imagination. Wordsworth, it turns out, is conflating two quite separate crimes, the recent one at Penrith, and one that had taken place a hundred years earlier, and that had indeed concerned 'A man, the murderer of his wife'. The first had left a gibbet which was still standing in 1775, and which the child is not specially likely to have been near, at least on the occasion described;[28] the second (the first in point of time) had left what by the late eighteenth century was a rotted but terrifying stump that stood in the water-meadows at Hawkshead, on the road that Wordsworth had daily to pass between his lodgings and the school.[29]

It is as imaginative writing that the version in the two-Part poem is so very much superior. The additional lines of *1805* are not only garrulous, but distracting, and oddly trivial in their associations. Wordsworth is seen playing up the murder-and-mystery ('fell deed', 'unknown hand', 'times long past') in a way that is not easy to justify. The new poetry has all the appearance of a versified guide-book entry: 'still from year to year by superstition of the neighbourhood the grass is cleared away.' The sense of expectation created at the beginning of the passage has gone. In order to get back to the frightened child stumbling down the moor, Wordsworth has now to insert a clumsy reminder: 'Faltering, and ignorant where I was, at length/I chanced to espy . . .'. There is no means of telling where or when he heard the detail of the letters engraved on the turf, or why he decided to insert it.[30] His concern in either version of the passage is presumably with 'the manner in which we associate ideas in a state of excitement' (Preface to *Lyrical Ballads*, 1800). The terror which we assume the child to have felt—it is never stressed—accounts for the heightened consciousness with which he transforms the landscape and his encounter with the woman on the hill, and the poet's evoking of the mouldered gibbet creates in the reader a parallel excitement that will then be transferred to the 'ordinary sight' which he is invited to regard as important. The process surely works best where the preparatory lines do not draw irrelevant attention to themselves. In the original version the poetry is beautifully homogeneous:

> down the rough and stony moor
> I led my horse, and stumbling on, at length
> Came to a bottom where in former times
> A man, the murderer of his wife, was hung
> In irons. Mouldered was the gibbet-mast;
> The bones were gone, the iron and the wood;
> Only a long green ridge of turf remained
> Whose shape was like a grave. I left the spot,
> And reascending the bare slope I saw
> A naked pool that lay beneath the hills,
> The beacon on the summit, and more near
> A girl who bore a pitcher on her head
> And seemed with difficult steps to force her way
> Against the blowing wind. It was in truth
> An ordinary sight, but I should need
> Colours and words that are unknown to man
> To paint the visionary dreariness
> Which, while I looked all round for my lost guide,
> Did at that time invest the naked pool,
> The beacon on the lonely eminence,
> The woman and her garments vexed and tossed
> By the strong wind.

(*1799*, i. 306–27)

It is probably the fussiness of the engraven letters that one most resents, and the fact that they delay the appearance of the inexplicably evocative figure who is to be the central focus of the landscape. The *1805* additions obscure the very nature of the poetry that Wordsworth is writing—poetry not of fact and guide-book detail but of strange imaginative power; poetry in which what is *not* seen, is as important as what is. 'The bones were gone, the iron and the wood' is not only beautiful in its rhythm, but reduces the unseen horrors of the gallows (the gruesome deterrent of a corpse swinging and rotting in its iron cage) to the elemental level on which Wordsworth's imagination plays. Similarly, 'the long green ridge of turf', perhaps actually a grave, perhaps just seeming one to the frightened child, is in either case a tranquil, reconciling, very Wordsworthian end to the violence of the past. The poetry in this version is all of a piece. In *1805* one has to clear one's mind of the superstition, mysteriousness, cluttering detail, before responding to the vision of the girl with her pitcher on the hill. In *1799*, one's mood has been prepared. One ascends the bare slope and meets almost without surprise the most purely imaginative of Wordsworth's solitaries.

It seems to be *The Thorn* that is at the back of the poet's mind as he writes. The mound where Martha Ray may have buried her child becomes the 'long green ridge of turf . . . Whose shape was like a grave'; the pond in which she may have drowned it becomes the 'naked pool that lay beneath the hills'; Martha on her hilltop, known to 'every wind that blows', suggests the garments that are 'vexed and tossed/ By the strong wind'. Again the background is one of murder, but the horrors inherited originally from Bürger, have quite disappeared. In *The Thorn*, whatever the writer's intention, we find ourselves forced to ask 'Did it really happen?' 'What *is* it all about?'. Here no questions are raised. Martha is on the hill because she was jilted, or because she is mad, or because she is a murderess: the woman with her garments vexed and tossed simply exists. If we look for them we can see that she has affinities to Martha, and even in a different way to Margaret of *The Ruined Cottage*; but the wind that blows her clothing implies no suffering, the water she carries, no relationship. It is unthinkable, for instance, that she should befriend the child, put her pitcher down to give him a drink. Even the Leech Gatherer, part stone, part sea-beast as he is, may be approached; but not this haunting dream-like presence. One responds to her almost as an emanation of the child's mind, not merely acted upon, but produced, by the 'visionary dreariness' that is his mood. And yet finally it is the fact that she is winning that gives her her peculiar fascination—the fact that however difficult her steps, however much her clothing may be vexed, she is forcing her way with success against the blowing wind. The child, lost, lonely, terrified, looks up and sees her, not as a reassuring human-being, but as something totally other, at one with the alien landscape. And yet she is admirable, is felt in her otherness to have a secret strength. Whether Wordsworth is conscious of it or not, it seems wholly appropriate that behind his lines is a vision of 'heavenly Truth /with gradual steps winning her difficult way'.[31]

If one turns to the Waiting for the Horses, which concludes the sequence, it is to find a still further development away from objective reality towards a poetry purely of the mind. Wordsworth, aged 12, has climbed a crag to keep watch for the groom who has been sent to bring him and his brothers home from school:

> 'Twas a day
> Stormy, and rough, and wild, and on the grass
> I sate, half sheltered by a naked wall.
> Upon my right hand was a single sheep,
> A whistling hawthorn on my left, and there,
> Those two companions at my side, I watched
> With eyes intensely straining, as the mist
> Gave intermitting prospects of the wood
> And plain beneath.
>
> (*1799*, i. 341–9)

One wall, one sheep, one tree—the ingredients of Wordsworth's poetry can seldom have been less exciting; and yet we read on, waiting expectantly as the child himself is waiting. This time there is to be no Drowned Man bobbing up with his ghastly face, nor even the much less palpable presence of the Woman on the Hill. Wordsworth has moved on. With the Drowned Man, much of the beauty of the poetry lies in the child's anticipation—

> meanwhile the calm lake
> Grew dark with all the shadows on its breast . . .
>
> (*1799*, i. 271–2)

—but something *does* happen, and we are invited to think that the incident is intensified within the memory by the waiting. Even the discovery of the murderer's grave has some basis in reality: the child in his dread presumably fixes upon a particular long green ridge of turf. With the Woman on the Hill we enter another, far more imaginative, realm, in which the distinction between perception and projection is blurred. Wordsworth is talking now clearly about the mind, not the external world. And yet the formula is still the same as in the crude earlier 'spots of time': heightened emotion leading to heightened response and the fixing in the memory of an event not as it was, but as at the time it seemed. In the Waiting for the Horses there is a further, very surprising, extension. Out of the unpromising details described in the passage quoted above, the mind *later* creates an important and formative experience.

'I have been struck', writes De Quincey in *Suspiria de Profundis*,

> with the important truth that far more of our deepest thoughts and feelings pass to us through perplexed combinations of concrete objects, pass to us as *involutes* (if I may coin that word) in compound experiences incapable of being disentangled, than ever reach us directly and in their own abstract shapes.
>
> (Ward, 130)

There is no better gloss on the major 'spots of time'. De Quincey is meditating on personal associations with the death of his sister Elizabeth, but as the one Romantic to be influenced by the long-unpublished *Prelude* (Coleridge of course knew it, but was not in the same sense influenced), he could well have had in mind the grouping of

> the naked pool,
> The beacon on the lonely eminence,
> The woman and her garments vexed and tossed
> By the strong wind . . .
>
> (*1799*, i. 324–7)

or the parallel scene in which the stone wall, tree, and sheep—irrelevent concrete objects if ever there were—become involutes in the death of Wordsworth's father:

> Ere I to school returned
> That dreary time, ere I had been ten days
> A dweller in my father's house, he died,
> And I and my two brothers, orphans then,
> Followed his body to the grave. The event,
> With all the sorrow which it brought, appeared
> A chastisement; and when I called to mind
> That day so lately passed, when from the crag
> I looked in such anxiety of hope,
> With trite reflexions of morality,
> Yet with the deepest passion, I bowed low
> To God who thus corrected my desires.

And afterwards the wind and sleety rain,
And all the business of the elements,
The single sheep, and the one blasted tree,
And the bleak music of that old stone wall,
The noise of wood and water, and the mist
Which on the line of each of those two roads
Advanced in such indisputable shapes—
All these were spectacles and sounds to which
I often would repair, and thence would drink
As at a fountain. And I do not doubt
That in this later time, when storm and rain
Beat on my roof at midnight, or by day
When I am in the woods, unknown to me
The workings of my spirit thence are brought.
(*1799*, i. 349–74)

Wordsworth is disentangling his compound memory, showing us how his improbable involutes have gained their power.

We never hear which road from Cockermouth the groom had chosen, or even that the horses finally came. The waiting exists to arouse a border expectation, an intensity within the mind that is carried over as the verse switches suddenly to another scene and a different event. Nothing of emotional relevance happens to the child in the ten days between the waiting and his father's death, and the reader experiences in the narrative a cut that the memory had long ago made. Wordsworth views his former self with sympathy and detachment, entering into his suffering, making clear his terrible wrongness, and retrieving from the experience that which is of permanent value.[32] The child has not killed his father; God has not corrected his desires; and the moral reflections with which he abases himself are not just trite ('Set not your heart upon the things of this world'), they are the appalling products of remorse. Yet the passion is important all the same—very important. The intensity of hope changes to an intensity of guilt, turns briefly to misplaced and ignorant fervour, and becomes at last the emotional charge that creates a 'spot of time'. As a result the remembered scene, at which nothing happened, and which has in itself no significance, becomes a lasting source of imaginative strength.[33] Wordsworth does not on this occasion heighten his poetry by telling us how difficult it was to write—

I should need
Colours and words that are unknown to man
To paint the visionary dreariness . . .

(*1799*, i. 320–2)

—but as with the Woman on the Hill he dwells in his conclusion a second time upon the elements of the landscape, slightly changing the details. The effect of this second description is to imply the changes of memory. The familiar 'whistling hawthorn' becomes 'the one blasted tree', and in general there is a rendering down ('The noise of wood and water'). Not all the new details are drearier, but the move is certainly towards the visionary. The wall loses its chilly nakedness, yet offers now a 'bleak music' that is a sort of prelude to the poetry that will one day be made out of this uncomfortable material; and the mist forms itself into shapes whose power is uncanny and quite unexplained.

What, one wonders, was in Wordsworth's mind as he wrote of

the mist
Which on the line of each of those two roads
Advanced in such indisputable shapes . . .

Earlier the mist had obscured the child's view, causing the strained attention that is typical of so many of the border experiences, and that almost invariably prefaces the unexpected.[34] Now, it advances along the roads by which the horses should have come, and—according to what is presumably the simplest interpretation—advances in shapes that indisputably resemble them. But what should one make of the *Hamlet* echo:

Thou com'st in such a questionable shape
That I will speak to thee. I'll call thee Hamlet,
King, father, royal Dane. O answer me!

(I. iv. 43–5)

It seems an odd chance that this of all passages in Wordsworth's poetry should be linked to the ghost of a murdered father. But in fact there is one other passage, similarly linked, and just as important. Looking backwards to the 'spots of time' in the great ninth stanza of *Intimations*, the poet in 1804 gives thanks not for 'the simple creed/Of childhood' (delight, liberty, new-born hope),

But for those blank misgivings of a creature
Moving about in worlds not realized,
High instincts before which our mortal nature
Did tremble like a guilty thing surprized—
    But for those first affections,
    Those shadowy recollections
  Which, be they what they may,
Are yet the fountain light of all our day,
Are yet the master light of all our seeing . . .

(ll. 142–50)

In this case it seems we have a quotation consciously used, but oddly misapplied: why should the child (as representative of our mortal nature) be connected with the Ghost who at the crowing of the cock 'started like a guilty thing/Upon a fearful summons' (*Hamlet*, I. i. 148-9)? The answer can only be that at some level the poet associated the 'blank misgivings' and 'high instincts' of childhood with his father's death, and with the guilt that has been taken over from the Ghost.

Infusing the unimportant remembered scene above Hawkshead with emotions occasioned by his father's death, the child gives it lasting power; evoking this power (and consciously deriving it from misplaced guilt), the adult poet visualizes the mist as 'advancing' in shapes that are connected by verbal echo to the ghost of a father who returned to seek revenge. On the level of the poet's intention one assumes that the mist-shapes were unquestionably horses;[35] on another, one indisputably can, and perhaps should, take them to be something far less comfortable. Presumably as an honest pre-Freudian Wordsworth would have been surprised to think of the forms he had created in the mist, and of the similarly 'advancing' mountain on Ullswater, in terms of his father; but the man who could write 'and I grew up/*Fostered* alike by beauty and by fear' (*1805*, i. 305–6) was not very far from knowing that Nature in her 'gentle visitations' had been a replacement for his mother, or that he associated his father with 'severer interventions'. Nor would everybody at this period have looked for the origins of adult creativity among 'Blank misgivings of a creature/Moving about in worlds not realized'. Wordsworth in fact clearly made allowance for elements in his make-up and development that he did not understand, or expect to be understood:

> those first affections,
> Those shadowy recollections
> Which, *be they what they may*,
> Are yet the fountain light of all our day,
> Are yet the master light of all our seeing . . .
>
> (*Intimations*, 146–50)

> All these were spectacles and sounds to which
> I often would repair, and thence would drink
> As at a fountain. And I do not doubt
> That in this later time, when storm and rain
> Beat on my roof at midnight, or by day
> When I am in the woods, *unknown to me*
> *The workings of my spirit thence are brought.*
>
> (*1799*, i. 368–74)

No one would now doubt that Wordsworth was right to put so much emphasis on the formative value of early experience; was he perhaps also right to think that his own creative powers were nourished in adulthood by particular childhood memories? When expressed in general terms—

> There are in *our* existence spots of time
> That with distinct preeminence retain
> A fructifying virtue . . .
>
> (*1799*, i. 288–90)

—the claim is not easy to support; but as in other cases in *The Prelude* Wordsworth may surely have been right about his own development, though wrong to regard it as typical human experience.[36] It seems wholly likely that incidents to which his mind recurred over the years in a form of repetition-compulsion (that had as its basis the need to assuage the mother's oedipal loss, and later death, or make acceptable the father's revengeful presence) should have come to be valued because the emotional intensity they derived from repression created for them an especial vividness. Contrasted with the drabness of adult sense-perception such vividness would have seemed a guarantee that his childhood had been characterized by a border vision, that he had truly been—and still must be—among the elect. It was this that Wordsworth needed above all to believe, and if the 'spots' gave him such confidence, they were indeed a source of power.

Chapter 3

The Child as Father

How do I study now, and scan
Thee, more than ere I studied man,
And only see through a long night
Thy edges, and thy bordering light!
(Vaughan: *Childhood*)

Wordsworth's human borderers are drawn from the extremes of life's pilgrimage—nearness either to the beginning or to the end of the road introducing the possibility of border vision—but the young are more important than the old, because within a single life-span only the child can be father. The old may be in touch with another world, but if they cross the border their wisdom goes with them. They make the grander symbolic figures because they represent attainment, that which may be achieved by suffering humanity; but such optimism as can be derived from them is muted and qualified. The child on the other hand stands for hope, hope that vision may *persist*, innocence be carried on into experience—in the poet's own case, hope that imagination will be pre-eminent till death, and will justify in its continued power his sense of election. To the adult who is his descendant the child can bequeath confidence and creative joy; the difficulty is to believe that he has done so. *The Rainbow*, though impressively enigmatic, offers no very convincing evidence:

My heart leaps up when I behold
A rainbow in the sky:
So was it when my life began,
So is it now I am a man,

So be it when I shall grow old,
Or let me die.
The child is father of the man;
And I should wish that all my days may be
Bound each to each by natural piety.

All *must* be well because the poet's heart has performed in the past, and is still capable of performing in the present, a spontaneous act of worship—or so it seems to Wordsworth in the late evening of 26 March 1802. At breakfast the next morning he feels differently:

There was a time when meadow, grove, and stream,
The earth, and every common sight,
To me did seem
Appareled in celestial light,
The glory and the freshness of a dream.
It is not now as it has been of yore:
Turn wheresoe'er I may
By night or day
The things which I have seen, I see them now no more.[1]
(*Intimations*, 1–9)

Wishful-thinking one day, the next a moving sense of loss; but the needs implied are the same, and so are the border assumptions. Childhood vision, whether or not one retains it, is felt by Wordsworth to have a peculiar intensity. This may at times be held to derive from a specific source—harmony with the natural world, or the mother's love, or pre-existence—but sources of power matter only insofar as they enable the poet to believe at a given moment in the continuity asserted by *The Rainbow*.

Like so much else in Wordsworth's poetry, the child-borderers have their beginnings at Alfoxden. The little maid of *We Are Seven* is imaginatively right in her refusal to accept an adult view of death—

'How many are you then', said I,
'If they two are in heaven?'
The little maiden did reply,
'O master, we are seven.'

'But they are dead—those two are dead . . .'
(ll. 61–5)

—but *We Are Seven*, like *Anecdote for Fathers*, is chiefly an example of the somewhat quirky interest in psychology that crops up at this period. The questioning—

> And five times did I say to him,
> 'Why, Edward, tell me why?'
>
> (*Anecdote for Fathers*, 47–8)

—shows very clearly Wordsworth's border preoccupation, but the little maid and Edward are a long way from being imaginatively developed borderers. The obvious example of course is the Pedlar, who is capable as a boy of the full border experience, drinking in the landscape before his eyes, and being himself drawn into it:

> Sound needed none,
> Nor any voice of joy: his spirit drank
> The spectacle. Sensation, soul, and form,
> All melted into him; they swallowed up
> His animal being. In them did he live,
> And by them did he live—they were his life.
>
> (*Pedlar*, 101–6)

The interesting fact in this case, however, is that instead of preserving the wisdom of childhood, the Pedlar has acquired *as a child* the perceptions of an adult:

> In such communion, not from terror free,
> While yet a child *and long before his time*,
> He had perceived the presence and the power
> Of greatness . . .
>
> (ll. 27–30)

A glance at *Tintern Abbey* shows very clearly what has happened. Wishing to give expression to his belief in the One Life, yet conscious that in fact he values above all an earlier stage when Nature was

> An appetite—a feeling and a love
> That had no need of a remoter charm
> By thought supplied . . .
>
> (ll. 81–3)

Wordsworth ascribes to the Pedlar as a boy views that he had only very recently come to hold. Belief in the One Life derives the millenarian hopefulness that is celebrated in *The Pedlar* (and that should have been the theme of *The Recluse*) from assumptions about human perfectibility and education that are totally opposed to the border instincts of the poet.[2]

The true child-borderer of Alfoxden has learnt nothing, and will never learn anything. Like the infant at the London theatre in *Prelude*, Book VII, he is 'A sort of alien scattered from the clouds', 'destined to live,/To be, to have been, come and go, a child' (vii. 378, 402–3). Adults may question him, and he will answer, and they will be none the wiser—though, if they wish, they may choose to ascribe to him wisdom:

> while they all were travelling home
> Cried Betty, 'Tell us Johnny, do,
> Where all this long night you have been,
> What you have heard, what you have seen—
> And Johnny, mind you tell us true.'
>
> Now Johnny all night long had heard
> The owls in tuneful concert strive;
> No doubt he too the moon had seen,
> For in the moonlight he had been
> From eight o'clock till five.
>
> And thus to Betty's question he
> Made answer like a traveller bold
> (His very words I give to you):
> 'The cocks did crow to-whoo, to-whoo,
> And the sun did shine so cold.'
> Thus answered Johnny in his glory,
> And that was all his travel's story.
>
> (*Idiot Boy*, 447–63)

The framework of the mock-heroic in which the idiot is 'like a traveller bold', the taunting of the reader with his expectation that Johnny might be in some romantic relationship with the owls and moon, the ridiculous emphasis on fact ('His very words'), together with the mocking possibility of Johnny's 'glory', all point to the existence of a different set of values according to which the Idiot Boy may indeed have a wisdom to offer. Wordsworth's famous later comment—'I have often applied to idiots, in my own mind, that sublime expression of Scripture that, "*their life is hidden with God*'" (*EY* 357; W.'s italics)—seems ponderous beside the comedy and tenderness of the poem. Johnny with his holly-bough, Johnny at the waterfall, has a privateness that hardly seems to need a scriptural authority. Yet the poetry, through its mockery of expectation and its hinting of numinous possibilities, has been able to suggest that beyond the mongol inarticulacy lies a special capacity to relate—a capacity that for most would be destroyed in the process of education, acquiring language, forming ordinary relationships and assumptions.

In his perpetual childhood Johnny the idiot very frequently reminds one of the actual child who was present at Alfoxden, and who was again and again to be noticed for his border qualities—not Basil Montagu, the Edward of *Anecdote for Fathers*, who was living with the Wordsworths, but Hartley Coleridge. Hartley makes his appearance in his father's poetry as the cradled infant of *Frost at Midnight* (February 1798):

> Whose gentle breathings, heard in [the] deep calm,
> Fill up the interspersèd vacancies
> And momentary pauses of the thought.
>
> (ll. 45–7)

Already in Coleridge's fatherly prediction, which is surely akin to prayer or blessing, he is gifted with natural attributes—'thou, my babe, shalt wander like a breeze'—and has without earning, or learning, it, the power of reading the language of God's presence:

> so shalt thou see and hear
> The lovely shapes and sounds intelligible
> Of that eternal language, which thy God
> Utters, who from eternity doth teach
> Himself in all, and all things in himself.
>
> (ll. 58–62)

Lamb too, in *This Lime-Tree Bower*, had been given the power of reading the Berkeleyan signs, but Hartley as child-borderer is part of what he beholds. His role six or eight weeks later in *The Nightingale* is important too—less numinous, more admonitory[3]—but it is *Frost at Midnight* that leads onwards, pointing towards the border poetry of Goslar in its imaginative freeing of the child from restriction and actuality. Hartley as the breeze, wandering 'By lakes and sandy shores, beneath the crags / Of ancient mountain', has floated away from time.[4] There is no sense that like the boy Pedlar he will grow into an awareness of the One Life: understanding in him is innate. He will see and hear directly 'The lovely shapes and sounds intelligible', making no act of interpretation, unaware that others are toiling all their lives to find the truths that rest so lightly upon him.[5]

Ceasing to put so much emphasis on the One Life, the Wordsworth of Goslar reconciles (presumably without intending to do so) the conflict between the didactic needs of his poetry, and his border emphasis on childhood as the period of inspiration. The beginnings of *The Prelude* show him looking backward for the sources of creativity, and the great lyrics of the period produce a succession of fully imaginative child-borderers, Lucy in her different manifestations, the girl of *Two April Mornings* whose 'hair was wet/With points of morning dew', and the strange, not fully realized, *Danish Boy*:

Between two sister moorland rills
There is a spot that seems to lie
Sacred to flowrets of the hills,
And sacred to the sky.
And in this smooth and open dell
There is a tempest-stricken tree,
A corner-stone by lightning cut
(The last stone of a cottage-hut),
And in this dell you see
A thing no storm can e'er destroy,
The shadow of a Danish boy.

(ll. 1–11)

According to Wordsworth's later explanation the poem, which extends to 66 lines but was printed in 1800 as 'A Fragment', was to have been the introduction to a ballad about a Danish prince who fled from battle (presumably in Cumbria), took refuge in a cottage, and was there murdered for his valuables. It is not at all surprising that the story was never written. The stanzas that survive are in effect *post*-ballad; they pick up spooky bits and pieces from *The Thorn*, and take them only half satisfactorily into a more imaginative world:

A harp is from his shoulder slung;
He rests the harp upon his knee,
And there in a forgotten tongue
He warbles melody.
Of flocks and herds both far and near
He is the darling and the joy,
And often when no cause appears
The mountain-ponies prick their ears:
They hear the Danish boy,
While in the dell he sits alone
Beside the tree and corner-stone.

When near this blasted tree you pass
Two sods are plainly to be seen
Close at its root, and each with grass
Is covered fresh and green.
Like turf upon a new-made grave
These two green sods together lie;
Nor heat, nor cold, nor rain, nor wind
Can these two sods together bind,
Nor sun, nor earth, nor sky,
But side by side the two are laid
As if just severed by the spade.

(ll. 34–55)

The poetry reads like an interim stage between *The Thorn* and the last two Goslar 'spots of time'. Purged of their spookiness, the sods will become the 'long green ridge of turf . . . Whose shape was like a grave' (*1799*, i. 312–3), and the blasted tree will evoke a far different mood in the Waiting for the Horses. The boy similarly is half-way imaginative. In fact he is the most self-conscious borderer that Wordsworth ever created. Though spirit rather than flesh, he is audible to mountain-ponies and visible to passers-by, and in the final stanza it appears that he is capable not only of singing, but of taking pleasure in his immortal semi-human existence:

There sits he. In his face you spy
No trace of a ferocious air,
Nor ever was a cloudless sky
So steady or so fair.

The lovely Danish boy is blest
And happy in his flowery cove;
From bloody deeds his thoughts are far,
And yet he warbles songs of war—
They seem like songs of love,
For calm and gentle is his mien;
Like a dead boy he is serene.

(ll. 56–66)

The last line must surely have been intended to shock: it is less clear how it was intended to work. Perhaps the ballad would have gone on to say that he *is* a dead boy, but in terms of the poetry as written the important thing is that he isn't. He is a poet—indeed *the* poet—singing agelessly in childhood, warbling to his harp in a forgotton tongue that has the power of turning war to love, pain to joy. Past violence, transmuted, becomes a source of unending creativity.[6]

Seven years later, Wordsworth found a perfect expression for his wish-fulfilment in *The Solitary Reaper*, when the song of another of these child-borderers, also uncomprehended, drew from him his most beautiful lyric-poetry:

Will no one tell me what she sings?
Perhaps the plaintive numbers flow
For old, unhappy, far-off things,
And battles long ago . . .

(ll. 17–20)

Meanwhile, at Sockburn at the end of 1799, he created the Infant Babe—nobody's favourite sequence of *The Prelude*, but one of the most important nonetheless. The child in this case is a borderer three times over: as a (fairly) ordinary infant, and thus a new arrival; as one who, like the boy of the earlier 'spots of time', seems to verge upon the transcendental; and as an ante-type of the poet, capable astonishingly of exercising the full powers, perceptive and creative, of the primary imagination.

Oddly enough it seems again to have been one of Coleridge's children—Berkeley this time—who caused Wordsworth to think of infancy in such very unusual terms. Coleridge heard the news of Berkeley's death in early April 1799, and motivated by grief, and guilt at having been away from home, and a desire not to accuse God of inhumanity, he made some astonishing claims as to what the child in his year of life must have achieved. 'My baby has not lived in vain', he wrote, 'this life has been to him what it is to all of us, education and developement' (Griggs, i. 479). And again:

> What a multitude of admirable actions . . . it learnt even before it saw the light? and who shall count or conceive the infinity of its thoughts and feelings, it's hopes and fears, and joys, and pains, and desires, and presentiments, from the moment of it's birth to the moment when the glass, through which we saw him darkly, was broken . . .?
>
> (Griggs, i. 482)

Passing through Göttingen on their way home to England two weeks later, the Wordsworths would no doubt hear both of Berkeley's death, and of his father's consoling speculations. On the basis of these Wordsworth, with his quite different needs and preoccupations, arrived at a new theory of infant psychology.

Berkeley, for Coleridge, had been busy deserving an after-life: the Infant Babe is busy equipping himself for an ordinary one—as elsewhere in *The Prelude*, Wordsworth's concern is with

> the very world which is the world
> Of all of us, the place in which, in the end,
> We find our happiness, or not at all.
>
> (*1805*, x. 725–7)

After finishing *1799*, Part I, at Goslar at the beginning of the year, Wordsworth apparently wished to go straight on, but was unable to do so without encouragement from Coleridge.[7] We can't tell whether he had specific questions in mind that he wished to discuss, but there was one very large one that was bound sooner or later to be asked. The polytheist spirits of Part I, whether or not one can take them with full seriousness, must represent fairly late environmental influences upon the child; going back beyond these, why had the child been able to respond so imaginatively? What had been the source of those powers that in the twilight of memory he seemed already to possess? *MS JJ* shows that for a brief moment in October 1798 Wordsworth had been prepared to answer these questions in terms of a pantheist world-soul; but for some reason the passage concerned was edited out in an immediate revision.[8] Part I stands—and stands perfectly well—with no discussion of first principles: in the early section the spirit-world seems to exist mainly as a framework, in the second half the 'spots of time' doctrine has no supernatural implications, and in any case casts forward in its thinking rather than back. But the poet's border preoccupations are always with him, and always likely to provoke questions that it would be convenient to ignore.

As he begins work on Part II, after an eight months' interval, Wordsworth seems merely to be extending his poem to take in the period of adolescence. The first two hundred lines he composes are memorable for the beautiful and untroubled 'spots' that show the boy's response to the song of the wren at Furness Abbey (*1799*, ii. 98–139), and to the flute-playing on Windermere:

> oh, then the calm
> And dead still water lay upon my mind
> Even with a weight of pleasure, and the sky,
> Never before so beautiful, sank down
> Into my heart and held me like a dream.
>
> (*1799*, ii. 210–14)

The poet is not at this stage seeking explanations. He is recording —making permanent—moments of deep but relatively uncomplex emotion, aware that for him they are border experiences, yet linking them to no theory. Indeed one can see in the poetry a wish precisely to avoid speculation. At line 239, Wordsworth is hastening on

> to tell
> How Nature, intervenient till this time
> And secondary, now at length was sought
> For her own sake.

Then he pauses, as if to face the inevitable, and evasion gives place to almost petulant defensiveness:

> But who shall parcel out
> His intellect by geometric rules,
> Split like a province into round and square?
> Who knows the individual hour in which
> His habits were first sown even as a seed?
> Who that shall point as with a wand, and say
> 'This portion of the river of my mind
> Came from yon fountain'?
>
> (*1799*, ii. 242–9)

'Thou, my friend', Wordsworth goes on, addressing Coleridge, whose thinking can give to such questions a sense of proportion,

> art one
> More deeply read in thy own thoughts, no slave
> Of that false secondary power by which
> In weakness we create distinctions, then
> Believe our puny boundaries are things
> Which we perceive, and not which we have made.
> To thee, unblinded by these outward shews,
> The unity of all has been revealed,
> And thou wilt doubt with me, less aptly skilled
> Than many are to class the cabinet
> Of their sensations . . .[9]
>
> (*1799*, ii. 249–59)

Past feelings become in this last contemptuous phrase museum-pieces, dead and ready for cataloguing. The point that Wordsworth is making is quite easily missed: to those who have a unified apprehension of life, past and present are not distinct, because the one lives within the other; intellectual history cannot be parcelled out, habits can have no beginning, and progress can derive from no specific source. Coleridge in all this is a support. He will share Wordsworth's doubts as to the possibility of cataloguing exhibits of the mind, because to him 'The unity of all has been *revealed*'. His established Unitarianism lends authority to a position that is based in Wordsworth on a much more intuitive sense of over-all harmony. But, not surprisingly now that he has at last accepted the challenge to give his own account of beginnings, Wordsworth is writing also with an eye upon Milton. 'Hard task to analyse a soul', he comments, and his allusion to Raphael's words—'High matter thou enjoinest me, O prime of men,/Sad task and hard' (*PL* v. 563–4)—suggests that he does so in some anxiety. Milton had written of the universe in its infancy; Wordsworth is now presuming to claim a comparable grandeur for the dawning of an individual consciousness.

'Blessed the infant babe', Wordsworth starts abruptly, 'For with my best conjectures I would trace/The progress of our being'. Human development will be traced on this occasion not from Adam but from an ordinary child. And in place of hallowed

Christian tradition, the account will be based upon guesswork—the poet's 'best conjectures':

                                        blest the babe
Nursed in his mother's arms, the babe who sleeps
Upon his mother's breast, who, when his soul
Claims manifest kindred with an earthly soul,
Doth gather passion from his mother's eye.
Such feelings pass into his torpid life
Like an awakening breeze, and hence his mind
Even in the first trial of its powers,
Is prompt and watchful, eager to combine
In one appearance all the elements
And parts of the same object, else detached
And loth to coalesce. Thus day by day
Subjected to the discipline of love,
His organs and recipient faculties
Are quickened, are more vigorous; his mind spreads
Tenacious of the forms which it receives.
In one beloved presence—nay and more,
In that most apprehensive habitude
And those sensations which have been derived
From this beloved presence—there exists
A virtue which irradiates and exalts
All objects through all intercourse of sense.
No outcast he, bewildered and depressed;
Along his infant veins are interfused
The gravitation and the filial bond
Of Nature that connect him with the world.
Emphatically such a being lives
An inmate of this *active* universe.
From Nature largely he receives, nor so
Is satisfied, but largely gives again;
For feeling has to him imparted strength,
And—powerful in all sentiments of grief,
Of exultation, fear and joy—his mind,
Even as an agent of the one great mind,
Creates, creator and receiver both,
Working but in alliance with the works
Which it beholds. Such, verily, is the first

Poetic spirit of our human life—
By uniform control of after years
In most abated and suppressed, in some
Through every change of growth or of decay
Preeminent till death.

(*1799*, ii. 267–310; W.'s italics)

The tones and rhythms are expository, the diction is sometimes very pompous,[10] and altogether it is difficult to give this thoughtful passage the attention it requires. Nor does it any longer seem as astonishing as it was at the end of the eighteenth century to suggest than an infant 'gather[s] passion from his mother's eye', that her 'feelings pass into his torpid life/Like an awakening breeze'. We are so accustomed to thinking of the mother-child relationship as formative that even the magnificent intuition that a baby is 'Subjected to the discipline of love' comes as no surprise. Yet Wordsworth the infant psychologist is surely 100 years ahead of his time—his best conjectures in this case are very largely right.

More idiosyncratic are the powers that Wordsworth sees the infant as deriving from his mother's love. His organs and faculties are 'quickened'—given life—'his mind spreads/*Tenacious of the forms which it receives*'. Like the adult of *Tintern Abbey*—.

These forms of beauty have not been to me
As is a landscape to a blind man's eye . . .

(ll. 24–5)

—the child is busy storing up the visual shapes and images on which Wordsworthian security depends.[11] Though the poet is not consciously saying so, clear verbal echoes reveal that in this process the mother has taken the place of God. In the child's 'apprehensive habitude', and the feelings he derives from relationship,

there exists
A virtue which irradiates and exalts
All objects through all intercourse of sense.

Objects of the external world are irradiated by the mother's 'virtue' (power) just as for the Wordsworth of *Tintern Abbey* they had been permeated by the One Life:

I have felt
A presence that disturbs me with the joy
Of elevated thoughts, a sense sublime
Of something far more deeply interfused . . .
A motion and a spirit that impels
All thinking things, all objects of all thought . . .
(ll. 94–7, 101–2)

To confirm that there was at least an unconscious link in Wordsworth's mind, the word 'interfused' (not elsewhere recorded in his work until a *Prelude* revision of 1832) appears two lines further on in the Infant Babe:

No outcast he, bewildered and depressed;
Along his infant veins are interfused
The gravitation and the filial bond
Of Nature that connect him with the world.

Richard Onorato has suggested that Wordsworth's odd reference to the child as potentially an 'outcast' reflects his traumatic sense of desertion at the time of his mother's death.[12] Resentment is not as close to the surface as it is for a moment in *1805*, Book V—

Early died
My honoured mother, she who was the heart
And hinge of all our learnings and our loves;
She left us destitute, and as we might
Trooping together.
(v. 256–60)

—but its presence in the Infant Babe is confirmed by the original reading of *MS RV*: 'No outcast he, *abandoned* and depressed' (Parrish, 188–9). The origins of the poet's border preoccupation become for a moment unusually clear. Feelings of desertion had left Wordsworth with more than usual need to believe himself part of an integrated whole. There is clearly a sense in which Nature who 'never did betray / The heart that loved her' (*Tintern Abbey*, 123–4) is a substitute for the mother who had done just that. In July 1798 the need to belong could be satisfied by pantheist affirmation, in autumn 1799 there was much less certainty; and so we get a bond connecting the child to the world that is both straightforwardly human ('filial' by virtue of the child's relationship to his mother) and potentially transcendental, in that the mother has been replaced, and the child is now a son of Nature. The original single-line version of ll. 274–5 shows just how close these two ways of thinking were for Wordsworth:

> Such feelings pass into his torpid life
> *Like* an awakening breeze

had earlier been quite simply, 'This passion *is* the awakening breeze of life' (Parrish, 188–9).

Berkeley Coleridge, according to his father's speculations, might have learned 'a multitude of admirable actions' in the womb, not to mention 'the infinity of [his] thoughts and feelings', hopes, fears, joys, pains, desires, and presentiments, in the months that followed his birth. But even this paternal extravagance cannot match the powers ascribed to the Infant Babe. To some slight extent Coleridge feels himself restricted by the fact that Berkeley died at 10 months old (he is after all writing to Sara), and he intends merely to prove to himself that his child had embarked on the process of 'education and developement'. Wordsworth is under no such restriction; and, as a borderer, the Infant Babe is not of course being educated. 'Even in the first trial of his powers', he is

> prompt and watchful, eager to combine
> In one appearance all the elements
> And parts of the same object, else detached
> And loth to coalesce.

In terms of child psychology Wordsworth makes the wrong guess: an infant's problem is not with forming parts into wholes, but with perceiving differences, distinguishing between self and other. And in terms of his own life he regards the urge towards unity as a creative power implanted by his mother very early on, when we should probably associate it with trauma that followed her death at a considerably later (normally post-oedipal) stage. But these terms have very limited relevance. The Infant Babe is a baby only insofar as he sleeps upon his mother's breast. He embodies Wordsworth's intuition as to the paramount importance of maternal love, but his formidable qualities have little to do with this. They are the powers which the adult poet at the time of writing needs to believe that he himself possesses. In defining the child's border role, he is defining what he hopes to be his own, and at the same time chanting to himself:

> So was it when my life began,
> So is it now I am a man . . .

At this stage he is even prepared to add, 'So shall it be when I grow old':

> Such, verily, is the first
> Poetic spirit of our human life—
> By uniform control of after years
> In most abated and suppressed, in some
> Through every change of growth or of decay
> Preeminent till death.

Earlier in the year the 'spots of time' had 'with distinct *preeminence* retain[ed]/A fructifying virtue'; now Wordsworth hopes the poetic spirit, which the 'spots' had 'nourished and invisible repaired', will be 'preeminent till death'. It won't, of course, but the echo-link is interesting. Wordsworth is talking of imagination, founded in the past and lasting forward. The Infant Babe enables him to define the remoter origins, answer the question as to where the imaginative power displayed in the 'spots' had actually come from, and thereby creates in him a qualified assurance for the future. The passage represents Wordsworth's final position during the period of early *Prelude* composition when he is seemingly in retreat from the full pantheist assumptions of Alfoxden. Two reservations have to be made: as always, it is likely that we are dealing not with radically altered positions, but with different ways of expressing the same intuitions; and (again, as always) Coleridge's thought is likely to be in the background. *1799* will end with a return to pantheism, as Wordsworth borrows from *The Pedlar* to describe the feelings of his 16-year-old self—'in all things/I saw one life, and felt that it was joy' (ii. 459–60)—but the Infant Babe looks forward, not back. His is an 'active universe' in which there is no shared life-force. The love which he receives from his mother is all-important, but not universal: his mind functions merely '*in alliance* with the works/Which it beholds'—they are out there, different, distinct. The role of the individual is still defined in terms of his relationship with God, but the presence to be felt at once in the blue sky and the mind of man has been replaced by a quite separate divinity for whom man's best hope is to work as an agent. This new 'one great mind' could scarcely be further from the 'ebbing and . . . flowing mind,/Expression ever varying' that the Pedlar had traced in the 'fixed and steady lineaments' of Nature (ll. 55–7).

'Tis the sublime of man,/Our noontide majesty', Coleridge had written in *Religious Musings* early in 1795, 'to know ourselves/ Parts and proportions of one wond'rous whole'. And just in case anyone got it wrong, he had added, ' 'tis God/Diffused through all, that doth make all one whole' (ll. 135–40). For Wordsworth in *The Pedlar* and *Tintern Abbey* man's highest achievement had been 'see[ing] into the life of things', seeing that things *had* life, seeing that the life they had was God, seeing that one was oneself a part of it all. The creativity of the individual, like all his other powers, would be subordinated to this achievement. Now, suddenly, creativity becomes not sharing *with* God, but acting *like* God—not being at one with external Nature, but working merely in alliance with it:

> powerful in all sentiments of grief,
> Of exultation, fear and joy—his mind,
> Even as an agent of the one great mind,
> Creates, creator and receiver both,
> Working but in alliance with the works
> Which it beholds.

There had been hints towards a definition of imagination in Wordsworth's earlier poetry, and the faculty had been implied in Coleridge's Berkeleyan assumption that the symbol-language of Nature could be interpreted,[13] but in the Infant Babe one hears for the first time the tones of the famous later pronouncements. As 'creator and receiver both', the child anticipates the creative and perceptive 'higher minds' of *1805*, Book XIII:

> They from their native selves can send abroad
> Like transformation, for themselves create
> A like existence; and, whene'er it is
> Created for them, catch it by an instinct.
>
> (ll. 93–6)

And one should not be afraid to say that he anticipates too the greatest of all Romantic border statements, Coleridge's definition of the primary imagination as 'the living power and prime agent of all human perception . . . a repetition in the finite mind of the eternal act of creation in the infinite I AM' (*BL* xiii. 167). Coleridge's craving for unity is quite as urgent as Wordsworth's, but he writes as a Christian, and is capable of philosophical, doctrinal, reassurance in a way that Wordsworth hardly ever is. Border preoccupations with him derive typically from a sense of personal exclusion: it was easier to believe that a harmony existed, than to feel himself part of it. Often they seem to be speculative—

> And what if all of animated Nature
> Be but organic harps diversely framed . . .?
>
> (*Eolian Harp*, 44–5)

—attempting to define the forms in which God may be present, and apprehended, in order to define Coleridge himself as belonging. At other times the poet—in the guise of Lamb, or Hartley, or the Mariner, or even himself—appears in situations that portray the redemptive possibility of communion. Effectively of course all these seekings to understand, and creative/perceptive acts of sympathy, are definitions of imagination. The language used in *Biographia Literaria* is evocative, expressive of need and hope rather than certainty, because Coleridge is ascribing to the human mind a godlike quality in which he only half dares to believe. Though so frequently quoted, his words have not always been well understood, or at least their less immediate implications have not been taken. Despite the ordering of the definitions, and the perfectly clear statement that the secondary imagination is an echo, scholar after scholar has contrived to think that for Coleridge the primary came second. Shawcross notes in his learned and much-reprinted edition of 1907:

> The distinction appears to be this. The primary imagination is the organ of common perception, the faculty by which we have experience of an actual world of phenomena. The secondary imagination is the same power in a heightened degree, which enables its possessor to see the world of our common experience in its real significance.[14]

Richards in 1934 says the same in rather more evocative terms:

The primary imagination is normal perception that produces the usual world of the senses,

> That inanimate cold world allowed
> To the poor loveless ever-anxious crowd

the world of motor-buses, beef-steaks and acquaintances, the framework of things and events within which we maintain our everyday existence, the world of the routine satisfaction of our minimum exigencies. The secondary imagination, re-forming this world gives us not only poetry—in the limited sense . . . —but every aspect of the routine world in which it is invested with other values than those necessary for our bare continuance as living beings . . .[15]

And Basil Willey, though no scholar has been more sympathetic to Coleridge's needs and achievements, adopts the same position, both in 1946 and 1972 referring with Richards to 'the inanimate cold world' of the primary imagination.[16] The run is broken in 1950 by Walter Jackson Bate, who as always is very much to the point:

the entire direction of Coleridge's criticism is opposed to the belief that he regarded the poetic imagination as merely an 'echo' of a capacity common to us all. [The primary imagination] is rather the highest exertion of the imagination that the 'finite mind' has to offer; and its scope . . . necessarily includes universals which lie beyond the restricted field of the 'secondary' imagination. For the appointed task of the 'secondary' imagination is to 'idealize and unify' its objects; and it can hardly 'unify' the universals.[17]

As a practical critic, Richards might well have taken a closer look at Coleridge's extraordinary use of language. Why should a man describe 'the world of the routine satisfaction of our minimum exigencies' as the result of 'a repetition in the finite mind of the eternal act of creation in the infinite I AM'? It seems a little extravagant. Willey gives to Coleridge's words their full seriousness of purpose, but even he seems not to go far enough in his conclusions. 'This is not to be dismissed as metaphysical babble', he writes,

a whole philosophy, lies beneath each phrase. Coleridge is here summarizing the great struggle and victory of his life—his triumph over the old tradition of Locke and Hartley, which had assumed that the mind in perception was wholly passive, 'a lazy looker-on on an external world'.[18]

This no doubt is true: the mind is in a philosophical sense creative of the world it sees, because it does not see objects, it sees objects upon which it puts its own constructions, imposes its own categories. And certainly Coleridge prized the victory which this Kantian viewpoint gave him over 'the sandy sophisms of Locke, and the mechanic dogmatists' (Griggs, iv. 574); but his language is asking us to see it all in a far less humdrum context. The imagination is not merely creative (and godlike in its creation), but perceptive too; it is 'the living power and prime agent of *all* human perception', including—or primarily—the perception of God. Jehovah named himself to Moses in Exodus as I AM; to do so was creative because self-consciousness implies the existence of something beyond the self, and as God's thoughts are acts, that which is implied is necessarily created. This process, eternal because an infinite being is not subject to time, is repeated within the finite human mind, and constitutes the primary imagination. Coleridge's definition had been prepared for in the 'Theses' of the preceding chapter of *Biographia* (xii), where there is not only a long footnote claiming that Jehovah in his self-consciousness 'revealed the fundamental truth of all philosophy' (p. 152), but also a statement which confirms that man's achievement of a comparable awareness is for Coleridge the means of attaining to ultimate religious truth: 'We begin with the I KNOW MYSELF, in order to end with the absolute I AM. We proceed from the self, in order to lose and find all self in GOD' (p. 154). It is of course precisely what happens in the 'serene and blessed mood' of *Tintern Abbey*—a mood that has not merely been experienced by the poet himself, but is assumed to be accessible to all. 'Laid asleep in body', the individual finds his true self as 'a living soul'. In this state of mystical awareness, he can 'see into the life of things' because he shares the joy and harmony which are the life-giving presence of God.

The traditional view of the primary imagination as relatively unimportant, 'the organ of common perception', makes nothing of the drama of Coleridge's presentation—his stage-managing of the bogus, and very funny, letter from a friend; his threat that a proper treatment of the subject could not 'amount to so little as an hundred pages'; and of course his simple placing of the primary first, where its extraordinary language and extraordinary claims meet the full impact of the reader's built-up curiosity. Nor does such a view take into account the linking of the three definitions: it seems logical to suppose that in choosing to end with fancy Coleridge meant to proceed from most to least important, most to least vital. And, as Professor Bate points out, it makes nonsense of the secondary imagination's *echo*ing the primary:

> The secondary I consider as an echo of the former, co-existing with the conscious will, yet still as identical with the primary in the kind of its agency, and differing only in degree, and in the mode of its operation.
>
> (*BL* xiii. 167)

If man's self-consciousness, though a positive *repetition* of God's first (and eternal) creative act, amounts to awareness of an inanimate cold world, membership of 'the poor loveless ever-anxious crowd', where does it leave the poet who echoes it?—and indeed does so by a decision of the conscious will. It seems a good deal easier not to ask such questions, but to put the primary first, and accept that (as for Blake and Wordsworth and Shelley, in their different ways) the poet for Coleridge is a prophet. His role is immensely important—

> to contemplate the Ancient of Days and all His works with feelings as fresh as if all had then sprang forth at the first creative fiat. . . . To carry on the feelings of childhood into the powers of manhood . . .
>
> (*BL* iv. 49)

—but it is secondary, an echo, because it consists in giving form to the apprehension of God, not in the apprehension itself;[19] and because it is conscious. It isn't that Coleridge doesn't value the conscious will—it is the basis of the Kantian imperative that supports his entire moral philosophy—but like Wordsworth he craves the immediacy of border experience in which 'We . . . lose and find all self in God'. Of course his definition of the primary imagination covers the whole range of human experience, offers the means by which ordinary things too (beef-steaks, if hardly motor-buses) are perceived in their full banality; but he places it first, gives it its prominence and magniloquence, because it contains a border hope that goes back, as so much of *Biographia* goes back, to his earlier shared ideals and shared assumptions.[20]

'Even as an agent of the one great mind', the Infant Babe 'creates, creator and receiver both'. Already in the autumn of 1799 the child embodies 'the living power and prime agent of all human perception', and does so because of his closeness to God.

His creativity is not in so many words said to be a repetition of God's; but it both derives from, and reproduces, the life-giving power of the mother that is so clearly linked in the poet's mind to the immanent presence of *Tintern Abbey*:

> Thus day by day
> Subjected to the discipline of love,
> His organs and recipient faculties
> Are quickened, are more vigorous; his mind spreads,
> Tenacious of the forms which it receives.
> In [that] beloved presence . . .
> there exists
> A virtue which irradiates and exalts
> All objects through all intercourse of sense.

There exists, that is, imagination. One is bound to wonder what conversation had centred on at Göttingen in April, apart from the death of Berkeley. Coleridge had not yet read the Germans—Leibnitz, Tetens, Kant, Fichte, Schlegel, Schelling—who were to be the basis of his later definitions; but there he was in Germany, in a university-town, and given his preoccupations he can hardly not have been talking to people about philosophy.[21]

Of those border sequences that follow the Infant Babe in *1799* two are embedded *Pedlar* material from Alfoxden, presented now as the poet's own boyhood experience—first *In storm and tempest*, with its evocation of 'possible sublimity';[22] then, sadly hedged about with qualification and apology, the pantheist sequence, 'From Nature and her overflowing soul'. Alongside, or rather between, these comes a passage of great power that was presumably written shortly after the Infant Babe in autumn 1799. Recalling moments at Hawkshead when he sat alone in the early morning stillness of the hills, Wordsworth returns to his earlier questioning:

> How shall I trace the history, where seek
> The origin of what I then have felt?
> Oft in those moments such a holy calm
> Did overspread my soul that I forgot
> The agency of sight, and what I saw
> Appeared like something in myself, a dream,
> A prospect in my mind.

(*1799*, ii. 395–401)

This is not a case of landscape internalized, as in *There was a boy* and the flute-playing on Windermere; in his solipsism the boy goes out to meet the view, sees it as if it were part of himself. There is the characteristic merging of inner and outer, but mind is now the dominant partner. It is a little surprising that this dominance should be portrayed as a religious experience—'a holy calm/Did overspread my soul'—but the poetry makes, and reiterates, this point:

> 'Twere long to tell
> What spring and autumn, what the winter snows,
> And what the summer shade, what day and night,
> The evening and the morning, what my dreams
> And what my waking thoughts, supplied to nurse
> That spirit of religious love in which
> I walked with Nature.
>
> (*1799*, ii. 401–7)

Questioning has been replaced by disingenuous refusal to relate, "'Twere long to tell'; and in order to evoke the task he has no intention of undertaking, Wordsworth produces lines and rhythms whose beauty seems rather too obviously rhetorical. Imagination apparently did not seem to him to have required any very special nourishment during adolescence, and he hasn't a lot to say. There is no attempt to link back amid this ordinary, seasonable, pleasurable experience to the traumatic 'spots' of Part I, though presumably they would have been held to be working at some deeper level, ready later to exercise their fructifying power upon the adult. For the moment it is not the means by which imagination has been sustained that is important, but the fact that nothing has changed:

> let this at least
> Be not forgotten, that I still retained
> My first creative sensibility,
> That by the regular action of the world
> My soul was unsubdued.
>
> (*1799*, ii. 407–11)

The 'uniform, control of after years' has been withstood; 'the first poetic spirit of our human life' has become autonomous, even capricious. The infant who had been 'creator and receiver both' is possessed by the unruly power of his own creativity:

A plastic power
Abode with me, a forming hand, at times
Rebellious, acting in a devious mood,
A local spirit of its own, at war
With general tendency, but for the most
Subservient strictly to the external things
With which it communed. An auxiliar light
Came from my mind, which on the setting sun
Bestowed new splendour; the melodious birds,
The gentle breezes, fountains that ran on
Murmuring so sweetly in themselves, obeyed
A like dominion, and the midnight storm
Grew darker in the presence of my eye.
Hence my obeisance, my devotion hence,
And *hence* my transport.[23]

(*1799*, ii. 411–25; W.'s italics)

Nowhere is mind so dominant, or at least, nowhere is dominance of mind so clearly recognized. From *Tintern Abbey* onwards many of the borderers *half*-create 'the mighty world/Of eye and ear'; this one first subjects it to his dominion and then, astonishingly, gives Nature his devotion for being thus subjected. It was a very confident moment.

The Infant Babe is in many ways the most important of the child-borderers, but the most famous, the 'Mighty prophet, seer blest' of the second half of *Intimations* (1804), stands all his assumptions quietly on their head. He too is godlike in his infancy, but his is a power that cannot be sustained. Childhood is once more fully symbolic; though curiously, as at Goslar, it becomes so while the poet is specially aware of the sharpness of early memory. The mythic child who is born into 'a sleep and a forgetting', and 'daily farther from the east/Must travel', is flanked on the one side by Wordsworth's 1802 lament for lost innocent vision—'Where is it gone, the glory and the dream?'—and on the other by his 1804 rejection of nostalgia:

The thought of our past years in me doth breed
Perpetual benedictions; not indeed
For that which is most worthy to be blest,
Delight and liberty, the simple creed
Of childhood . . .

Not for these I raise
The song of thanks and praise,
But for those blank misgivings of a creature
Moving about in worlds not realized . . .
(*Intimations*, 134–43)

Wordsworth had been reworking the 'spots of time' for the five-Book *Prelude* when he wrote these lines, yet despite the value that he set upon the 'blank misgivings' of actuality he chose to create a symbol-child who has nothing to do with personal experience, and little enough with observation. In the words of the Fenwick Note, 'I took hold of the notion of pre-existence as having sufficient foundation in humanity for authorising me . . . to make for my purpose the best use of it I could as a poet' (Grosart, iii. 195). As a poet he wished to evoke his overwhelming sense of loss—lost vision, lost creativity—and he wished too, though this presumably was unconscious, to comfort himself with the border implication that if we come 'trailing clouds of glory . . . From God who is our home', then we can presently go back to 'that imperial palace whence [we] came' (*Intimations*, 64–5, 84). This was the period at which he wrote,

Our destiny, our nature, and our home,
Is with infinitude—and only there;
With hope it is, hope that can never die,
Effort, and expectation, and desire,
And something evermore about to be.
(*1805*, vi. 538–42)

and wrote also:

Oh mystery of man, from what a depth
Proceed thy honours! I am lost, but see
In simple childhood something of the base
On which thy greatness stands . . .
(xi. 328–31)

Valuing above all the aspiring mind, but having (still) no conviction of that towards which it can finally aspire, he turns his sense of loss to gain by deducing what may be, from what was.

Alone of the borderers, the child of *Intimations* has known direct contact with God, and is actually said to be in possession of the truths for which the poet strives:

O thou, whose outward seeming doth belie
Thy soul's immensity;
Thou best philosopher, who yet dost keep
Thy heritage, thou eye among the blind,
That, deaf and silent, read'st the eternal deep,
Haunted for ever by the eternal mind—
Thou mighty prophet, seer blest,
On whom those truths do rest,
Which we are toiling all our lives to find . . .

(*Intimations*, 108–16)

Coleridge's '*mental* bombast'—'thoughts and images too great for the subject'—seems on the face of it a fair assessment. In the previous stanza Wordsworth has offered a family scene, which, though appallingly sentimental, is clearly an effort at naturalism:

Behold the child among his new-born blisses,
A four-years' darling of a pigmy size—
See where mid work of his own hand he lies,
Fretted by sallies of his mother's kisses,
With light upon him from his father's eyes . . .

(ll. 85–9)

Now suddenly he switches to the symbolic, producing merely heightened incongruity. 'Not to stop at the daring spirit of metaphor', Coleridge writes,

which connects the epithets 'deaf and silent' with the apostrophized eye . . . we will merely ask, what does all this mean? In what sense is a child of that age a philosopher? In what sense does he read 'the eternal deep'? In what sense is he declared to be 'for ever haunted' by the Supreme Being? or so inspired as to deserve the splendid titles of a mighty prophet, a blessed seer? By reflection? by knowledge? by conscious intuition? or by any form or modification of consciousness? These would be tidings indeed . . .

(*BL* xxii. 260)

'Children at this age', he continues, 'give us no such information. . . . There are many of us that still possess some remembrances. . . . ' Not for a moment does he pause to think that Wordsworth too has his early memories, that he may in this case have chosen to write a poetry that is removed from experience. The fact that the writing is clumsy makes Coleridge's literal-minded commentary appear less obtuse than it otherwise would, but it seems to be the theology not the quality that worries him. Wordsworth's utterly non-theological epithets provoke him to a further page of speculation. Spinoza, Boehme, Jacobi, Lessing are invoked, and the outcome is still more rhetorical questions:

> In what sense can the magnificent attributes above quoted be appropriated to a child, which would not make them equally suitable to a bee, or a dog, or a field of corn; or even to a ship, or to the wind and waves that propel it? The omnipresent Spirit works equally in them as in the child; and the child is equally unconscious of it as they.
>
> (*BL* xxii. 261–2)

Coleridge's thoughts have turned to pantheism partly no doubt because it is the central preoccupation of *Biographia*, but also because it is a non-symbolic border state. To his own dogged satisfaction he establishes that Wordsworth's claims for the child can be true in this one limited sense. He knows of course that this was not the sense that Wordsworth intended, but doesn't let it deter him. It is almost as if he is deliberately excluding the possibility that the terms used might have an imaginative validity, or at least have for the poet himself a symbolic force that he was failing to communicate. Can he really have had no understanding of Wordsworth's border preoccupation, or no sympathy with it? What makes the situation odder is that, though thinking in symbolic terms, Wordsworth had once again had a particular child in mind as he wrote, and once again it had been Hartley Coleridge. Hartley had been the 'four-years' darling of a pigmy size . . . Fretted by *sallies*' of his mother Sara's kisses (one hopes the pun was not intended), and Coleridge himself had been the indulgent father who completed the family scene. This part of *Intimations* in fact fits into a sequence of Hartley border-poems that goes back to within days of his birth in September 1796. Before Coleridge had ever seen his child he wrote a sonnet speculating on his pre-existence—'some have said/We lived ere yet this *fleshly* robe we wore' (Griggs, i. 246)—and the following month he justified his doing so in almost exactly the terms that Wordsworth would later use of *Intimations*: 'Now, that the thinking part of man, i.e. the soul, existed previously to its appearance in its present body, may be very wild philosophy; but it is very intelligible poetry.'[24] Hartley does not come trailing clouds of glory; no more than his talented younger brother, who learns a multitude of admirable habits *in the womb*, is he capable at any stage of catching gleams of past existence. His childhood does, however, take on a border quality remarkably soon. In succession, there is Hartley in *Frost at Midnight* (aged 17 months) wandering like a breeze, seeing and hearing 'The lovely shapes and sounds intelligible' of God's eternal language; Hartley who two months later, in *The Nightingale*, hushes his sobs and laughs most silently at the sight of the moon; Hartley at the conclusion to *Christabel*, Part II—by now

> A little child, a limber elf,
> Singing, dancing to itself,
> A fairy thing with red round cheeks,
> That always finds, and never seeks . . .
>   such a vision to the sight
> As fills a father's eyes with light.
>
> (ll. 656–61)

There is a difference of tone of course as the border claim that Hartley could find without seeking becomes in Wordsworth's solemn envious terms,

> Thou mighty prophet, seer blest,
> On whom those truths do rest
> Which we are toiling all our lives to find . . .
>
> (*Intimations*, 114–16)

but the claim itself doesn't seem very different.

To both Wordsworth and Coleridge, Hartley clearly just *was* a borderer. As Coleridge puts it in a letter to Poole of October 1803

> Hartley is what he always was—a strange, strange boy—'*exquisitely wild*'! An utter visionary! Like the moon among thin clouds, he moves in a circle of light of his own making—he alone, in a light of his own.
>
> (Griggs, ii. 1014)

The quotation that Coleridge italicizes comes significantly from a recent Wordsworth poem, published in 1807 as *To H. C: Six Years Old*, but in its composition very closely connected with the Ode:

> O thou, whose fancies from afar are brought,
> Who of thy words dost make a mock apparel,
> And fittest to unutterable thought
> The breeze-like motion and the self-born carol;

Thou faery voyager that dost float
In such clear water that thy boat
May rather seem
To brood on air than on an earthly stream,
Suspended in a stream as clear as sky
Where earth and heaven do make one imagery;
O blessed vision, happy child,
Thou art so exquisitely wild,
I think of thee with many fears
For what may be thy lot in future years.

(ll. 1–14)

Suspended in his midway existence between heaven and earth, floating on water whose clarity shows the power of imaginative vision yet undimmed, Hartley contains within him the central myth of *Intimations*. He also explains, as nothing else could, how Wordsworth came to create the symbol-child to whom Coleridge so much objected. If one places *To H.C.* next door to (or perhaps in between) stanzas VII and VIII of the Ode it becomes suddenly clear why the child has brought his fancies 'from afar', why his words are 'mock-apparel'. He is acting life,

As if his whole vocation
Were endless imitation,

(*Intimations*, 106–7)

living according to the 'plan or chart' (*Intimations*, 90) of his fantasy, not yet subject to the weight of custom, and not yet tied to its restricting forms of language. The thought he has is truly unutterable, and still finds its natural expression in 'Singing, dancing *to itself*'—'The breeze-like motion, and the *self-born* carol'.[25]

So far from Coleridge's being unable in *Biographia* to comprehend the border implications of the Ode ('In what sense is a child of that age a philosopher? In what sense does he read the eternal deep?'), he is shown to be behaving exactly as he did over the Preface to *Lyrical Ballads*, and ridiculing in Wordsworth a way of thinking which had originally been his own—or, at least, to which he had originally contributed very much.[26] Perhaps it was this fact that irritated him especially: he had himself shown Wordsworth how to go too far. Through fatherhood, and through the special qualities of Hartley's childhood, he had sought a greater understanding, in terms that might have been at times indulgent, but which had never been far from the safely theological. Wordsworth had taken Hartley on beyond these connections, crediting him with powers that had (and, for him, needed) no philosophical basis, and yet addressing him, in a way that Coleridge had every reason to find affronting, as 'Thou *best* philosopher'.

It would have been so much more valuable to have Coleridge's opinion of the great poetry of the end of *Intimations*, especially perhaps of the conclusion to stanza IX. Here memory and myth come together in a beautiful and fully imaginative expression of the special border importance of childhood:

> Not for these I raise
> The song of thanks and praise . . .
> But for those first affections,
> Those shadowy recollections,
> Which, be they what they may,
> Are yet the fountain light of all our day,
> Are yet the master light of all our seeing,
> Uphold us, cherish us, and make
> Our noisy years seem moments in the being
> Of the eternal silence—truths that wake
> To perish never,
> Which neither listlessness, nor mad endeavour,
> Nor man, nor boy,
> Nor all that is at enmity with joy,
> Can utterly abolish or destroy.
>
> (ll. 140–1, 146–58)

In the Waiting for the Horses, early emotions ('first affections') and twilight memories had been 'spectacles and sounds to which/ [the poet] often would repair, and thence would drink/*As at a fountain*' (*1799*, i. 368–70); now five years later they are 'the fountain-light' of adult vision. There is a surprising consistency in Wordsworth's thinking and imagery, but whereas at Goslar, autobiography (*1799*, Part I) and symbol (Lucy, the Danish Boy) had been normally distinct, now the poetry can bond the two. Taking over the role of the mother, as Nature had earlier done, memory upholds and *cherishes* adult imagination, providing the essential border reassurance that human existence is part of a totality. The vivid phrase 'Our noisy years', though on one level standing for life as a whole, draws attention especially to the unthinking boyhood that Wordsworth looked back upon so enviously; while 'the being/Of the eternal silence' magnificently evokes the harmony for which he craved. But, impressive as it is, this merging of personal experience into myth merely prepares the way for the child-borderers who sport upon the shores of immortality. In seven lines Wordsworth creates a spot of visionary time, a gleam not of past, but of ideal, existence:

> Hence, in a season of calm weather,
> Though inland far we be,
> Our souls have sight of that immortal sea
> Which brought us hither,
> Can in a moment travel thither
> And see the children sport upon the shore,
> And hear the mighty waters rolling evermore.
> (*Intimations*, 159–65)

The poetry is strangely visual, yet imaginative in its every detail and suggestion. The season of calm weather offers the characteristic pause as the narrative of a 'spot' begins to develop. 'Inland', though implying distance travelled away from the sea of pre-existence and into middle age, is a word that has already its border associations: the Wye above Tintern has 'a sweet *inland* murmur' the landscape at Furness listens to the sea in 'more than *inland* peace'. On this occasion it prefaces the assurance that through an act of imagination the presence of the transcendental can still be perceived—that borderers we remain. No contact though is possible, no joining in with the children in their games and unself-consciousness. The adult is for ever deprived of those joys 'That had no need of a remoter charm,/By thought supplied' (*Tintern Abbey*, 82–3). But if his soul is not deafened with the drumming of a fleshly ear, it can hear in the past a promise for the future. The mighty waters of eternity ring life round, linking the end to the beginning.

Yet the intimations of the Ode are not of Christian immortality. A year later, in February 1805, belief in an afterlife was to become for Wordsworth a matter of urgent personal need. Prompted by the death of John, he was to lead the *Prelude* river of imagination into an ocean of rest and reward.[27] There are hints in the Ode of such pious acceptance—strength is to be found 'In the faith that looks through death,/In years that bring the philosophic mind' (ll. 178–9)—but this is not what the poem is about. Wordsworth's Fenwick Note, apart from its much (and rightly) quoted account of the poet on his way to school grasping at walls and trees to rescue himself from the 'abyss of idealism', offers the extraordinary detail of his fantasy about bodily assumption:

> Nothing was more difficult for me in childhood than to admit the notion of death as a state applicable to my own being. . . it was not so much from the source of animal vivacity that my difficulty came as from a sense of the indomitableness of the spirit within me. I used to brood over the stories of Enoch and Elijah, and almost to persuade myself that, whatever might become of others, I should be translated in something of the same way into heaven.
> (Grosart, iii. 194)

Enoch and Elijah do not die, they cross the border *as their terrestial selves*—and as a tribute to man's unconquerable mind. For once a memory of Wordsworth's old age adds something of real importance to our understanding of the poetry.

The child-borderers of the earlier period had existed to provide evidence of election; those of the Ode show these upholding and cherishing memories being themselves carefully cherished:

> Oh joy that in our embers
> Is something that doth live,
> That nature yet remembers
> What was so fugitive.
> (ll. 130–3)

The visionary gleam has gone—'the hour/Of splendour in the grass, of glory in the flower' (ll. 172–3)—but the fact that it was once there is infinitely precious. Though the mood now is unremittingly elegiac, childhood memories continue their work of nourishment and invisible repair. For the moment, too, they continue to fructify.

Chapter 4

Visions of Paradise: Spring 1800

Domestic happiness, thou only bliss
Of Paradise that has survived the Fall!
(Cowper: *The Task*)

I. 'THE EARTH IS ALL BEFORE ME' (THE PREAMBLE AND PROSPECTUS)

On the morning of 18 November 1799 Coleridge was sitting beside Ullswater near the house of Thomas Clarkson, the abolitionist, with whom he and Wordsworth had spent the previous night. His thoughts were cheerful, self-indulgent, and so bawdy as to need the veiling decency of German and Greek when committed to his notebook:

> Monday morning—sitting on a tree stump at the brink of the lake by Mr Clarkson's—perfect serenity. That round fat backside of a hill ጠ with its image in the water made together *one* absolutely undistinguishable form . . . . The road appeared a sort of suture, in many places exactly as the weiblich τετραγραμματον is painted in anatomical books! I never saw so sweet an image![1]

Though Coleridge's mood might not reflect it, it was a moment of great importance: not a final parting of the ways between him and Wordsworth—that was delayed for ten troubled, yet often supportive and productive, years—but a moment at which for the first time their differing temperaments and differing needs had been acknowledged.

In making '*one* absolutely undistinguishable form', the round fat double backside of the hill appeals to the desire in Coleridge for unity, the struggle 'at all events . . . to idealize and to unify'. The preoccupation appears again in more serious, but no less characteristic, tones in the entry that follows:

If I begin a poem of Spinoza, thus it should begin. I would make a pilgrimage to the burning sands of Arabia, or etc etc to find the man who could explain to me [how] there can be *oneness*, there being infinite perceptions—yet there must be *one*ness, not an intense union but an absolute unity, for etc

(*Notebooks*, i, no. 556)

For a time the man to reconcile oneness and infinite individual perceptions had seemed to be Wordworth. Confronted with *There was a boy*—Wordsworth's very different reflections on reflections in a lake—Coleridge had written in December 1798: 'That "uncertain heaven received/Into the bosom of the steady lake" I should have recognised any where; and had I met these lines running wild in the deserts of Arabia, I should instantly have screamed out "Wordsworth!"' (Griggs, i. 452–3). At Alfoxden in spring 1798 Wordsworth's intuition of harmony had been offered the support of dogma by Coleridge's Unitarianism; and as early as the previous autumn it had been clear that Coleridge drew support from Wordsworth's (and Dorothy's) unmediated intuitions. Nature's 'melodies of woods, and winds, and waters', her 'general dance and minstrelsy' (*Osorio*, Act V; *Dungeon*, 24, 27), must surely be a case of the Wordsworths' influence appearing in his poetry, and in a more famous context these become the redemptive love and sharing of *The Ancient Mariner*. But the clearest example is presumably *Frost at Midnight*, where Hartley receives as his father's blessing the Wordsworthian childhood that Coleridge himself had lacked:

For I was reared
In the great city, pent mid cloisters dim,
And saw nought lovely but the sky and stars.
But *thou*, my babe! shalt wander like a breeze
By lakes and sandy shores, beneath the crags
Of ancient mountain, and beneath the clouds . . .

(ll. 51–6)

There is no reason to think that in the early German period to which *There was a boy* belongs Coleridge would have been less convinced, or less reassured, by Wordsworthian reciprocity. The voice of mountain torrents 'carried far into [the] heart', the 'solemn imagery' of Nature entering unawares into the mind, would have been in some sense a guarantee of 'the one and indivisible' for which he yearned. But the German separation dragged on. 'I am sure I need not say how you are incorporated into the better part of my being', Coleridge wrote *c.* December 1798, 'how, whenever I spring forward into the future with noble affections, I always alight by your side' (Griggs, i. 453); yet he lingered in Göttingen till the following July, and then—though daily expected by the Wordsworths—didn't go north on his return till the end of October.

By 18 November, when Coleridge was sitting on his tree-stump, a decision had been taken that despite all their plans to live near to each other, re-enact on a permanent basis the closeness of Alfoxden and Nether Stowey, he and Wordsworth should go their separate ways. Wordsworth should return to Grasmere and rent the house (Dove Cottage) which they had seen to let earlier in their walking-tour, and Coleridge would go south to become a journalist in London. The decision was of course reversed when Coleridge came to live at Greta Hall, Keswick, in July 1800, but was nonetheless important. The official reason for separating was Coleridge's need of a library, but the two men had grown apart. Wordsworth in concluding the 1799 *Prelude* at the end of November could write movingly of their having attained by different roads 'The self-same bourne' in the love of Nature, but there are hints of wishful-thinking alongside the dignified sorrow of his final address:

thou hast sought
The truth in solitude, and thou art one
The most intense of Nature's worshippers,
In many things my brother, chiefly here
In this my deep devotion. Fare thee well:
Health and the quiet of a healthful mind
Attend thee, seeking oft the haunts of men—
But yet more often living with thyself,
And for thyself—so haply shall thy days
Be many, and a blessing to mankind.

(*1799*, ii. 505–14)

The last five lines admit Coleridge's difference, and need for different conditions of work; the first five show Wordsworth's personal need (more obvious still in the conclusion of *1805*, Book XIII: 'Prophets of Nature, we to them will speak . . . ') to believe that his 'deep devotion' is fully shared. No doubt it still could be so at times, but there was to be no prolonged recapturing of the mood of Alfoxden. It is difficult not to think that Coleridge had Wordsworth in mind when he distinguished 'intense union' from the true oneness that consists in 'absolute unity'.

By chance an eye-witness account has been preserved of how Wordsworth and Coleridge seemed at this important moment in their relationship; in fact it is almost the only account of what they were like when together. Catherine Clarkson, their hostess on the night of 17 November, wrote on 12 January 1800 to Priscilla Lloyd (later wife of Wordsworth's brother Christopher):

> I must tell you that we [had] a visit from Coleridge and W. Wordsworth. They spent a whole day with us. C was in high spirits and talked a great deal. W was more reserved, but there was neither hauteur nor moroseness in his reserve. He has a fine commanding figure, is rather handsome, and looks as if he was born to be a great prince or a great general. He seems very fond of C, laughing at all his jokes and taking all opportunities of shewing him off . . .[2]

It is difficult to know quite what should be made of this very personal impression, but the Clarksons were Coleridge's friends, and it is interesting that Catherine, who had never met Wordsworth before, should regard him as showing Coleridge off. One could certainly read unease into Wordsworth's behaviour, but affectionate understanding seems quite as likely. It could be that in their different ways both men were in fact relieved that a decision had been reached. Coleridge's high spirits we know persisted on the eighteenth, and they seem to have lasted. His return to Sockburn on the twenty-first, *en route* for London, was followed by the evening of 'conundrums and puns and stories and laughter' with the Hutchinsons, on which to judge from Coleridge's later Notebook entry (this time in Latin) he seems to have shown a good deal of self-confidence: 'pressed the hand of Sara [Hutchinson] for a long time behind her back—and then, for the first time, love pricked me with its light arrow, alas poisoned and hopeless!'[3]

Wordsworth meanwhile had set off for Grasmere, and *his* new life—his 'heart/Joyous, nor scared at its own liberty'. On the way he composed the first version of the Glad Preamble, the quite separate 'effusion' which in January 1804 was incorporated in the five-Book *Prelude*, and which is known to us as *1805*, i. 1–54.[4] The opening lines both image, and in an unexpected way *demonstrate*, the powers of the creative imagination:

Oh there is blessing in this gentle breeze,
That blows from the green fields and from the clouds
And from the sky; it beats against my cheek,
And seems half conscious of the joy it gives.
O welcome messenger! O welcome friend!
A captive greets thee, coming from a house
Of bondage, from yon city's walls set free,
A prison where he hath been long immured.
Now I am free, enfranchised and at large,
May fix my habitation where I will.

(*1805*, i. 1–10)

The gentle, half-human, external wind that brings joy, and seems almost to feel it, is of course associated in lines 39–47 with a creative breeze within the poet himself, a breeze initially gentle, but which becomes 'A tempest, a redundant energy/Vexing its own creation'.[5] The power of Wordsworth's imagination could not be more impressively evoked, more impressively displayed; its oddity is more likely to pass unnoticed. The city of line 7 is apparently full in view. It reappears at line 98, is surrounded by new detail in *1850*, i. 87–9—

casting then
A backward glance upon the curling cloud
Of city smoke, by distance ruralized . . .

—and in viii. 347–50 (*1850*, viii. 209–15) is firmly connected with Goslar:

A glimpse of such sweet life
I saw when, from the melancholy walls
Of Goslar, once imperial, I renewed
My daily walk . . .

Yet we know that Wordsworth was in the Lake District as he wrote the Preamble lines, far from a city of any kind, and across the sea from Goslar. One is misled at first, and surprised later when one finds out what has happened, partly because of the circumstantial detail, partly because of Wordsworth's reputation for 'clinging to the palpable', measuring ponds with comic exactitude. He himself had no doubt as to priorities, taking pride in his 'unwillingness to submit the poetic spirit to the chains of fact and real circumstance'.[6] Within a year of composing the Preamble he began a poem to his country-bred future sister-in-law, 'Amid the smoke of cities did you pass/Your time of early youth' (*To Joanna*, 1–2); to us it seems an odd thing to do, to Wordsworth and his circle presumably it didn't—'by the imagination the mere fact is exhibited as connected with that infinity without which there is no poetry' (Morley, i. 191).

The city is a way of life, a state of mind, a mood from which Wordsworth had suffered in London, and Goslar, and elsewhere (in the country, no doubt, during the moral crisis of the early Racedown period), and from which he now suddenly felt free. It is 'That burthen of my own unnatural self' (*1805*, i. 23), 'the heavy and the weary weight/Of all this unintelligible world' (*Tintern Abbey*, 40–1). In terms specifically of 18 November 1799, it is also the choice that Coleridge had made in returning to the south, 'seeking . . . the haunts of men' (*1799*, ii. 511). Coleridge was going back to the environment of his own early years at Christ's Hospital, in the centre of London, implicitly preferring it to the pattern of Wordsworthian childhood which at Alfoxden had been accepted as the shared ideal. Wordsworth was left asserting that all was well, both in the relationship, and, still more important, in the choice that he himself had made. The conclusion of *1799*, written ten days to a fortnight after the Preamble, is a direct address to Coleridge for whom the poem has been written. With formal neatness, it refers him back to *Frost at Midnight*, his own most Wordsworthian work, which in the different circumstances of October 1798 had been quoted in the opening lines (i. 8) as an allusion to their continuing discussion, and even more perhaps as a talisman, a tender guarantee that their conversation and friendship would always be there. The concluding reference to *Frost at Midnight* is disquieting. Coleridge had conferred on the sleeping Hartley a Wordsworthian upbringing amid the scenes of Nature, then contrasted this with his own stunting early experience: Wordsworth in his poem reaches a climactic statement of personal faith, then turns to Coleridge to affirm that his feelings are shared—

Thou [Nature] hast fed
My lofty speculations, and in thee
For this uneasy heart of ours I find

A never-failing principle of joy
And purest passion.

Thou, my friend, wast reared
In the great city, mid far other scenes,
But we by different roads at length have gained
The self-same bourne.

(*1799*, ii. 492–9)

The phrase 'far other scenes' had been used in *Frost at Midnight* to refer to the country, and is used by Wordsworth to refer to the town. It is a small change, but has the effect of pointing up the fact that Coleridge had not himself enjoyed the blessings he wished for his son, and casting doubt on the claim that the self-same Nature-worshipping bourne has indeed been reached.

The larger context of Wordsworth's lines is important too. His statement of faith in Nature's 'never-failing principle of joy' follows a passage of rare political concern, taken almost verbatim from a recent Coleridge letter. Thinking specifically of James Mackintosh, the now turncoat author of *Vindiciae Gallicae* (1791) about whom Hazlitt was to write brilliantly in *The Spirit of the Age*, Coleridge had urged Wordsworth to

> write a poem, in blank verse, addressed to those, who, in consequence of the complete failure of the French Revolution, have thrown up all hopes of the amelioration of mankind, and are sinking into an almost epicurean selfishness, disguising the same under the soft titles of domestic attachment and contempt for visionary *philosophes*.

'It would do great good', he continued, 'and might form a part of *The Recluse*' (Griggs, i.527). Whether Wordsworth thought at some future date to write such a polemic we cannot know, but his immediate reaction was to give thanks to Nature that despite all the dreadfulness of the contemporary political scene he himself retained 'A more than Roman confidence':

if in these times of fear,
This melancholy waste of hopes o'erthrown,
If, mid indifference and apathy
And wicked exultation, when good men
On every side fall off we know not how
To selfishness, disguised in gentle names
Of peace and quiet and domestic love—

> Yet mingled, not unwillingly, with sneers
> On visionary minds—if, in this time
> Of dereliction and dismay, I yet
> Despair not of our nature, but retain
> A more than Roman confidence, a faith
> That fails not, in all sorrow my support,
> The blessing of my life, the gift is yours
> Ye mountains, thine O Nature. Thou hast fed
> My lofty speculations, and in thee
> For this uneasy heart of ours I find
> A never-failing principle of joy
> And purest passion.
>
> (*1799*, ii. 478–96)

It was the thought of writing *The Recluse* that supported Wordsworth in his isolationist position. The Preamble records a mood of extraordinary exaltation, because the prospect of going to live with Dorothy at Grasmere filled him with confidence in his poetic role. In October 1798 he had begun the *Prelude* drafts of *MS JJ* because he felt unable to write *The Recluse*, and guilty at his inability ('was it for *this* . . .'); now, thirteen months later, he suddenly felt certain that he could go ahead. Like his earlier anxieties, the new confidence can be measured in his relationship to Milton. For a start, Coleridge's reference to being 'pent' in the great city (directly alluded to by Wordsworth at the end of November, and presumably in his mind on the eighteenth) takes us to *Paradise Lost*, Book IX, where Satan is momentarily confused by the beauty of Eden and Eve:

> Much he the place admired, the person more.
> As one who long in populous city pent,
> Where houses thick and sewers annoy the air,
> Forth issuing on a summer's morn to breathe
> Among the pleasant villages and farms
> Adjoined, from each thing met conceives delight,
> The smell of grain, or tedded grass, or kine,
> Or dairy, each rural sight, each rural sound . . .
>
> (ll. 444–51)

There is no way of proving that Wordsworth while composing the Preamble was conscious of these lines. They were, however, a very famous example of London and the country being used to represent opposing states of mind, bondage versus freedom; and, given his detailed knowledge of *Paradise Lost*, it is virtually certain that he would have read (and reiterated) Coleridge's 'pent' as deliberate quotation. At line 15 of the Preamble, reference to Milton becomes explicit. 'The earth is all before me', Wordsworth writes, setting up not just an echo of the conclusion to *Paradise Lost*, but a comparison of his own position to that of Adam and Eve:

> Some natural tears they dropped, but wiped them soon;
> *The world was all before them*, where to choose
> Their place of rest, and providence their guide:
> They hand in hand, with wandering steps and slow,
> Through Eden took their solitary way.

Wordsworth too is setting out on a new life. And he too has his guide:

> The earth is all before me—with a heart
> Joyous, nor scared at its own liberty,
> I look about, *and should the guide I chuse*
> *Be nothing better than a wandering cloud*
> *I cannot miss my way.*
>
> Long months of ease and undisturbed delight
> Are mine in prospect. Whither shall I turn,
> By road or pathway, or through open field,
> *Or shall a twig or any floating thing*
> *Upon the river point me out my course?*

(*1805*, i. 15–19, 28–32)

Wordsworth's tones are playful, in keeping with the joyousness of the day, but his replacement of Milton's Christian Providence by cloud, twig, or floating object does more than merely tease the reader with his different expectations. It offers Nature as a serious alternative guide—Nature not at her grandest ('The mountain's outline and its steady form'), but in shapes which, like Peter Bell's leaf, achieve their effect through the human imagination which half-creates the things it sees. Above all, it is the rebirth of imagination that Wordsworth is celebrating in the Preamble. Odd as it may be to think of the previous year—the year of *1799*,

Part I and the Lucy Poems—as unproductive, it had failed to create *The Recluse*, and therefore to the poet seems 'a long-continued frost'. Now, however, the burden has been shaken off, his mood changed 'As by miraculous gift'.[7]

Adam at the end of *Paradise Lost* had been granted visions of the Incarnation, Eve had been comforted in dreams; putting behind them their recent infected thoughts (brought to Eden by Satan from the city of Hell), they had moved hand in hand out of Paradise and the poem. But however touching they may seem in their new-won humanity, and whatever the future might hold for their remote descendants, they had been cast out. The world might be all before them, but Eden was behind, and at their backs was the Covering Cherub with his sword blazing to prevent their return. By contrast, Wordsworth at this moment is moving *into* a poem (not *The Prelude*, but *The Recluse*) and is about to *enter* Paradise.

> If not a settler on the soil, at least
> To drink wild water, and to pluck green herbs,
> And gather fruits fresh from their native bough.[8]
>
> (*1805*, i. 36–8)

With him will go the 'gift that consecrates [his] joy', dedicates it to a higher cause—the inward breeze of imagination, which corresponds to, and by implication is conferred by, the sweet external 'breath of Heaven':

> 'Tis a power
> That does not come unrecognised, a storm
> Which, breaking up a long-continued frost,
> Brings with it vernal promises, the hope
> Of active days, of dignity and thought,
> Of prowess in an honorable field,
> Pure passions, virtue, knowledge, and delight,
> The holy life of music and of verse.
>
> (i. 47–54)

Wordsworth and Milton are writing at the end of two great periods of English political millennialism and disappointment. Milton, left at the Restoration with an understandable need to justify the ways of God, adopts the stance of the blind seer Tiresias. More surprisingly, he also permits himself in fantasy an active involvement in the conflict against evil: not only does

Abdiel reject the blandishments of Satan ('Among the faithless, faithful only he', *PL* v. 897), he has the privilege of striking the first blow in the battle that follows. Wordsworth, who was to note Milton's identification with Abdiel in Book III of *1805*, similarly casts himself as the champion of right. He receives no divine congratulations—'Servant of God, well done' (*PL* vi. 29)—but in the sudden heroic concept of 'prowess in an honorable field' presents himself as the knight preparing in solitude to do battle for mankind.

Wordsworth's ideals and aspirations are of course most clearly expressed in the Prospectus to *The Recluse*, the inspired sequence of Miltonic verse which became in 1806 the concluding section of *Home at Grasmere*, and which gets its name because in 1814 it was printed separately in the Preface to *The Excursion* as an advertisement for the poet's over-all scheme. There has been much discussion of the dating of the Prospectus, but far the most likely period is January 1800.[9] Like the Preamble, the Prospectus was no doubt originally a free-standing effusion. The Preamble was composed in a mood of exalted confidence just before the Wordsworths' arrival at Dove Cottage; the Prospectus was in all probability written just after, when the poet's hopes seemed all to have been fulfilled, and while the practical difficulties and discouragements of working on *The Recluse* were still in the future:

> On man, on Nature, and on human life,
> Thinking in solitude, from time to time
> I find sweet passions traversing my soul
> Like music; unto these, where'er I may,
> I would give utterance in numerous verse.
> Of truth, of grandeur, beauty, love, and hope,
> Of joy in various commonalty spread,
> Of the individual mind that keeps its own
> Inviolate retirement, and consists
> With being limitless, the one great life,
> I sing; fit audience let me find, though few.
>
> (Prospectus, 1–11)

The Preamble had shown Wordsworth eager to win prowess in the honourable field of *The Recluse*, and it had shown him in a mood to challenge Milton with a new redemptive vision. The Prospectus does just this:

'Fit audience find, though few'—thus prayed the bard,
Holiest of men. Urania, I shall need
Thy guidance, or a greater muse, if such
Descend to earth or dwell in highest heaven;
For I must tread on shadowy ground, must sink
Deep, and ascend aloft, and breathe in worlds
To which the heaven of heavens is but a veil.
All strength, all terror, single or in bands,
That ever was put forth by personal forms—
Jehovah, with his thunder, and the choir
Of shouting angels, and the empyreal thrones—
I pass them unalarmed. The darkest pit
Of the profoundest hell, night, chaos, death,
Nor aught of blinder vacancy scooped out
By help of dreams, can breed such fear and awe
As fall upon me often when I look
Into my soul, into the soul of man,
My haunt, and the main region of my song.
(Prospectus, 12–29)

Wordsworth is neither parodying Milton, nor writing pastiche; he is, as usual, placing his own work alongside *Paradise Lost*, and he is using a comparable grandeur of style to evoke a purpose comparably grand. Blake, for all his disapproving comment that 'Solomon when he married Pharoh's daughter . . . talked exactly in this way of Jehovah',[10] offers the closest parallels to what Wordsworth is actually saying. The heaven of heavens, and with it the celestial hierarchy (strength put forth in personal forms) and cosmology, is a veil that stands between man and an understanding of his own capacity for response. 'If the doors of perception were cleansed every thing would appear to man as it is, infinite'[11]—to be more specific, man would discover himself to be surrounded by the paradise that Milton thought to be lost:

Beauty, whose living home in the green earth,
Surpassing far what hath by special craft
Of delicate poets been culled forth and shaped
From earth's materials, waits upon my steps,
Pitches her tents before me as I move,
My hourly neighbour. Paradise and groves
Elysian, blessed islands in the deep,

Of choice seclusion-wherefore need they be
A history, or but a dream, when minds
Once wedded to this outward frame of things
In love, find these the growth of common day?

(ll. 30–40)

Because the lines that follow in the later texts are so famous,[12] and because the Prospectus tends anyway to be discussed in the context of *The Prelude* and imagination, this moving statement has received very little comment. The equation of paradise and Grasmere anticipated in the Preamble, experienced now in the joy of day-to-day life at Dove Cottage, has become the basis of Wordsworth's faith in the future of mankind. Poets who have created golden ages and other-worldly perfection from the materials they saw on earth should have taken the implication that earth itself can be perfect. Paradise is not a place, or a stage in the history of man, but a state of mind, a true perception which the individual will carry with him. Behind this redefinition lies one of God's, or Milton's, more surprising concessions to Adam. Michael in *Paradise Lost*, Book XII, first presents the distant future on earth as superior to God's original creation—

for then the earth
Shall all be paradise, far happier place
Than this of Eden, and far happier days.

(*PL* xii. 463–5)

—and then tells Adam that he is capable of achieving as a psychological state the happiness for which the world as a whole will have to wait till the apocalypse:

then will thou not be loath
To leave this Paradise, but shalt possess
A paradise within thee, happier far . . .[13]

(*PL* xii. 585–7)

Turning from the regained paradise of Grasmere to think of other less favoured scenes, Wordsworth in this earliest version of the Prospectus asks significantly that he may see human suffering as it appears to God:

Such pleasant haunts foregoing, if my song
Must turn elsewhere, and travel near the tribes
And fellowships of men, and see ill sights

Of passions ravenous from each other's rage,
Insult and injury and wrong and strife,
Wisdom be thou my guide. And if so tasked
I hear humanity in fields and groves
Pipe solitary anguish, or must hang
Brooding above the fierce confederate storm
Of sorrow, barricadoed ever more
Within the walls of cities, to these sounds
Do thou give meaning more akin to that
Which to God's ear they carry, that even these
Hearing, I be not heartless, or forlorn.

(ll. 41–54)

A Milton echo in 'barricadoed' (*PL* viii. 241) establishes the city once again as the Hell of Wordsworth's imagination, and the contemporary associations of *confédérés* and barricades must surely bring with them thoughts of the Revolution that had recently failed to achieve political utopia. Hope is seen to lie in a godlike perspective in which suffering is a temporary part of the total scheme. The poet accepts it as his task to hang brooding over the chaos of city life (like the Holy Spirit in this case), because in the slower millenarian process that he envisages he is to have a prophetic role that cannot ignore the less congenial. He stands between suffering mankind and a compassionate God, has affinities with both, and may thus through his poetry transmute the 'passions ravenous from each other's rage' into something permanent and assuaging.

Readings of the Prospectus have invariably depended on the later texts, and invariably taken it for granted that Wordsworth's redemptive principle is imagination. The two facts are connected because the major 1806 addition is so dominant in its assertions. Wordsworth in 1800 had stated clearly that 'minds/Once wedded to this outward frame of things/In love' find paradise 'the growth of common day'; in 1806 he decides, characteristically, to elaborate his earlier metaphor:

I, long before the blessèd hour arrives,
Would sing in solitude the spousal verse
Of this great consummation, would proclaim—
Speaking of nothing more than what we are—

How exquisitely the individual mind,
(And the progressive powers perhaps no less
Of the whole species) to the external world
Is fitted; and how exquisitely too—
Theme this but little heard of among men—
The external world is fitted to the mind;
And the creation (by no lower name
Can it be called) which they with blended might
Accomplish, this is my great argument.
(*Home at Grasmere*, 1002–14)

It is not Wordsworth at his most subtle, or most likeable, but it is a big, quotable, and very much quoted, policy-statement. The parenthesis, 'Speaking of nothing more than what we are', and the reference to 'the progressive powers' of the species are attempts to tie the poetry back into the concerns of 1800, but the central proclamation is a rather crude restatement of positions reached in the final Books of *The Prelude*: the 'ennobling interchange/Of action from within and from without' (xii. 376–7). Blake was absolutely right in his rejection—'You shall not bring me down to believe such fitting and fitted, I know better and please your lordship'[14]—but Wordsworth himself would not have been so mechanical in 1800. In his original wedding metaphor, man and Nature instead of being fitted to each other (by the Great Joiner, presumably), had been united in love—love that had rendered the actualities of the surrounding world a paradise, and done so without changing them. Fear and awe had fallen upon the poet when he looked into his own soul because of its capacity for such love, and obviously he could have used the term imagination for this godlike human power that cleanses the doors of perception. He didn't, though; he called it love, because that was how it felt. Imagination is the name given to such experience at periods when it is abnormal, felt to be a transcending of limitation, a crossing of the border.

The concept of the external world as a creation that man and Nature 'with blended might accomplish' is duly impressive, fine for those 'higher minds' whose achievements resemble the mist on Snowdon; but one no more thinks that the progressive powers of the species will reach such a level than one believes the sinking nations in the final lines of *1805* will understand

how the mind of man becomes
A thousand times more beautiful than the earth
On which he dwells . . .

(xiii. 446–8)

The terms employed are millenarian, but empty—or if not empty, full of the poet's own passion, not of a credible promise. It is not so with the poetry of 1800. Here too we are bound to think Wordsworth optimistic; but he is infinitely more approachable, and the paradise that he offers is one that must be to a large extent our own ideal, even if we know it can never be reached. Instead of imagination distant and grand we are shown 'dear imaginations', in the plural, realized in a personal relationship 'Up to their highest measure' (*Home at Grasmere*, 127–8). Instead of being asked to believe that all God's people could be prophets, we are told that they have all a potential for happiness. Joy, deriving from personal love and love of place, may be diffused throughout society, 'in various commonalty spread'; the poet's mind though it 'keeps its own/Inviolate retirement', special solitude, coexists 'With being limitless, the one great life'. For a moment this last reference may look like pantheism, but the world-soul belongs to man in 1800, not to God, as is clear in the first of the two moving prayers with which the Prospectus ends:

Come thou, prophetic spirit, soul of man,
Thou human soul of the wide earth, that hast
Thy metropolitan temple in the hearts
Of mighty poets; unto me vouchsafe
Thy foresight, teach me to discern, and part
Inherent things from casual, what is fixed
From fleeting, that my song may live, and be
Even as a light hung up in heaven to chear
The world in times to come.

(ll. 55–63)

In the second half of the quoted passage Wordsworth is putting his faith in 'the qualities which are common to all men as opposed to those which distinguish one man from another',[15] drawing attention as he will do in the Preface to *Lyrical Ballads* to that which is permanent and inherent in human experience, and may therefore be built upon. It is far less clear what goes on in the opening lines. There is a temptation as one reads to behave as

Coleridge did over the child who was 'Mighty prophet, seer blest', and ask literal-mindedly in what sense the soul of man can be either prophetic, or pervasive, or have the godlike power of answering prayers. As in the Ode, Wordsworth is being deliberately evocative in order to establish the grandeur of his credentials, and in some sense perhaps define the nature of prophecy—which is fine if he can get away with it. On this occasion, however, he is doing so at a period that deals normally with actualities; symbolic writing (poets whose hearts are metropolitan temples) easily seems incongruous. The lines that follow return to the personal mode, as Wordsworth reminds his readers of the extent to which vision—the vision that he hopes will sustain *The Recluse*—emerges from private experience:

> And if [with] this
> I mingle humbler matter, with the thing
> Contemplated describe the mind and man
> Contemplating, and who he was, and what,
> The transitory being that beheld
> This vision—when, and where, and how he lived,
> In part a fellow citizen, in part
> An outlaw and a borderer of his age—
> Be not this labour useless. O great God
> (To less than thee I cannot make this prayer),
> Innocent mighty spirit, let my life
> Express the image of a better time,
> Desires more wise and simpler manners nurse
> My heart in genuine freedom, all pure thoughts
> Be with me, and uphold me to the end.
>
> (ll. 63–77)

Wordsworth lives half within his age, half upon its borders. The coupling of 'borderer' with 'outlaw' suggests a dominant meaning of political exile; but insofar as his life expresses the image of a better time he is a borderer too in a different sense, between the unregenerate present and a millenarian future.

II. PARADISE REGAINED (*Home at Grasmere*, 1–667)

The task of *Home at Grasmere*—Book I of *The Recluse*, begun in March 1800—was surely to offer the poet living up to the claims of the Prospectus.[16] Appropriately the opening lines take us back to his first sight of the valley that was to become his earthly paradise:

> Once on the brow of yonder hill I stopped,
> While I was yet a schoolboy . . .
> At sight of this seclusion, I forgot
> My haste—for hasty had my footsteps been,
> As boyish my pursuits—and sighing said,
> 'What happy fortune were it here to live!
> And if a thought of dying, if a thought
> Of mortal separation could come in
> With paradise before me, here to die.'
> I was no prophet, nor had even a hope,
> Scarcely a wish, but one bright pleasing thought,
> A fancy in the heart of what might be
> The lot of others, never could be mine.
>
> (ll. 1–2, 6–16)

To judge from his stilted juvenilia, Wordsworth could well have moralized like this in early adolescence,[17] but the boy's response is interesting chiefly for what it tells us about the poet of 1800. The Wordsworth of the Preamble—'The earth is all before me'—had seemed a new and luckier Adam, joyous in heart and free to seek his own Eden; now, two months or so later, he is a second Moses, but one who has reached his promised land, where the Moses of Deuteronomy had been granted only a glimpse. It is all delicately implied—wittily in the double-meaning of 'prophet', tenderly in the poet's recreation of the 'one bright pleasing thought'. The poetry is so confident that it does not need to be arrogant. As he goes back into the mind of the boy looking down for the first time on Grasmere (from Red Bank, the fell opposite Dove Cottage across the lake), Wordsworth allows himself for once to evoke the superficial early moods for which the Ode refuses to give thanks:

> Delight and liberty, the simple creed
> Of childhood, whether fluttering or at rest,
> With new-born hope for ever in his breast . . .
>
> (*Intimations*, 137–9)

It is the world of the Preamble that he is offering, but it is a child's version:

> I thought of clouds
> That sail on winds; of breezes that delight
> To play on water, or in endless chase
> Pursue each other through the liquid depths
> Of grass or corn, over and through and through
> In billow after billow evermore;
> Of sunbeams, shadows, butterflies and birds,
> Angels, and wingèd creatures that are lords
> Without restraint of all which they behold.
> I sate, and, stirred in spirit as I looked,
> I seemed to feel such liberty was mine,
> Such power and joy . . .
>
> (ll. 25–36)

Breezes that might have stirred and symbolized imagination have no border implications here. The angels may be monarchs of all they survey, but they are products of the fancy, suggested not by the creative struggle to unify different orders of experience, but because like the butterflies and birds they are 'wingèd creatures'. Liberty and power and joy may be conferred—'but only for this end', so that the boy himself may

> *Flit* from field to rock, from rock to field,
> From shore to island, and from isle to shore . . .
>
> (ll. 36–8)

The poet has been chosen, has been given a sight of the promised land, and has responded with the wonder of childhood; as yet he can have no awareness of an adult mission to be performed.

Grasmere, however, lives on in the memory:

> From that time forward was the place to me
> As beautiful in thought as it had been
> When present to my bodily eyes . . .
>
> (ll. 44–6)

And, like the valley of the Wye above Tintern Abbey, it lives on *essentially unchanged*, valued for what it is, not for what the mind has made it.[18] The midnight storm of *1799*, Part II, grows darker in the presence of the poet's eye, and it is for this reason that he offers obeisance to Nature; but Grasmere was, is, and will always be, ideal. It is the same within the mind, and without:

> a haunt
> Of my affections, oftentimes in joy
> A brighter joy, in sorrow (but of that
> I have known little) in such gloom, at least,
> Such damp of the gay mind as stood to me
> In place of sorrow, 'twas a gleam of light—
> And now 'tis mine for life! Dear vale,
> One of thy lowly dwellings is my home.[19]
>
> (ll. 46–53)

The gleam has come true, and Wordsworth's exaltation rises to a height that not even the Preamble and Prospectus can match. Settling at Grasmere, which at one stage might have seemed a sacrifice, is 'an act/Of reason that exultingly aspires':

> This solitude is mine; the distant thought
> Is fetched out of the heaven in which it was.
> The unappropriated bliss hath found
> An owner, and that owner I am he!
>
> (ll. 81–6)

The poetry has become a song of triumph, but modulates with surprising ease into a statement of gain and loss, a balancing of accounts. Half-way between the affirmation of spring 1798 and the regret of 1802—'It is not now as it has been of yore'—Wordsworth in measured tones announces:

> in my day of childhood I was less
> The mind of Nature, less, take all in all,
> Whatever may be lost, than I am now?
>
> (ll. 94–6)

It is thoughtful and moving statement, and Wordsworth is perfectly clear what is the basis of his confidence. 'For proof', he writes,

> behold this valley—and behold
> Yon cottage, where with me my Emma dwells.
> Aye, think on that, my heart, and cease to stir . . .
>
> (ll. 97–9)

Home at Grasmere in its original impulse is Dorothy's poem, thanksgiving for a love, deep, and untroubled, and totally supportive:

> Long is it since we met to part no more,
> Since I and Emma heard each other's call
> And were companions once again . . .
>
> (ll. 171–3)

We cannot know to what extent this love had a sexual basis,[20] but in the early days at Grasmere it inspired in Wordsworth confidence in his poetic role, and poetry of astonishing tenderness:

> Mine eyes did ne'er
> Rest on a lovely object, nor my mind
> Take pleasure in the midst of happy thoughts,
> But either she whom now I have, who now
> Divides with me this loved abode, was there
> Or not far off. Where'er my footsteps turned
> Her voice was like a hidden bird that sang;
> The thought of her was like a flash of light
> Or an unseen companionship, a breath
> Or fragrance independent of the wind . . .
>
> (ll. 104–13)

Wordsworth's language associates Dorothy with the 'gleam of light' that Grasmere had seemed in anticipation. More surprisingly, at least at first sight, it associates her with the 'secret ministry' that frost performs for Coleridge, 'unhelped by any wind'.[21] And by a subtler link she is connected too with the wren at Furness Abbey—'the invisible bird' that 'one day sang so sweetly in the nave/Of the old church':

> Our steeds remounted, and the summons given,
> With whip and spur we by the chantry flew
> In uncouth race, and left the cross-legged knight
> And the stone abbot, and that single wren
> Which one day sang so sweetly in the nave
> Of the old church that, though from recent showers
> The earth was comfortless, and, touched by faint
> Internal breezes, from the roofless walls

The shuddering ivy dripped large drops, yet still
So sweetly mid the gloom the invisible bird
Sang to itself that there I could have made
My dwelling-place, and lived for ever there,
To hear such music.

(*1799*, ii. 118–30)

Like Keats in *Bright Star*, Wordsworth is using the background presence of Shakespeare to enhance a moment of border vision. The famous metaphor of Sonnet lxxiii—'Bare ruined choirs where late the sweet birds sang'—is made actual, just as in *The Ruined Cottage* the broken pitcher of Ecclesiastes becomes the useless fragment of a wooden bowl. But though the choirs become the nave of a palpable abbey, the bird remains invisible, intangible, its sourceless song implying possible sublimity. In *Home at Grasmere* a further extension has been achieved into a lived reality. The voice of the hidden bird is Dorothy's now,[22] and the poetry is full of exultation at the thought of living for ever to hear it in the joy of the present. It is extraordinary the extent to which Dorothy in 1800 calls out the border associations in her brother's language. Insofar as she was Lucy she had inspired the symbolic and elegiac writing of Goslar the previous year, but now she represents aspirations that have been fulfilled. Song, light, breath, fragrance, wind, all of them frequently carry border implications, and they cannot fail to do so when qualified by the three times repeated emphasis on sourcelessness—not just '*hidden* bird', but '*unseen* companionship', and the beautiful 'fragrance independent of the wind'. *Three years she grew* had shown the border vision curiously striving to be alive:

And hers shall be *the breathing balm*,
And hers the silence and the calm
Of mute insensate things.

(ll. 16–18)

Now, in the great love-poetry of *Home at Grasmere*, it has fully come to life.

Dorothy was quite as central to the paradise of Grasmere as Eve to Eden. Her brother in fact contrived to think his happiness in one respect superior to Adam's:

surpassing grace
To me hath been vouchsafed. Among the bowers
Of blissful Eden this was neither given,
Nor could be given—possession of the good
Which had been sighed for, antient thought fulfilled,
And dear imaginations realized
Up to their highest measure . . .

(ll. 122–8)

For Wordsworth, of course, this was not a merely personal happiness; the grace had been vouchsafed for a purpose. On their way from Sockburn, through Wensleydale, to Grasmere on 17 December 1799, he and Dorothy had stopped at Hart-leap Well, and heard the story of the hunted stag, whose last amazing leaps had been commemorated by the huntsman in a pleasure-house, now ruined. The resulting ballad, which was written in January, concludes in a strange pantheist reconciling vision—more literary than the pantheism of *Tintern Abbey*, more Christian than the spirit-world of *1799*, Part I:

This beast not unobserved by Nature fell,
His death was mourned by sympathy divine.

The being that is in the clouds and air,
That is in the green leaves among the groves,
Maintains a deep and reverential care
For them the quiet creatures whom he loves.

The pleasure-house is dust—behind, before,
This is no common waste, no common gloom—
But Nature, in due course of time, once more
Shall here put on her beauty and her bloom.

She leaves these objects to a slow decay
That what we are, and have been, may be known;
But at the coming of the milder day
These monuments shall all be overgrown.

(*Hart-leap Well*, 163–76)

We respond to the hint of apocalypse in 'the coming of the milder day', but Wordsworth's purposes here are local, and a hint it remains. A final stanza plays the poem out with the moral earnestness of *Lines Left Upon a Seat in a Yew-tree* (*c.* May 1797):

> One lesson, shepherd, let us two divide,
> Taught both by what she shews, and what conceals,
> Never to blend our pleasure or our pride
> With sorrow of the meanest thing that feels.[23]
>
> (ll. 177–80)

The ballad's disproportionate intensity is explained by a passage of *Home at Grasmere* which has not had the attention it deserves. Through their shared response to the death of the stag, Wordsworth and Dorothy, it seems, experienced at Hart-leap Well a moment of vision at once prophetic and confirming—received a positive 'intimation' of 'the milder day':

> And when the trance
> Came to us as we stood by Hart-leap Well,
> The intimation of the milder day
> Which is to come, the fairer world than this,
> And raised us up, dejected as we were
> Among the records of that doleful place
> By sorrow for the hunted beast who there
> Had yielded up his breath—the awful trance;
> The vision of humanity and of God
> The mourner, God the sufferer, when the heart
> Of his poor creatures suffers wrongfully—
> Both in the sadness and the joy we found
> A promise and an earnest that we twain,
> A pair seceding from the common world,
> Might in that hallowed spot to which our steps
> Were tending, in that individual nook,
> Might even thus early for ourselves secure,
> And in the midst of these unhappy times,
> A portion of the blessedness which love
> And knowledge will, we trust, hereafter give
> To all the vales of earth and all mankind.
>
> (ll. 236–56)

The Coleridge letter quoted above, and incorporated in *1799*,

Part II three weeks before the experience at Hart-leap Well,[24] had asked Wordsworth to involve himself in the contemporary scene, reprove Mackintosh and others for their apostasy. Had he been willing to use his poetry for this purpose, Wordsworth would no longer have been striking a blow for France (the French invasion of republican Switzerland in January 1798 had put an end to such thoughts) but he would have been consenting to see his 'hopes of the amelioration of mankind' in political terms. Refusal to do so, implicit in the parting of the ways on 18 November and choice of seclusion at Grasmere, left Wordsworth open to the first of the two charges that Coleridge had levelled at the apostates: selfishness disguised under the soft name of domestic attachment. The Preamble confidence was a support, but not a rationale, for his choice. This was provided by the moment of shared trance—almost the only one that he records[25]—at Hart-leap Well. He and Dorothy were not escaping from active responsibilities, they were 'seceding from the common world' in order to anticipate the non-political millennium of love and knowledge. By implication, the knowledge referred to has to be that which they themselves had gained:

> The vision of humanity and God
> The mourner, God the sufferer, when the heart
> Of his poor creatures suffers wrongfully . . .
>
> (ll. 244–6)

Wordsworth's terms are surprising, and so is the ordering of his sentence. The vision achieved is not of God and man, or even of man and God, but of 'humanity and God/The mourner'—humanity meaning at once human-kind, and the human compassion that God is shown to be sharing. The 'intimation of the milder day' is an intimation neither of immortality, nor of dramatic apocalypse to come, but simply that God cares, in effect that he is human too. There are no borders to be crossed in 1800 through the grandeur of imagination; but a trance not so very different in its effect and implications from that of *Tintern Abbey* may be attained through depth of imaginative sympathy. There is no pantheist life-force now, yet once more it is confirmed that the poet is part of the total harmony he craves. God is a supportive presence, not very supernatural, and conforming to no obvious doctrinal position, who validates the joys because he shares the sorrows of human existence.

Read with this in mind, *Hart-leap Well* becomes an allegory of man's self-destructive impulse. Sir Walter, representing pride and power, hunts to its death innocence, beauty, natural strength, embodied in the hart, which dies at its place of birth, its natural cycle unnaturally completed. Seeing the stag's last galvanic leaps as a tribute to himself, Sir Walter creates at the spot a pleasure-house, nominally a record of the animal's achievement, actually a mockery of its pain. A crude moral structure had been present in Wordsworth's source, *Der Wilde Jäger*, but the extravagances of Bürger have been rejected: the crops, cattle, and herdsmen, trodden under foot; the Good and Bad Angels that ride with the Huntsman; the explicit self-damnation ('Not God himself shall make me turn'); the voice of judgement spoken from the clouds; the reversal of roles, in which the Huntsman will be hunted nightly by hell-hounds 'Till time itself shall have an end'.[26] Sir Walter in Wordsworth's poem, though he wears out horses and hounds, hunts nobody down, and brings no sudden judgement on his head; he and his paramour are even, rather surprisingly, allowed pleasure in their pleasure-house, unreproved, amid dancers and minstrel's song. But his 'silent joy' in the death of the hart had been blasphemy all the same—'This beast not unobserved by Nature fell'.[27] Nature does not assimilate the bower and pleasure-house, take them over with 'her plants, her weeds and flowers,/And silent overgrowings' *Ruined Cottage*, 505–6); she leaves them to a slow decay, amid 'no common waste, no common gloom . . . That what *we* are, and have been, may be known'. Such is the power of man's destructiveness and pride that not till the coming of 'the milder day' can the monuments be overgrown.

Hart-leap Well does not say why 'the milder day' should ever come if Sir Walter's behaviour truly shows us 'what we are', but *The Recluse* cannot leave the question unanswered. Nor indeed does Wordsworth wish to do so. Personal happiness has given him the confidence to bring it out into the open. He discusses it easily, thoughtfully, at times with a wry, self-knowing humour. His instinct is to present Grasmere as unique in possessing already the virtues that will one day be shared, and in the early part of the poem he allows himself to assert that this is in fact the case. Here only, is to be felt

> the sense
> Of majesty and beauty and repose,
> A blended holiness of earth and sky,
> Something that makes this individual spot . . .
> A whole without dependence or defect,
> Made for itself, and happy in itself,
> Perfect contentment, unity entire.
>
> (ll. 161–4, 168–70)

Even at this stage, however, in the midst of his song of love and triumph at the regaining of paradise, he feels a need to qualify his assertions:

> Nowhere (*or is it fancy*?) can be found—
> The one sensation that is here . . .
>
> (ll. 155–6)

The happiness the poet feels creates the happiness he sees; the unity he perceives is an extension of the unity that he shares with Dorothy. In Coleridge's terms, we have 'intense union' leading to a sense (or sensation) of oneness, not the 'absolute unity' that both of them crave. In its different idiom it is no less fanciful to make the earth and sky of Grasmere into a blended holiness, than to create '*one* absolutely undistinguishable form' from the round fat backside of a hill and its image in the water. What is surprising is that Wordsworth should be so conscious of this. Much as he would like to think of his neighbours as sharing in the 'Perfect contentment, unity entire' of the landscape in which they live, he knows that it is not so. And he knows that wish-fulfilment is no basis for his poem:

> Ah, if I wished to follow where the sight
> Of all that is before my eyes, the voice
> Which is as a presiding spirit here,
> Would lead me, I should say unto myself,
> 'They who are dwellers in this holy place
> Must needs themselves be hallowed.'
>
> (ll. 362–7)

This is a Wordsworth who is astonishingly self-aware. The

swans on the lake, as he is at pains to point out, may have been shot despite his tender identification:

> They came, like Emma and myself, to live
> Together here in peace and solitude,
> Chusing this valley, they who had choice
> Of the whole world . . .
> They strangers, and we strangers—they a pair,
> And we a solitary pair like them.
> They should not have departed . . .
>
> (ll. 326–9, 340–2)

And, whatever he might like to believe, the voice he hears from the distant heights is no presiding spirit, but a shepherd, who may really be drunken and cursing:

> not betrayed by tenderness of mind
> That feared, or wholly overlooked, the truth
> Did we come hither, with romantic hope
> To find in midst of so much loveliness
> Love, perfect love . . .
> Nor from such hope, or aught of such belief,
> Hath issued any portion of the joy
> Which I have felt this day. An awful voice,
> 'Tis true, I in my walks have often heard
> Sent from the mountains . . .
>
> (ll. 398–409)

As in the Preamble, Wordsworth is seen in a playful mood, teasing the reader with expectations of providential guidance; but it is interesting that in this case he is clearly also mocking himself in his wish for border implication. He would like to treat the shepherd's probably drunken and blasphemous voice as an apocalyptic message, but to do so would be fanciful.[28]

Not that fancy is undervalued, just that Wordsworth at this period of actualities knows it very precisely for what it is:

> *Thus do we soothe ourselves*, and when the thought
> Is passed, we blame it not for having come.
> What if I floated down a pleasant stream
> And now am landed, and the motion gone,
> Shall I reprove myself? Ah no, the stream

Is flowing and will never cease to flow,
And I shall float upon that stream again.
By such forgetfulness the soul becomes
Words cannot say how beautiful.

(ll. 379–87)

And yet? It seems incredible after these evocative final lines, but in 1800 the soul made beautiful by self-forgetfulness has nowhere to go, no border to cross. In Blake's phrase, Wordsworth the spiritual man is at this moment subordinated to Wordsworth the natural man. The value he sets on present happiness precludes for a time his sense of higher imaginative possibilities. There is no seeing into the life of things, and there is no 'something evermore about to be'. Instead there is an almost dispassionate awareness of what is to be lost as well as gained in yielding to the stream of personal response: 'Hail to thee,/Delightful valley',

And to whatever else of outward form
Can give us inward help, can purify
And elevate and harmonize and soothe,
And steal away and for a while deceive
And lap in pleasing rest, and bear us on
Without desire in full complacency,
Contemplating perfection absolute
And entertained as in a placid sleep.

(ll. 388–97)

The passage is a strange mixture. As at Alfoxden, the poet floats down the stream of tendency in a calm mood of holy and beneficial indolence;[29] and as in *Tintern Abbey*, while laid asleep in body he is especially responsive to the moral influence of external forms. Yet this pleasing rest is no longer simply a wise receptive passiveness, it is at the same time a wilful yielding to deception. Though Grasmere for Wordsworth *is* perfection absolute, and though its outward forms *can* give inward help, the poet's contemplation will not bring about the millennium. Neither the depth of his happiness, nor the increase of his moral awareness, is any guarantee that the state of mind that he himself has achieved can become universal.

The shepherd's voice comes in these circumstances to stand for the possibility of accepting self-delusion:

That voice, the same, the very same, that breath
Which was an utterance awful as the wind,
Or any sound the mountains ever heard . . .
(ll. 420–2)

Used with deliberate incongruity, the border language shows at once the strength of the temptation, and the extent of the poet's self-consciousness. He will not on this occasion be deceived by himself or anyone else:

I came not dreaming of unruffled life . . .
I shrink not from the evil in disgust,
Or with immoderate pain. I look for man,
The common creature of the brotherhood,
But little differing from man elsewhere . . .
(ll. 428–35)

The clear-sightedness is impressive, but hardly prophetic or redemptive. As Wordsworth moves on, one senses in his tones an almost desperate awareness of the need to make much larger claims:

Yet is it something gained—it is in truth
A mighty gain—that labour here preserves
His rosy face, a servant only here
Of the fireside or of the open field,
A freeman, therefore sound and unenslaved;
That extreme penury is here unknown,
And cold and hunger's abject wretchedness,
Mortal to body and the heaven-born mind . . .
(ll. 439–46)

There is a touch of sentimentality no doubt in the fireside and the rosy face of labour;[30] but we are now very close to the mere facts of Wordsworth's situation. In his choice of Grasmere he feels himself to be 'enfranchised and at large' (Preamble), and he perceives in the life of the Cumbrian 'statesman' a similar freedom. He wishes of course to believe that the shepherd's 'heaven-born mind' will share his own aspirations, but he makes no claim that this can ever be so. As this first movement of *Home at Grasmere* comes to an end, he is forced back upon the unpretentious, non-millenarian, position that will form the basis of *Michael* and the Preface to *Lyrical Ballads*:

he who tills the field,
He, happy man, is master of the field
And treads the mountain which his father trod.

And hence,

In this enclosure many of the old
Substantial virtues have a firmer tone
Than in the base and ordinary world.

(ll. 462–8)

It is not a forward-looking view.[31]

In his effort to portray 'the old/Substantial virtues' of the Grasmere peasant's life in a way that has some bearing on *The Recluse* (and the future of mankind), Wordsworth turns at this point to narrative. Two of the resulting stories were later transferred to *Excursion*, Book VI, but their presence in *MS R* of *Home at Grasmere* shows them to belong to 1800;[32] though they fit perfectly well in *The Excursion*, their idiom is that of the Matron's Tale (*1805*, viii. 222–311) and the more priggish early parts of *Michael*. The poetry is unremarkable save for a brief, tender portrait of Dorothy in the guise of a hardy shepherd-girl, companion of her father on the hills;[33] the tone is frequently unctuous—

Unhappy man—
That which he had been weak enough to do
Was misery in remembrance . . .

(ll. 507–9)

—and the form is far too obviously moral exemplum. The first story is sentimentally wretched, the second sentimentally happy. The third is barely under way when the poet's anxiety breaks suddenly into the verse:

She then began
In fond obedience to her private thoughts
To speak of her dead husband. *Is there not*
An art, a music, and a stream of words
That shall be life, the acknowledged voice of life . . . ?

(ll. 618–22)

The shift in the final line is important. Art cannot *be* life, but life might still have its acknowledged voice—a language that has the special appropriateness, and thus the permanence, which Wordsworth at both ends of the Preface to *Lyrical Ballads* states to be the aim of his poetry.[34] 'Was human life perfect', Hartley writes in a part of the *Observations on Man* that has obvious relevance to *Home at Grasmere*,

> our happiness in it would be properly represented by that accurate knowledge of things which a truly philosophical language would give us. And if we suppose a number of persons thus making a progress in pure unmixed happiness, and capable both of expressing their own feelings, and of understanding those of others, by means of a perfect and adequate language, they might be like new senses and powers of perception to each other, and both give to and receive from each other happiness indefinitely.[35]

The philosophical language which should at once arise out of, and support, this 'progress in pure unmixed happiness' 'would as much exceed any of the present languages as a paradisiacal state does the mixture of happiness and misery, which has been our portion ever since the fall'. 'And', Hartley continues,

> It is no improbable supposition, that the language given by God to Adam and Eve, before the fall, was of this kind; and though it might be narrow, answered all their exigencies perfectly well.[36]

It is difficult to know whether Wordsworth would have accepted as a matter of fact the biblical tradition of a single original language;[37] but indirectly it may well have given support to his extraordinary statement in the Preface that countrymen 'hourly communicate with the *best* objects from which the *best* part of language is originally derived'.[38] It seemed to him axiomatic that 'where the passions of men are incorporated'—his characteristic metaphor of embodying—'with the beautiful and permanent forms of Nature' a language will evolve to give them their perfect expression. In their personal relationship he and Dorothy had achieved such a language—they were indeed 'like new senses and powers of perception to each other'—and he like Hartley saw in language a millenarian possibility.[39] Why should not the regained paradise of Grasmere have its acknowledged voice?

Wordsworth's mood is wistful, but not self-indulgent; he knows just how far his wishes are fanciful. The idiom he yearns for—and *needs* as poet of *The Recluse*—would transcend that of Eden not merely in its breadth, but in its powers of creative reconciliation.

It would bring into harmony the actualities of fallen, unideal, ordinary existence,

> speak of what is done among the fields,
> Done truly there, or felt, of solid good
> And real evil, *yet be sweet withal* . . .
>
> (ll. 623–5)

If language could render evil harmonious it would be fully prophetic, a guarantee that in life as well as literature harmony exists, and will one day be perceived. The poet would be seen to possess the godlike vision of the Prospectus; his poetry would truly be 'a stream of words/That *shall be* life'. But for the Wordsworth of *Home at Grasmere* there can be no such reliance on the achievements of imagination. For a moment it seems that dignity and grace, the social virtues that look forward to the 'milder day' of *The Recluse*, might indeed be conferred; but then, in a line of insistent monosyllables that force themselves on the reader's attention, Wordsworth asks the question that has for so long been implied:

> Is there such a stream,
> Pure and unsullied, flowing from the heart
> With motions of true dignity and grace—
> *Or must we seek these things where man is not?*
>
> (ll. 628–31)

To readers of Blake, the line is a flat contradiction of *The Marriage of Heaven and Hell*—'Where man is not, Nature is barren'—and it is a contradiction too of what Wordsworth himself at other periods seems often to believe.[40] The special circumstances of *The Recluse* demand that man shall possess, and be seen to possess, social qualities that Romantic poets do not normally find themselves stressing. For a few more lines Wordsworth tries to get the widow's story under way, then gives up in awkwardness and confusion:

> Be this
> A task above my skill; the silent mind
> Has its own treasures, and I think of these,
> Love what I see, and honour humankind.
>
> (ll. 642–5)

Once again a section of the poem, begun with confidence, has come to an end as Wordsworth refuses to evade the questions that cannot be answered. And once again he turns to Dorothy—not to ask for support, and not on this occasion to celebrate their private happiness, but with the instinct that if an answer is indeed to be found to his problem, the clue must be contained in personal relationship:

> No, we are not alone; we do not stand,
> My Emma, here misplaced and desolate,
> Loving what noone cares for but ourselves.
> We shall not scatter through the plains and rocks
> Of this fair vale and o'er its spatious heights
> Unprofitable kindliness, bestowed
> On objects unaccustomed to the gifts
> Of feeling, that were cheerless and forlorn
> But few weeks past, and would be so again
> If we were not. We do not tend a lamp
> Whose lustre we alone participate. . . .
> Look where we will, some human heart has been
> Before us with its offering . . .
>
> (ll. 646–60)

In the background is the Hartleyan position on which Coleridge as long ago as May 1795 had based his attack on Godwin in the *Lectures on Revealed Religion*. Personal love is no mere 'domestic attachment', but the centre of ever-widening circles:

> Jesus knew our nature—and that expands like the circles of a lake—the love of our friends, parents and neighbours lead[s] us to the love of our country, to the love of all mankind. The intensity of private attachment encourages, not prevents, universal philanthropy . . .
>
> (*CC* i. 163)

Wordsworth had assimilated the view at Alfoxden, extending it with Coleridge's approval to provide a reason for believing that love of Nature will lead to love of man. At that moment (the moment at which *The Recluse* was originally planned) the problem had been to see why a pantheist apprehension of the joy in Nature—

the pure joy of love,
By sound diffused, or by the breathing air,
Or by the silent looks of happy things,
Or flowing from the universal face
Of earth and sky.

(*Pedlar*, 82–6)

—should have social implications, help to bring about the millennium. The answer, as formulated by Wordsworth in early March 1798 and immediately quoted by Coleridge, had been that the man who is truly in sympathy with 'things that hold/An inarticulate language'

needs must feel
The joy of that pure principle of love
So deeply, that, unsatisfied with aught
Less pure and exquisite, he cannot chuse
But seek for objects of a kindred love
In fellow-natures . . .[41]

(Griggs, i. 397–8)

Love of the one kind *must* become love of the other, if it is deeply enough felt. In *Home at Grasmere* the focus of Wordsworth's concern has shifted. Pantheism has gone, the millennium is thought of in less excited terms as 'the coming of the milder day'; yet the rationale remains the same:

Joy spreads and sorrow spreads; and this whole vale,
Home of untutored shepherds as it is,
Swarms with sensation, as with gleams of sunshine,
Shadows or breezes, scents or sounds.

(ll. 664–7)

III. THE SERPENT IN EDEN (*Home at Grasmere*, 667–1048)

Wordsworth did not find it easy to believe that untutored Grasmere shepherds were capable of creative and forward-looking love, but he knew that he had to do so. When he allowed himself to identify with their way of life there was no problem—Michael

had been alone
Amid the heart of many thousand mists
That came to him and left him on the heights.

(ll. 58–60)

—but at other times he was betrayed into hectoring assertion. 'And grossly that man errs', he writes, just two lines further on in *Michael*,

who should suppose
That the green valleys, and the streams and rocks,
Were things indifferent to the shepherd's thoughts.[42]
(ll. 62–4)

The tones of *Home at Grasmere* are less on edge, and Wordsworth's position is quite carefully thought out. The shepherd's feelings, 'though subservient more than ours/To every day's demand for daily bread' (condescension nicely offset by wit), have the power to 'lift the animal being',

do themselves
By Nature's kind and ever present aid
Refine the selfishness from which they spring,
Redeem by love the individual sense
Of anxiousness with which they are combined.
(ll. 667–8, 673–7)

The child of *1799*, Part I, had stocked his mind with grand and beautiful forms not as a result of direct response to Nature but through 'collateral interest' (ll. 375–9); the poet aged 23 had captured the landscape of the Wye despite being 'more like a man/Flying from something that he dreads, than one/Who sought the thing he loved' (*Tintern Abbey*, 71–3); now shepherds too are seen to be capable of unconscious assimilation, and of refining or transmuting inconsequential energies within the mind. Though the Wordsworth of *Home at Grasmere* does not stress the point, this is an imaginative process, and it results in feelings that

Are fit associates of the worthiest joy,
Joy of the highest and the purest minds.
(ll. 680–1)

In arriving at his needful theory of other minds as similar to his own, Wordsworth was inspired by the presence of his brother John, the 'never-resting pilgrim of the sea'.[43] John was a link with the ordinary; in effect he stood half way between the poet himself and his neighbours. There was no doubting the depth of his responses, the quality of his love, yet he was content to be a merely silent poet, and to earn his living in the customary way. If John's silence was mere inarticulacy, could not the peasant's apparent incomprehension also conceal an underlying love? In a draft of *Michael* written at the end of the year, there is a touching scene in which the representative peasant is first awkwardly questioned—

> No doubt if you in terms direct had asked
> Whether he loved the mountains, true it is
> That with blunt repetition of your words
> He might have stared at you, and said that they
> Were frightful to behold . . .

—and then induced more subtly to reveal

> That in his thoughts there were obscurities,
> Wonders and admirations, things that wrought
> Not less than a religion in his heart.[44]

This is not the gratuitous questioning of *We Are Seven* or *The Leech Gatherer*, where the ineptitude that is portrayed shows Wordsworth himself to be craving for border wisdom; it is a necessary and moving attempt to prove that the poet's message makes sense to others. The peasant of 1804 will point out to Wordsworth the horse that is 'an amphibious work of Nature's hand'; the peasant of 1800 stands waiting to be educated. If he can be shown to be receptive, the poet's work is not elitist, his millenarian hopes have a basis, *The Recluse* can proceed. For a moment Wordsworth allows himself to believe that Michael, like John, may be a poet too:

> And if it was his fortune to converse
> With any who could talk of common things
> In an unusual way, and give to them
> Unusual aspects, or by questions apt
> Wake sudden recognitions, that were like
> Creations in the mind, and were indeed
> Creations often, then, when he discoursed
> Of mountain sights, this untaught shepherd stood
> Before the man with whom he so conversed
> And looked at him as with a poet's eye.[45]

For the purposes of *Home at Grasmere*, the peasant does not have precisely to turn poet, but his feelings are nevertheless defined in terms of their fitness to associate with 'Joy of the highest and the purest minds', and their effect is thought of as being vitally creative:

> Calmly they breathe their own undying life,
> Lowly and unassuming as it is,
> Through this, their mountain sanctuary. . .
> giving to the moments as they pass
> Their little boons of animating thought,
> That sweeten labour, make it seem and feel
> To be no arbitrary weight imposed,
> But a glad function natural to man.
>
> (ll. 683–92)

John may indeed have had such feelings, and they could be attributed confidently enough to the frugal and industrious families of Michael and 'the homely priest of Ennerdale',[46] but it was less easy to believe that labour seemed a glad and natural function to all the inhabitants of Grasmere. 'Fair proof of this, newcomer though I be,/Already have I seen', Wordsworth announces; but no proof is forthcoming. There is further defiance—

> and what if I . . .
> Am sometimes forced to cast a painful look
> Upon unwelcome things . . . ?
>
> (ll. 710–13)

—and there are some remarkably unconvincing assertions:

> The more I see the more is my delight.
> Truth justifies herself; and as she dwells
> With Hope, who would not follow where she leads?
>
> (ll. 717–19)

And finally there is a section that seems at first sight to be wholly irrelevant: eighty-five lines on the subject not of sensitive human-beings, but of animals and birds. Writing of his new attachments, Wordsworth at times is laughably (or painfully) unguarded:

I begin
Already to inscribe upon my heart
A liking for the small grey horse that bears
The paralytic man; I know the ass
On which the cripple, in the quarry maimed,
Rides to and fro: I know them and their ways.
(ll. 723–8)

What the reviewers and the parodists would have made of such lines one can only guess, but the poet himself seems to have taken them quite seriously—indeed, there is evidence in the drafts of *MS R* that he saw them as clearly related to his over-all scheme. Before the small grey horse there was originally an introduction of forty lines: 'Happy is he who lives to understand/Not human nature only . . .'.[47] By taking this out of his poem—presumably during the fair-copying of *MS B* in 1806—Wordsworth obscured a number of important links that had been in his mind at the time of writing. Happiness in the drafts is seen to lie in observing (with Ulysses) the workings of degree:

To every class its station and its office,
Throughout the mighty commonwealth of things,
Up from the stone, or plant, to sovereign man . . .

'Such converse', Wordsworth goes on, in his most didactic tones, 'teaches love;/For knowledge is delight, and such delight/Is love'. Love, it seems is to be derived from a fervent understanding of the Great Chain of Being. By an odd chance Wordsworth had before him as he wrote lines that should have made him especially aware of the barrenness of the position that he found himself adopting. *MS R* is no ordinary notebook, but a volume of Coleridge's *Poems* 1796 that has been interleaved with blank paper.[48] Whether by design or otherwise, the drafts of *Home at Grasmere* are written between (and frequently on top of) pages from *Religious Musings*, the apocalyptic poem which had been a fore-runner to *The Recluse*.[49] The first draft of 'Happy is he who lives to understand' is roughed out alongside the grandest of all Coleridge's pantheist claims:

'Tis the sublime of man,
Our noontide majesty, to know ourselves
Parts and proportions of one wond'rous whole:

This fraternises man, this constitutes
Our charities and bearings.

(ll. 135–9)

Wordsworth can hardly have been unaware of these lines on the page, and hardly have been unaware that the claims that he himself now felt able to make were very much less impressive. And yet there is an evident seriousness of purpose about the way in which he puts forward his new positives of love and knowledge. Behind it lies the trance at Hart-leap Well, 'The vision of humanity and God/The mourner, God the sufferer', out of which had emerged the promise on which *Home at Grasmere*—and life at Grasmere—was felt to depend:

Both in the sadness and the joy we found
A promise and an earnest that we twain,
A pair seceding from the common world,
Might in that hallowed spot to which our steps
Were tending, in that individual nook,
Might even thus early for ourselves secure . . .
A portion of *the blessedness which love*
And knowledge will, we trust, hereafter give
To all the vales of earth, and all mankind.

(ll. 247–56)

Though the pairing of love with knowledge (as words, and as the source of millenarian hopes about the future) belongs only to *Home at Grasmere*, it had been anticipated in Wordsworth's very first statements about *The Recluse*.[50] Knowledge then had been of a pantheist universe, in which 'love' was very frequently the name given to the transcendental force that bonded man and Nature.[51] Among the poems of the period had been of course *The Ancient Mariner* and *Peter Bell*; the ballad of *Hart-leap Well* takes up where these leave off, and the trance in *Home at Grasmere* similarly offers its truths about love and knowledge in what might seem the limited context of cruelty to animals. To Coleridge and Wordsworth it did not seem limited. The shooting of the albatross and the swans on Grasmere Lake, the beating of Peter Bell's ass and the hunting to death of the stag, are supposed equally to show man as 'a jarring and a dissonant thing' amid the general harmony of Nature—which doesn't mean that they achieve, or are likely to achieve, a comparable imaginative importance. Only in *Hart-leap Well* does cruelty take on any of the symbolic power that it has in *The Ancient Mariner*, and the fact that it does so there has much to do with the un-Wordsworthian origins of the story—its legendary character, and the residue of Bürger's bad-and-good-angel, black-and-white morality. The 'clinging to the palpable' which in 1798 allowed Wordsworth to think that he could usefully replace the killing of the albatross with ill-natured donkey-beating has the effect of limiting the symbolic possibilities of the poetry, restricting its moral implications to the local and the actual. Sometimes of course metaphor and moral connotation win through, strengthened by the plainness of their surroundings; but often they don't. The Wordsworth of *Home at Grasmere*, dedicated to celebrating the paradise of common day, was especially likely to over-rate the literary power of ordinariness. In writing of the small grey horse and paralytic man, the ass and the cripple, he was following up the positive implications of the lesson of Hart-leap Well—offering man not hunting animals down, but forming with them a mutually supportive relationship. Just as the sea-beast of *The Leech Gatherer* loses some of his vital qualities to approximate him to the stone, the paralytic and cripple have become closer to the animals they ride; and the animals in their turn have taken on something like human responsibilities. Because of the special circumstance of the men's handicaps, there is the sort of interdependence that would ideally be normal 'Throughout the mighty commonwealth of things /Up from the stone, or plant, to sovereign man'. It is hardly surprising that in his attempt to show Grasmere as possessed already of this happy state, the poet should turn to dogs—'The famous sheep-dog, first in all the Vale', and 'the blind man's guide'—but there is a shortage of such ready-made examples of man and animal in partnership, and he is forced very soon into stressing instead unfunctional, in fact whimsical, relationships that have much less bearing on his theme:

> Whoever lived a winter in one place,
> Beneath the shelter of one cottage-roof,
> And has not had his redbreast or his wren?

I have them both; and I shall have my thrush
In spring-time . . .

(ll. 733–7)

Once again the poetry has failed to move beyond the personal. Not that it is the worse for that—as poetry. By this stage of *Home at Grasmere* it has long been clear that moments which evoke the poet's own pleasure in his surroundings—his sense that whatever may be true for others, and whatever the distant future may hold, he at least has regained his paradise—are far more likely to be rewarding than efforts to support the argument. The attempt to show man and animals in relationship, though a welcome rest from man himself, was not much helped by the fact that except in certain moods of self-indulgence Wordsworth valued the natural world precisely in its aloofness. Which perhaps explains the speed, and certainly explains the rise in quality of the writing, as he moves away from animals that may form particular attachments to men, and individual birds for which friendship may be claimed, to the extended and vividly imaginative description of the waterfowl:

And ye as happy under Nature's care,
Strangers to me and all men, or at least
Strangers to all particular amity . . .

(ll. 753–5)

The birds are incapable of relationship with man, and yet the very use, and repetition, of the word 'Strangers' as a means of saying so is a sign that the poet has for them a special admiration. The swans on the lake had been strangers too—

They strangers, and we strangers—they a pair,
And we a solitary pair like them.
They should not have departed!

(ll. 340–2)

—but the tender identification of the earlier passage, though surely now recalled, has given place to poetry of quite another kind. In a beautiful phrase, the waterfowl are said to come, 'the gift of winds':

Wild creatures, and of many homes, that come
The gift of winds, and whom the winds again
Take from us . . .

(ll. 761–3)

Where before, the strangeness had evoked the wonder of commitment, now—four hundred lines further into a poem that couldn't be made to work—it has come to be associated with the sourceless, restless condition of imagination itself.[52] Inspired by the wheeling and plunging of the ducks, Wordsworth writes with a sudden vivid excitement that has nothing to do with the argument that he has for so long been trying to put forward:

> Witness the delight
> With which erewhile I saw that multitude
> Wheel through the sky, and see them now at rest,
> Yet not at rest, upon the glassy lake.
> They cannot rest—they gambol like young whelps,
> Active as lambs, and overcome with joy;
> They try all frolic motions, flutter, plunge,
> And beat the passive water with their wings.
>
> (ll. 766–73)

The poetry becomes a celebration of the return of spring, and also surely of the return of inspiration. Thomson, not surprisingly, is felt strongly in the background as Wordsworth evokes the sharing not just of the ducks, but of the incongruous ravens too, in the joys of the coming year:

> Admonished of the days of love to come,
> The raven croaks and fills the sunny air
> With a strange sound of genial harmony . . .[53]
>
> (ll. 795–7)

But what does it all add up to? 'I leave them to their pleasure', Wordsworth concludes, happily, and with no sense of problems yet unsolved:

> and I pass,
> Pass with a thought the life of the whole year
> That is to come—the throngs of mountain flowers
> And lilies that will dance upon the lake.
>
> (ll. 803–6)

It looks very much as if Wordsworth is trying to bring his poem—or this Book of it, if already he is thinking in Books—to an end. In terms of his original intentions no conclusion has been arrived at, but pleasure in writing once again the poetry of excited personal response carries him on into claims which for the moment can *seem* to be appropriate:

> Then boldly say that solitude is not
> Where these things are . . .

Community now appears to consist in imaginative sympathy; the social implications essential to the scheme of *The Recluse* have been forgotten. Conveniently it is the Londoner, not the Grasmere peasant, who is alone:

> Then boldly say that solitude is not
> Where these things are: he truly is alone,
> He of the multitude, whose eyes are doomed
> To hold a vacant commerce day by day
> With that which he can neither know nor love—
> Dead things, to him thrice dead . . .

Love and knowledge are redefined as the enlivening power of imagination—the power that had been welcomed in the Preamble in the twin metaphors of escape from the city, and shaking off of the burden of the poet's own unnatural self. London, though, is more than a state of mind: it is difficult not to think that in these vehement, unbalanced allusions, characteristic only of 1800, there is the fear that Wordsworth and Dorothy, for all their mutual love and shared response to their surroundings, have indeed been running away.[54] Their right to be 'A pair seceding from the common world' was to have been established in the setting up of Grasmere, and the countryman's way of life, as a pattern for the future; the claim to have done anything of the kind now rested solely on the power of assertion:

> Society is here:
> The true community, the noblest frame
> Of many into one incorporate;
> That must be looked for here; paternal sway,
> One household under God for high and low,
> One family and one mansion . . .
>
> (ll. 818–23)

The terms, and tones, have a splendid resonance, but hardly more.

For the moment, though, their emptiness is not apparent to the poet himself. As the final sequence of *MS R* begins, he looks back to the Prospectus confident that 'Paradise and groves/Elysian' have indeed become 'the growth of common day'. His first draft is very rough:

> Dismissing therefore all Arcadian dreams,
> All golden fancies borrowed from the time
> That was before all time—that perfect age
> How dear to think of when we wish to part
> With all remembrance of a jarring world—
> Take we at once this hope unto ourselves,
> This chearful hope
> How goodly, how exceeding fair, how pure
> From all reproach, is this etherial frame
> And this deep vale, its counterpart below,
> By which and under which we are enclosed
> To breathe in peace
>   we shall also prove
> If rightly we observe and justly weigh,
> The inmates not unworthy of their home[55]

As before, Grasmere is offered to the reader as the paradise of everyday-life, distinct in its actuality from the creations of myth and the products of literary nostalgia. The first ten lines of the passage quoted were tidied up on a separate page of *MS R* bringing Wordsworth once again to his central problem—the 'inmates' (Grasmere peasants), who had for the sake of his redemptive scheme to be shown, at the very least, as 'not unworthy of their home'. No previous attempt in the poem had been a success, but it comes as a shock nonetheless to find him at this stage suddenly inserting lines which suggest that he has given up all hope:

> Dismissing therefore all Arcadian dreams,
> All golden fancies of the golden age . . .
> Give entrance to the sober truth, avow
> That Nature to this favoured spot of ours
> Yields no exemption, but her awful rights
> Enforces to the utmost and exacts
> Her tribute of inevitable pain,
> And that the sting is added—man himself,
> For ever busy to afflict himself.[56]

In *Tintern Abbey* it had been Nature's 'privilege/Through all the years of this our life to lead/From joy to joy' (ll. 124–6). In the Prospectus, though it had been conceded that humanity might experience 'solitary anguish' in the countryside as well as 'the fierce confederate storm/Of sorrow . . . Within the walls of cities', it had been implied very strongly that Grasmere itself was exempt:

> *Such pleasant haunts foregoing*, if my song
> Must turn elsewhere, and travel near the tribes
> And fellowships of men, and see ill sights
> Of passions ravenous . . .
>
> (ll. 41–4)

It is the writing of *Home at Grasmere* that has brought the poet to accept the existence of 'inevitable pain' and 'passions ravenous' amid the pleasant haunts that surround him. Gradually, it appears, he has come to identify the presence of Satan in his Eden. As Donne puts it, sardonically, in *Twicknam Garden*—

> And that this place may thoroughly be thought
> True Paradise, I have the serpent brought.
>
> (ll. 8–9)

In *Hart-leap Well*, man's destructive tendencies had been directed against Nature; presumably they had not been a help, but nor had they precluded 'the coming of the milder day'. The 'sting' of man 'For ever busy to afflict himself' is something new. Wordsworth counters the thought, of course, but his claims now carry no conviction:

> Yet temper this with one sufficient faith
> (What need of more?), that we shall neither droop
> Nor pine for want of pleasure in the life
> Which is about us, nor through dearth of aught
> That keeps in health the insatiable mind—
> That we shall have for knowledge and for love
> Abundance, and that feeling as we do[57]

Here the drafts of *MS R* come to an end. The final words are supposed to tie back into the passage quoted above:

and that feeling as we do
How goodly, how exceeding fair, how pure
From all reproach, is this etherial frame
And this deep vale its counterpart below . . .
we shall also prove
If rightly we observe, and justly weigh,
The inmates not unworthy of their home

The peasants of Grasmere are to be thought of as worthy of the place in which they live, not because of anything they are, or do, or achieve, but because the vale is an earthly counterpart of heaven (or the sky) and thus reflects its purity.[58] It was not much to offer in the face of the poet's intuition of man the serpent, self-destructive and ineducable; and there is a special pathos in the poet's assertion—probably the last words of *Home at Grasmere* actually to be composed in *MS R*—that he and Dorothy will have 'for knowledge and for love/Abundance'. The great claims and high millenarian hopes have dwindled into private anxiety. He is concerned now that Grasmere shall produce enough pleasure, enough stimulus to keep healthy his insatiable mind. There is no longer any mention of spreading love and knowledge, or even of sharing them—they are now personal qualities that need to be sustained. In the contraction of his aims, only Dorothy's presence saves Wordsworth from feeling a Coleridgean despair—a 'decrease of hope and joy' that leaves 'the soul in its round and round flight forming narrower circles, till at every gyre its wings beat against the *personal self*' (*Notebooks*, ii, no. 2531).

It is tempting to think that it was at this point that Wordsworth broke off work in 1800. The fact that he didn't go on to write the central section of *The Recluse* is itself evidence that he was disheartened; and the progress of *Home at Grasmere*, culminating in the drafts of *MS R*, shows very clearly why he should have become so. When transcribed in *MS B*, however, the material drafted in *R* is followed at once by a paragraph (ll. 859–74) including tender references to the presence to John Wordsworth at Dove Cottage (January–September 1800), and looking forward to the first visit of Coleridge (on 6 April). The fact that these lines, though not preserved in *R*, belong undoubtedly to 1800, raises the question as to whether the rest of the hundred-line sequence of *Home at Grasmere* leading up to the Prospectus in *MS*

B may not also contain early material. One section especially—the chastened and muted new estimate of the poet's vocation—seems to reflect the need in April 1800 to scale down aspirations, think in less exalted terms than had recently seemed appropriate. Coming after the tender fantasy of the mountains rejoicing 'with open joy' at the arrival of Coleridge, the opening lines seem almost pitiful in their humbleness:

> These mountains will rejoice with open joy.
> Such is our wealth: O vale of peace, we are
> And must be, with God's will, a happy band!
>   *But 'tis not to enjoy, for this alone*
> *That we exist; no, something must be done . . .*
> Each being has his office, lowly some
> And common, yet all worthy if fulfilled
> With zeal . . .
> Of ill advised ambition and of pride
> I would stand clear, yet unto me I feel
> That an internal brightness is vouchsafed
> That must not die, that must not pass away.
>
> (ll. 872–87)

A quiet dignity comes into the verse as the poet returns to define once again his sense of election—the steady underlying confidence which is proof against discouragement, and which so often becomes the theme of his poetry when he is most in need of reassurance:

> Possessions have I, wholly, solely mine,
> Something within, which yet is shared with none—
> Not even the nearest to me and most dear—
> Something which power and effort may impart.
> I would impart it; I would spread it wide,
> Immortal in the world which is to come.
> I would not wholly perish even in this,
> Lie down and be forgotten in the dust,
> I and the modest partners of my days
> Making a silent company in death.
> It must not be, if I divinely taught
> Am privileged to speak as I have felt
> Of what in man is human or divine.
>
> (ll. 897–909)

The poet, it seems, has settled for Coleridge's 'intense union', as opposed to the 'absolute unity' which has been the ideal of his poem. Even with 'the modest partners of [his] days'—Dorothy and John, Coleridge, Mary and Sara—he cannot share that which is to him most precious. Yet the faith remains that he *is* divinely taught, that a special virtue resides in what he personally has felt, that for all his godlike qualities man is important first in his humanity.

In the text of *MS B*, of course (which is presumably the first completed version of *Home at Grasmere*), this calm and modest reassessment is followed within fifty lines by the grandiloquent claims of the Prospectus. It is a strange juxtaposition, and not one that could have been intended when the Prospectus was originally written.[59] With its echo of the terms in which Wordsworth first mentions his plan for *The Recluse*—'My object is to give pictures of Nature, man and society' (March 1798)—the Prospectus is obviously a beginning; and there is manuscript evidence to suggest that the poet not only wrote it first, but thought of it as a preface.[60] The Pisgah-sight of Grasmere—'Once on the brow of yonder hill . . . ' would have followed logically as an introduction to the regained paradise which the Prospectus had already celebrated in its high-flown and very general terms. But *Home at Grasmere* did not develop as it should have done. The early lines contain some of the most tender and beautiful love-poetry in the language ('Her voice was like a hidden bird that sang') and later there is much to be admired—intermittently in the quality of the writing, and at all times in the honesty of the poet as he refuses to give in and falsify the none-too-promising lives that his neighbours are living. Gradually, though, he must have become aware that acting out his personal role as the Recluse, however much it might remind him of 'the bowers/Of blissful Eden', was not going to provide him with the material that he needed. Something grander—perhaps more, in Coleridge's sense of the word, philosophical[61]—would have to be found to justify his millenarian claims. At this point *Home at Grasmere* and the Prospectus would in effect change places. *Home at Grasmere* would come to be seen as a stock-taking made before *The Recluse* proper could get under way,[62] and the Prospectus would have to go at the end in order to fulfil its original purpose as an introduction.

Everything points to summer 1806 as the moment at which the Prospectus was actually transferred to the end of *Home at Grasmere*. The question remains as to what Wordsworth had done in 1800 when his poem refused to take the form, or move in the direction, that had at first been intended. Coleridge's visit to Dove Cottage on 6 April may well be significant. We don't know what he thought of *Home at Grasmere*, but in a letter written on the tenth he tells Southey that Wordsworth has decided to publish 'a second volume of Lyrical Ballads and Pastorals'. It is not a decision that would have been taken—and certainly not one that would have been encouraged by Coleridge—if the writing of *The Recluse* had been going well. Wordsworth in fact went on to compose major work of three quite different kinds before the end of the year, all associated with *Lyrical Ballads: Poems on the Naming of Places*, *Michael*, and the Preface. In each of the three it is possible to see the ideals of the spring taking a less exalted, but no less passionate, form. The first brings together some quietly impressive poems under a very dull heading, and shows the poet exploring his paradise—naming and claiming places within it, as Adam names his fellow inhabitants of Eden. With its curious blend of propaganda and tragedy, *Michael* continues the attempt made in *Home at Grasmere* to give value to the peasant's way of life. While the Preface asserts not only that the feelings of such men are more 'sane, pure and permanent' but that their language—the medium the poet himself has chosen—will be so too.

At the beginning of the year Wordsworth had prayed in the Prospectus that his verse might be 'Even as a light hung up in heaven to chear/The world in times to come' (ll. 62–3). At a defiant moment in the spring when *Home at Grasmere* wasn't going too well, he had written

> No, we are not alone; we do not stand,
> My Emma, here misplaced and desolate,
> Loving what no one cares for but ourselves. . . .
>   We do not tend a lamp
> Whose lustre we alone participate . . .
>
> (ll. 646–8, 655–6)

And in *Michael* the lamp of course reappears as the 'aged utensil', 'Surviving comrade of uncounted hours' (l. 120), that has given the cottage its name, the Evening Star. In its humbler, domestic way, it is still symbolic:

> The light was famous in its neighbourhood,
> And was a public symbol of the life
> The thrifty pair had lived; for, as it chanced,
> Their cottage on a plot of rising ground
> Stood single, with large prospect north and south . . . [63]
>
> (ll. 136–40)

As he worked on *Michael* in October–December 1800, Wordsworth probably did not think *The Recluse* had come seriously to a halt. One day, he must surely have felt, the lamp that he and Dorothy tended at Dove Cottage would similarly have 'large prospect north and south', telling the world not of a private paradise regained, but of one available to all whose minds were 'wedded to this outward frame of things/In love'.

Chapter 5

Joy and Jollity: Spring 1802

I never saw daffodils so beautiful; they grew among the mossy stones, about and about them; some rested their heads upon these stones as on a pillow for weariness, and the rest tossed and reeled and danced and seemed as if they verily laughed with the wind that blew upon them over the lake, they looked so gay—ever glancing, ever changing.

(Dorothy Wordsworth: April 1802)

The Barberry-Tree

Late on a breezy vernal eve
  When breezes wheeled their whirling flight
I wandered forth, and I believe
  I never saw so sweet a sight:

It nodded in the breeze,
  It rustled in mine ear—
Fairest of blossomed trees
  In hill or valley, far or near.

No tree that grew in hill or vale
  Such blithesome blossoms e'er displayed:
They laughed and danced upon the gale,
  They seemed as they could never fade—
As they could never fade they seemed,
  And still they danced, now high, now low.
In very joy their colours gleamed,
  But whether it be thus or no,
That while they danced upon the wind
They felt a joy like humankind,
That this blithe breeze which cheerly sung
While the merry boughs he swung
Did in that moment while the bough

Whispered to his gladsome singing
Feel the pleasures that even now
In my breast are springing—
And whether, as I said before,
These golden blossoms dancing high,
These breezes piping through the sky,
Have in themselves of joy a store,
And, mingling breath and murmured motion
Like eddies of the gusty ocean,
Do in their leafy morris bear
Mirth and gladness through the air,
As up and down the branches toss,
And above and beneath and across
The breezes brush on lusty pinion
(Sportive struggling for dominion)—
If living sympathy be theirs,
And leaves and airs,
The piping breeze and dancing tree,
Are all alive and glad as we—
Whether this be truth or no
I cannot tell, I do not know;
Nay, whether now I reason well,
I do not know, I cannot tell.
But this I know, and will declare,
Rightly and surely *this* I know,
That never here, that never there,
Around me, aloft, or alow,
Nor here, nor there, nor anywhere,
Saw I a scene so very fair.
And on this food of thought I fed
Till moments, minutes, hours, had fled,
And had not sudden the church-chimes
Rung out the well-known peal I love,
I had forgotten Peter Grimes,
His nuts and cyder in the apple-grove:
I say, and I aver it true,
That had I not the warning heard
Which told how late it grew
(And I to Grimes had pledged my word),

In that most happy mood of mind
There like a statue had I stood till now—
And when my trance was ended
And on my way I tended,

  Still so it was, I know not how,
But passed it not away, that piping wind.

For as I went, in sober sooth,
    It seemed to go along with me—
I tell you now the very truth,
  It seemed part of myself to be—
That in my inner self I had
Those whispering sounds which made me glad.
Now if you feel a wish dear Jones
  To see these branches dancing so,
Lest you in vain should stir your bones,
  I will advise you when to go—
That is, if you should wish to see
This piping, skipping barberry
(For so they call the shrub I mean,
Whose blossomed branches thus are seen
  Uptossing their leafy shrouds
    As if they were fain to spring
    On the whirl-zephyr's wing,
        Up to the clouds).
If Jacob Jones you have at heart
  To hear this sound and see this sight
[Then this] advice I do impart,[1]
  [That] Jacob you don't go by night,
[For then 'tis] possible the shrub so green
[To toss and b]low, may not well be seen—
[Nor Jaco]b would I have you go
When the blithe winds forbear to blow;
I think it may be safely then averred
  The piping leaves will not be heard.
    But when the wind rushes
    Through brakes and through bushes,
  And around, and within, and without,
    Makes a roar and a rout,
      Then may you see
      The barberry-tree,
    With all its yellow flowers
    And interwoven bowers,
    Toss in merry madness
    Every bough of gladness
And dance to and fro to the loud-singing breeze
The blithest of gales, and the maddest of trees;
    And then like me

Even from the blossoms of the barberry,
Mayst thou a store of thought lay by
For present time and long futurity,
And teach to fellow men a lore
They never learned before—
The manly strain of natural poesy.

The *Barberry-Tree* turned up in 1964 in the Library at Christ Church, Oxford. Wordsworth never published it, and no copy is preserved among his extant manuscripts, but it is undoubtedly his, and belongs almost certainly to the end of May 1802.[2] Its self-revelation, and the blending of serious and comic, may seem to us uneasy, but don't appear to worry the poet. He is composing fast, and with evident enjoyment—composing for himself, for Dorothy, for Coleridge perhaps especially, and with no thought of a wider audience that might laugh in the wrong places. The resulting poem is partly very fluent, partly very clumsy, and tells us a great deal about the moods of this odd yet important period.

Most obviously successful are the passages of strong personal response (ll. 29–40, and especially 95–106), as Wordsworth evokes the tossing branches and yellow flowers of the berberis dancing in the wind. In the background is Dorothy's recent prose account of the daffodils, source of the later poem—'the rest tossed and reeled and danced, and seemed as if they verily laughed with the wind' (15 April 1802)—and there are clear connections with *The sun has long been set*, written by Wordsworth on 8 June:

The sun has long been set,
The stars are out by twos and threes,
The little birds are piping yet
Among the bushes and the trees;
There's a cuckoo, and one or two thrushes,
And a noise of wind that rushes,
With a noise of water that gushes,
And the cuckoo's sovereign cry
Fills all the hollow of the sky . . .

(ll. 1–9)

Least acceptable, presumably, are the facetious moments of *The Barberry-Tree*, in which the poet descends to doggerel in the manner of 'I do not love thee, Doctor Fell' (ll. 41–4), makes doubly inexplicable references to Peter Grimes (ll. 55–6, 60),[3] or advises the ludicrous Jacob Jones not to visit the berberis in the dark in case he can't see it (ll. 85–90). No doubt much of the clumsiness is self-mockery on the part of the poet, but Southey's unkind remark about *Lyrical Ballads*, 1798, remains as true as ever: 'The author should be warned that he who personates tiresome loquacity becomes tiresome himself.'[4]

The idiom of *The Barberry-Tree* belongs exclusively to spring 1802, and was clearly evolved to allow the maximum flexibility in sound-effects and mood. At its most formal it produces *Intimations*, i–iv (27 March/17 June), at its jolliest, *The Tinker* (27–9 April):

> Right before the farmer's door
> Down he sits, his brows he knits,
> Then his hammer he rouzes:
> Batter! batter! batter!
> He begins to clatter,
> And while the work is going on
> Right good ale he bouzes.
> And when it is done, away he is gone,
> And in his scarlet coat
> With a merry note
> He sings the sun to bed,
> And without making a pother
> Finds some place or other
> For his own careless head.
>
> (ll. 9–22)

The Barberry-Tree shares with *The Tinker* its gaiety and feebleness,[5] its abrupt changes of pace and rhythm and length of line; but it is both much more facetious, and facetious about much more surprising material. This is hardly the context in which one would expect to find a discussion of animism, a 'spot of time', and the Wordsworthian storing up of pleasure for future restoration. Not all the comedy in *The Barberry-Tree* is ponderous—the guying of the poet's trance, for instance ('Till moments, minutes, *hours*, had fled'), is nicely done—but the poem as a whole forces one to ask what Wordsworth thought he was doing. Why the self-mockery? To what extent are serious beliefs undercut by the garrulous questioning (or refusals to question)?—

> *But whether it be thus or no,*
> That while they danced upon the wind
> They felt a joy like humankind,
> That this blithe breeze which cheerly sung
> While the merry boughs he swung
> Did in that moment while the bough
> Whispered to his gladsome singing
> Feel the pleasures that even now
> In my breast are springing—
> *And whether, as I said before,*
> These golden blossoms dancing high,
> These breezes piping through the sky,
> Have in themselves of joy a store,
> And, mingling breath and murmured motion
> Like eddies of the gusty ocean,
> Do in their leafy morris bear
> Mirth and gladness through the air,
> As up and down the branches toss,
> And above and beneath and across
> The breezes brush on lusty pinion
> (Sportive struggling for dominion)—
> If living sympathy be theirs,
> And leaves and airs,
> The piping breeze and dancing tree,
> Are all alive and glad as we—
> *Whether this be truth or no*
> *I cannot tell, I do not know;*
> *Nay, whether now I reason well,*
> *I do not know, I cannot tell.*
>
> (ll. 16–44)

Spring 1802 is the moment before Wordsworth set out with Dorothy to visit Annette and his French daughter Caroline as a prelude to getting married to Mary Hutchinson.[6] It is also, importantly, the moment that produced the first version of Coleridge's *Dejection*, lamenting the hopelessness of his love for Mary's sister Sara, his increasing sense of exclusion from the Wordsworth household, his loss of imaginative certainty and power. It has long been recognized that the first four stanzas of *Intimations*, together with *Dejection* and *The Leech Gatherer*, form a sequence, provoking and answering each other, and showing in the process a widening gap between the two poets; but Coleridge's magnificent despair—

> My genial spirits fail—
> And what can these avail
> To lift the smothering weight from off my breast? . . .
> I may not hope from outward forms to win
> The passion and the life, whose fountains are within!
> (*Dejection*, 44–6, 50–1)[7]

—has tended to prevent questions as to the nature of Wordsworth's countering optimism. Because Coleridge evokes in such impressive tones his inability to feel the certainties that they had earlier shared, it is assumed that Wordsworth on his side would have had no difficulty. This is not the case.

At Alfoxden in 1798, and at Grasmere in the early days of 1800, Wordsworth had lived a vision; at Goslar in 1798–9, though (or because) day-to-day life provided no inspiration, he had evolved an imaginative mode that led him back to the primal sources of his creativity—and very much the same was to be true again in 1804. In 1802 happiness itself was a temptation. Life at Dove Cottage offered countless tender feelings and episodes that could too easily be tied into Nature at the level of fancy, and into the past in terms of nostalgia. Understandably the poet was reluctant to go for more. Why risk becoming the self-driven neurotic of the *Castle of Indolence* stanzas, vexed by the 'tempest, [the] redundant energy' of his own imagination:

> happier soul no living creature has . . .
> But verse was what he had been wedded to;
> And his own mind did like a tempest strong
> Come to him thus, and drove the weary man along.
> (ll. 30, 34–6)

Wordsworth's vision in spring 1802 was wilfully limited: he did not wish to be disturbed. 'In youth from rock to rock I went', he wrote in the first of the Daisy poems,

> From hill to hill in discontent
> Of pleasure high and turbulent,
> Most pleased when most uneasy;

But now my own delights I make,
My thirst at every rill can slake,
And gladly Nature's love partake
Of thee, sweet daisy.

(ll. 1–8)

There were the deeper moments, too, times when his thirst was not so easily slaked; but the poet who partook of love from celandines and daisies was making his own delights in quite a different sense from the man who in *1799* had given his devotion to Nature because 'the midnight storm/Grew darker in the presence of [his] eye' (ii. 422–3). Behind the period of pleasing discontent Wordsworth now saw not the childhood of guilt and pain and 'visionary dreariness' recorded at Goslar, but golden days spent, as his days were again being spent, beneath the tender civilizing influence of Dorothy:

The blessing of my later years
Was with me when a boy:
She gave me eyes, she gave me ears,
And humble cares, and delicate fears,
A heart the fountain of sweet tears,
And love, and thought, and joy.

(*The Sparrow's Nest*, 15–20)

The disturbing primal experiences of *1799*, Part I had been held to retain 'a fructifying virtue', and in the great imaginative work of 1804–5 Wordsworth was again to regard them as the source of adult creative power—

Fair seed-time had my soul, and I grew up
Fostered alike by beauty and by fear

(*1805*, i. 305–6)

—but for the moment vision consisted merely of childish wonderment prolonged. Past and future could be linked by pleasure in rainbows.[8]

Even the first four stanzas of *Intimations*, aside from *The Leech Gatherer* unquestionably the greatest poetry of this period, seem to find difficulty in transcending this level of fancy and nostalgia. The poet's sense of loss, generalized at first ('There was a time . . .'), but finally specific ('there's a tree, of many *one*,/A *single* field . . . '), is often very moving. And there is the one moment of vividly imaginative border poetry, in which the 'sounding cataracts' of *Tintern Abbey* come into their own, and the poet is able beautifully to evoke the hidden sources of his power:

> The cataracts blow their trumpets from the steep,
> No more shall grief of mine the season wrong;
> I hear the echoes through the mountains throng,
> *The winds come to me from the fields of sleep*,
> And all the earth is gay . . .
>
> (ll. 25–9)

But after such resolution, such inspiration, why does he then choose to treat returning strength, joyfulness, harmony, on a level of determined superficiality?

The key mood, and word, of spring 1802 is found in the lines that follow:

> Land and sea
> Give themselves up to jollity . . .

The joy of communion ('Love now from heart to heart is stealing'), seen in its different forms at Alfoxden and in the early Grasmere days, has given place to incongruous jollity. The poet is surrounded now by lambs that 'bound/As to the tabor's sound', beasts that 'keep holiday', and 'blessed creatures' with whom the heavens laugh in their 'jubilee'. It is all very literary, and not very persuasive; few can read

> My heart is at your festival,
> My head hath its coronal . . .
>
> (ll. 39–40)

without some sense of unease. Wordsworth, who believes himself to be excluded from the jubilee by loss of childhood vision, is felt to be excluded in fact by lack of imaginative sympathy.

There are exceptions of course—usually where the poetry is least ambitious:

> The cock is crowing,
> The stream is flowing,
> The small birds twitter,
> The lake doth glitter,
> The green field sleeps in the sun . . .

The cattle are grazing,
Their heads never raising,
There are forty feeding like one.

(ll. 1–5, 8–10)

—but very often the attempt to recapture 'the glory and the dream' leads at this period to whimsy and self-congratulation. The second Daisy is given 'many a fond and idle name' so that finally Wordsworth can salute it with its own ('Sweet flower . . . Sweet silent creature'), but the poem depends on our willingness to share in the 'web of similes' that has been woven *en route*:

And many a fond and idle name
I give to thee for praise or blame,
As is the humour of the game,
    While I am gazing.

A nun demure of lowly port,
Or sprightly maiden of Love's court,
In thy simplicity the sport
    Of all temptations;
A queen in crown of rubies drest,
A starvling in a scanty vest,
Are all, as seem to suit thee best,
    Thy appelations.

(ll. 13–24)

It is not just that the poetry remains on the level of fancy—fairly impoverished fancy—but that while imagination transcends the self, fancy is a form of self-pleasure.

Wordsworth in spring 1802 was easily pleased; and, surprisingly, the fault must largely have been Dorothy's. Their love was as deep as ever, but the exalted sharing of the early days at Dove Cottage had been overtaken by domesticity. Dorothy's *Journal* of this period is probably the best of all, but the vividness of her perceptions doesn't seem ever to have made her critical of her brother. Whatever one might wish to believe, she doted on him; and she accepted his work at his own valuation. She was a force for good in that her responsiveness was a stimulus to the outgoing poetry (*The cock is crowing*, and the dancing of the berberis), but she did nothing to allay the self-regard. 'Dear

Sara', she wrote in June to Sara Hutchinson, who, of all things, had been bored by *The Leech Gatherer*,

> When you happen to be displeased with what you suppose to be the tendency or moral of any poem which William writes, ask yourself whether you have hit upon the real tendency and true moral, and above all never think that he writes for no reason but merely because a thing happened—and when you feel any poem of his to be tedious, ask yourself in what spirit it was written—whether merely to tell the tale and be through with it, or to illustrate a particular character or truth etc etc.
>
> I am glad that you have found out how to bake bread in my way . . .
>
> (*EY* 367)

Dorothy does not pause for a moment to consider that Sara could be right, or that her responses could have their own validity. William has been criticized; her defence is wholly automatic, and leaves her so ruffled that she cannot even phrase acceptably her pleasure at having been able to help with the baking. Wordsworth's art derived from moods of abnormal imaginative intensity, and Dorothy's protectiveness shows clearly the shape of things to come in the too comfortable later years. Nothing could have been more obstructive of great poetry—except her brother's willingness to be protected.

Spring 1802 has sometimes been portrayed as a moment of crisis. In his forthcoming marriage Wordsworth, we are told, was proposing to jilt Annette, who was the mother of his child, and to betray Dorothy (to whom he was bound by a love incestuous or not according to the critic's personal taste)—and then there was Coleridge, intruding private unhappiness, and casting doubt on all that was, or had been, sacred. If Wordsworth and Dorothy hadn't appeared quite so unconcerned, the case would be open and shut. The most recent claims are made by Jared Curtis:

> The spring of 1802 is for Wordsworth a period of great uncertainty and momentous decision, of intense delight and anxious doubt and disappointment. It was a time when not only the poem on his own life lay fallow and seemed threatened by silence, but his way of life and its emotional and spiritual continuity suddenly faltered, under the new internal and external pressures, under his deep sense of changes within himself, and under his awareness of shifting relationships with persons both near and distant.[9]

If Wordsworth was indeed worried at this period about *The Recluse*, it must surely have been about the central section not the subordinate 'poem on his own life',[10] and it would require more evidence than is produced to support this sudden faltering of 'emotional and spiritual continuity'. The decision to get married to Mary Hutchinson had by 1802 been on the cards for so long that it must have been losing some of its momentousness; and there is no reason to suppose that it shifted Wordsworth's relationship with 'persons' either 'near' (Dorothy), or 'distant' (Annette). The pattern of the 'ménage à trois' had been taken for granted as early as 1793,[11] and it is clear that Dorothy had never thought that her brother's marriage would be a time of parting. At that period the cottage of the future was to be shared with Annette and Caroline; but it likely that Mary had at a still earlier stage seemed the logical wife for William, and she must surely have done so again during, and after, her six months' stay at Racedown in 1796–7.[12] Dorothy's feelings about the impending marriage are probably well represented by the end of the daffodils entry in her *Journal* (15 April 1802): 'We had a glass of warm rum and water. We enjoyed ourselves and wished for Mary.' One can if one chooses posit in her an unconscious resentment, but it is a different thing to infer that her relationship with her brother was changed by the prospect of his marriage—and a still larger step to assume that he felt himself to be betraying her.[13]

That Wordsworth should be brought to crisis-point in spring 1802 by worry over Coleridge seems on the face of it more likely. His next, and last, great creative period in 1804–5 was certainly given an impetus by Coleridge's seeming nearness to death, and by the emotional need to be doing something for him at the time of his departure for the Mediterranean; and in 1802 there is tangible evidence of anxiety both in Dorothy's *Journal*, and in Wordsworth's poetic response to *Dejection*. But in this connection it is interesting that the first version of *The Leech Gatherer*, written in early May, is not only less impressive as a poem, it is also far less convincing as part of a dialogue. The two versions have the same opening section (ll. 1–54), and the same final stanza; the early poem is thus as clearly offered to Coleridge as the later, in response to the 'untoward thoughts' of *Dejection*. In form, however, it is a rather feeble latter-day lyrical ballad. It is quite without an imaginative centre, presenting as the 'leading from above', the 'something given', merely a pathetic old man 'For chimney-nook, or bed, or coffin meet', who has trouble finding leeches, yet bears it all with pious fortitude:

> 'I yet can gain my bread, though in times gone
> I twenty could have found where now I can find one.
>
> Feeble I am in health these hills to climb,
> Yet I procure a living of my own:
> This is my summer work; in winter-time
> I go with godly books from town to town . . .'
>
> (ll. 125–30)

Neither version shows in Wordsworth an ability to focus his mind specifically on Coleridge's troubles, offer him reassurance that might actually be supportive, but in the final poem the images of the stone/sea-beast/cloud (ll. 64–84), the reverie ('soon his voice to me was like a stream/Scarce heard', ll. 121–2), and the beautiful myth in which the old man is internalized as the wanderer—

> In my mind's eye I seemed to see him pace
> About the weary moors continually,
> Wandering about alone and silently . . .
>
> (ll. 143–5)

—would, if anything could, substantiate the poet's claim that 'By our own spirits are we deified'.[14] It might perhaps be argued that these inspired revisions show in Wordsworth an awareness that he has not done enough for Coleridge, but to judge from his protestations—'Good God! Such a figure, in such a place, a pious self-respecting, miserably infirm, and [ ] old man, telling such a tale!' (*EY* 367)—it seems far more likely that Sara Hutchinson needled him into having second thoughts.

Even the first version of *The Leech Gatherer* (3–9 May) is a very delayed reply to *Dejection*, which, as Dorothy records, had been repeated at Dove Cottage on 21 April. Hers is both the first, and the most obviously heartfelt, response that has been preserved:

> William and I sauntered a little in the garden. Coleridge came to us and repeated the verses he wrote to Sara. I was affected with them and was on the whole, not being well, in miserable spirits. The sunshine, the green fields, and the fair sky made me sadder; even the little, happy, sporting lambs seemed but sorrowful to me.

Coleridge's references to *Intimations* (*Dejection*, 42–3, 136) have been taken, and Dorothy can no longer share her brother's pleasure in the lambs and the jubilee of spring. The three of them, however, 'sate comfortably' together that evening, and seem to have enjoyed the days that followed, Coleridge finding a bower, 'the sweetest that was ever seen', in which they decided to plant flowers, and the next day (24th) damming a rill by the roadside to make a miniature lake. It is especially interesting that two days after hearing *Dejection* Dorothy should be able to write quite simply, 'We wished for Mary and Sara.' The power of the poem had been oppressive, but none of its revelations would have been new to the Wordsworths. They had lived with every aspect of Coleridge's tortured love, and it remained natural to Dorothy that when they found a bower of unusual beauty they should all of them wish the Hutchinson sisters—Mary whom Wordsworth was about to marry, Sara whom Coleridge couldn't[15]—to be there too.

On 22 April Dorothy makes a cryptic reference in her *Journal* to the second of two brief poems, *These chairs, they have no words to utter* and *I have thoughts that are fed by the sun*, which show in a very personal light her brother's moods of this period, and which may well have been written after Coleridge's reading of *Dejection*. The first is a pushing away of experience, partly whimsical, partly reflective; the second, headed in the manuscript, 'Half an hour afterwards', is beautiful and assured in its acceptance. Dorothy's *Journal* tells of a walk in Easedale with William and Coleridge, and of William's coming back to her at one stage, 'repeating the poem *I have thoughts that are fed by the sun*'. 'It had been called to his mind', she adds—which could presumably mean either that he had just written it in his head, or that it had been *re*called—'by the dying away of the stunning of the waterfall when he came behind a stone.' In different forms, death is in fact at the centre of both poems. The mood of *These chairs* is seemingly one of pure escapism. The poet is 'alone,/Happy and alone', undistracted because his surroundings are mute and make no demands—and that is how he wishes permanently to be:

These chairs they have no words to utter,
No fire is in the grate to stir or flutter,
The ceiling and floor are mute as a stone;

My chamber is hushed and still,
And I am alone,
Happy and alone.

Oh, who would be afraid of life,
The passion, the sorrow, and the strife,
When he may lie
Sheltered so easily?—
May lie in peace on his bed,
Happy as they who are dead.

The silliness of the opening thought, mimed in the feminine rhyme of 'utter'/'flutter', betrays one into assuming that the poem will be trivial; and there is a sense in which Wordsworth himself wishes it to be so. The presence of *Frost at Midnight* in the very second line, however, makes it clear that this cannot be—that the poet will not (and knows he will not), be permitted to 'lie/Sheltered so easily'. 'The passion, the sorrow, and the strife' of existence have to be acknowledged, because they are part of the world of an active imagination. Like the many references in *Dejection* that go back to the poetry and shared assumptions of Alfoxden, Wordsworth's allusion to the 'stranger' fluttering in the grate in *Frost at Midnight* is a reminder in a mood of weakness of an earlier moment of strength.[16] If it was not already in his mind, the thought of past sharing would inevitably bring with it Coleridge's present despair—the 'grief without a pang, void, dark, and drear', evoked not only in *Dejection*, but again and again in the letters and notebooks of the period. His first impulse is to shut it out, deny its threatening implications by denying that he himself *needs* 'the sole unquiet thing' that is imagination. He will do without it, buy himself peace by being positively pleased that there is no fire in the grate. But from the first the poetry tells us that this won't do. The border words 'mute', 'stone', 'still', 'alone', are being abused, deprived of their resonance; the poet knows that to lie sheltered in bed *is* to be afraid of life. The peace it offers is the peace of wish-fulfilment. The sequel had to come.

I have thoughts that are fed by the sun is a very personal, Wordsworthian, facing of facts. That the dying noise of the waterfall should have prompted, or recalled, the poem is a measure of its distance from the mood of the earlier lines. Death comes to be seen not as happiness, escapism, but as separation—

separation from the sun as source of spiritual energy, from the poet's surroundings, from his love and hopes. He wishes still for its peace, but is no longer denying its sharpness:

> I have thoughts that are fed by the sun—
> The things which I see
> Are welcome to me,
> Welcome every one;
> I do not wish to lie
> Dead, dead,
> Dead, without any company.
> Here alone on my bed
> With thoughts that are fed by the sun,
> And hopes that are welcome every one,
> Happy am I.
>
> O life there is about thee
> A deep delicious peace;
> I would not be without thee,
> Stay, oh stay—
> Yet be thou ever as now,
> Sweetness and breath, with the quiet of death,
> Be but thou ever as now,
> Peace, peace, peace.

Perhaps it is not great poetry, but it is very moving because Wordsworth has taken us—as Coleridge does in *Dejection*—into a mood so private that it can barely be controlled by the formal beauty that contains it. At this level, despite 'The passion, the sorrow, and the strife' that goes on about him, Wordsworth is felt to have a right to his own sense that there is in life 'A deep delicious peace'. Above all it seems to be the silent quotation from Chaucer that gives him this right. After the poem's initial fluency of rhythm, the lines

> I do not wish to lie
> Dead, dead,
> Dead, without any company.

have an odd, half clumsy power. 'I do not wish' could be a calm declaration, but instead appears almost an act of rebellion against the inevitable; the repetition, 'Dead, dead, dead', is impressive, but its vehemence is quite unexplained and seems to verge on uncontrol; and the phrase 'without any company' is felt to be doing more for the poet than has been made explicit. (Does he mean without 'The things which [he] see[s]'? or without human company in general? or is it particular friends that death will take from him?) None of this *needs* an explanation—the poetry can stand without support—but it certainly takes one closer to the sources of its peculiar intensity if one hears in the background the tones of Arcite's dying speech in *The Knight's Tale*. On his deathbed, pointlessly deprived of life and love, Arcite addresses to Emily the unanswerable question that Wordsworth has in mind:

> 'What is this world? what asketh men to have?
> Now with his love, now in his colde grave
> Allone, withouten any compaignye?'
>
> (*Canterbury Tales*, Group A, 2777–9)

The deep delicious peace of Wordsworth's life with Dorothy, and the welcome hopes (that must surely include his marriage to Mary Hutchinson), are valued more intensely for his awareness of their precariousness. The poem is written out of a moment of equipoise, 'Sweetness and breath' on the one hand, 'the quiet of death' on the other. It is not a moment of imaginative power—no border state, no profound insight, or loss of self, has been achieved—but one of poignant tranquillity.[17] Instead of the reaching out for something evermore about to be, the sense of possible sublimity, there is a beautiful affirmation of the fulness of life. The poet's wish is that transience should be arrested, that he may be allowed to remain for ever in peace *on this side of the border*. Though allowed its sharpness in the Chaucer allusion, death is finally the muted participation seen in the fantasy that Dorothy records in her *Journal* at end of the month:

> *Thursday 29th* A beautiful morning. The sun shone and all was pleasant. . . . We then went to John's Grove, sate a while at first. Afterwards William lay, and I lay, in the trench under the fence—he with his eyes shut and listening to the waterfalls and the birds. . . . William heard me breathing and rustling now and then, but we both lay still, and unseen by one another. He thought that it would be as sweet thus to lie so in the grave, to hear the *peaceful* sounds of the earth, and just to know that our dear friends were near.[18]

Dorothy's tender factual prose, and Wordsworth's strange imagining of an eternity of loving relationship and responsiveness, between them evoke all that Coleridge in April 1802 felt himself to be excluded from. Surprisingly, for all its comic idiom, *The Barberry-Tree* has a far better claim than most poems of the period to be taking a serious view of Coleridge's position. If the first version of *The Leech Gatherer* is to be thought of as in any sense a reply to *Dejection*, the encourgement it offers is remarkably heavy–handed. Coleridge is presented with a good and godly exemplum: domestic tranquillity, joy, imagination have all been drastically cut down like the supply of leeches, so the thing to do is laugh oneself to scorn and be henceforth of firmer mind. Presumably no argument or advice could really have helped—Coleridge was not wrong about his gloomy situation[19]—but playfulness was surely more appropriate than didacticism, and *The Barberry-Tree* does take notice of the anxiety that is at the centre of *Dejection*, rather than treating it as a question of moral weakness. To Coleridge's most anguished, most impressive lines—

> O Sara, we receive but what we give,
> And in *our* life alone does Nature live.
> Our's is her wedding-garment, our's her shroud . . .
>
> (*Dejection*, 296–8)

—Wordsworth answers:

> Whether this be truth or no
> I cannot tell, I do not know . . .
>
> (ll. 41–2)

On the face of it, this may not seem a very sensitive response, and *The Barberry-Tree* can easily be seen as trivial and facetious, a refusal to take seriously views that are not only important to Coleridge, but which at another period the poet himself would have treated very differently. The poetry should be given a chance, though.

For a start one has to ask the very difficult question as to what Coleridge and Wordsworth are likely to have believed in spring 1802—not what they said, or claimed, or appeared to claim, about imagination, but what in practice they may have thought or felt. At one extreme, represented later by the primary imagination of *Biographia*, it was possible to argue that the mind was both perceptive and creative—that perception and creation were a single act—in which case human powers were godlike, and projection was a logical impossibility. At the other, imagination, however pleasurable, or however intense the experience, could be nothing other than projection: 'in our life *alone* does Nature live'. At Alfoxden the first position, or something like it, had been supported for both poets by faith in the One Life; it could be felt with confidence only in the most exalted moments, but was at other times the ultimate border possibility (besides being obviously the claim that it was most attractive to make). Even though projection could in certain moods be enjoyed *as* projection—'The moon doth with delight / Look round her when the heavens are bare' (*Intimations*, 12–13)[20]—the second position was infinitely less flattering. Between the two, however, lay an undefined area in which creativity could be valued apparently in its own right, but in fact the more highly because the border possibility was never closed. It was the equation of creativity with 'genial spirits', joy, that allowed the more awkward and specific definitions to be evaded:

> O pure of heart! thou needst not ask of me
> What this strong music in the soul may be,
> What and wherein it doth exist,
> This light, this glory, this fair luminous mist,
> This beautiful and beauty-making power!
> JOY, innocent Sara! Joy that ne'er was given
> Save to the pure, and in their purest hour . . .
>
> (*Dejection*, 308–14)

Though in the moment of his deepest personal anguish Coleridge has dismissed imagination as projection, he allows himself to re-instate it with all its positive force by conferring upon Sara (and by implication on Wordsworth too)[21] the joy that he himself has lost:

> Thus, thus should'st thou rejoice!
> To thee would all things live from pole to pole,
> Their life the eddying of thy living soul.
>
> (ll. 334–6)

The poetry is curiously scrupulous in not saying that things will have an independent life, but at the same time it is able triumphantly to over-ride such distinctions. Sara, as 'the conjugal and mother dove', is allied to the Holy Spirit brooding over Chaos; her 'genial warmth' has become the life-force that 'rolls through all things' in *Tintern Abbey*.

Dejection is not finally a very dejected poem—or at least it is dejected because Coleridge feels his own genial spirits to have failed, not because of a denial of shared beliefs. Wordsworth in *The Barberry-Tree*, adopting a comic idiom and offering his criticism in the form of self-parody, attempts to laugh him out of taking himself and his loss too seriously. His rhythms as he evokes the tossing branches carry the same message as the comedy:

> whether it be thus or no,
> That while they danced upon the wind
> They felt a joy like humankind,
> That this blithe breeze which cheerly sung
> While the merry boughs he swung
> Did in that moment while the bough
>   Whispered to his gladsome singing
> Feel the pleasures that even now
>   In my breast are springing—
> And whether, as I said before,
>   These golden blossoms dancing high,
>   These breezes piping through the sky,
> Have in themselves of joy a store,
> And, mingling breath and murmured motion
> Like eddies of the gusty ocean,
> Do in their leafy morris bear
> Mirth and gladness through the air,
> As up and down the branches toss,
> And above and beneath and across
> The breezes brush on lusty pinion
> (Sportive struggling for dominion)—
> If living sympathy be theirs,
>   And leaves and airs,
> The piping breeze and dancing tree,
> Are all alive and glad as we—
> Whether this be truth or no
> I cannot tell, I do not know;
> Nay, whether now I reason well,
> I do not know, I cannot tell.
> But this I know, and will declare,
>   Rightly and surely *this* I know,
> That never here, that never there,
>   Around me, aloft, or alow,

Nor here, nor there, nor anywhere,
Saw I a scene so very fair.
(ll. 16–50)

Dejection of course has all the answers: one needs one's genial spirits in order to make such an act of response, and these (as Wordsworth himself has pointed out in *Tintern Abbey*)[22] depend on loving companionship. Coleridge *has* tried to respond; he just cannot do so wholeheartedly.[23] Yet *The Rape of the Lock* is not a lesser poem for its failure to laugh the Fermors and the Petres together again. Wordsworth's lines and rhythms are not uniformly successful—some will feel that the sound-effects go on too long, others that the comedy blends in uneasily—but the poetry catches exuberantly the writer's pleasure as he stands before the dancing berberis:

As up and down the branches toss,
And above and beneath and across
The breezes brush on lusty pinion
(Sportive struggling for dominion) . . .
(ll. 32–5)

One feels that for once the emotion is truly joy not jollity, that whether or not it is shared, it is an act of imaginative sympathy. Best of all is the concluding sequence, as the poet turns back to the tree after his clowning:

But when the wind rushes
Through brakes and through bushes,
And around, and within, and without,
Makes a roar and a rout,
Then may you see
The barberry-tree,
With all its yellow flowers
And interwoven bowers,
Toss in merry madness
Every bough of gladness
And dance to and fro to the loud-singing breeze
The blithest of gales, and the maddest of trees . . .
(ll. 95–106)

It must be one of the most compelling and beautifully varied rhythmic passages that Wordsworth ever wrote. The tree and the wind, for all the questioning earlier in the poem, are now certainly, totally, joyful.[24]

At the centre of *The Barberry-Tree* is a 'spot of time' that seems peculiarly empty:

> on this food of thought I fed
> Till moments, minutes, hours, had fled,
> And had not sudden the church-chimes
> Rung out the well-known peal I love . . .
> In that most happy mood of mind
> There like a statue had I stood till now—
> And when my trance was ended
> And on my way I tended,
> Still so it was, I know not how,
> But passed it not away, that piping wind.
>
> (ll. 51–4, 61–6)

Wordsworth sets out in self-mockery. After laughing at the Coleridgean folly of asking philosophical questions, he will laugh at his own tendency to 'spots' and trances and storing up pleasure for future restoration: by implication, Coleridge destroys response by 'thinking too precisely on the event', he himself makes too much of it. The idea of the poet standing for hours before the berberis is delicately ludicrous, as is his compulsion to turn the experience into 'food of thought'; but gradually the poetry ceases to be comic. The thought of standing like a statue till the time of writing is whimsical and evidently humorous, but 'that most happy mood of mind' is inappropriately touching. Wordsworth it seems can't be, or stay, wholly unserious; the pleasure has been real, and comes back to him as he writes. The poetry never quite settles into his highest lyric mode, but in succession come anticipations of the second half of the Ode,

> And by the vision splendid
> Is on his way attended . . .
>
> (ll. 73–4)

and of *The Solitary Reaper*:

> The music in my heart I bore,
> Long after it was heard no more.[25]
>
> (ll. 31–2)

Despite its greater imaginative engagement *The Barberry-Tree*, like so much of the work of spring 1802 seems finally to be pulled back, limited by its context. This time, though, it is not so much that deeper levels of commitment have been repressed, as that parody and self-mockery are never wholly transcended. There was no reason why they should be. Anticipations of the great lyric-poetry of 1804–5 may suggest to us that the poem could have become something different, but for Wordsworth and his very small, very private, original audience it was no doubt fine as it was. Looked at in one way, it provides the only possible answer to *Dejection*: dance with the berberis, as the poetry is dancing, and it will not matter whether or not (or in what sense) 'we receive but what we give'. Looked at another way, it belongs not with the poetry of serious philosophical discussion, but with the affectionate, facetious, thoroughly frivolous, doggerel of Coleridge's *Soliloquy of the Full Moon*:

> They're my torment and curse
> And harass me worse
> And bait me and bay me far sorer I vow
> Than the screech of the owl,
> Or the witch-wolf's long howl,
> Or sheep-killing butcher-dog's inward bow wow.
> For me they all spite, an unfortunate wight,
> And the very first moment that I came to light
> A rascal called Voss, the more to his scandal,
> Turned me into a sickle with never a handle.
> A night or two after a worse rogue there came,
> The head of the gang, one Wordsworth by name . . .
> I saw him look at me most terribly blue . . .
> [And he] changed me at once to a little canoe[26]
>
> (ll. 16–32)

If one is looking for the great poetry of spring 1802 one has to go to those rare instances in which something occurs to take Wordsworth outside, or beyond, his too supportive roles and relationships. Even *Dejection* did not deeply trouble him. Only the Leech Gatherer succeeded in doing that, and then it was on second thoughts, and after unprecedented criticism from a member of the group on whose love and approval he so much depended. Perhaps one shouldn't give too much credit to Sara

Hutchinson, but after the banal original version that she had dared to say was boring the poet's imagination, for whatever reason, suddenly took charge. Wordsworth seems to re-enact the process, allow the reader for a moment very close to the creative workings of his mind, in the beautiful 'spot of time' that brings the final poem to a climax:

> The old man still stood talking by my side,
> But soon his voice to me was like a stream
> Scarce heard, nor word from word could I divide,
> And the whole body of the man did seem
> Like one whom I had met with in a dream . . .
>
> While he was talking thus, the lonely place,
> The old man's shape and speech, all troubled me:
> In my mind's eye I seemed to see him pace
> About the weary moors continually,
> Wandering about alone and silently.
>
> (ll. 120–4, 141–5)

The old man turns to myth before our eyes[27]—but not without some resistance. There is about him an obstinate physicality. His words may be reducible to 'a stream/Scarce heard', but he himself has to be taken bodily into the dream-world of the poet's reverie: 'the whole body of the man' has a cumbersome appropriateness, and is not at all the same as the pronoun 'he', that Wordsworth could easily have used. 'The old man's *shape*' is similarly unexpected, similarly appropriate; but most important are the simple words, 'all *troubled* me'. It is as if the fight to subdue the Leech Gatherer's obstrusive physical presence gives Wordsworth the energy to create his myth—or that the figure has become imaginatively so dominant that a myth has to be created to contain and explain his power. As a Wordsworthian Wandering Jew the Leech Gatherer cannot lose his corporeal existence, but has achieved permanence, moved across into that other world that had seemed to be his proper realm in the great border images of the stone, sea-beast, and cloud earlier in the poem.

At first sight it may be surprising to find the Leech Gatherer in 1802, amid poetry so lacking in imaginative involvement, so untroubled; but the borderers are characteristic chiefly of periods at which on a conscious level the poet feels unable to 'see into the life of things'. The big problems have been glossed over, driven down, but force themselves up from the unconscious in poetry of uncomprehended beauty and power. Wordsworth spent time and energy defending the first version of *The Leech Gatherer*, and would himself have seen no distinction between the strange, impressive disproportion of *To a Butterfly*—

> I've watched you now a full half-hour
> Self-poized upon that yellow flower,
> And little butterfly indeed
> I know not if you sleep or feed.
> How motionless! Not frozen seas
> More motionless—and then,
> What joy awaits you when the breeze
> Shall find you out among the trees
> And call you forth again.
>
> (ll. 1–9)

and the abysmal final stanza of *To a Skylark*:

> Happy, happy liver,
> With a soul as strong as a mountain river,
> Pouring out praise to th'Almighty Giver,
> Joy and jollity be with us both!
> Hearing thee, or else some other,
> As merry a brother,
> I on earth will go plodding on
> By myself chearfully till the day is done.
>
> (ll. 24–31)

Though applied to an insect, 'Not frozen seas/More motionless' is felt to be a moment of vision (the universe in a grain of sand), where 'soul as strong as a mountain-river' seems a mere nod towards inspiration, the language without the passion. The poetry of the first quotation has an intensity because at some level one perceives the butterfly in his stillness to be a borderer, waiting (as the poet himself is unconsciously waiting) to be sought out by the joyous and creative breeze of imagination. The second passage is simply of the surface. Sustained by his jollity, and the fellowship of brother lark, the poet plods chearfully into the future. Fortunately his day was not yet done.

Chapter 6

Usurpation and Reality: Spring 1804

To develope the powers of the Creator is our proper employment—and to imitate creativeness by combination, our most exalted and self-satisfying delight. But we are progressive and must not rest content with present blessings. Our Almighty Parent hath therefore given to us imagination . . .

(Coleridge, 1795)

Three times in the space of six or eight weeks in the spring of 1804 Wordsworth makes use of the metaphor of usurpation. He is saying different things—or at least his standpoint varies—but the contexts are identical, and, though it may be unconscious, there is clearly a connection in his mind. The first of these usurpations is found in the Climbing of Snowdon, finally the opening of Book XIII of the 1805 *Prelude*, but written in late February 1804 as a climax for the five-Book version of the poem. The poet, aged 21, is ahead of his companions as they climb the mountain, and is startled by a light that falls like a flash upon the turf:

I looked about, and lo,
The moon stood naked in the heavens at height
Immense above my head, and on the shore
I found myself of a huge sea of mist,
Which meek and silent rested at my feet.
A hundred hills their dusky backs upheaved
All over this still ocean, and beyond,
Far, far beyond, the vapours shot themselves
In headlands, tongues, and promontory shapes,
Into the sea, the real sea, that seemed
To dwindle and give up its majesty,
Usurped upon as far as sight could reach.

(*1805*, xiii. 40–51)

The fantasy ocean of mist is not just beautiful, but active: it may please to rest 'meek and silent' at the poet's feet, but it consists of 'dusky backs *upheaved*'—static, but full of strain—and in the distance a positive aggression is taking place. The vapours project themselves in 'headlands, tongues, and promontory shapes' (all pointed, all assertive) into the Irish Channel, which is visible in the moonlight, forcing it to surrender both its majestic appearance and its sovereignty to the usurper. After this affront to reality we scarcely need to be told a few lines further on that the mist shows Nature playing the part of the human imagination.

A second instance of usurpation—more famous still—belongs to late March, by which time Wordsworth has abandoned the scheme for a five-Book *Prelude*, reordered his material, sent the first five Books as we know them off to London for Coleridge to take with him to Malta, and begun work on Book VI. Among the first passages to be composed is the extraordinary sequence in which response to the anticlimax of having crossed the Alps unknowingly fourteen years before overwhelms the poet with a sense of present achievement and potential:

> Imagination!—lifting up itself
> Before the eye and progress of my song
> Like an unfathered vapour, here that power,
> In all the might of its endowments, came
> Athwart me. I was lost as in a cloud,
> Halted without a struggle to break through,
> And now, recovering, to my soul I say
> 'I recognise thy glory'. In such strength
> Of usurpation, in such visitings
> Of awful promise, when the light of sense
> Goes out in flashes that have shewn to us
> The invisible world, doth greatness make abode,
> There harbours whether we be young or old.
>
> (*1805*, vi. 525–37)

Again the imagination as a mist ('an unfathered vapour'), again the aggressive take-over, again the passive resignation; but here it is still more plain that reality has been transcended, not merely deposed—that majesty, greatness, sovereignty, lie with the usurping power.

In the third of these examples (also from Book VI, and written within the following two or three weeks) roles are reversed, and reality becomes the usurper:

> That day we first
> Beheld the summit of Mount Blanc, and grieved
> To have a soulless image on the eye
> Which had usurped upon a living thought
> That never more could be.
>
> (*1805*, vi. 452–6)

So much for the most famous, and most beautiful mountain of Western Europe; and so much for Wordsworth the Nature-poet. This time imagination itself has been taken over—displaced by reality, which, however beautiful, is dead. Instead of his 'living thought' Wordsworth sees, and, whether he likes it or not, will carry away in his memory, the static picture of a mountain. Quite suddenly we have the extreme Romantic view. As Blake puts it, commenting on *Poems* 1815, 'Natural objects always did and now do weaken, deaden and obliterate imagination in me. Wordsworth must know that what he writes valuable is not to be found in Nature.[1]

First, Nature enacting the transforming power of the human imagination; next, imagination totally dominant; and finally, this dominance emphasized by Wordsworth's grief at seeing what to most of us would be one of Nature's most impressive sights. Spring 1804 is a pivotal moment in Wordsworth's thinking. To it belong not only these great blank-verse passages, which are to be at the centre of the thirteen-Book *Prelude*, completed next year, but also stanzas v-xi of *Intimations*, and the whole *Ode to Duty*, with their strong implications for the Christian poet of the future. Behind it, but still offering their support, are the poetry and assumptions of Alfoxden and Goslar—seen for instance in the conclusion to the stealing of the boat in *1799*, Part I:

> twenty times
> I dipped my oars into the silent lake,
> And as I rose upon the stroke my boat
> Went heaving through the water like a swan—
> When from behind that rocky steep, till then
> The bound of the horizon, a huge cliff,

As if with voluntary power instinct,
Upreared its head. I struck, and struck again,
And, growing still in stature, the huge cliff
Rose up between me and the stars, and still,
With measured motion, like a living thing
Strode after me. With trembling hands I turned,
And through the silent water stole my way
Back to the cavern of the willow-tree.
There in her mooring-place I left my bark,
And through the meadows homeward went with grave
And serious thoughts; and after I had seen
That spectacle, for many days my brain
Worked with a dim and undetermined sense
Of unknown modes of being. In my thoughts
There was darkness—call it solitude,
Or blank desertion—no familiar shapes
Of hourly objects, images of trees,
Of sea or sky, no colours of green fields,
But huge and mighty forms that do not live
Like living men moved slowly through my mind
By day, and were the trouble of my dreams.

(*1799*, i. 103–29)

On this occasion the usurpation had been of quite another kind. The child's mind had been taken over all right, and taken over by imagination, but it is not reality that was being displaced. Just for a brief moment as the mountain first rises up between the child and the stars we see Nature herself being usurped upon; but in the later stage what we are shown is an active, aggressive imagination displacing what is in effect a passive one. The mountain, which had been threatening because though it stayed a mountain it had human attributes ('As if with voluntary power instinct', 'With measured motion, like a living thing,/Strode after me') begets in the child's mind a race of beings that are neither mountains nor humans—huge, inexorable, unspecific forms, that are so clearly alive that they can only be defined in human terms, but which 'do not live/Like living men'.

The child's terror and incomprehension are beautifully evoked, but more important from the present point of view is Wordsworth's account of what has been displaced:

In my thoughts
There was a darkness—call it solitude,
Or blank desertion—no familar shapes
Of hourly objects, images of trees,
Of sea or sky, no colours of green fields,
But huge and mighty forms . . .

The child has been deprived of *visual* reassurance—of the stability which for Wordsworth seems to have come from having a mind stocked with pictures, images, of ordinary, daily experienced, natural scenes. In the astonishing words of *1805*, Book VIII, he 'had forms distinct/To steady' him, 'a real solid world/Of images about' him (ll. 598–9, 604–5)—the 'solid world' being Nature taken into, or impressed upon, the mind. Like so much else that we associate with *The Prelude* and *Tintern Abbey*, this internalizing process is described for the first time in *The Pedlar*. 'Deep feelings', Wordsworth writes in spring 1798,

had impressed
Great objects on his mind with portraiture
And colour so distinct that on his mind
They lay like substances, and almost seemed
To haunt the bodily sense.

(ll. 30–4)

In the background is Hartleyan associationism; but this is a very idiosyncratic, and very Wordsworthian, version. The process starts, as one would expect, from strong emotion, which initiates what amounts to a form of colour-printing (the metaphor is Wordsworth's), as natural objects are stamped upon the mind. There they lie, not just in full colour, but so much felt that they appear to have substance, weight—the '*solid* world of images'.[2] Yet this would leave them inert, and for Wordsworth they are active, '*haunting* the bodily sense' just as the sounding cataract of *Tintern Abbey* will haunt him 'like a passion' (ll. 76–7).

Wordsworth himself might have preferred not to use the term imagination with reference to natural scenes stored up within the mind. 'Sensible objects really existing, and felt to exist', he commented to his nephew, 'are *imagery*. . . . imagination is a subjective term: it deals with objects not as they are, but as they appear to the mind of the poet.'[3] The same distinction is made in the Preface to *Poems* 1815:

Imagination, in the sense of the word as giving title to a class of the following poems, has no reference to images that are merely a faithful copy, existing in the mind, of absent external objects; but is a word of higher import, denoting operations of the mind upon those objects, and processes of creation or of composition, governed by certain fixed laws.

(*Prose Works*, iii. 30–1)

It was thus perhaps 'imagery' that was displaced as the 'huge and mighty forms' strode through the poet's childish mind, and 'imagery' that was impressed upon the Pedlar's by his deep feeling; in neither case do the shapes and colours of Nature seem to have been modified. *The Pedlar* and *1799*, Part I were written before either Wordsworth or Coleridge had formulated a theory of imagination as such, but it seems likely that for Wordsworth in 1798 the imaginative process was one of creative intensification. The Pedlar did not merely have imagery stamped on his mind, he himself 'attained/An *active* power to fasten images upon his brain',

and on their pictured lines
Intensely brooded, even till they acquired
The liveliness of dreams.

(*Pedlar*, 39–43; W.'s italics)

The word 'brooded'—which for Wordsworth has not lost its original egg-hatching, life-giving, force—ties this passage across to a draft conclusion for *The Ruined Cottage*, written a month or so later, and again featuring the Pedlar—now grown up, and displaying the wisdom he had gained as a child:

He had discoursed
Like one who in the slow and silent works,
The manifold conclusions of his thought,
Had brooded till imagination's power
Condensed them to a passion, whence she drew
Herself new energies, resistless force.

(Butler, 274–5)

In condensing thought to a passion, activating in imagery the liveliness of dreams, imagination—as Wordsworth must certainly have been aware—was playing the part of Milton's Holy Spirit, brooding over the deep and giving it life.[4]

For Wordsworth in spring 1798 this power within himself was a sign, perhaps a guarantee, of sharing the life-force

Whose dwelling is the light of setting suns,
And the round ocean, and the living air,
And the blue sky, and in the mind of man.
(*Tintern Abbey*, 98–100)

Inspired by Coleridge's Priestleyan Unitarianism, Wordsworth for a time believed in an immanent God present in, and imparting energy to, the entire material world.[5] Nothing could be dead, nothing could be still—they could only seem so. In the 'fixed and steady lineaments', of the natural world, the Pedlar 'traced an ebbing and a flowing mind,/Expression ever varying' (*Pedlar*, 55–7). *Tintern Abbey* is of course the best known embodiment of this belief, and it is important to notice that the first of its two great climactic moments is dependent on the process of storing up and enlivening mental images. Wordsworth in August 1793 had visited the spot on the river Wye where the poem is set in a particularly impressionable mood, and carried away with him images to which on his return five years later he attributes extraordinary formative properties:

Though absent long,
These forms of beauty have not been to me
As is a landscape to a blind man's eye;
But oft, in lonely rooms, and mid the din
Of towns and cities, I have owed to them
In hours of weariness, sensations sweet,
Felt in the blood and felt along the heart,
And passing even into my purer mind
With tranquil restoration.
(ll. 23–31)

Imagery at this stage, or on this level, provides recurrent pleasure, security, reassurance, is able to preserve the individual consciousness against the intrusions of city life—though perhaps not against walking mountains. The lines that follow offer first the moral effect of stored-up images (in terms that may seem unacceptably priggish: 'little, nameless, unremembered acts/Of kindness and of love'), and then the famous evocation of a mood in which the individual is enabled through loss of bodily awareness to merge into, and perceive himself as part of, the total pantheist harmony. 'Nor less I trust/To *them*', Wordsworth writes, 'I may have owed another gift/Of aspect more sublime '—that is, to the 'forms of beauty' preserved within the mind, and recalled at some point distant in time and space. It is quite a surprising claim:

> *To them* I may have owed another gift
> Of aspect more sublime—that blessed mood
> In which the burthen of the mystery,
> In which the heavy and the weary weight
> Of all this unintelligible world,
> Is lightened—that serene and blessed mood
> In which the affections gently lead us on,
> Until, the breath of this corporeal frame
> And even the motion of our human blood
> Almost suspended, we are laid asleep
> In body and become a living soul,
> While, with an eye made quiet by the power
> Of harmony and the deep power of joy,
> We see into the life of things.
>
> (ll. 36–50)

It is interesting to ask how much this mystical experience depends upon Nature, and how much on the mind. Wordsworth seems to be deliberately providing an answer as the image that has been directly responsible rises again before the mind's eye in the presence of the landscape from which it originates:

> And now, with gleams of half-extinguished thought,
> With many recognitions dim and faint,
> And somewhat of a sad perplexity,
> The picture of the mind revives again
> While here I stand . . .
>
> (ll. 59–63)

The landscape in front of him does not tally with the picture of the mind—hence the perplexity ('sad' meaning 'grave', 'serious', at this period, as well as 'unhappy')—but nor has it been transformed. Imagination no doubt has been at work, brooding and enlivening, but essentially it is '*these* forms', the shapes of actual Nature, that have been responsible for the three-fold effects, emotional, moral, and spiritual, within the absent poet's mind. The picture of the mind, despite its astonishing properties, is in no sense to be preferred to the scene from which it derives.[6] This might have been an early usurpation (Nature, in the form of the actual Wye landscape, displacing the product of imagination, as with Mont Blanc), but Wordsworth does not yet think in such terms. He is aware of his own creativity, values it, even regards it at times as a possible mode of perception, but has not yet erected it into the transcendent principle it is to become.

At the end of February, or very beginning of March 1804, Mary Wordsworth copied into *MS W* the opening sixty-five lines of the Climbing of Snowdon—the first of the usurpations with which this chapter started. As is well known, she headed the passage '5th Book', and there is no doubt that it was to be the beginning of the last part of the then nearly completed five-Book *Prelude*. As in the *1805* text, her transcription leads through the account of the mist lying at the travellers' feet into the magnificent, and much odder, description of the blue chasm, the

> deep and gloomy breathing-place, through which
> Mounted the roar of waters, torrents, streams
> Innumerable, roaring with one voice.
>
> (*1805*, xiii. 57–9)

Wordsworth takes over at this stage in the manuscript, but offers not the allegorization that is in the final text ('A meditation rose in me that night . . . '), which probably belongs to May 1805, but a version of lines 74–94, tracing

> The diverse manner in which Nature works
> Oft times upon the outward face of things . . .
> so moulds, exalts, endues, combines,
> Impregnates, separates, adds, takes away,
> And makes one object sway another so
> By unhabitual influence or abrupt,
> That even the grossest minds must see and hear
> And cannot chuse but feel.

The tones of the conclusion are not endearing, and the central lines needed the tidying-up they later got, but what Wordsworth is saying is important. 'The power which these/Are touched by', he continues

> which Nature thus
> Puts forth upon the senses . . .

is in kind
A brother of the very faculty
Which higher minds bear with them as their own.
These from their native selves can deal about
Like transformation, to one life impart
The functions of another, shift, create,
Trafficking with immeasurable thoughts.
(Norton *Prelude*, 497, ll. 10–26)

Nature—one should perhaps call her Dame Nature, for in this context she is a goddess—working upon the outward face of things, and making one object sway another by unhabitual influence, has caused the mist to lie above the slopes of the mountain and the coast of the Irish Channel. The human imagination, dealing about like transformation, and imparting to one life the functions of another, has perceived the mist as sea, and its overlapping presence as usurpation, giving life to Nature's world of objects:

A hundred hills their dusky backs upheaved
All over this still ocean, and beyond,
Far, far beyond, the vapours shot themselves
In headlands, tongues, and promontory shapes,
Into the sea, the real sea, that seemed
To dwindle and give up its majesty,
Usurped upon as far as sight could reach.
(*1805*, xiii. 45–51)

In the terms of *Biographia Literaria*, Nature and man are united in showing the power of the secondary, poetic, imagination, which 'dissolves, diffuses, dissipates, in order to recreate', which 'struggles to idealize and to unify', and which is 'essentially *vital*, even as all objects (as objects) are essentially fixed and dead' (*BL* xiii. 167). In his godlike role, Wordsworth the poet is conferring on the natural world the life which in 1798 he had believed it to possess, and to derive from the omnipresence of God. In this respect the Climbing of Snowdon confirms the change first seen in the account of the Infant Babe who (in 1799) had worked *but in alliance with* the works that he beheld. Also linking the two passages is Wordsworth's stress on the coexistence of creativity and perception. The 'higher mind' of 1804 is

By objects of the senses not enslaved,
But strengthened, rouzed, and made thereby more fit
To hold communion with the invisible world.[7]

What invisible world? Perhaps it is the sort of question one shouldn't ask; but the poet of *Tintern Abbey* would have had an answer, and it is by no means so clear that in 1804 Wordsworth would have known what to say. Pantheism had given him something to share and be in touch with, and see into the life of—something that had not been replaced when creativity took over as 'the sublime of man'. Wordsworth's instincts were still towards communion, but it had become easier to assert than to explain.

Coleridge's position ten or twelve years later offers some interesting parallels. He too was uncertain how far his intuitions were to be trusted. As he put it, in rather technical language, at the end of *The Statesman's Manual* (1816):

> Whether ideas are regulative only, according to Aristotle and Kant; or likewise CONSTITUTIVE, and one with the power and life of Nature, according to Plato, and Plotinus . . . is the highest *problem* of philosophy.
>
> (*CC* vi. 114)

The regulative idea was safe and orthodox, the constitutive was pantheist: in Kantian terms the regulative gave order to external appearances, rendered them meaningful by assigning them to categories (time, space, etc.), but did not penetrate to inherent qualities (the things in themselves); the constitutive, in the phrase that Coleridge so surprisingly added at this time to *The Eolian Harp*, was a demonstration of 'the one life within us and abroad'.[8] If they are accurately to parallel 'Aristotle and Kant', 'Plato and Plotinus' should of course read 'Plato and *Schelling*'—but then, Schelling did not by any means always get his due. The many pages of his work that reappear in *Biographia* show the pantheist in Coleridge as clearly as the plagiarist. Indeed the two are closely linked. Coleridge often lied about having got there first, but a great deal of the plagiarism in *Biographia* does reproduce thoughts and patterns that he had known in the 1790s through the different earlier pantheist influences of Boehme, Priestley, and Spinoza, and through Berkeley's prefiguring of German idealism.[9] His position in the later period was not often put so clearly as in the passage quoted from *The Statesman's Manual*.

More often, as with the plagiarism, one gets denials and concealments; the difference being that whereas many of the borrowings (much as one might wish it not to be the case) turn out to be quite blatantly covered up to prevent detection,[10] it often seems with the pantheism that Coleridge is concealing it from himself.

No doubt in general terms Coleridge thought plagiarism a bad thing; but pantheism was heresy. And so one gets on the one hand the frequent attacks on Unitarianism that overstate their rejection of his former views, and on the other the curious sense that *Biographia* is a justification, almost a reliving, of the golden age of Alfoxden, when the heart had lived in the head and the 'mere reflective faculty' had scarcely seemed a threat. And so one gets too, the characteristic border statements—statements, that is, that can just about be given an orthodox interpretation: the definition of the primary imagination, and its counterpart in *The Statesman's Manual*,

> that reconciling and mediatory power, which incorporating the reason in images of the sense, and organizing (as it were) the flux of the senses by the permanence and self-circling energies of the reason, gives birth to a system of symbols, harmonious in themselves, and consubstantial with the truths, of which they are the conductors.
>
> (*CC* vi. 29)

and the redefinition of reason in *The Friend* (1818), as

> an organ bearing the same relation to spiritual objects, the universal, the eternal, and the necessary, as the eye bears to material and contingent phaenomena . . . an organ identical with its appropriate objects.
>
> (*CC* IV. i. 155–6)

and, still more extreme in its language, the reference to

> intellectual re-union of the all in one, in that eternal reason whose fulness hath no opacity, whose transparency hath no vacuum.

On second thoughts this last passage worried Coleridge so much that he sent out an 'unfortunately omitted' extra paragraph, 'it's object being to preclude all suspicion of any leaning towards pantheism, in any of it's forms' (*CC* IV. i. 522 and n.).

It is interesting that Coleridge should have thought the obscurities in Kant might be 'hints and insinuations referring to ideas which . . . he did not think it prudent to avow';[11] but his own writing seems often to be more like brinksmanship. How close *dare* he go? Magniloquent imprecision could take him to the very edge—allow him the possibility that reason in its most exalted mood (the primary imagination) was *consubstantial* with the truths that it perceived—and yet at the same time allow him to tell himself as well as others that he'd been carried away, his intentions had been pure.[12] Logically the person most likely to repeat God's self-naming—the 'repetition in the finite mind of the infinite I AM'—must be God. If we read the *Biographia* definition in this way, we are back with *Tintern Abbey*: 'the living power and prime agent of all human perception' becomes God himself within 'the mind of man'. One cannot know if Coleridge was aware of this as a possible reading, but there can be no doubt that he was still drawn to his early belief that 'God/Diffused through all . . . make[s] all one whole'(*Religious Musings*, 139–40).[13]

And what of Wordsworth? What did he think he was saying when in February 1804 he wrote of the moonlit horse,

> We paused awhile
> In pleasure of the sight, and left him there,
> With all his functions silently sealed up,
> Like an amphibious work of Nature's hand,
> A borderer dwelling betwixt life and death . . .

Would it have surprised him that we should see this poetry as reflecting a wish for the confidence of an earlier period, when there had seemed to be no hard and fast borderlines, and when he had shared with Coleridge a faith in the One Life? Did he recognize that 'holding communion with the invisible world' was a problem not just because one might become enthralled by objects of the senses? Could he have accepted that his need to believe in an accessible other-world of truth did not at this moment have an adequate philosophical support? Again, we cannot know. The famous lines of *Prelude*, Book VI that were my second usurpation show Wordsworth's predicament in great poetry that verges on the empty and the sad. Imagination, as he is writing in March 1804, comes athwart him 'Like an unfathered vapour':

> I was lost as in a cloud,
> Halted without a struggle to break through,
> And now, recovering, to my soul I say

'I recognise thy glory'. In such strength
Of usurpation, in such visitings
Of awful promise, when the light of sense
Goes out in flashes that have shewn to us
The invisible world, doth greatness make abode,
There harbours whether we be young or old.
Our destiny, our nature, and our home,
Is with infinitude—and only there;
With hope it is, hope that can never die,
Effort, and expectation, and desire,
And something evermore about to be.

(*1805*, vi. 529–42)

Yet again Wordsworth is rewriting *Tintern Abbey*, defining in terms appropriate to the moment the essential border experience in which,

the breath of this corporeal frame,
And even the motion of our human blood
Almost suspended, we are laid asleep
In body and become a living soul.

(ll. 44–7)

Both passages describe the entrance, through loss of bodily awareness, into an invisible world of the soul; but the quiet confidence of 1798 has been replaced by poetry of magnificent assertiveness—the poetry of a rearguard action. The Wordsworth of 1804 turns to his soul and says 'I recognise thy glory', grandly claims that in such moods as his, 'greatness make[s] abode', that our destiny is with infinitude. Coleridge's thinking at this period is very close to the primary imagination—the first comparable definition belongs to 1801 (and behind that is the Infant Babe)—and Wordsworth draws on it to support the presentation in religious terms of what does not by the standards of 1798 appear to be a religious experience.

It is the underlying pathos that strengthens the poetry, one's sense that desperation is qualifying the grandeur of Wordsworth's claims. We just might believe that 'Our destiny, our nature, and our home/Is with infinitude', but to add 'and only there' was defiance. 'With hope it is, hope that can never die'—by now we surely know we are listening to a vulnerable human voice. Hope can die, and does; it is the poet's need, and his courage, that we respond to as he comes to his final assertion:

> Effort, and expectation, and desire,
> And something evermore about to be.

—something, that is, that will quite certainly never happen. Wordsworth makes the point in lines that are less often quoted, but very important to an understanding of his poetry at this moment:

> The mind beneath such banners militant
> Thinks not of spoils or trophies, nor of aught
> That may attest its prowess, *blest in thoughts*
> *That are their own perfection and reward*—
> Strong in itself, and in the access of joy
> Which hides it like the overflowing Nile.
>
> (*1805*, vi. 543–8)

The beauty of Wordsworth's concluding image of the overflowing, fertilizing Nile seems to some extent to qualify his central statement, but this *access* of joy is an internal flooding (just as the imagination that comes athwart him at the opening of the passage is internal), whereas the Pedlar's 'access of mind' in February 1798 had been a 'high hour/Of visitation from the living God' (*Pedlar*, 107–8). Despite his need to believe in an invisible world of revelation, in which 'the power/Of harmony, and the deep power of joy' lead to a recognition of total sharing, the poet is left with the limited joy of his own creativity—and with the 'visitings/Of awful promise' that he himself creates. At Alfoxden he had defined the condition of his greatest poetry, the 'obscure sense/Of possible sublimity' to which the mind aspires with growing faculties,

> With faculties still growing, feeling still
> That whatsoever point they gain, there still
> Is something to pursue.
>
> (*In storm and tempest*, 15–20)

Now, six years later, the aspiration is the same ('Effort, and expectation, and desire . . . '), but for a moment the poet concedes that perhaps sublimity is *not* possible—or not possible in the supportive earlier sense of the something to which one responds outside the self. There are few more moving statements in Wordsworth's poetry than his acceptance that the mind in the moods of shadowy exaltation which above all he values is 'blest in thoughts/That are their own perfection and reward'.

There used to be speculation as to whether the Crossing of the Alps, the lines upon imagination, and the Simplon Pass were in fact written in that order. They were; but the pencil drafts of *MS WW* show that between the first two passages there was a highly important intervening piece of poetry.[14] Imagination did not arise 'Before the eye and progress of [Wordsworth's] song' as he recalled the anticlimax of crossing the pass—or at least it didn't arise until he had attempted to evoke his original feelings in the great epic smile of the cave that finally appears in Book VIII:

As when a traveller hath from open day
With torches passed into some vault of earth,
The Grotto of Antiparos, or the den
Of Yordas among Craven's mountain tracts,
He looks and sees the cavern spread and grow,
Widening itself on all sides, sees, or thinks
He sees, erelong, the roof above his head,
Which instantly unsettles and recedes—
Substance and shadow, light and darkness, all
Commingled, making up a canopy
Of shapes, and forms, and tendencies to shape,
That shift and vanish, change and interchange,
Like spectres—ferment quiet and sublime,
Which, after a short space, works less and less
Till, every effort, every motion gone,
The scene before him lies in perfect view
Exposed, and lifeless as a written book.

(*1805*, viii. 711–27)

Crossing the Alps should have been for Wordsworth a moment of creativity released, a moment in which the bounds of ordinary experience spread and grew, substance and shadow interchanging in a 'ferment quiet and sublime'. Instead he had been left in the world of perfect view, a world utterly dull and null, 'Exposed, and lifeless as a written book'. It is this last phrase—appalling in its implications for the writer (and the reader too)[15]—that leads on to the thought of imagination as 'an unfathered vapour'.

Wordsworth in August 1790 had promised himself an imaginative experience. A letter to Dorothy written the following month shows him to have been at this period conscientiously impressing great objects on his mind, storing up visual memories of the Alps, and reflecting as he did so, 'perhaps scarce a day of my life will pass [in] which I shall not derive some happiness from these images' (*EY* 36). He had 'fathered' imagination upon the moment of crossing the Simplon because at some level he assumed that to cross one kind of border was to cross the other. Fourteen years later he could see the nature of his mistake: imagination cannot be 'tracked and fathered', imaginative experience cannot be arranged. His sympathy for an earlier self led him to evoke the expectations and disappointment, and in so doing he came to see with abnormal vividness what imagination meant to him in March 1804. But the simile of the cave does not merely enact the anticlimax that took place, it implies that whether or not Wordsworth had been conscious of crossing the Alps, his achievement would have been empty because it was a fact. Roofs of caves when too clearly visible, scenes in perfect view, written books (which while still unwritten had embodied 'effort, and expectation, and desire'), all disallow the sense of 'something evermore about to be'. The border quality of imminence has become for Wordsworth a guarantee of human potential. Mont Blanc and the lines that follow (my third usurpation) show very neatly how in 1804 this requirement is reflected in his response to the natural world:

That day we first
Beheld the summit of Mount Blanc, and grieved
To have a soulless image on the eye
Which had usurped upon a living thought
That never more could be. The wondrous Vale
Of Chamouny did, on the following dawn,
With its dumb cataracts and streams of ice—
A motionless array of mighty waves,
Five rivers broad and vast—make rich amends,
And reconciled us to realities.

(*1805*, vi. 452–61)

The last statement is more than doubtful. It is not reality that Wordsworth is reconciled to by the glacier, but a symbolic enactment of the potential in which he needed to believe. Mont Blanc, however beautiful, remains Mont Blanc, a 'soulless image' because it is itself and no more. The mountain represents stasis, the death of imagination, as opposed to stillness, which for Wordsworth contains the possibility of development, change, rebirth. Clearly the distinction is idiosyncratic, but it is none the less felt. As it dies into perfect view, 'every effort, every motion gone', its shifting and vanishing 'tendencies to shape' hardening into fact, the cave is linked by an echo to the horse of the previous month ('breath, motion gone . . . all but shape and substance gone'), in whom shape had been essential, and stillness a border condition. It is the 'living thought' that gives the distinction its validity. Had Wordsworth looked forward to seeing the horse, it could not have lived up to his expectation; had he come upon Mont Blanc unexpectedly, its image would not have been soulless. The glacier of Chamouny was especially well designed to stir the living thought, release the poet from realities. It is truly, 'a ferment' that is 'quiet and sublime'. Its 'dumb cataracts' may sound again, once more haunt the listener like a passion; its 'streams of ice' may flow again, frozen though they be; and the 'five rivers broad and vast' may be motionless, stopped for ever in their course, but the poet's imagination perceives them still as waves, for ever ready to move on. Like the 'dusky backs upheaved' of the mist on Snowdon, and 'the stationary blasts of waterfalls' in the Simplon Pass, these images of latent power enact and correspond to a need within the poet himself.[16]

Wordsworth's terror of fixity, stasis, death, objects as objects, raises the fascinating question as to how far he is and is not like Blake. Clearly Nature did on occasion deaden and obliterate imagination in him too, and he thought of this as did Blake in terms of enslavement by the senses, especially of succumbing to the tyranny of the eye. One part of Wordsworth (this certainly is an essential difference between the two poets) did value Nature for her permanence—seen in the trees of *The Ruined Cottage* that have no part in human suffering; seen in 'earth's diurnal course' and Nature's cyclical process; seen in 'the forms/Perennial of the ancient hills' that can give simple grandeur to the soul. But very seldom does he allow himself to rest upon this permanence. In the forms perennial 'He trace[s] an ebbing and a flowing mind'; it is the pathos of human transience, and the too closely allied grandeur of human aspiration, that stir him to creativity. Images stored in the memory know no decay because the mind revisits them, not because they are, or can be, as permanent as their archetypes; and the craving for permanence in language and emotion shows above all the borderer's wish that it might be so. Wordsworth may not see the sun as a company of the heavenly host, but no more than Blake does he respond to an object-world. In no ordinary sense is he a Nature-poet. He rarely celebrates, almost never describes, natural beauties; he does not even wonder at his response *to the object seen*, he wonders at the power and quality of the response itself. Imagination in him is nourished by imagination. Blake distinguished in his annotation to *Poems* 1815 between Wordsworth the natural man (in effect the poet seduced by Vala), and Wordsworth the spiritual man (whose creativity finds its true counterpart in Jerusalem).[17] It is not a false distinction, but, like his other contemporaries except for Coleridge and De Quincey, Blake didn't know *The Prelude*, which contains the bulk of Wordsworth's spiritual poetry. For Wordsworth at his most creative, Nature is not Vala, who represents the temptation to be content with soft delusion and lifeless response, but Albion, who is at once man and the external world, and who falls into disunity and the sleep of death (Coleridge's Ulro of parts) as soon as any one of his faculties begins to dominate. For Wordsworth as for Blake the world is held together, prevented from the spiritual disintegration that is to be seen going on all round the poet himself, by the divine vision, imagination.[18] And his poetry too seeks again and again to define the prophetic role in the process of reconstruction, a bringing about of the creative harmony that will result from parts (Albion's faculties) knowing and accepting their true relation to the whole.

Wordsworth's account of the Simplon Pass as it mounts towards its famous conclusion becomes in a curiously precise sense apocalyptic. As one reads one is aware chiefly of the urgency of the poet's wish to reconcile the disparate, warring elements—

the sick sight
And giddy prospect of the raving stream,
The unfettered clouds and region of the heavens,
Tumult and peace, the darkness and the light . . .

—and such is the building up of rhythm and rhetoric that one probably gives no individual attention to the strange assortment of similes that brings the reconciliation about:

> Were all like workings of one mind, the features
> Of the same face, blossoms upon one tree,
> Characters of the great apocalypse,
> The types and symbols of eternity,
> Of first, and last, and midst, and without end.
> (*1805*, vi. 564–72)

The image of the ravine as a face, though certainly suggesting one way in which different parts may form a whole, has to the mind's eye a bizarre effect reminiscent of Hardy;[19] and the sudden Samuel Palmer tree is still more obstinately visual, reconciling in its profusion of identical blossoms the disparateness that has gone before, yet adding its own compelling, irrelevant presence to the mental landscape. More important, though, is the apocalyptic geology. In a rare moment of inspired *Prelude* revision Wordsworth for a time inserted between 'the raving stream' and 'The unfettered clouds' lines which are wholly in the spirit of his original text, and which footnote his cryptic reference to 'characters' (that is handwriting) of the great apocalypse:

> And ever as we halted, or crept on,
> Huge fragments of primaeval mountain spread
> In powerless ruin, blocks as huge aloft
> Impending, nor permitted yet to fall,
> The sacred death-cross, monument forlorn
> Though frequent of the perished traveller . . . [20]

The characters are (literally) the writing on the wall. To the followers of Thomas Burnet the Alps, and other horrid manifestations of Nature, were the 'powerless ruin' of a once perfect world, created by Divine Providence through the action of the Deluge;[21] they were also by the same token a reminder of the next and final apocalypse, when the blocks impending above man's head would be allowed to come down. The ravine thus speaks 'Of first, and last, and midst' (the position of man, the traveller, as he halts, or creeps along), and also of eternity—the 'without end'. It should come as no surprise that this final line is drawn from Milton, who applied it to God: '*Him* first, him last, him midst, and without end' (*PL* v. 165).[22] But Wordsworth does not apply it to God. He is not forecasting a Christian millennium, but evoking the apocalyptic quality of the human imagination, the 'something evermore about to be' of the previous passage. These thoughts too, however reassuring are the patterns that they make, must be their own perfection and reward.

Not that the patterns created in the Simplon Pass were all that reassuring. Wordsworth certainly felt the need to connect past, present, and future in one imaginative whole—the home of his poetry is with infinitude—but he could also see himself as the creeping, even the perished, traveller. One wonders what message the crags that spake by the wayside had for him. Overall harmony is not necessarily comfortable to the individual, and for all its astonishing productivity, spring 1804 was a period that had its more threatening side. What, for instance, is one to make of 'the fleet waters of the drowning world' that pursue the Arab Quixote with whom Wordsworth so deeply identifies in the dream of the stone and shell? Apocalypse is closer, more frightening, on this occasion. Geoffrey Hartman has argued that the flood from which the poet flees is imagination,[23] but this seems to be going far to seek disquietude. It is surely a threatened engulfment *of*, not by, imagination that causes the terror: 'the hiding-places of my power/Seem open', Wordsworth wrote this same month, 'I approach, and then they close' (*1805*, xi. 335–6). Time was running out on him. The dream is difficult to assess partly because we don't know in what form the material came to Wordsworth. In *1805* the dreamer is Coleridge, in *1850* he is the poet himself; and we know that in an earlier shape the dream had in fact belonged to Descartes, taking place not in a desert but in a library, amid actual books, two of which were held to contain the sum-total of scientific and poetic knowledge. It seems a little unlikely that Wordsworth, and more so that Coleridge, dreamed a second version of the original dream; but the material certainly came *via* Coleridge, and he could well have modified it in the telling, or even (at Grasmere in January 1804) discussed with Wordsworth how it might be changed. Somewhere along the line, the dreamer's initial reading of *Don Quixote*, the desert, the Arab, the dromedary, stone, shell, and flood, were all introduced, and there is really no means of knowing whose inspiration they were.

Wordsworth presents the dream, which was perhaps at first a separate poem, within a conventional framework that he presumably thought of in terms of the early Chaucer.[24] The dreamer falls asleep reading a book, which forms the starting-point of the dream, and which he finds lying open beside him when he wakes; to which one can add that on this occasion he is reading by the sea, which provides both the desert sands and the waters of the flood. *En route* (as for instance in *The Book of the Duchess*) we have an imaginary landscape, an encounter that takes place outside normal time, dialogue that carries uncomprehended truth in partly symbolic terms, and intermittent (very successful) attempts to portray a dreaming state of mind:

> Upon a dromedary, lance in rest,
> He rode, I keeping pace with him; and now
> I fancied that he was the very knight
> Whose tale Cervantes tells, yet not the knight,
> But was an Arab of the desart too,
> Of these was neither, and was both at once.
>
> (*1805*, v. 121–6)

The handling of the Quixote figure within the dream is vividly imaginative, and seems not at all to require the comments that Wordsworth adds on his madness in the concluding lines:

> Full often, taking from the world of sleep
> This arab phantom which my friend beheld,
> This semi-Quixote, I to him have given
> A substance, fancied him a living man—
> A gentle dweller in the desart, crazed
> By love, and feeling, and internal thought
> Protracted among endless solitudes—
> Have shaped him, in the oppression of his brain,
> Wandering upon this quest and thus equipped.
> And I have scarcely pitied him, have felt
> A reverence for a being thus employed,
> And thought that in the blind and awful lair
> Of such a madness reason did lie couched.
>
> yea, will I say,
> In sober contemplation of the approach

Of such great overthrow, made manifest
By certain evidence, that I methinks
Could share that maniac's anxiousness, could go
Upon like errand.

(*1805*, v. 140–52, 156–61)

The image of reason lying couched within the lair of blind and awful madness seems disproportionate both to the 'gentle dweller in the desart' and to the figure within the dream; and how is one to reconcile its obsessional quality with the poet's sense that he himself 'could go/Upon like errand'? Why despite regarding the Arab Quixote as mad did Wordsworth so easily and so strongly identify with him in his task of saving the stone and shell? One answer is perhaps suggested by the very odd definitions that are given to the two objects within the dream.[25] At first the stone is *Euclid's Elements*, while the shell produces in an unknown tongue

A loud prophetic blast of harmony,
An ode in passion uttered which foretold
Destruction to the children of the earth . . .

(*1805*, v. 96–8)

Both then become books, and each is redefined in a way that is wholly unexpected, yet oddly consonant with Wordsworth's own needs and ambitions:

the arab said
That all was true, that it was even so
As had been spoken, and that he himself
Was going then to bury those two books—
The one that held acquaintance with the stars,
And wedded man to man by purest bond
Of nature, undisturbed by space or time;
The other that was a god, yea many gods,
Had voices more than all the winds, and was
A joy, a consolation, and a hope.

(*1805*, v. 100–9)

Even if it could be proved that the major transformation of Descartes' dream had been carried out by Coleridge, the emphasis on the social implications of astronomy would have to be Wordsworth. The concept of science as a bond, linking man through Nature (and through his nature), yet *undisturbed by space or time*, has all the power and eccentricity of Wordsworth's need to believe: somewhere, out there, beyond ordinary experience, there *must* be destinal forces working for man's good. Mathematics spiritualized—'His triangles they were the stars of heaven,/The silent stars' (*Pedlar*, 166–7)—could bring the attractive, yet repugnantly inhuman, order of the Newtonian universe to the aid of man. Back at Alfoxden Wordsworth, in lines that were presumably to have been part of *The Recluse*, had foreseen a future in which science should be 'a precious visitant': as a result of 'general laws/And local accidents' a 'chain of good/ [Should] link us to our kind'. 'Was it ever meant', he had asked rhetorically,

> That this majestic imagery, the clouds,
> The ocean, and the firmament of heaven
> Should be a barren picture on the mind?

In the pantheist confidence of March 1798 the answer had been that,

> deeply drinking in the soul of things
> We shall be wise perforce, and we shall move
> From strict necessity along the path
> Of order and of good.[26]

As in *Tintern Abbey*, the connection between 'majestic imagery' and 'the soul of things' had seemed axiomatic, and the role of science had been to explain the workings of strict necessity, the 'chain of good'.

Perhaps none of this would have been in Wordsworth's conscious mind in February 1804 when he wrote of the stone, or book,

> that held acquaintance with the stars
> And wedded man to man by purest bond
> Of Nature, undisturbed by space or time . . .

His words would have taken a lot of explaining in terms of any belief held at the period; yet it may be that what they imply is not belief, but a way of thinking, a habit of mind that persisted because the need that it had been evolved to assuage had never disappeared. Much the same would surely be true of his second definition, of the shell,

> that was a god, yea many gods,
> Had voices more than all the winds, and was
> A joy, a consolation, and a hope.

As the poet who for six years now had been unable to write the centre-piece of *The Recluse* that should help to bring about the millennium, Wordsworth can no longer have found it easy to see his work as 'A joy, a consolation, and a hope'. On the other hand, the need to see it in this way—as the chearing lamp of the Prospectus and *Michael*—must have been very strong, given his new preoccupation with declining powers. Wordsworth's earnest sharing of the maniac's anxiousness, his sense that he himself would go on a similar errand, his definitions of the stone and shell—the first effectively the philosophical basis of *The Recluse* (man linked to man by purest bond of Nature), the second its poetic and prophetic mode—all tend to suggest that the fleet waters from which the two books must be saved are the sea of time, or death, either being symbolic of the final loss of vision.

When he was writing *1799* it had seemed that the 'poetic spirit' might for the chosen few survive 'Through every change of growth or of decay/Preeminent till death' (ii. 309–10); in spring 1804, Wordsworth knows this is not to be. And so alongside, sometimes indeed within, the great *Prelude* affirmations of the period one hears other more tentative voices: 'O joy that in our embers/Is something that doth live' (*Intimations*, 130–1). Wordsworth does not doubt his former vision, but there is something almost symbolic about the way *Intimations* pushes it back and back until it sports on the shore of a previous immortality. As he reworks the 'spots of time' of *1799*, Part I for the first and last Books of the five-Book *Prelude*, he feels again their power, and renders thanks for the shadowy recollections of childhood, 'Which, *be they what they may*,/Are yet the fountain light of all our day' (*Intimations*, 147–9). And in between the Woman on the Hill and the Waiting for the Horses he inserts a passage that beautifully evokes his sense at once of human grandeur and personal loss:

> Oh mystery of man, from what a depth
> Proceed thy honours! I am lost, but see
> In simple childhood something of the base
> On which thy greatness stands; but this I feel—

That from thyself it is, that thou must give
Else never canst receive. The days gone by
Come back upon me from the dawn almost
Of life; the hiding-places of my power
Seem open, I approach, and then they close;
Yet have I singled out—not satisfied
With general feelings, here and there have culled—
Some incidents that may explain whence come
My restorations . . . [27]

The voice that had so confidently explained, 'There are in our existence spots of time' (*1799*, i. 288), now tells us 'I am lost,/But see in simple childhood *something of the base* . . . '. The 'spots', though in the five-Book *Prelude* they were to form the climax of the poem, are merely 'Some incidents that *may* explain . . . '. The honesty and tentativeness are very moving, the more so if one realizes that they form part of a discussion with Coleridge, whose despair had in 1802 been seen in the context of Wordsworth's continued strength. Wordsworth's 'but this I feel . . . that thou must give/Else never canst receive' tacitly accepts the sad implications of *Dejection*:

These mountains too, these vales, these woods, these lakes . . .
I were sunk low indeed, did they *no* solace give;
But oft I seem to feel, and evermore I fear,
They are not to me now the things which once they were.

O Sara! we receive but what we give,
And in *our* life alone does Nature live.
Our's is her wedding garment, our's her shroud . . .
(*Dejection*, 290, 293–8)

Though written six months before as part of a love-poem for Sara Hutchinson, these lines in their first published form had been addressed to Wordsworth on his wedding-day (4 October 1802)—'Edmund, we receive but what we give'—and there is a sense in which Wordsworth had from the first been the natural audience of *Dejection*.[28] Coleridge's reference to *Intimations*, 9 ('The things which I have seen I see them now no more') draws deliberate attention to itself, and further back must surely lie the wedding-image of the 1800 Prospectus: 'Paradise and groves/ Elysian',

wherefore need they be
A history, or but a dream, when minds
Once wedded to this outward frame of things
In love find these the growth of common day?

(*Prospectus*, 35–40)

In a typically clumsy transition between paragraphs Wordsworth had written in July 1798,

Nor, perchance,
If I were not thus taught, should I the more
Suffer my genial spirits to decay . . .

(*Tintern Abbey*, 112–14)

He and Coleridge had at Alfoxden shared their genial spirits, outgoing joy, relating them to participation in the One Life, but drawing them one suspects chiefly from each other's company. In 1800 the same power, spreading outwards from personal ties had seemed to Wordsworth in his regained paradise of Grasmere to hold millennial promises. In 1802 there had been poignancy in the lament for lost vision—

But there's a tree, of many one,
A single field which I have looked upon,
Both of them speak of something that is gone . . .

(*Intimations*, 51–3)

—but Wordsworth's position had seemed enviably secure beside Coleridge's 'Grief without a pang, void, dark and drear':

My genial spirits fail . . .
I may not hope from outward forms to win
The passion and the life, whose fountains are within!
These lifeless shapes, around, below, above,
O what can they impart?

(*Dejection*, 44, 50–3)

Now, in 1804, while concluding *Intimations* with dignified stoicism—

What though it be past the hour
Of splendour in the grass, of glory in the flower,
We will grieve not, rather find
Strength in what remains behind. . .

(ll. 172–5)

—Wordsworth slips into the poem he is writing to and for Coleridge, the concession:

> but this I feel,
> That from thyself it comes, that thou must give
> Else never canst receive.

He is lost, sees in childhood a source of imaginative strength, but feels bound to qualify any hope with a new realization of the precariousness of joy. The hiding-places of his power close when he approaches because he no longer feels confidence in his ability to give. It is in this mood, and this same extraordinary month of February 1804, that Wordsworth writes the beautiful and very personal lyric poem, *Ode to Duty*, which because of its proto-Victorian title, and opening, so few people now read with sympathy:

> I, loving freedom, and untried,
> No sport of every random gust,
> Yet being to myself a guide,
> Too blindly have reposed my trust.
> Resolved that nothing e'er should press
> Upon my present happiness,
> I shoved unwelcome tasks away—
> But thee I now would serve more strictly if I may.
>
> Through no disturbance of my soul,
> Or strong compunction in me wrought,
> I supplicate for thy controul,
> But in the quietness of thought.
> Me this unchartered freedom tires—
> I feel the weight of chance desires—
> My hopes no more must change their name,
> I long for a repose which ever is the same.
>
> (ll. 25–40)

'Me this unchartered freedom tires'; some of Wordsworth's very greatest poetry was still to come when this line was composed—he had not yet written, for instance,

> Our destiny, our nature, and our home,
> Is with infinitude—and only there;
> With hope it is, hope that can never die,

Effort, and expectation, and desire,
And something evermore about to be.
(*1805*, vi. 538–42)

It is clear, however, that poised against the border aspiration, restlessness, was a banal wish to settle down. Perhaps one shouldn't be surprised that the two existed for a moment side by side, or that the period at which they did so, was so productive. Great art cannot go on longing for repose that ever is the same, but there is no reason why the moment just before controls become too welcome should not be especially creative. Even the word 'usurpation' looks both ways. The force of Wordsworth's poetry in its grand affirmation of human potential has after all persuaded one to ignore its normal connotations. In another sense imagination is indeed the usurper—takes over from a less exciting reality that must now be acknowledged to have a rightful claim.

Chapter 7

As With the Silence of the Thought

But who can paint
Like Nature? Can imagination boast
Amid its gay creation, hues like hers?
Or can it mix them with that matchless skill,
And lose them in each other, as appears
In every bud that blows? If fancy then
Unequal fails beneath the pleasing task,
Ah, what shall language do?

(Thomson: *The Seasons*)

'Oh, why hath not the mind', Wordsworth writes early in *Prelude*, Book V,

Some element to stamp her image on
In nature somewhat nearer to her own?

(*1805*, v. 45–6)

The lines come from the clumsy, half powerful opening paragraph, in which the poet grieves with Hamlet for the state of man as 'paramount creature', but grieves more especially for the fate of his writings—'The consecrated works of bard and sage'. At the other end of the Book is a passage quite equally idiosyncratic in which Wordsworth, who has been unable to convince himself or his audience of the importance of literature as such in his education, comes out with the sudden, astonishing statement:

Visionary power
Attends upon the motions of the winds
Embodied in the mystery of words . . .

(*1805*, v. 619–21)

In their different odd ways the two passages raise the question of the relation in Wordsworth's poetry between mind, Nature, and language. It is a question for which there are not likely to be any specific answers; but, as with the metaphor of usurpation, the recurrence of certain words and clusters of words can provide interesting evidence if one chooses to play the game of following associations.

Back in 1799 Wordsworth had used the image of stamping in a rather more expected way:

> Yes, I remember when the changeful earth
> And twice five seasons on my mind had stamped
> The faces of the moving year . . .
>
> (*1799*, i. 391–3)

Wordsworth is not at his most original, yet for all their conventionality his lines are saved from tedium by their curious and characteristic physical emphasis. The child is acquiring the 'real solid world of images' (*1805*, viii. 604–5) that will 'steady' him in adult life, and seasonal landscapes are printed onto his mind like a series of woodcuts. The extent to which visual memory, and the experience it records, is solid in this poetry—actually *weighty*—is quite extraordinary. One is not too surprised to hear of 'The heavy weight of many a weary day' (*1805*, i. 24), or the weight of ages, custom, unintelligibility; but Wordsworth can feel a weight too in liberty, joy, pleasure, good humour, even in chance desires. All these are sustained by the mind; collectively they are 'life's mysterious weight', 'the burthen of the mystery'. Even where moods and states of mind in Wordsworth's poetry do not have palpable weight, the sense of their physical presence is exceptionally strong. Imagination *comes athwart* the poet, memory *rises up against him*, restoration comes

> Like an intruder knocking at the door
> Of unacknowledged weariness.
>
> (*1805*, iv. 147–8)

and terrors of the past can actually be touched:

> I thought of those September massacres,
> Divided from me by a little month,
> And felt and touched them, a substantial dread . . .
>
> (*1805*, x. 64–6)

Lacking Wordsworth's 'more than usual organic sensibility', at times we probably read more abstractly than he expected. The 'high objects' with which the child's emotions are intertwined in *The Prelude* (*1799*, i. 136) are not exalted aims, but chunks of the countryside—probably in fact mountains, with an unconscious pun on 'high'. 'Things', too, tend to have a very concrete thingness. Who else would call man a 'thinking thing'?—and if one continues the *Tintern Abbey* quotation,

> A motion and a spirit that impels
> All thinking things, all objects of all thought,
> And rolls through all things.
>
> (ll. 101–3)

it is clear that Wordsworth as himself a 'thinking thing' has in mind God's presence not in space, infinity, eternity, but in the separate blockish units of the material world. When he sees 'into the life of things', the last word should be taking a lot of the stress.

Similarly, it is doubtful whether the many printing images of Wordsworth's poetry are felt with their original force, whether we always receive, and carry away, the right impression:

> In these my lonely wanderings I perceived
> What mighty objects do *impress* their forms
> To build up this our intellectual being . . .
>
> (*Borderers*, IV. ii. 133–5)

> not vain
> Nor profitless, if haply they *impressed*
> Collateral objects . . .
>
> (*1799*, i. 421–3)

> deep feelings had *impressed*
> Great objects on his mind with portraiture
> And colour so distinct that on his mind
> They lay like substances . . .
>
> (*Pedlar*, 30–3)

The objects don't get *into* the memory, *into* the mind, they lie upon it, retaining not just form but substance—as Wordsworth elsewhere puts it, they are 'in their *substantial* lineaments/ Depicted' (*1799*, i. 430–1). Given the 'ennobling interchange/Of action from within and from without' (*1805*, xii. 376–7), perhaps one shouldn't be surprised that the printing process goes two ways. Hills which have impressed upon the mind of Michael 'So many incidents . . . Of hardship, skill or courage, joy or fear' become themselves a book preserving the memory of animals that he has saved (ll. 68–74). More numinous, yet in its different way as typically Wordsworthian, is the 'peak/Familiar with forgotten years',

> which shews
> *Inscribed, as with the silence of the thought,*
> Upon its bleak and visionary sides
> The history of many a winter storm,
> Or obscure records of the path of fire.
> (*Pedlar*, 169-173)

And of course there are the 'steep and lofty cliffs' of *Tintern Abbey* that impress not upon the mind, but upon the wild secluded scene, '*Thoughts* of more deep seclusion' (ll. 6–7). But even this is some way from the strange compelling wish that the mind of the poet himself might have

> Some element to stamp her image on
> In nature somewhat nearer to her own . . .

One can if one chooses give 'Nature' a capital 'n', and ask why the mind hasn't some element that is closer to her own *within the natural world* to print her image on. More probably Wordsworth meant some element that *in its own nature* was closer to the mind; but in fact the readings amount to very much the same. Either way he is asking, as no one else ever could or would have asked, why mind cannot print upon mind, why the human spirit in the grandeur and permanence of its achievement must be dependent upon such transient and destructible material as books and paper. Instead of asking with Keats and others why life cannot have the permanence of art, he is asking why art cannot have the permanence of life. Perhaps the passage should be given its fuller context: 'A thought is with me sometimes', Wordsworth begins,

> and I say,
> 'Should earth by inward throes be wrenched throughout,
> Or fire be sent from far to wither all
> Her pleasant habitations, and dry up

Old Ocean in his bed, left singed and bare,
Yet would the living presence still subsist
Victorious; and composure would ensue,
And kindlings like the morning—presage sure,
Though slow perhaps, of a returning day.'
But all the meditations of mankind,
Yea, all the adamantine holds of truth
By reason built, or passion (which itself
Is highest reason in a soul sublime),
The consecrated works of bard or sage . . .
Where would they be? *Oh, why hath not the mind*
Some element to stamp her image on
In nature somewhat nearer to her own?
Why, gifted with such powers to send abroad
Her spirit, must it lodge in shrines so frail?

(*1805*, v. 28–48)

Life it seems is indestructible. The embers of humanity—*Intimations* must have been completed this same month[1]—may be relied upon to rekindle. It is the works of bard and sage, consecrated at the altar of human achievement, that may perish. And so we get the dream of the Arab with his stone and shell, to which these are the introductory lines.

Can Wordsworth, one wonders, really be preoccupied with the transitoriness of books as such, or even of philosophy (the stone) and poetry (the shell) in their own right? His language in the introduction has about it a disproportionate intensity that will return at the end of the dream, where sympathy with the

gentle dweller in the desart, crazed
By love, and feeling, and internal thought
Protracted among endless solitudes . . .

turns into a moment of strange imbalance:

And I have scarcely pitied him, have felt
A reverance for a being thus employed,
And thought that in the blind and awful lair
Of such a madness reason did lie couched.

(*1805*, v. 144–52)

One hasn't in the dream thought of the Arab as mad at all, and neither the associations of Don Quixote nor the poet's own identification have led one to think of his mind as a 'blind and awful lair'. The image is violent, shocking, an intrusion of personal terrors into poetry that has seemed to be decorous and assured. The poet sets out to tell us of an underlying reasonableness, and ends by portraying reason as a wild beast and the mind as its den. After Parson Adams, Uncle Toby, Matthew Bramble—not to mention Johnny Foy—there was no actual need to point to the Arab as a holy fool, but there was still less call to use such violent imagery in doing so. One is left wondering whether at some level Wordsworth was confronting the possibility that he himself could be mad, crazed by protracted internal thought, deluded in his mission and his aspirations.[2] Be that as it may, he goes on with exemplary neatness to tie the episode back to the point from which he started:

> I methinks
> Could share that maniac's anxiousness, could go
> Upon like errand. Oftentimes at least
> Me hath such deep entrancement half-possessed
> When I have held a volume in my hand—
> Poor earthly casket of immortal verse—
> Shakespeare or Milton, labourers divine.
>
> (*1805*, v. 159–65)

It is interesting that the earthly casket should be virtually the same image as the shrines as the end of the introductory lines:

> Why, gifted with such powers to send abroad
> Her spirit, must it lodge in shrines so frail?
>
> (*1805*, v. 47–8)

In each case, traditional metaphors for the soul and body are used instead for mind and book. Or is it merely for mind and book? In the dream, the shell that the Arab is trying to save is not just a book, but a god,

> yea many gods,
> Had voices more than all the winds, and was
> A joy, a consolation, a hope.
>
> (*1805*, v. 107–9)

The godlike property of the shell is to give form, meaning, without trammeling inspiration. If one puts it to one's ear one hears not language but articulate sounds, 'A loud prophetic blast of harmony' that remains a blast though harmonious and fully comprehensible, 'An ode in passion uttered' that achieves the structure of art without qualifying the passion. The stone that is likewise a book and represents philosophy, though said to be less important, turns out to have very much the same attribute, 'wedd[ing] man to man by purest bond/Of nature, undisturbed by space or time' (*1805*, v. 105–6)—dispensing, as the poet would ideally wish to be able to do, with limiting temporal bonds and connections.

If the wish that mind should be able to print upon mind is at some level a wish to remove the impediment of language, one is left asking how much *did* Wordsworth the poet distrust his medium—he was, after all prone to make comments about 'the sad incompetence of human speech' and the need for 'Colours and words that are unknown to man' so that he could 'paint the visionary dreariness' of experience. Some of his pronouncements make it all seem quite simple, a question merely of the writer's selecting that which is natural, and avoiding 'those arbitrary connections of feelings and ideas with particular words, from which no man can altogether protect himself'. The poet

> will feel that there is no necessity to trick out or to elevate Nature: and, the more industriously he applies this principle, the deeper will be his faith that no words, which his fancy or imagination can suggest, will be to be compared with those which are the emanations of reality and truth.[3]

Through a redefinition of Hartley's millenarian claims, Wordsworth at the time of the Preface to *Lyrical Ballads* is able to think of writing as *positively* mechanical—a process in which the beneficent power of association, acting in both poet and audience, will of necessity lead to improvements. As is so often the case, it is the passage that qualifies a too-famous quotation which turns out to be most important:

> For all good poetry is the spontaneous overflow of powerful feelings; but though this be true, poems to which any value can be attached, were never produced on any variety of subjects but by a man who being possessed of more than usual organic sensibility had also thought long and deeply. For our continued influxes of feeling are modified and directed by our thoughts, which are indeed the representatives of all our past feelings; and as by contemplating the relation of these general representatives to each other, we discover what is really important to men, so by the repetition and continuance of this act feelings connected with

important subjects will be nourished, till at length, if we be originally possessed of much organic sensibility, such habits of mind will be produced that by obeying blindly and mechanically the impulses of those habits we shall describe objects and utter sentiments of such a nature and in such connection with each other, that the understanding of the being to whom we address ourselves, if he be in a healthful state of association, must necessarily be in some degree enlightened, his taste exalted, and his affections ameliorated.

(*Prose Works*, i. 126)

'Or, in other words, association'—as Hartley comments in Part I of the *Observations on Man*—'has a tendency to reduce the state of those who have eaten of the tree of the knowledge of good and evil, back again into a paradisiacal one.'[4]

A 'healthful state of association' in the reader is especially important to Wordsworth's thinking: poetry must be creatively read as well as creatively written. Composition, he writes in the second of the 1810 *Essays on Epitaphs*, speaks 'from the primary sensations of the human heart', and 'unless correspondent ones listen promptly and submissively in the inner cell of the mind to whom it is addressed, the voice cannot be heard . . . its highest powers are wasted' (*Prose Works*, ii. 70). It seems as if the problem of inducing such a response, subduing association to his purposes, came to seem increasingly difficult. Language, he comments in the *Essay, Supplementary to the Preface* (1815), is

a thing subject to endless fluctuations and arbitrary associations. The genius of the poet melts these down for his purpose; but they retain their shape and quality to him who is not capable of exerting, within his own mind, a corresponding energy.

(*Prose Works*, iii. 82)

As Stephen K. Land has remarked in his very useful article on 'The Silent Poet', 'Wordsworth's aim, for the theoretical purposes of poetry, is to divest language of all secondary associations and to confine (poetic) communication to the sphere governed by "the primary laws of our nature".'[5] The depth of the poet's anxiety is brought out most clearly in a passage that a number of recent critics have cited, but no one has so far looked at very closely, from the third of the 1810 *Essays*.[6] 'Words are too awful an instrument for good and evil to be trifled with', Wordsworth begins impressively, 'they hold above all other external powers a dominion over thoughts.' 'If words be not . . . an incarnation of the thought'—one hears the style becoming prophetic, sybilline, as he strives to express a feeling about the nature of language that once again is surely disproportionate—

> If words be not . . . an incarnation of the thought but only a clothing for it, then surely will they prove an ill gift; such a one as those poisoned vestments, read of in the stories of superstitious times, which had power to consume and to alienate from his right mind the victim who put them on. Language, if it do not uphold . . .

The tone has changed again. We are suddenly with the mother and her feeding child:

> Language, if it do not uphold, and feed, and leave in quiet, like the power of gravitation or the air we breathe, is a counter-spirit . . .

(Violence returns.)

> a counter-spirit, unremittingly and noiselessly at work to derange, to subvert, to lay waste, to vitiate, and to dissolve.
>
> (*Prose Works*, ii. 84–5)

Wordsworth's use of the term 'incarnation'—which can after all imply exactly the dualism that he is here rejecting[7]—causes De Quincey to comment thirty years later, 'Never in one word was so profound a truth conveyed.' He is writing about style and subjectivity, and recalls what was apparently a conversation with the poet at the time of the *Essays on Epitaphs*:

> In saying this, we do but vary the form of what we once heard delivered on this subject by Mr Wordsworth. His remark was by far the weightiest thing we ever heard on the subject of style, and it was this: that it is in the highest degree unphilosophic to call language or diction 'the *dress* of thoughts' . . . he would call it 'the *incarnation* of thoughts'. . . . The truth is apparent on consideration: for, if language were merely a dress, then you could separate the two; you could lay the thoughts on the left hand, the language on the right. But, generally speaking, you can no more deal thus with poetic thoughts than you can with soul and body. The union is too subtle, the inter-texture too ineffable—each coexisting not merely with the other, but each *in* and *through* the other. An image, for instance, a single word, often enters into a thought as a constituent part. In short, the two elements are not united as a body with a separate dress, but as a mysterious incarnation.[8]

The emphasis on mystery is especially interesting—the coexistence of thought and language '*in* and *through*' each other. Professor Land has argued persuasively that Wordsworth 'used the incarnation metaphor . . . with a clear awareness of its strong implicit dualism';[9] but De Quincey is not at all often wrong about Wordsworth the writer, however resentful he may sometimes be of the man. We cannot know whether he had read the unpublished third *Essay* of 1810, or whether the conversation he recalls had placed incarnation in a similar context, but he surely provides the best possible gloss on Wordsworth's original definition.

'Words', to go back to the beginning of the poet's solemn warning,

> are too awful an instrument for good and evil to be trifled with: they hold above all other external powers a dominion over thoughts.

It is a remarkable statement, but not apparently a hasty one. Words have more power even than the primary external forces of Nature—more than 'The mountain's outline and its steady form' which confer upon the mind a 'simple grandeur', more than the crag which, rising up between the steady outline and the stars can chase a child across a lake, filling his mind with 'grave/And serious thoughts', peopling it with alien forms, affecting his future development and future life. What is it that can give to language this extraordinary power?—and to Wordsworth's language in this instance such extraordinary vehemence? Two further cases of the word 'incarnation' in his writing may be a help. The first belongs to *Prelude*, Book VII, and seems a little pedestrian. Wordsworth is recalling how very limited his response had been to drama. Even tragedy, it appears, had not passed 'beyond the suburbs of [his] mind'.[10] The actors and action seen at the theatre had been an 'incarnation of the spirits that moved/Amid the poet's beauteous world' (vii. 510–11)—presumably, that is, in Shakespeare's beauteous world—but they had also been in their own right 'gross realities'. The world of imagination had been present to the mind only as a contrast. In the very ineptitude of the actors Wordsworth had recognized

> As by a glimpse, the things which [he] had shaped
> And yet not shaped, had seen and scarcely seen,
> Had felt, and thought of in [his] solitude.
>
> (*1805*, vii. 514–16)

The solitary reading of Shakespeare had led to imaginative shapings that were necessarily imprecise—a creative fusion of things made, seen, felt, and thought. The dramatist's *words* had thus been successful in their incarnation of the ideal in a way that ceased to be possible when the world of imagination was too literally 'embodied' in the theatre. But poetry too is circumscribed. The *Essay Supplementary to the Preface* of 1815 defines its powers and limitations in terms of an affinity with religion:

> The concerns of religion refer to indefinite objects, and are too weighty for the mind to support them without relieving itself by resting a great part of the burthen upon words and symbols. The commerce between man and his Maker cannot be carried on but by a process where much is represented in little, and the Infinite Being accommodates himself to a finite capacity. In all this may be perceived the affinity between religion and poetry . . . between religion, whose element is infinitude, and whose ultimate trust is the supreme of things, submitting herself to circumscription, and reconciled to substitutions; and poetry, ethereal and transcendent, yet incapable to sustain her existence without sensous incarnation.
>
> (*Prose Works*, iii. 65)

J. Hillis Miller in his essay on 'The Stone and the Shell' has asked himself the question: 'Does the meaning [in Wordsworth] pre-exist the signs for it, so that it is only expressed, copied or represented by them, or does it come into existence only in its signs? Does Word precede words, or is it the other way round?'[11] The answer must surely be yes, meaning does pre-exist, Word does precede words, at least insofar as what is being talked about is Wordsworth's most deeply felt, underlying, attitudes to language. The Word becomes incarnate in Christ; drama becomes incarnate in the actors; poetry, in its nature ideal, can *sustain* the existence it has in the imagination only through the 'sensuous incarnation' of language. Words take on an extraordinary responsibility and extraordinary power. Only they can 'fix in a visible home', endue 'with a frame of outward life', the 'phantoms of conceit' that float loose in the poet's mind, thus expressing and assuaging 'The many feelings that oppressed [his] heart' (*1805*, i. 127–33). Choice of language that is mere clothing to the thought is a betrayal of the original creative impulse, a denial of that which has been ethereal and transcendent. It can be seen as a settling for poetic diction, but where that term usually implies a language that is glossy and inert—and had indeed done so for Wordsworth himself in the 1802 Appendix to the Preface to *Lyrical Ballads*—the force that is evoked in the *Essay on Epitaphs* is active and threatening. To falsify is to surrender control over one's own mind. Falsification once accepted becomes indistinguishable from fact, becomes a habit, a way of thinking, a poison that maddens and seemingly lacks all antidote. In its way the force let loose resembles the apocalyptic dulness of *Dunciad*, Book IV, but it is felt as a personal fear: 'a counter-spirit unremittingly and noiselessly at work to derange, to subvert, to lay waste, to vitiate, and to dissolve'.

There is a sense in which this negative and negating power runs counter to the human spirit itself, but it is counter especially to the spirit of the poet's own creativity—the 'plastic power' which in Part II of the 1799 *Prelude* is also personified, also maverick, also at work within the mind, and which exemplifies the most confident, expansive moment in Wordsworth's early relationship with Nature:

> A plastic power
> Abode with me, a forming hand, at times
> Rebellious, acting in a devious mood,
> A local spirit of its own, at war
> With general tendency, but for the most
> Subservient strictly to the external things
> With which it communed. An auxiliar light
> Came from my mind, which on the setting sun
> Bestowed new splendour; the melodious birds,
> The gentle breezes, fountains that ran on
> Murmuring so sweetly in themselves, obeyed
> A like dominion, and the midnight storm
> Grew darker in the presence of my eye.
> (*1799*, ii. 411–23)

One spirit enhances everything it touches, the other lays waste, subverts, dissolves; one plainly is the imagination, the other is its daemonic antithesis. The 'plastic power' is *of* the mind, and, though displaying at times an autonomy, subservient on the whole to the general forces of Nature: the 'counter-spirit' is external—words after all are common property—but may establish a hold *within* the mind as a result of creativity misused.

Behind the statement that 'words hold above all other external powers a dominion over thoughts' is the poet's surprise that *any* power outside the mind could be strong enough to dominate. 'Great God', he wrote of the moment of entry into London at the end of *1805*, Book VIII,

> That aught *external* to the living mind
> Should have such mighty sway . . .
>
> (ll. 700–2)

We may be inclined with Coleridge to say that it didn't, that this was a case in which

> power streamed from [him], and [his] soul received
> The light reflected as a light bestowed . . .
>
> (*To William Wordsworth*, 18–19)

but it does not alter the fact that the experience is *felt* to be external. To continue the quotation,

> yet so it was:
> A weight of ages did at once descend
> Upon my heart—no thought embodied, no
> Distinct remembrances, but weight and power,
> Power growing with the weight.
>
> (*1805*, viii. 702–6)

Power, as De Quincey points out, again thinking of Wordsworth, though not this time referring to him directly, is the 'exercise and expansion [of the individual's] latent capacity of sympathy with the infinite'.[12] Power cannot stay still, and it has to find expression. In the immediate experience there will be 'no thought embodied', but thought comes as a secondary stage, and with it, if the process is uncontaminated, will come (to return to the *Essay on Epitaphs*):

> expressions which are not what the garb is to the body but what the body is to the soul, themselves a constituent part and power or function in the thought . . .[13]
>
> (*Prose Works*, ii. 84)

If, as a critic, and presumably as a writer, one wishes to test language to see if it is truly an incarnation, the second of the 1810 *Essays* tells us confidently that there is an 'art of bringing words rigorously to the test of thoughts; and these again to a comparison with things, their archetypes' (*Prose Works*, ii. 77). Pre-Jungian archetypes were not especially numinous: in the *Guide to the Lakes* a man on horseback is the archetype of his reflection in the water beside the road (*Prose Works*, ii. 192); in the 1799 *Prelude*, stored-up mental images are said to have the permanence of their archetypes, which are the natural scenes from which they derive (i. 283–7). It is clear that Wordsworth is thinking in his customarily physical terms. If one has a word, one should test it against a thought; if one has a thought, one should test it against a thing—it is all really very satisfactory, a sort of literary or critical equivalent of grasping at walls and trees. There are of course those who are not in a position to carry out such tests. Musing in *1805*, Book VI, on what went wrong for Coleridge in his University career, the poet writes:

> I have thought
> Of thee, thy learning, gorgeous eloquence . . .
> Thy subtle speculations, toils abstruse
> Among the Schoolmen, and Platonic forms
> Of wild ideal pageantry, *shaped out*
> *From things well matched, or ill, and words for things*—
> The self-created sustenance of a mind
> Debarred from Nature's living images,
> Compelled to be a life unto itself . . .
>
> (ll. 305–14)

Debarred from Nature's images, Coleridge had been unable to make the comparisons which alone can show language to be susbstantial, and which had been at the centre of the Pedlar's early training:

> He had received
> A precious gift, for as he grew in years
> With these impressions would he still compare
> All his ideal stores, his shapes and forms . . .

(That is, the creations of his own imagination)

> And, being still unsatisfied with aught
> Of dimmer character, he thence attained
> An *active* power to fasten images
> Upon his brain . . .
>
> (*Pedlar*, 34–41; W.'s. italics)

Coleridge had been seduced by language, creating his own sustenance of wild ideal pageantry because he had no things—or no natural things—to test his words against. His situation had been unfortunate, but he can hardly have been at fault. Godwin, by contrast, is said in the fragment of an *Essay on Morals* (1798) to have knowingly abused the powers of language: 'The whole secret of this juggler's trick lies not in fitting words to things (which would be a noble employment), but in fitting things to words' (*Prose Works*, i. 103). By such standards the ultimate crime is that of Macpherson's *Ossian*. Claiming himself never to have been taken in by this great opportunist pre-Romantic fake,[14] Wordsworth writes in 1815:

> From what I saw with my own eyes, I knew that the imagery was spurious. In Nature every thing is distinct, yet nothing defined into absolute independent singleness. In Macpherson's work it is exactly the reverse; every thing (that is not stolen) is in this manner defined, insulated, dislocated, deadened—yet nothing distinct.

'It will always be so', he adds, 'when words are substituted for things' (*Prose Works*, iii. 77).

There is a very important distinction to be made between the substitution of words for things that takes place as the result of failure to connect them to their archetypes, and the tendency of words when being creatively used to achieve in their own right the status of things. In the first case words have become counters, and (at the risk of false etymology) the power they wield is a counter-spirit; in the second, they have become so enriched that they take on an imaginative life of their own. Wordsworth's defence of tautology in his 1800 note to *The Thorn* offers an insight into the very personal relationship with words that one sees being built up in his poetry. 'Repetition and apparent tautology are frequent[ly] beauties of the highest kind', because 'poetry is passion', and because words 'ought to be weighed in the balance of feeling and not measured by the space which they occupy upon paper'. 'Among the chief of these reasons', Wordsworth concludes,

> is the interest which the mind attaches to words, not only as symbols of the passion, but as *things*, active and efficient, which are themselves part of the passion. And further, from a spirit of fondness, exultation, and gratitude, the mind luxuriates in the repetition of words which appear successfully to communicate its feelings.

As one might expect at the period of the Preface to *Lyrical Ballads*, Coleridge's thinking is in the background.[15] A matter of weeks before, he had written to Godwin: 'I wish you to write a book on the power of words, and the processes by which human feelings form affinities with them.' The processes as he sees them are philosophical, or psychological—' Is *thinking* impossible without arbitrary signs? and how far is the word "arbitrary" a misnomer?' (Griggs, i. 625)—but his final piece of advice is that Godwin should ' endeavour to destroy the old antithesis of *words* and *things*, elevating, as it were, words into things, and living things too' (Griggs, i. 626). For Coleridge, words will be living things if it can be proven that their use is part of the organic process of human existence—'Are not words etc parts and germinations of the plant?' (Griggs, i. 625)—for Wordsworth they are so because their repetition brings out fondness, exultation, gratitude, in the writer. Coleridge's thought is much more far-reaching. In effect he is positing the existence of an unconscious; whereas Wordsworth, characteristically taking over what he wants and leaving the rest on one side, is telling us how he values and feels the language of his own poetry.

Wordsworth's position appears limited beside Coleridge's speculation, and is certainly a long way from the thinking of the *Essay on Epitaphs*, in which language will take on a quite different autonomy and become at its best an incarnation of the thought. It may be, however, that he does not want to stray too far from his discussion of tautology and *The Thorn*. Already at this early period there are signs that he would like to make much larger claims. A group of four closely related fragments of blank verse belonging to summer 1799 is especially interesting in this respect.[16] The first three are concerned with the poet's failure to give form to his ideas, and may refer either to work on *The Recluse* or to inability to get going on the second Part of the 1799 *Prelude*. The fourth presents this failure, very surprisingly for the period, as a relapse from full participation in the One Life:

> I seemed to learn
> That what we see of forms and images
> Which float along our minds, and what we feel
> Of active or recognizable thought,
> Prospectiveness, or intellect, or will,

Not only is not worthy to be deemed
Our being, to be prized as what we are,
But is the very littleness of life.

'Such consciousness', Wordsworth continues, switching into the present tense to give still further emphasis,

I deem but accidents,
Relapses from the one interior life
That lives in all things, sacred from the touch
Of that false secondary power by which
In weakness we create distinctions, then
Believe that all our puny boundaries are things
Which we perceive, and not which we have made—
In which all beings live with God, themselves
Are God, existing in one mighty whole,
As undistinguishable as the cloudless east
At noon is from the cloudless west, when all
The hemisphere is one cerulean blue.

The passage is remarkable not only in taking up the extreme pantheist position which Spinoza and all his descendants down to Priestley, Coleridge, and Schelling, seek desperately to avoid—'themselves/*Are* God'—but in its out-and-out rejection of the life of the mind. The internalized forms and images of Nature, which in *Tintern Abbey* had led through recollection to mystical experience, have come to seem mere littleness; the poet's intellectual life now appears to be a Urizenic fall into division, a creating of distinctions and categories in place of sharing in the totality of God.

The first of these extraordinary fragments had presented the poet's sense of failure no less powerfully, but in literary terms:

nor had my voice
Been silent—oftentimes had I burst forth
In verse which with a strong and random light
Touching an object in its prominent parts
Created a memorial which to me
Was all sufficient, and, to my own mind
Recalling the whole picture, seemed to speak
An universal language. Scattering thus
In passion many a desultory sound,

I deemed that I had adequately cloathed
Meanings at which I hardly hinted, thoughts
And forms of which I scarcely had produced
A monument and arbitrary sign.

Again there is the failure to achieve universality, but this time it is a universal language. The poet's bursting forth in verse ought to have been the river of imagination, flowing steadily, not 'oftentimes', in gushes. Because of its randomness, the light too, however strong, has failed in its task.[17] The passion has found no true embodiment—scarcely even an epitaph.[18] In effect what has been created is a personal note, fit only to recall the original feelings and circumstances to the poet himself. If it were not that the mood is placed firmly in the past, it would be among the most despairing passages that Wordsworth ever wrote. As it is, it is the brief second fragment that is finally most impressive.[19] This time we are in the present; the poet is referring to the patient laborious act of composition, describing what can be—perhaps indeed has been—achieved:

In that considerate and laborious work,
That patience which, admitting no neglect,
[?By] slow creation doth impart to speach
Outline and substance, even till it has given
A function kindred to organic power—
The vital spirit of a perfect form.

Through the long-drawn-out creative process the writer imparts to language (in effect, to his work) not just a circumscribing outline, but also substance. In the terms of the *Essay on Epitaphs*, he has found out 'those expressions which are not what the garb is to the body, but what the body is to the soul, themselves a constituent part and power or function in the thought.' Wordsworth's use of the word 'function' is personal, and not always easy to define,[20] but the last two all-important lines show the imparted substance as possessing a power, essence, spirit, analogous to life itself—achieving, in the poet's final paradox, a vital spirit, by virtue of the fact that it has achieved a perfect form. The Romantic doctrine of organic form, normally associated with Coleridge's Shakespeare Lectures of 1812 and his unacknowledged debt to Schlegel, had seemingly been anticipated by Wordsworth as early as summer 1799.[21] Obviously it is tempting to think that Coleridge arrived at the idea earlier than has been assumed, and passed it on to Wordsworth when he and Dorothy came through Göttingen in April 1799. The case would then be exactly and conveniently parallel to the sudden appearance of the primary imagination in the account of the Infant Babe (*1799*, ii. 267–310).[22] But whereas Coleridge becomes preoccupied with imagination, if not at once, at least quite soon after it appears in the 1799 *Prelude*, there is little evidence of his thinking in terms of organic form until the second course of Shakespeare Lectures thirteen years later.[23] It seems very possible that despite its resemblance to later positions, Wordsworth's thinking on this occasion is entirely his own, and should be taken to imply not a critical concept or viewpoint, but a wish that he may himself participate in the One Life through writing that has achieved a universal, and therefore an organic, language. If Coleridge's influence is present at all, perhaps instead of looking forward to the period of his critical lectures, one should look back to the time when speculation of every kind had seemed to find energy and support in a pantheist life-force:

And what if all of animated Nature
Be but organic harps diversely framed,
That tremble into thought as o'er them sweeps
Plastic and vast, one intellectual breeze,
At once the soul of each, and God of all?

(*Eolian Harp*, 44–8)

As a representative of animated nature, the poet trembles into thought; as a creator in his own right, he imparts to his work,

A function kindred to organic power—
The vital spirit of a perfect form.

In practice the life that Wordsworth gave, or hoped to give, in his poetry was a storing-up—a making permanent, and making available—of impressions:

and I would give
While yet we may, as far as words can give,

A substance and a life to what I feel:
I would enshrine the spirit of the past
For future restoration.

(*1805*, xi. 338–42)

The emotions of the moment, often themselves deriving from the past, are to be treasured in a 'casket of immortal verse', for the sake of the poet himself, and for the sake of those that follow. The wish that feeling may have the permanence of the natural forms with which it is associated leads in the Preface to *Lyrical Ballads* to a quest for language that shall have a corresponding permanence. At one moment Wordsworth goes so far as to claim that 'the *best* part of language is originally derived' from objects with which the peasant is in contact (*Prose Works*, i. 124). Coleridge's derision in *Biographia* is well-known and to the point, but as with his commentary on the 'seer blest' of *Intimations*, he ignores what is taking place beneath the overstatement.[24] The child is a symbol not a prodigy; and language at its purest is felt to derive from natural objects, not because the poet is unaware of the limits of a peasant's vocabulary, but because he associates such objects with the sources of his own power and wish to communicate. Within the mind they have established their permanence: they are the 'forms of beauty' which in *Tintern Abbey* 'have not been. . . . As is a landscape to a blind man's eye' (ll. 23–5), the forms which in Part I of the 1799 *Prelude*

exist with independent life,
And, like their archetypes, know no decay.

(*1799*, i. 285–7)

Whether the images are knowingly and pleasurably 'fastened' upon the brain (*Pedlar*, 39–41), or stamped upon it through painful experience (the 'spots of time'; *1799*, i. 258–374), or merely left there as unconscious, 'collateral' impressions (*1799*, i. 418–26), they are already a kind of language, a silent poetry of the mind that recalls emotion and experience to which only words can give an outward life. Wordsworth was no doubt aware of replacing Hartley's millenarian associationism with his own more personal brand:

The earth
And common face of Nature spake to me
Rememberable things—sometimes, 'tis true,
By quaint associations, yet not vain
Nor profitless, if haply they impressed
Collateral objects and appearances,
Albeit lifeless then, and doomed to sleep
Until maturer seasons called them forth
To impregnate and to elevate the mind.

(*1799*, i. 418–26)

Rememberable things do not have to be remembered—they have to be linked by associations, however quaint, that will later call them back to a mind that can give them their true Wordsworthian value. In a magnificent phrase, the child's immediate joy, 'Wearied itself out of the memory', but

The scenes which were a witness of that joy
Remained, in their substantial lineaments
Depicted on the brain, and to the eye
Were visible, a daily sight.

(*1799*, i. 427–32)

It is of course to the inward eye—the eye that will come to seem 'the bliss of solitude'—that the scenes are daily visible. In bringing them repeatedly to mind, the poet revisits and revalues past emotions 'purifying thus/The elements of feeling and of thought' (*1799*, i. 137–8), and preserving for the future that which could not originally have been known to be precious:

And thus
By the impressive agency of fear,
By pleasure and repeated happiness—
So frequently repeated—and by force
Of obscure feelings representative
Of joys that were forgotten, these same scenes,
So beauteous and majestic in themselves,
Though yet the day was distant, did at length
Become habitually dear, and all
Their hues and forms were by invisible links
Allied to the affections.

(*1799*, i. 432–42)

In the 'obscure feelings representative/Of joys that were forgotten' lie not just the sources of adult confidence, but the 'obscure sense/Of possible sublimity' that is the poet's inspiration as he writes. Whether or not associationism can be in general a force for good, there is no reason to doubt that in the development of Wordsworth's own mind—and in the poetry that records that development—it is extremely important. It is in such a context that one should read the strange, at first sight largely incomprehensible, sequence from the end of *Prelude*, Book V, that was quoted at the beginning of this chapter:

> Visionary power
> Attends upon the motions of the winds
> Embodied in the mystery of words.
> There darkness makes abode, and all the host
> Of shadowy things do work their changes there
> As in a mansion like their proper home.
> Even forms and substances are circumfused
> By that transparent veil with light divine,
> And through the turnings intricate of verse
> Present themselves as objects recognised
> In flashes, and with a glory scarce their own.
> (*1805*, v. 619–29)

On a superficial level the passage shows Wordsworth in March 1804 trying to excuse himself for not having succeeded in writing a Book about 'Books'. He has just alleged, not very convincingly, that those who have been brought up in the country get a special pleasure from what he terms 'the great Nature that exists in works/Of mighty poets'—hence apparently his reference to 'the motions of the winds/Embodied in the mystery of words'. But this train of thought hardly seems to explain the preoccupations of the poetry. How much effect are the winds really felt to have in Wordsworth's sentence? Where is it that the enigmatic 'darkness makes abode'—in winds? or in words? What would be the difference if one left the winds out, and read: 'Visionary power/ Attends upon . . . the mystery of words'? A great deal falls into place if one realizes that the mighty poet whom Wordsworth has in mind is not Shakespeare, or Milton, or even the Coleridge of *The Eolian Harp*, but his own earlier self. A cluster of verbal echoes refers us back to Alfoxden, and what may well be the earliest lines in *The Prelude*:

and I would stand
Beneath some rock, listening to sounds that are
The ghostly language of the ancient earth
Or make their dim abode in distant winds.
Thence did I drink the visionary power.[25]

(*1799*, ii. 356–60)

The Wordsworth of Book V is looking back to spring 1798 as the period at which it had seemed possible to perceive directly the transcendental forces of Nature. But his concern now is with language—not the unarticulated 'sounds that are/The ghostly language of the ancient earth', but the mystery of words in which he had been able to embody his response. In effect he is saying, visionary power is inherent in the language I then used. The reassuring corollary is to be found in lines written a day or two later, that connect the original 'spots of time' through to the later period of happiness, wandering with Mary Hutchinson and Dorothy 'in daily presence of . . . the naked pool and dreary crags/And . . . melancholy beacon' that had been the 'involutes' of his early traumatic experience:

So feeling comes in aid
Of feeling, and diversity of strength
Attends us if but once we have been strong.

(*1805*, xi. 325–7)

Wordsworth is seen drawing strength from his own inspired earlier poetry in very much the same way that he draws it from memories of an imaginative childhood. The phrase, 'There darkness makes abode', comes to be a reference to the 'obscure sense/Of possible sublimity' with which the earlier experience had left him. At the same time it is the expression of a new hope that in the uncomprehended workings of language itself there are creative powers. The 'darkness' in which the host of shadowy things are working their changes is the first cousin of the 'greatness' that will similarly 'make abode' in the much more famous piece of verse that was written a few weeks later directly about imagination:

I was lost as in a cloud,
Halted without a struggle to break through,
And now, recovering, to my soul I say
'I recognize thy glory'. In such strength

Of usurpation, in such visitings
Of awful promise, when the light of sense
Goes out in flashes that have shewn to us
The invisible world, doth greatness make abode . . .

(*1805*, vi. 529–36)

The cloud that halts the mental traveller in the lines from Book VI is specifically the 'unfathered vapour' of imagination. It is, one feels, far better understood by the poet himself, as well as far more impressive, than the darkness of the earlier passage. Yet this darkness has very positive properties. It leads as in the later sequence to flashes of recognition, but *en route* has been described much less predictably as a veil. In Book IV—

Gently did my soul
Put off her veil, and self-transmuted, stood
Naked as in the presence of her God.

(iv.140–2)

—he had used the traditional veil that closes off perception, preserving decencies and distance; but here the veil is an active force that circumfuses the external world of forms and substances with light divine— 'apparels' them 'with celestial light', adds to them 'The light that never was, on sea or land' (*Peele Castle*, 15).[26] Wordsworth is writing about the making of poetry, and it might be convenient to think of the darkness of Book V as defining the secondary, or poetic, imagination, so as to prepare the way for definition of the primary in Book VI. It isn't so. Both passages deal with the primary, but in the earlier it is seen in the workings of language. Like Coleridge's secret ministry of frost, or the sea of mist on Snowdon, language is for Wordsworth a silent transforming power. Veiled (in the conventional sense)behind the lines of Book V is the border hope that neither he nor Coleridge ever dared to express that poetry itself, the act of writing, is 'a repetition in the finite mind of the eternal act of creation in the infinite I AM'—a repetition that does not always, or merely, co-exist 'with the conscious will' (*BL* xiii. 167). It is for this reason that the correspondent breeze of the Preamble becomes incarnate in the mystery of words, and for this reason that one hears so many echoes from Book V when Wordsworth comes to define the 'visitings of awful promise', and that very special hope that consists of

Effort, and expectation, and desire,
And something evermore about to be.
(*1805*, vi. 541–2)

No wonder that language out of control should appear to vitiate and dissolve (where the imagination struggles at all events to idealize and to unify), and that Wordsworth should think it able, if rightly and creatively used, to 'uphold, and feed, and leave in quiet, like the power of gravitation, or the air we breathe'. At its best Wordsworth's prose can be as rich in associations as his verse—as full of shadowy things that are working their changes in the darkness of the language. 'Uphold' is certainly a word that he repeats 'from a spirit of fondness, exultation, and gratitude', and which is felt to have its own especial resonance, partly acquired through this repetition, partly innate. In *Prelude*, Book X, Nature and human love have *upheld* the poet in his hour of crisis, and *uphold* him still at the time of writing (ll. 921–9). In a most untypical passage of Book III we hear of

visitings
Of the *upholder*, of the tranquil soul,
Which underneath all passion lives secure
A steadfast life.
(ll. 115–18)

Margaret in *The Ruined Cottage* had '*upheld* the cool refreshment, drawn' from a well that came to symbolize outgoing love and the brotherhood of Nature and man (ll. 98–103). Then,there are 'those first affections' of the Ode,

Those shadowy recollections
Which, be they what they may
Are yet the fountain light of all our day,
Are yet the master light of all our seeing—
Uphold us, cherish us, and make
Our noisy years seem moments in the being
Of the eternal silence . .
(*Intimations*, 147–53)

And, among may further instances, there is Wordsworth's confident description in *1805*, Book XII, of poets as 'Men . . . of other mold',

> Who are *their own upholders*, to themselves
> Encouragement, and energy, and will,
> Expressing liveliest thoughts in lively words
> As native passion dictates.
>
> (*1805*, xii. 260–4)

These men who are 'their own upholders' have surely achieved a Wordsworthian ideal. They have a power that is self-sufficing and self-supporting; they are 'blest in thoughts/That are their own perfection and reward' (*1805*, vi. 545–6),and they are capable of transforming these into poetry that is the natural incarnation of their passion. And yet for all their qualities and attainments, and despite the fact that this is the group to which Wordsworth himself belongs, one should expect to find them taking a second place. 'Others too/There are among the homely walks of life', the passage continues, '*Still higher*':

> Theirs is the language of the heavens, the power,
> The thought, the image, and the silent joy;
> Words are but under-agents in their souls—
> When they are grasping with their greatest strength
> They do not breathe among them.
>
> (*1805*, xii. 270–4)

To speak on earth the language of the heavens is indeed 'to make/Our noisy years seem moments in the being/Of the eternal silence'. For poets in general, words are 'external things' that may at any time assume dominion over thoughts: in silent poets, language is a function of the soul. The prefix 'under' ('Words are but *under*—agents') works in different ways. It implies of course the unimportance of words as such, for those who speak the language of the heavens; but it suggests while doing so that the silent poet is peculiarly in touch with Wordsworthian sources of power—the 'under-soul' that is 'hushed' as imagination sleeps at Cambridge (*1805*, iii. 539–40), the 'under-presence' of Snowdon that is 'The sense of God, or whatso'er is dim/Or vast in its own being' (*1805*, xiii. 71–3). When grasping with their greatest strength—the physicality of Wordsworth's metaphor has more than usual appropriateness—silent poets have transcended not just ordinary speech but the liveliest embodiments of native passion. They are fully perceptive; and fully creative too, in so far as perception *is* creation. John Wordsworth, the original silent poet, brings 'from the solitude/Of the vast sea' 'an eye practiced like a blind man's touch' (*When to the attractions of the busy world*, 80–3); and a similar perceptiveness heightened into creativity can be brought out in the shepherd Michael, who is his counterpart on land.[27] Such men have the spontaneity that the vocal poet would have if mind could print upon mind, if it were possible to inscribe as with the silence of the thought. Even when words are truly an incarnation, the creative process implies in practice a standing back.[28] In effect the silent poet is a child who can prolong the state of innocence because he does not have responsibilities—or has them only within a limited sphere. Wordsworth as a teacher has accepted the obligation to communicate; however envious he may be, he is bound to the tools of his trade. If his work is truly to become 'A power like one of Nature's' (*1805*, xii. 312), he must find the colours and words hitherto unknown to man—a barrier must be broken down, a border crossed. 'Is there not', he asks poignantly in *Home at Grasmere*, at a moment when things are not going too well,

> An art, a music, and a stream of words,
> That shall be life—the acknowledged voice of life . . . ?[29]

'Language if it do not uphold, and feed, and leave in quiet, like the power of gravitation, or the air we breathe'—perhaps one hardly needs to go on with the game of associations, but it cannot fail to be significant that the single place in Wordsworth's poetry where the word 'gravitation' appears, is the *Prelude* account of the Infant Babe and the origins of imagination in the love of a mother for her child:

> [In] this beloved presence, there exists
> A virtue which irradiates and exalts
> All objects through all intercourse of sense.
> No outcast *he* . . .

(Unlike the adult poet; and unlike Wordsworth the child after the early death of his mother.)

> No outcast he, bewildered and depressed;
> Along his infant veins are interfused
> The *gravitation* and the filial bond
> Of Nature that connect him with the world.
> (*1799*, ii. 288–94)

Such for Wordsworth is the power and function of language. It is a primal reassurance of belonging, a connection with the world that is at the same time a source and guarantee of adult vision. In its highest form it is imagination itself, the corresponding internal energy of the *Essay Supplementary* that coincides with, and balances, the external correspondent breeze. If only it could be inscribed as with the silence of the thought—if mind could stamp its image upon mind as in the days when the poet himself had 'held mute dialogues with his mother's heart', and possessed as of right the 'virtue which irradiates . . . All objects through all intercourse of sense'.

Chapter 8

Versions of the Fall

No more of talk where God or angel guest
With man, as with his friend, familiar used
To sit indulgent . . .
                                        I now must change
Those notes to tragic; foul distrust, and breach
Disloyal on the part of man, revolt,
And disobedience . . .

(Milton: *Paradise Lost*)

As one who, long in thickets and in brakes
Entangled, winds now this way and now that
His devious course uncertain, seeking home;
Or, having long in miry ways been foiled
And sore discomfited, from slough to slough
Plunging, and half despairing of escape;
If chance at length he find a greensward smooth
And faithful to the foot, his spirits rise . . .
So I, designing other themes . . .
Have rambled wide. In country, city, seat
Of academic fame (howe'er deserved),
Long held, and scarcely disengaged at last.
But now, with pleasant pace, a cleanlier road
I mean to tread. I feel myself at large . . .

The lines could almost be from *The Prelude*—the last assertion is pure Wordsworth, even if the use of 'country' a little earlier on doesn't sound quite right—but are in fact Cowper's opening to Book III of *The Task*. Wordsworth's version of the passage is found at the beginning of *1805*, Book IX:

As oftentimes a river, it might seem,
Yielding in part to old remembrances,
Part swayed by fear to tread an onward road
That leads direct to the devouring sea,
Turns and will measure back his course—far back,
Towards the very regions which he crossed
In his first outset—so have we long time
Made motions retrograde, in like pursuit
Detained. But now we start afresh: I feel
An impulse to precipitate my verse . . .

So far the poetry has been astonishingly close to Cowper, but the style now changes. 'Fair greetings to this shapeless eagerness,/Whene'er it comes', Wordsworth writes, mocking his new resolution, and moves abruptly from *The Task* to *Paradise Lost*:

needful in work so long,
Thrice needful to the argument which now
Awaits us—oh, how much unlike the past—
One which, though bright the promise, will be found
Ere far we shall advance, ungenial, hard
To treat of, and forbidding in itself.

(*1805*, ix. 11–17)

Wordsworth is not merely acknowledging his precursors, he is standing back from *The Prelude* and imposing a structure. The bulk of Book IX belongs almost certainly to late April–May 1804;[1] but these lines, with their reference to doubling back to infancy, must be later than the composition of VIII in October, and it seems very likely that in fact they belong to the period of tidying-up and copying that followed the poem's completion in May 1805. In these circumstances it is especially interesting that the inserted lines should juxtapose *The Prelude*'s two great structural metaphors, the river of imagination, and the Fall.

The river of Book IX, with which Wordsworth so strongly identifies—

Yielding in part to old remembrances,
Part swayed by fear to tread an onward road
That leads direct to the devouring sea . . .

—has a clear rhetorical function. It is an image at once of the poem, and of the mind that is the subject of the poem, and of the poet's mind that is controlling, or failing to control, the narrative. It is also (in terms of the finished poem) a guide, pointing us forward towards the famous river-image of Book XIII in which Wordsworth will look back over the full course of his work:

> we have traced the stream
> From darkness, and the very place of birth
> In its blind cavern, whence it faintly heard
> The sound of waters; followed it to light
> And open day, accompanied its course
> Among the ways of Nature . . .[2]
>
> (xiii. 172–7)

The poet's allusion to *Paradise Lost* at the beginning of Book IX is similarly very deliberate, and similarly an attempt to pull together recurrent images and implications within the poem, and impose a firmer structure. 'No more of talk', Milton had written at the beginning of *his* ninth Book,

> where God or angel guest
> With man, as with his friend, familiar used
> To sit indulgent . . .
> I now must change
> Those notes to tragic; foul distrust, and breach
> Disloyal on the part of man . . .

And he had moved on into his account of the Fall, commenting as he did so on *his* relation to poetic predecessors:

> sad task, yet argument
> Not less but more heroic than the wrath
> Of stern Achilles on his foe pursued
> Thrice fugitive about Troy wall; or rage
> Of Turnus for Lavinia disespoused . . .
>
> (*PL* ix. 13–17)

Wordsworth in his cross-reference is reminding the audience that *The Prelude* is a further redefinition of the heroic. Like Milton he is not just a strong poet, but one who knows his strength. By his transumption of the precursor—to adopt Harold Bloom's terminology—he places himself in a very distinguished line: Homer—Virgil—Milton—Wordsworth.

Broadly, of course, one knows what all this means. Milton takes on from the poetry of battle—'hitherto the only argument/ Heroic deemed' (*PL* ix. 28–9)—and makes a Christian epic: Wordsworth takes on from Christian epic and creates a spiritual autobiography:

> Not of outward things
> Done visibly for other minds—words, signs,
> Symbols or actions—but of my own heart
> Have I been speaking . . .
>
> (*1805*, iii. 174–7)

Similarly, it is clear in general terms that what the Fall means to Wordsworth is loss of vision;[3] but not every reader of *The Prelude* could say where and when and for what reason such a Fall occurs within the poem. Wordsworth tells us in Book IX that it is coming, but does not in fact use the phrase 'Imagination Impaired' until the heading to XI, by which time he has bypassed the period of Godwinism and subsequent despair with which most readers assume it to be connected. The truth is that there are many Falls within *The Prelude*, imposed upon the narrative at different times and for different reasons. Those of Books III, IV, and XI come ready-made into *1805*, representing in fact successive attempts to structure the five-Book *Prelude* on a Miltonic basis. In the later French Books (IX and Xa)[4] the patterning is less evident, but innocent vision is for a time obscured as the poet loses his way in the political world of experience. The Fall of Xb is different again, convincing in biographical terms, yet curiously isolated in relation to the poem's over-all structure. It is difficult to think that any one of these Falls is really effective as a turning-point in the narrative; and yet there is no doubt that Wordsworth intended to impose on his poem the paradise-lost-and-regained pattern that was innate in his mature thinking, and that would establish his succession to Milton. Given the facts of his biography (as seen with least distortion in *Tintern Abbey*) there seems to be little reason why he should not have done so more impressively. But alongside his preoccupation with loss, and with the possible sublimity of primal vision restored, there is an extraordinary refusal to believe that his imagination has ever truly been impaired. Again and again Wordsworth brings himself to a point in his autobiography when he seems to be about to show significant deterioration; and then he steps back and says no, I can't, I won't, it wasn't so.

I. 'INTO A POPULOUS PLAIN': THE FIVE-BOOK *Prelude* (JANUARY-MARCH 1804)

The two-Part *Prelude* of 1798–9 contains no version of the Fall. Though following closely on *Tintern Abbey*'s elegiac tones, and emerging from a moment of self-accusation and self-doubt, it is one of Wordsworth's most optimistic poems. The 'spots of time' of Part I successfully nourish adult creativity, and the babe of Part II who is 'creator and receiver both', unlike the child of *Intimations* who will convict the poet of his loss, is shown in his imaginative power to be a source of confidence:

> Such, verily, is the first
> Poetic spirit of our human life—
> By uniform control of after years
> In most abated or suppressed, in some
> Through every change of growth or of decay
> Preeminent till death.
>
> (*1799*, ii. 305–10)

The final implications of *1799* are that childhood and adolescence lead forward to a period of fuller awareness; and this is still Wordsworth's position when in December 1801 he extends his poem into a third Part in order to take in the concluding lines of *The Pedlar*. 'I had an eye', he writes, adapting the third-person narrative of Alfoxden,

> Which from a stone, a tree, a withered leaf,
> To the broad ocean and the azure heavens
> Spangled with kindred multitudes of stars,
> Could find no surface where its power might sleep . . .
>
> (*1805*, iii. 161–4)[5]

As perhaps one would expect, the metaphor of lost paradise appears first at the beginning of 1804 when Wordsworth resumes work on Part III, intending now to create a *Prelude* in five Parts (or Books). Almost at once there are reminders that this is the period in which *Intimations* was completed—

> O heavens, how awful is the might of souls,
> And what they do within themselves while yet
> The yoke of earth is new to them . . .
>
> (*1805*, iii. 178–80)

—but loss of vision was not merely a preoccupation of the moment, it had structural implications too. The first three Books of the five-Book *Prelude* are preserved as *1805*, I–III; Book IV was expanded to form *1805*, IV and V, and must have contained most of their important material; it was the last Book that gave the poem its unique and satisfying shape. Book V was to consist of the Climbing of Snowdon, followed by the 'spots of time' sequence that had been extracted from *1799*, Part I. The poem was thus to begin and end in childhood, the source of Wordsworth's adult power; and *en route* it was to portray and exemplify the loss and regaining of paradise. Imagination, nourished in childhood, sustained in adolescence, was to be impaired for a while by the poet's entry into adult life, yet shown once more in its full glory in the epiphany of Snowdon when he was 21.[6]

Wordsworth's immediate task in January 1804 was to take his poem on from the high-point of 18 year-old communion, or creative perception, reached in the *Pedlar* insertions of 1801. By now he may well have felt that shades of the prison-house would have closed rather earlier round the growing boy, but in any event he lost no time in switching his story onto a downward course:

> And here, O friend, have I retraced my life
> Up to an eminence, and told a tale
> Of matters which not falsely I may call
> The glory of my youth . . . .
> Enough, for now into a populous plain
> We must descend.
>
> (iii. 168–71, 195–6)

There is no lack of confidence as Wordsworth descends from his eminence. The glory of his youth is defined in claims that Blake could not have taken an inch further, and that are (as they would be in Blake) a deliberate affront to Milton:

> Of genius, power,
> Creation, and divinity itself,
> I have been speaking, for my theme has been
> What passed within me.
>
> (iii. 171–4)

And as if the implications might be missed, Wordsworth adds a defiant, almost truculent, allusion—'*This* is in truth heroic argument,/And genuine prowess'—which relegates Milton as firmly as Milton had once relegated Virgil and Homer, to a now outmoded past. It does not mean that he is any the less dependent on his predecessor, just that he can use him now for his own purposes. Wordsworth by this stage has clearly decided to include a version of the Fall that will demonstrate a need for restoration through the 'spots of time'. The populous plain of Cambridge turns out to have much in common with the 'spacious plain, whereon/Were tents of various hue' which is shown by Michael to Adam from the 'hill/Of Paradise the highest' (*PL* xi. 556–7 and 377–8). Wordsworth the freshman—

> I was a chosen son.
> For hither I had come with holy powers
> And faculties, whether to work or feel . . .
>
> (*1805*, iii. 82–4)

resembles the just men of Milton's poem, 'all their study bent/ To worship God aright', who are seduced by the 'bevy of fair women richly gay' (*PL* xi. 577ff.) that represent false pleasures. And the test to which he is being submitted is surely implied in the terms of Michael's rebuke to Adam:

> Judge not what is best
> By pleasure, though to nature seeming meet,
> Created, as thou art, to nobler end
> Holy and pure, conformity divine.
> Those tents thou saw'st so pleasant, were the tents
> Of wickedness . . .
>
> (*PL* xi. 603–8)

The five-Book *Prelude* was to take Wordsworth's autobiography only to the age of 21, and he clearly started out with the intention of showing imagination impaired at, and by, Cambridge. In the event, however, he failed to portray a convincing deterioration in Book III, and had to make further attempts in IV and V. The problem was not that he didn't see the university as a temptation—his warnings to De Quincey six weeks later about Oxford were as moral as anyone could wish[7]—but that he couldn't feel that he himself had yielded. An odd see-saw movement is set up within the verse as the poet struggles to meet the demands of his chosen structure, yet is unable to bring himself to describe a fall from grace. 'It hath been told already how my sight/Was dazzled by the novel show', he writes of the early Cambridge days, but adds in haste, 'and how erelong/I did into myself return' (iii. 202–4). There was

> a treasonable growth
> Of indecisive judgements that impaired
> And shook the mind's simplicity. *And yet*
> This was a gladsome time . . .
>
> (iii. 214–17)

And so it goes on; or at least, the alternation goes on—the degree of blame attaching to the negative side of the balance gets progressively less and less. One moment of self-criticism does stand out—

> Yet could I only cleave to solitude
> In lonesome places—if a throng was near
> That way I leaned by nature, for my heart
> Was social and loved idleness and joy.
>
> (iii. 233–6)

—but it is not easy at this stage in the poem to give the words full weight. The reader's final impression of Cambridge is contained in the typical statement *plus* retraction: 'Imagination slept,/And yet not utterly . . .' (iii. 260–1). Wordsworth it would seem was seldom deeply touched,[8] but one never feels that the sleeping imagination has truly been impaired, or that the activities of the day-to-day mind have power to cause it injury. They are a continuation, inappropriate perhaps but not harmful, of the boyhood pleasures of Book II:

> We sauntered, played, we rioted, we talked
> Unprofitable talk at morning hours,
> Drifted about along the streets and walks,
> Read lazily in lazy books, went forth
> To gallop through the country in blind zeal
> Of senseless horsemanship, or on the breast
> Of Cam sailed boisterously, and let the stars
> Come out perhaps without one quiet thought.
>
> (iii. 251–8)

Wordsworth makes one last attempt to show impairment at Cambridge in the bizarre simile of the floating island of Derwentwater:

> Rotted as by a charm, my life became
> A floating island, an amphibious thing,
> Unsound, of spungy texture, yet withal
> Not wanting a fair face of water-weeds
> And pleasant flowers.
>
> (iii. 339–43)

The lines stand out both as eccentric poetry (a case in which vivid personal memory has not been successfully transmuted),[9] and because the implications of the image are felt to be too extreme. In the passage that follows, Wordsworth effusively takes on himself all blame for lack of academic commitment—

> I should in truth,
> As far as doth concern my single self,
> Misdeem most widely, lodging it elsewhere . . .
>
> (iii. 355–7)

—then slides into self-justification: as a spoilt child of Nature, used to rambling like the wind, he was 'ill-tutored for captivity' (iii.363). Presumably he is unaware of meaning also that he was 'ill-tutored *in* captivity', but he goes on at once to

> shape
> The image of a place which—soothed and lulled
> As [he] had been, trained up in paradise
> Among sweet garlands and delightful sounds . . .

should have 'bent [him] down/To instantaneous service' (iii. 375–83), drawn from him the homage that he had been used to give to Nature. Paradise it now seems has not been actively *lost* at all, merely left behind in childhood and the Lake District. When Wordsworth does for a moment return to his structural metaphor of the Fall, it is as if he has forgotten what it is there for:

> For me, I grieve not; happy is the man
> Who only misses what I missed, who falls
> No lower than I fell.
>
> (iii. 504–6)

Having failed to portray a Fall at Cambridge with any conviction, Wordsworth is left with the more difficult task of showing one on his return to the Lake District for the summer vacation of 1789. Book IV of the five-Book *Prelude* cannot be reconstructed in every detail;[10] but certainly present was the Hawkshead consecration scene, 'I made no vows, but vows/Were then made for me'. None of the great *Prelude* sequences is more lamely, more negatively, introduced:

> And yet, in chastisement of these regrets,
> The memory of one particular hour
> Doth here rise up against me.
>
> (iv. 314–16)

Wordsworth the poet has been making another attempt to show 'an inner falling-off':

> sure it is that now
> Contagious air did oft environ me,
> Unknown among these haunts in former days.
> The very garments that I wore appeared
> To prey upon my strength, and stopped the course
> And quiet stream of self-forgetfulness.
>
> (iv. 289–94)

To Wordsworth the student in this mood of Hamlet-like depression, man

> Seems but a pageant plaything with vile claws,
> And this great frame of breathing elements
> A senseless idol.
>
> (iv. 302–4)

The imagery is impressively vehement,[11] but as at Cambridge it is not clear what the falling-off amounts to, and as before the poet shies away from the implications of what he has said. A memory—no mere recollection, but a daemonic power within the self—on this occasion rises up against him like the mountain on Ullswater rather than let him tell us that imagination has been seriously impaired.

In Wordsworth's mind, though he does not say so, is Milton once again. For a moment he had seemed to be recounting his personal Fall, as his undergraduate self, environed by contagious air within the paradise of Hawkshead, came to see Nature ('this great frame of breathing elements') as a senseless idol. Instead he presents an incident that implies not just that no Fall has taken place, or could ever have taken place, but that he Wordsworth has been chosen as Milton's successor. The opening lines show a connection in the poet's mind that is possibly unconscious: he had passed the night dancing amid a 'promiscuous rout,/A medley of all tempers', and all four words are Miltonic in this usage.[12] The lines that follow, however, are conscious without doubt in their weighing of the language and landscape and assumptions of Wordsworth against those of *Paradise Lost*:

> Magnificent
> The morning was, a memorable pomp,
> More glorious than I ever had beheld.
> The sea was laughing at a distance; all
> The solid mountains were as bright as clouds,
> Grain-tinctured, drenched in empyrean light;
> And in the meadows and the lower grounds
> Was all the sweetness of a common dawn—
> Dews, vapours, and the melody of birds,
> And labourers going forth into the fields.
>
> (iv. 330–9)

The landscape has two levels, two imaginative worlds—Milton's celestial one, in which solid mountains turn to clouds drenched in crimson light from the empyrean, seat of the pure element of fire; and Wordsworth's own, where the sea laughs like daffodils with the pleasure of the poet, where dawn 'in the meadows and the lower grounds' is full of its normal infinite sweetness, and where 'labourers going forth into the fields' as the poet himself will now go forth, wear their biblical associations very lightly, just tenderly hinting at the fitness of things:

> And out of what one sees and hears and out
> Of what one feels, who could have thought to make
> So many selves, so many sensuous worlds,
> As if the air, the mid-day air, was swarming
> With the metaphysical changes that occur,
> Merely in living as and where we live.[13]

Wordsworth is as aware as Stevens and the rest of us just how rare it is to see a common dawn as he sees it. Indeed he takes the depth of his response, as he had taken the imaginative experiences of *1799*, Part I, to be evidence of his election:

> need I say, dear friend, that to the brim
> My heart was full? I made no vows, but vows
> Were then made for me: bond unknown to me
> Was given that I should be—else sinning greatly—
> A dedicated spirit. On I walked
> In blessedness, which even yet remains.
>
> (iv. 340–5)

The effect of the dedication-scene has been to identify the power within the self that refuses to let the poet structure his work in terms of a Fall. So strong is it, that it is felt to have been imposed from without—truly daemonic. Harold Bloom in passing defines the superego as 'the One who commands us', and this would seem a peculiarly dominant example. Wordsworth records not merely a sense of vocation (of having been called), but a feeling that his very answer to that call had been made for him. In the circumstances, failure to live according to the dictates of this power would be the only Fall that could matter, and by implication even at the time of writing (February 1804) there had still been no such failure.

No further attempt is made in Book IV of this intermediate *Prelude* to portray imagination impaired. The fifth, and last, Book may not have been completed when Wordsworth decided in early March 1804 to reorganize his material and work towards a longer poem, but it must have consisted broadly of the first third of *1805*, XIII followed by the last two-thirds of XI. The Climbing of Snowdon showed mature imagination at its height, and the 'spots of time' sequence demonstrated the sources of Wordsworth's adult strength—more particularly, the sources of the mind's power of self-restoration. It was seemingly this last factor that led the poet to make a final attempt to introduce a Fall into his narrative. The 'spots of time' doctrine had from the first been associated with the invisible repair as well as the nourishment of the mind, but merely in the context of 'trivial occupations and the round/Of ordinary intercourse'; now Wordsworth inserted between the two central 'spots' the great lines, 'Oh mystery of man, from what a depth/Proceed thy honours' (*1805*, xi. 328–44), ending in their original version:

> The days gone by
> Come back upon me from the dawn almost
> Of life; the hiding-places of my power
> Seem open, I approach, and then they close;
> *Yet have I singled out–not satisfied*
> *With general feelings, here and there have culled—*
> *Some incidents that may explain whence come*
> *My restorations, and with yet one more of these*
> *Will I conclude.*[14]

If the poem was to end as well as begin in childhood memories chosen because Wordsworth believed them to have had a restorative effect, it was more than ever necessary that he should demonstrate a need for restoration. The central section in which he attempts to do so is the part of the final Book that may never have been completed, but drafts reveal the normal short uneasy motion in the verse. Wordsworth tries successively to show 'The unremitting warfare from the first/Waged' against imagination, his own 'Sad perplexity/In moral knowledge', enslavement to analytic reason, and (most incongruous) a tendency to aesthetic judgements of Nature. But as each attempt to put a negative position prompts a positive one, we get interspersed a series of trubutes to Nature for her care and protection. Both the senses and the objects of their perception have apparently been subordinated by her 'To the great ends of liberty and power', and Mary Hutchinson is offered as a type of the natural piety which it now seems that the poet has shared all along. The 'spots of time' are finally introduced by a statement that Wordsworth's imagination has never seriously been impaired. All his efforts to impose a structure go by the board as he announces:

> In truth the malady of which I speak
> Though aided by the times, whose deeper sound
> Without my knowledge sometimes might perchance
> Make rural Nature's milder minstrelsies
> Inaudible, did never take in me
> Deep root or larger action. I had received
> Impressions far too early and too strong
> For this to last: I threw the habit off
> Entirely and for ever, and again
> In Nature's presence stood as I do now
> A sensitive and creative soul.[15]

The Fall, it seems had been no more than a passing phase. Early 'impressions'—'spots of time' imprinted on the mind—had merely to reassert themselves, for all to be well.

The poet's vehemence—'*far* too early and too strong/For this to last'—carries an implication that the child's impressions were stronger for being early, closer to the hiding-places of power. Wordsworth is clearly thinking in terms of a Fall into experience, and yet he states categorically that a mind protected, or supported, by memories of primal vision contains within itself a redemptive principle which the world of experience cannot seriously affect. Once again his position is very close to De Quincey's in *Suspiria*. 'Of this, at least', De Quincey writes,

> I feel assured, that there is no such thing as *forgetting* possible to the mind; a thousand accidents may and will interpose a veil between our present consciousness and the secret inscriptions on the mind. Accidents of the same sort will also rend away this veil; but alike, whether veiled or unveiled, the inscription remains forever . . .
>
> (Ward, 91)

The great image of the palimpsest—vellum used for successive layers of manuscript, all remaining legible despite the effects of time, and efforts to erase them—shows that for De Quincey, as for Wordsworth, such inscriptions owe their power to the sense they give of an ultimate harmony:

> What else than a natural and mighty palimpsest is the human brain? Such a palimpsest is my brain; such a palimpsest, O reader, is yours. Everlasting layers of ideas, images, feelings, have fallen upon your brain softly as light. Each

> succession has seemed to bury all that went before. And yet, in reality, not one has been extinguished. . . . The fleeting accidents of a man's life and its external shows may indeed be irrelate and incongruous; but the organizing principles which fuse into harmony and gather about fixed predetermined centers whatever heterogeneous elements life may have accumulated from without will not permit the grandeur of human unity greatly to be violated or its ultimate repose to be troubled . . .
>
> (Ward, 169–70)

It is all, in many ways, extremely Wordsworthian. 'The grandeur of human unity'—that of the individual human consciousness, as well as of humanity in general—rests upon the oneness of disparate experience. Harmony is to be perceived through the recovery of underlying layers: 'I, the child', as De Quincey puts it elsewhere in a footnote, 'had the feelings; I, the man, decypher them. In the child lay the handwriting mysterious to *him*, in me the interpretation and the comment' (Ward, 139). The interpretation does, however, vary, and so does the optimism with which the two writers confront the Fall into experience. Both portray an education through suffering that is guided, and presided over, by beneficent powers.[16] Both seek out ways in which their writing may express 'the mighty abstractions that incarnate themselves in all individual sufferings of man's heart' (Ward, 174). But for De Quincey suffering persists as the condition of human life—it is the source of adult recognitions, and in itself a connection with the past[17]—whereas for the Wordsworth of the five-Book *Prelude* recollections of early pain, fear, discomforture, can positively enhance the joys of a later period. The Woman on the Hill is now for the first time followed by reminiscences of the poet's 'time of early love' with Mary Hutchinson and Dorothy in the summer of 1789:

> When, in the blessèd time of early love,
> Long afterwards I roamed about
> In daily presence of this very scene,
> Upon the naked pool and dreary crags,
> And on the melancholy beacon, fell
> The spirit of pleasure and youth's golden gleam—
> And think ye not with radiance more divine
> From these remembrances, and from the power
> They left behind?

'So feeling comes in aid/Of feeling', Wordsworth adds, 'and diversity of strength/Attends us, if but once we have been strong'(*1805*, xi. 317–27). The sense that border vision can be retrieved, or at least that a secondary imaginative strength ('O joy that in our embers/Is something that doth live') can be derived from strong impressions surviving of the first, is deeply at odds with the structure that he has been trying to impose upon his poem. It would have been convenient to be able to show the 'populous plain' of Cambridge as having for a time truly impaired the imagination, or to have been able to portray some convincing Fall in the Hawkshead Long Vacation, but a nameless force was at work as he wrote that would not permit the unity of human grandeur greatly to be violated. Reading back through the palimpsest of his mind—

> The days gone by
> Come back upon me from the dawn almost
> Of life . . .
>
> (*1805* xi. 333–5)

—it seemed to the poet as he was making the five-Book *Prelude* that feeling had always come in aid of feeling, and always would. He was conscious of the hiding-places of his power as closing when he approached, but did not at this moment doubt that the power itself persisted.[18]

II. POLITICAL INNOCENCE AND EXPERIENCE: 'I WITH HIM BELIEVED DEVOUTLY' (1805, IX AND XA)

The five-Book *Prelude* was broken up in March 1804, chiefly one suspects because Wordsworth could not face the implication that if this subordinate poem were completed he would have to go ahead with the centrepiece of *The Recluse*, and do so in the absence of Coleridge whom he still believed capable of providing the desperately needed philosophical material.[19] But there were two further causes: a sense of having omitted important parts of his autobiography, and memories of his own travel brought to mind by Coleridge's leaving for Malta. Both these pointed towards an account of the French trip of 1790, which had been bypassed in the five-Book poem in order to reach the climactic Ascent of Snowdon in 1791. Wordsworth's decision to reorganize his material was taken about 10 March; by the eighteenth his fourth Book, finished less than three weeks before, had been split in two and reworked, and the first five Books of *1805* had been despatched to Coleridge in almost their final shape. Ten days later Book VI ('Cambridge and the Alps') was under way; and by 29 April, if not before, it was complete. By early June when composition paused for the summer Wordsworth seems to have written a version of Book IX as well, and the first half of X, carrying him through his second visit to France, his return to England at the end of 1792, and up to the death of Robespierre in August 1794.[20]

It is very difficult to know what implications Wordsworth thought this new burst of writing had for the structure of his poem. The Climbing of Snowdon had been left on one side, presumably to form the conclusion of the new longer *Prelude*, but otherwise he was moving forward in an orderly chronological progression. Book VI—centering on the Crossing of the Alps, Cave of Yordas, the lines upon imagination, and the Simplon Pass[21]—asserted the primacy of imaginative power very much as Snowdon had done, showing it in the poet's second Long Vacation (1790) to have been unimpaired by Cambridge, and of course showing it at its height in spring 1804. The move into Book IX was an important one. Wordsworth may well have thought of himself merely as extending his French memories, but the introduction of politics into the poem offered the possibility of a new version of the Fall. Cambridge, though initially portrayed as the populous plain of experience, had proved merely 'a privileged world/Within a world, a midway residence' between youth and 'the conflicts of substantial life' (iii. 553ff.). The French visit of 1790 had similarly been protected from realities—by the speed of the tour, and by the abnormal situation:

> France standing on the top of golden hours,
> And human nature seeming born again.
>
> (vi. 353–4)

The Book IX descriptions of French politics in 1792 are the first true poetry of experience written for *The Prelude*. They have also the air—one can't say more—of being very close to biographical fact.

Wordsworth aged 21 seems to have arrived in Paris in

December 1791 with no sense of purpose, except to get away from family pressures and avoid taking a job, and no more than a vague general sympathy for the Revolution. He did the sights as a matter of course, and the poet looking back is able beautifully to catch the emptiness of the moment. 'Where silent zephyrs', he writes, mocking the trite poetic level on which he had then reacted to historic change,

> sported with the dust
> Of the Bastile I sate in the open sun
> And from the rubbish gathered up a stone,
> And pocketed the relick in the guise
> Of an enthusiast; yet, in honest truth . . .
> I looked for something which I could not find,
> Affecting more emotion than I felt.
>
> (ix. 63–71)

Very probably in Wordsworth's mind as he made his token gesture was the address to the Bastile in Cowper's *Task*, published only seven years before:

> Ye horrid towers, the abode of broken hearts;
> Ye dungeons and ye cages of despair,
> That monarchs have supplied from age to age
> With music such as suits their sovereign ears—
> The sighs and groans of miserable men!
> There's not an English heart that would not leap
> To hear that ye were fallen at last . . .
>
> (*Task*, v. 384–90)

Wordsworth may possibly have been aware that neither the fortress nor its razing to the dust had had any political significance, but in any case he responded habitually not to symbols and gestures but to people. Eighteen months before he had not found it difficult to join the delegates in dancing by the Rhône on their way back from Paris and the Fête de la Fédération:

> We rose at signal given, and formed a ring,
> And hand in hand danced round and round the board;
> All hearts were open, every tongue was loud
> With amity and glee. We bore a name

Honoured in France, the name of Englishmen,
And hospitably did they give us hail
As their forerunners in a glorious course;
And round and round the board they danced again.
(vi. 406–13)

It is a mark of his political naïvety in 1790–1 that Wordsworth would probably have shared with the rejoicing delegates, and with Cowper, an assumption that the Glorious Revolution of 1688 had created in England something like a just society.

Writing in 1804, though no longer a republican, the poet is shocked at having been quite so protected—

a parlour-shrub
When every bush and tree the country through
[Was] shaking to the roots . . .
(ix. 89–91)

Neither of the explanations he offers for not having noticed the workings of privilege is at all convincing. The scholars and gentlemen of Cambridge did not form a single community in which 'wealth and titles were in less esteem/Than talents and successful industry' (ix. 235–6): the scholars, like their tutors, were intent on bettering themselves through academic success and positions in the Church, the gentlemen were moneyed and had no such concerns.[22] And though Hawkshead may have retained an 'ancient homeliness', the claim scarcely to have seen anyone vested with respect by rank or wealth seems odd when the poet had been born in the largest and most elegant house in Cockermouth, and returned there duly for the holidays because his father was agent to one of the biggest land-owners in the country. There would have been plenty of social injustice about for those with eyes to see it. Except in rather standard literary contexts Wordsworth in fact seems scarcely to have questioned the *status quo* until at Blois in spring 1792 he came under the influence of Michel Beaupuy.[23] Curiously, despite his immense importance—no one save Coleridge made a greater impact on Wordsworth's thinking—Beaupuy seems very probably to have been introduced into the *Prelude* account as an afterthought.[24] At first it seems the poet wished to portray his sympathy for the French republicans as part of the natural course of events, the result of innate strength and favoured education. Even in its final shape Book IX introduces his royalist fellow-officers before Beaupuy, and shows Wordsworth as unaffected by their arguments before it reveals (by implication) that he had all along been hearing the alternative point of view. The impression created is a little confusing, and the account of Wordsworth's inherent republicanism becomes rather pointless in retrospect. One interesting result, however, of the way the material is presented, is that before reaching Beaupuy one meets his satanic opposite—the defender of the *ancien régime* who has been destroyed, where Beaupuy was exalted, by the times:

> One, reckoning by years,
> Was in the prime of manhood, and erewhile
> He had sate lord in many tender hearts,
> Though heedless of such honours now, and changed:
> His temper was quite mastered by the times,
> And they had blighted him, had eat away
> The beauty of his person, doing wrong
> Alike to body and to mind. His port,
> Which once had been erect and open, now
> Was stooping and contracted, and a face
> By nature lovely in itself, expressed,
> As much as any that was ever seen,
> A ravage out of season, made by thoughts
> Unhealthy and vexatious. At the hour,
> The most important of each day, in which
> The public news was read, the fever came,
> A punctual visitant, to shake this man,
> Disarmed his voice and fanned his yellow cheek
> Into a thousand colours. While he read,
> Or mused, his sword was haunted by his touch
> Continually, like an uneasy place
> In his own body.
>
> (ix. 143–64)

And so Wordsworth leaves him, his social standing threatened and personal confidence gone, fingering his sword for reassurance as a child will finger his penis. There is much of Godwin's broken Falkland about him; he is a sort of inverted borderer waiting for news, subject not to 'visitings/Of awful promise' but to the punctual visitation of fever, that can fan his cheek to a thousand unnatural colours, but cannot repair the 'ravage out of season'. Wordsworth's observation is nowhere more acute.

To such men there could be no greater contrast than Michel Beaupuy, similarly well-bred (he came from the minor nobility), but a dedicated patriot, and

> thence rejected by the rest,
> And with an oriental loathing spurned
> As of a different cast.
>
> (ix. 296–8)

If the royalist is an utterly defeated Satan, Beaupuy has something Christ-like about him. For Wordsworth he is an ideal, one who sacrificed rank and wealth, carried innocence into the world of experience, never betrayed his standards, and died fighting for his cause. Half-echoes of Chaucer's *General Prologue*—'A meeker man/Than this lived never', 'Somewhat vain he was,/ Or seemed so' (ix. 298–9, 320–1)—suggest that the poet is a little self-conscious in building up his formal portrait, and Beaupuy in fact comes through to us in a single vivid moment of response to social injustice:

> And when we chanced
> One day to meet a hunger-bitten girl
> Who crept along fitting her languid self
> Unto a heifer's motion—by a cord
> Tied to her arm, and picking thus from the lane
> Its sustenance, while the girl with her two hands
> Was busy knitting in a heartless mood
> Of solitude—and at the sight my friend
> In agitation said, ''Tis against *that*
> Which we are fighting', I with him believed
> Devoutly that a spirit was abroad
> Which could not be withstood, that poverty,
> At least like this, would in a little time
> Be found no more, that we should see . . .
> All institutes for ever blotted out
> That legalised exclusion . . .
> And finally, as sum and crown of all,
> Should see the people having a strong hand
> In making their own laws . . .
>
> (ix. 511–33)

Beaupuy was 36, an accomplished soldier, administrator, and philosopher as well; Wordsworth was 21, and had precious little accomplishment of any kind. No doubt they were drawn together by their isolation (Beaupuy as a patriot among royalists, Wordsworth as an Englishman abroad), and if Beaupuy was a little vain perhaps he was flattered by the emotional response that he roused in his disciple, and that comes through so strongly in Wordsworth's account of the starving girl. It is one of those pieces of writing that would seem inept if they didn't so obviously work. At first the girl is subject of the central relative clause, then with no grammatical transition the heifer turns out to have displaced her:

> a hunger-bitten girl
> Who crept along fitting her languid self
> Unto a heifer's motion—by a cord
> Tied to her arm, and picking thus from the lane
> Its sustenance . . .

No punctuation could contain or imply the poet's meaning, but we become aware through the movement of the syntax that the girl in her poverty and despair has yielded to the dominance of the heifer, which of course is feeding, while she is 'bitten' with hunger. The detail of the cord, not held and controlled, but tied to her as if she were the animal, brings home the cruelty of the situation. The heifer is the stronger, and in every way the luckier, of the two.

Wordsworth had not been moved by the grander gestures of the Revolution—by the razing of the Bastile, or the oratory of the National Assembly, to which it seems he had been introduced by a member (*EY* 71)—but with Beaupuy he had felt the rightness of the cause as a local human fact. Beaupuy's words, ' " 'Tis against *that*/Which we are fighting" ', express an emotion that has been unstated in the previous description; and the emotion, transferring itself to his companion, turns before our eyes to political idealism. Because he sees and shares Beaupuy's agitation, the Wordsworth of 1792 believes that everyone else will do the same, that a spirit is abroad that cannot be withstood, that poverty and privilege are about to disappear. Looking back, the poet is quite as moved by his former self as he is by the starving girl, but indulgence is not allowed to qualify his over-all position. By his commitment he had been self-doomed to the impotence and disappointment of the political innocent. Book IX in its original form of summer 1804 would have contained no signposts: the reader had yet to be told that the way ahead was 'ungenial, hard/To treat of, and forbidding in itself' (ix. 16–17). But history was there to do this job, as long as Wordsworth stuck to its expected course. His audience did not have to be told that revolutionary politics was an area in which the innocent would be duly punished for trespassing. The surprising elements in Wordsworth's treatment of his theme are the inclusion of *Vaudracour and Julia* (ix. 556–935), personal at one remove in that it touches in his relationship with Annette Vallon (as well as exemplifying the injustice of the *ancien régime* and need for revolution), and the honesty with which he records the fear, rage, bitterness, disillusion, and false hope he suffered after becoming a patriot.

The first half of Book X, which Wordsworth may be presumed to have composed before he left off writing for the summer, was originally a single unit as it is in *1850*. It is perhaps chiefly Robespierre's Book, but contains three magnificent studies of the poet himself, isolated in his political commitment, and subjected to extremes of emotion. Terror comes first, as he breaks his journey in Paris in October 1792. The room he sleeps in is 'high and lonely'—

a place of fear,
Unfit for the repose of night,
Defenceless as a wood where tigers roam . . .
(x. 80–2)

—and the city is quiet, but waiting for the return of violence:

The fear gone by
Pressed on me almost like a fear to come.
I thought of those September massacres,
Divided from me by a little month,
And felt and touched them, a substantial dread . . .
(x. 62–6)

Past becomes future as fear reverses the process of time, but still more strange and powerful is Wordsworth's *touching* of the Massacres. It is not that he doubts them, has with Thomas to prove them flesh and blood, but that the idea has taken on an extraordinary physical presence, a corporeality unusual even for him.[25] Reliving his substantial dread of the Massacres, Wordsworth produces five sudden purely apocalyptic lines of interior monologue that are quite unlike anything else he ever wrote:

> 'The horse is taught his manage, and the wind
> Of heaven wheels round and treads in his own steps;
> Year follows year, the tide returns again,
> Day follows day, all things have second birth;
> The earthquake is not satisfied at once'—
> And in such way I wrought upon myself,
> Until I seemed to hear a voice that cried
> To the whole city, 'Sleep no more!'
>
> (x. 70–7)

The horse is schooled by man against its nature to turn upon the spot (as Danton may induce spontaneous bloodshed to come round), and 'the wind of heaven', that should be freer still, wheels in its steps, constricted to the movements of a horse. In his nightmare reverie the poet can turn anything to evidence of cyclical return. Years, tides, days, add their more obvious corroboration, till the argument so commonly and tendentiously used for the Christian afterlife ('all things have second birth') betrays us suddenly into the power of insatiable violence: 'The earthquake is not satisfied at once.'

'The ease and light-heartedness of my youth were for ever gone', Godwin (or his hero) had written in *Caleb Williams, or Things As They Are Now* (1794), 'The voice of an irresistible necessity had commanded me to "sleep no more."'[26] Caleb had lost his innocence: as a result of inquiring too far, he was burdened for ever with the knowledge that his 'beneficent divinity', Falkland, who had seemed to embody every human quality, and in whom his own hopes rested for the future, was a murderer. The Revolution, Wordsworth's beneficent divinity, had in September 1792 become a murderer too—more than 1,000 prisoners, many of them not in fact royalists, had been taken from the prisons of Paris and butchered by the mob after farcical trials—and for Wordsworth too 'The ease and light-heartedness of . . . youth were for ever gone'. Back in England he was doomed, after the execution of Louis XVI in January 1793 and immediate declarations of war, to be a guiltless outcast (again like Caleb, though one shouldn't push the parallels too far):

> It was a grief—
> Grief call it not, 'twas any thing but that—
> A conflict of sensations without name,
> Of which he only who may love the sight
> Of a village steeple as I do can judge,
> When in the congregation, bending all
> To their great Father, prayers were offered up
> Or praises for our country's victories,
> And, mid the simple worshippers perchance
> I only, like an uninvited guest
> Whom no one owned, sate silent—shall I add,
> Fed on the day of vengeance yet to come!
>
> (x. 263–74)

The congregation bending all to *their* great Father stand for a harmony, ignorant but enviable, from which the poet is as firmly excluded as the Ancient Mariner (also burdened with knowledge that means he can never again fit back into the society from which he came). The 'conflict of sensations without name' included guilt—guilt for English loyalties transgressed, perhaps less acknowledged guilt by association for crimes in France—and in the background again is *Macbeth*: 'wherefore could not I pronounce "Amen"?' (II. ii. 31).

The prospective vengeance on which the poet feeds is presumably French victory, to be followed by the setting up of a revolutionary government in England. This was not to be, but Wordsworth did later have one moment of exultant revenge, as he heard, while crossing Levens Sands, the news of Robespierre's execution:

> Great was my glee of spirit, great my joy
> In vengeance, and eternal justice, thus
> Made manifest. 'Come now, ye golden times',

> Said I, forth-breathing on those open sands
> A hymn of triumph, 'as the morning comes
> Out of the bosom of the night, come ye.
> Thus far our trust is verified: behold,
> They who with clumsy desperation brought
> Rivers of blood, and preached that nothing else
> Would cleanse the Augean Stable, by the might
> Of their own helper have been swept away'.
>
> (x. 539–49)

It was a moment not just of personal vengeance, sweet though that was, but of hope suddenly renewed. The blood-river, as is shown by countless gory prints, started at the guillotine; it could, and did, cease to flow.[27] For Wordsworth and many other British radicals Robespierre was the false leader, the man whom it was convenient to think solely responsible for diverting the Revolution from its peaceful course. This first half of Book X is in fact very much about leadership. On the morning that followed his night of terror in Paris the poet had been greeted by hawkers 'Bawling, *Denunciation of the crimes/Of Maximilian Robespierre*' (x. 87–8); the broadsheet they were selling gave an account of Louvet's famous accusation in the Assembly, concluding in the words 'Je t'accuse d'avoir évidement marché au suprême pouvoir.'[28] Louvet, standing alone in the *Prelude* account against the forces of evil, takes on the role of Abdiel in *Paradise Lost*, but where Milton allows himself to bask in divine congratulations—'Servant of God, well done' (*PL* vi. 29)—Wordsworth's fantasies have no such fulfilment. He muses to himself, 'How much the destiny of man [has] still/Hung upon single persons' (x. 137–8), but knows the risk of perishing 'A poor mistaken and bewildered offering', with his reputation as a poet yet unmade (x. 194–201).

And so the opportunity is lost. Louvet is deserted by his friends—neither Wordsworth nor anyone else comes forward to be the man of destiny—evil triumphs (as it cannot do in *Paradise Lost*), ordains the Terror in France, and in England strengthens a reactionary government by seeming to show that change could lead only to violence. Unlike Satan, Robespierre is for a time permitted actual control; but Wordsworth's references as he builds up to the scene on Levens Sands show clearly that he wishes us to link the two figures. First there is a flash-back to 1790, and France apparently 'standing on the top of golden hours'. Wordsworth is introducing his serpent by taking us momentarily back to Paradise, and especially recalls 15 July, the day after the Fête de la Fédération, 'when through an arch that spanned the street,/A rainbow made of garish ornaments', he and Jones had

> walked, a pair of weary travellers,
> Along the town of Arras—place from which
> Issued that Robespierre, who afterwards
> Wielded the sceptre of the atheist crew.
>
> (x. 451–7)

The fallen angels singled out for Abdiel's attentions in the War in Heaven had similarly been dismissed as 'The atheist crew' (*PL* vi. 370) and Wordsworth's allusion is followed almost at once by a second Miltonic reference:

> O friend, few happier moments have been mine
> Through my whole life than that when first I heard
> That this foul tribe of Moloch was o'erthrown,
> And their chief regent levelled with the dust.[29]
>
> (x. 466–9)

Milton is thus very much in evidence, and it soon turns out that Wordsworth wishes to make broader connections than those between Robespierre and Satan, the guillotine and human-sacrifice. Before the news of Robespierre's death is heard, there is unexpectedly a close parallel to the dawn consecration scene of Book IV. Again the landscape has two levels, the upper one of mountains and indistinguishable clouds highlighted in Miltonic glory, and beneath it Wordsworth's own:

> [The] distant prospect among gleams of sky
> And clouds, and intermingled mountain-tops,
> In one inseparable glory clad—
> Creatures of one ethereal substance, met
> In consistory, like a diadem
> Or crown of burning seraphs, as they sit
> In the empyrean. Underneath this show
> Lay, as I knew, the nest of pastoral vales
> Among whose happy fields I had grown up . . .
>
> (x. 477–85)

If vows are not so explicitly made for the poet on this occasion, a reassuring confirmation of the earlier ones is offered by a voice from the grave. Among the pastoral vales lay Hawkshead and its grammar-school, and Wordsworth had that morning visited Cartmell Priory where his old headmaster was buried:

> A week, or little less, before his death
> He had said to me, 'My head will soon lie low';
> And when I saw the turf that covered him,
> After the lapse of full eight years, those words,
> With sound of voice, and countenance of the man,
> Came back upon me . . .
>
> (x. 500–5)

Taylor, though only 30, had been prepared for death, and chosen some lines from Gray to be inscribed on his headstone. 'And now', Wordsworth continues,

> Thus travelling smoothly o'er the level sands,
> I thought with pleasure of the verses graven
> Upon his tombstone, saying to myself
> 'He loved the poets, and if now alive
> Would have loved me, as one not destitute
> Of promise, nor belying the kind hope
> Which he had formed . . .'
>
> (x. 506–13)

As in the consecration scene ('On I walked/In blessedness, which even yet remains'), admiration for Milton's world, 'drenched in empyrean light', is followed in Wordsworth by a sense of his own vocation, and finally by unusual calm:

> Without me and within as I advanced
> All that I saw, or felt, or communed with,
> Was gentleness and peace.
>
> (x. 515–17)

It is in this context that he hears of Robespierre's execution, greeting the news with joy as the fulfilment of private vengeance, but also taking it for granted that eternal justice has prevailed and that golden times will now return to France. False hope is juxtaposed with true. There were to be no political solutions, as of course the audience is aware; and political dedication, however deeply felt, was secondary. Commitment to a life of the imagination had come far earlier, and been of far greater importance. In his fantasies about becoming a man of action Wordsworth had forgotten the sphere in which he truly had been singled out as leader and chosen son. Writing ten years later in May/June 1804 the poet is able quietly to assume that Taylor's confidence has been justified.

As the Book ends, and work on *The Prelude* is laid aside for the summer, Wordsworth aged 24 pursues his way along the coast where he had galloped as a boy. He is still framing delusive schemes for 'The mighty renovation' that will proceed (x. 556), but they are calmer now, and his presence amid the scenes of Book II is felt as a guarantee that older values will reassert themselves. Once more we have a version of the Fall that has no lasting adverse consequences, indeed one that the poet himself barely regards as a Fall. Beaupuy had been no tempter; and it had not been wrong to believe devoutly with him that a better future was in store. For a time, however, Wordsworth had mistaken the part that he himself had to play in bringing this future about. The mistake had been painful and potentially dangerous.

III. 'BIGOT TO A NEW IDOLATRY': IMAGINATION UNIMPAIRED (*1805*, XB AND XI)

'I saw the spring return', writes Wordsworth at the beginning of *1805*, Book XI, 'when I was dead/To deeper hope' (ll. 24–5), and in the slight, inevitable pause for the line-ending one feels the absoluteness of past despair.[30] He is looking back nine years to the spring of 1796 at Racedown:

The morning shines,
Nor heedeth man's perverseness; spring returns—
I saw the spring return, when I was dead
To deeper hope, yet had I joy for her
And welcomed her benevolence, rejoiced
In common with the children of her love,
Plants, insects, beasts in field, and birds in bower.
(xi. 22–8)

Biblical rhythms and phraseology are used, as elsewhere, to create a sense of the fitness of things. Man in his perverseness stands outside the harmony of seasonal change, renewal, but does not need to do so. The original text of *MS Z* is clearest in its wording:

> *So neither stillness, beauty or repose,*
> *Order or peace, were wanting for my good*
> In those distracted times: in Nature still
> Glorying, I found a counterpoise in her
> Which, when the spirit of evil was at height,
> Maintained for me a secret happiness.[31]

As a chosen son, a child of Nature's love, the poet had been offered a private order and peace, immunity from the nameless spirit of evil. It is a characteristic Wordsworthian assertion, and perhaps we should expect too the lines that follow:

> Her I resorted to, and loved so much
> I seemed to love as much as heretofore—
> *And yet* . . .
>
> (xi. 35–7)

Once again there is the conflict between Wordsworth's obstinate sense that nothing had ever gone wrong, and the structural needs of his poem that require him to show imagination (his own imaginative response to Nature) as having been impaired. The questions raised in this case are particularly interesting, for some form of crisis surely did take place in 1796, and if any version of the Fall can give coherence to the paradise-lost-and-regained pattern within the full-length *Prelude* it has to be this one.

Discussion must inevitably start from the climactic lines of X(b) in which Wordsworth, using in turn images of the operating-theatre and law-court, recalls the moment, or period, of crisis. The lines that surround these two striking and famous metaphors, however, need more attention than they usually get:

> a shock had then been given
> To old opinions, and the minds of all men
> Had felt it . . . my mind was both let loose,
> Let loose and goaded . . .
> from the first
> Having two natures in me (joy the one,
> The other melancholy), and withal
> A happy man, and therefore bold to look
> On painful things—slow, somewhat, too, and stern

In temperament—I took the knife in hand,
And, stopping not at parts less sensitive,
Endeavoured with my best of skill to probe
The living body of society
Even to the heart. I pushed without remorse
My speculations forward; yea, set foot
On Nature's holiest places.

(x. 860–3, 867–78)

Wordsworth in March 1796 had been working on an imitation of Juvenal which could well be said to 'probe/The living body of society', and certainly shows a goaded mind reacting to 'old opinions';[32] but 'Nature's holiest places' could have nothing to do with so superficial and external a reading—

Of genius, power,
Creation, and divinity itself,
I have been speaking, for my theme has been
What passed within me.

(iii. 171–4)

At the centre of the living body of society, and at the heart too of his own hopes for the future both in 1796 and at the time of writing, was the individual. Wordsworth needed to be strong enough to look at painful things because in effect he was seeking the causes of human degradation 'in the place/The holiest that [he] knew of—[his] own soul' (x. 379–80).

It is with this in mind that we should read on into the account of desperation and despair, as Wordsworth portrays his former self attempting rationally to establish *proof* that all is well:

Time may come
When some dramatic story may afford
Shapes livelier to convey to thee, my friend,
What then I learned—or think I learned—of truth,
And the errors into which I was betrayed
By present objects, and by reasonings false
From the beginning, inasmuch as drawn
Out of a heart which had been turned aside
From Nature by external accidents,
And which was thus confounded more and more,
Misguiding and misguided.

(x. 878–88)

It is nice and clear that the Fall in this case lies in turning aside from Nature, but one could equally well read 'nature' with a small 'n'—the poet's own nature. It can have been only two months since he had written of his entry into London, 'Great God!/That aught *external* to the living mind/Should have such mighty sway' (viii. 700–2; W.'s italics), and 'external accidents' in the passage quoted are political creeds and events that are extraneous both to the natural world, and to the natural order of the mind. The image of the law-court catches brilliantly a mood of frenzied introspection:

Thus I fared,
Dragging all passions, notions, shapes of faith,
Like culprits to the bar, suspiciously
Calling the mind to establish in plain day
Her titles and her honours, now believing,
Now disbelieving, endlessly perplexed
With impulse, motive, right and wrong, the ground
Of moral obligation—what the rule,
And what the sanction—till, demanding *proof*,
And seeking it in everything, I lost
All feeling of conviction, and, in fine,
Sick, wearied out with contrarieties,
Yielded up moral questions in despair,
And for my future studies, as the sole
Employment of the inquiring faculty,
Turned towards mathematics, and their clear
And solid evidence.

(x. 888–904)

As to what really happened there is almost no 'clear/And solid evidence'. A letter of 21 March 1796 to William Mathews shows Wordsworth apparently in high spirits. He asks for books, condemns Southey (whom he had earlier liked) as 'certainly a coxcomb',[33] predicts an Ovidian metamorphosis of himself and Dorothy into cabbages, sends messages to friends in London, and concludes: 'Give me some news about the theatre. I have attempted to read Holcroft's *Man of Ten Thousand*, but such stuff! Demme, hey, humph!' One fact does, however, stand out. The second edition of *Political Justice* has just arrived:

I have received from Montagu, Godwyn's second edition. I expect to find the work much improved. I cannot say that I have been encouraged in this hope by the perusal of the second preface, which is all I have yet looked into. Such a piece of barbarous writing I have not often seen. It contains scarce one sentence decently written. I am surprized to find such gross faults in a writer who has had so much practice in composition.

(*EY* 170–1)

No further letters are preserved from this period; in fact almost the next positive news that we have of Wordsworth is when on 7 June he has supper in London with Godwin himself. As always, Godwin's Diary is non-committal; what they discussed we cannot know.

There is much in Godwin's thinking that Wordsworth would have found inevitably sympathetic. Hazlitt's definition of his ideals in *The Spirit of the Age* is at once elegant and generous:

The author of *Political Justice* took abstract reason for the rule of conduct, and abstract good for its end. He places the human mind on an elevation, from which it commands a view of the whole line of moral consequences; and requires it to conform its acts to the larger and more enlightened conscience which it has thus acquired. He absolves man from the gross and narrow ties of sense, custom, authority, private and local attachment, in order that he may devote himself to the boundless pursuit of universal benevolence.

(Howe, xi. 18–19)

Hazlitt's prose is gently ironic; he knows the weaknesses of Godwin's system, yet chooses to praise the aspirations:

The fault, then, of Mr Godwin's philosophy, in one word, was too much ambition. . . . He conceived too nobly of his fellows . . . he raised the standard of morality above the reach of humanity.

(Howe, xi. 18)

Very much the same could be said of Wordsworth—though the wish to conceive so nobly of his fellows may at times have been stronger than his power to do so.

Wordsworth may or may not have given the advice that Hazlitt recalls, to a student of the Inner Temple—'Throw aside your books of chemistry . . . and read Godwin on Necessity' (Howe, xi. 17)—but it was certainly the necessitarianism of *Political Justice*, brought over from Godwin's years as a dissenting minister, that gave the work its immediate appeal:

Truth is in reality single and uniform. There must in the nature of things be one best form of government, which all intellects, sufficiently roused from the slumber of savage ignorance, will be irresistibly incited to approve.

(*PJ* i. 181–2)

Shaken by the execution of Louis XVI on 21 January 1793, and by the French declaration of war ten days later, English liberals had every reason to be grateful for a book that came out in mid-February telling them that progress was 'in the nature of things', and would be made not through violent social change, but through the innate rationality of man. He

> who regards all things past, present and to come as links of an indissoluble chain, will, as often as he recollects this comprehensive view, be superior to the tumult of passion; and will reflect upon the moral concerns of mankind with the same clearness of perception, the same unalterable firmness of judgement, and the same tranquillity as we are accustomed to do upon the truths of geometry. (*PJ* i. 316–17)

The central democratic ideals of *Political Justice* had been current among followers of the Revolution,[34] but not the comprehensive view that could stand 'superior to the tumult of passion'. Wordsworth's personal need for such reassurance was heightened by first-hand experience of post-revolutionary politics, and by separation from Annette and Caroline. His *Letter to the Bishop of Llandaff* depends on Thomas Paine, and was probably written too early in the spring to show Godwin's influence;[35] but *Salisbury Plain* of late summer 1793 ends in a call to British 'Heroes of Truth' to raise undaunted, and 'Resistless in [their] might, the herculean mace/Of Reason' (Gill, 38, ll. 543–4). That Wordsworth at this stage became a Godwinian is clear from two letters of May and June 1794, that show him set on founding a new monthly miscellany, to be named *The Philanthropist*. 'You know perhaps already', he writes to his intended co-editor, Mathews, in the first of these, 'that I am of that odious class of men called democrats, and of that class I shall for ever continue' (*EY* 119). He is, he says two weeks later, 'a determined enemy to every species of violence'; he wishes to avert revolution, and work through 'gradual and constant reform'; 'the enlightened friend of mankind' should diffuse 'a knowledge of those rules of political justice, from which the farther any government deviates the more effectually must it defeat the object for which government was ordained' (*EY* 124). One did not need to capitalize or underline the words 'political justice' in 1794.

Wordsworth seems actually to have met Godwin for the first time on 27 February 1795. We hear nothing of their conversations, but they met ten times before Wordsworth left

London at the end of August. His expectation that the second edition of *Political Justice* would be an improvement suggests that he had been impressed by the author, and the new version of *Salisbury Plain* in the autumn confirms that Godwin's influence is still strong.[36] Wordsworth's next two major works in fact bracket the period of crisis described in *The Prelude*. In each the central figure is Godwinian, but the sailor of *Adventures on Salisbury Plain* (November 1795), though a murderer, has been driven to crime by social injustice, and is correctly benevolent, whereas Rivers of *The Borderers* (November 1796–March 1797) exists to show how the rationalist ideal of *Political Justice* is unbalanced by denial of emotional values. Coleridge, who had never truly been his disciple, defined the faults of Godwin's theory in terms of New Testament Christianity: 'whatever is just in it, is more forcibly recommended in the Gospel, and whatever is new is absurd' (*CC* i. 164). Instead of a theory of general benevolence, to which personal relationship was a hindrance, he offered the Hartleyan view of love radiating outwards from the individual consciousness:

> Jesus knew our nature—and that expands like the circles of a lake—the love of our friends, parents and neighbours lead[s] us to the love of our country to the love of all mankind. The intensity of private attachment encourages, not prevents, universal philanthropy.
>
> (*CC* i. 163)

Wordsworth had no such Christian framework for his thinking, but only at a time of great emotional stress, or intellectual enthusiasm, could he have disagreed with Coleridge's final sentence.[37] After his reunion with Dorothy at Racedown in autumn 1795 he must have been more than ever aware that Godwin's theory cut across his own experience. Presumably in 1793 the ideal of general benevolence had been taken pretty much for granted by one who in France had become a patriot and given his heart to the people (*1805*, ix. 123–6). But for Wordsworth even republicanism had had its origins in personal relationship, and as the inspiration of Beaupuy became more distant, and political events more discouraging, it was likely that commitment to theory would grow weaker.

Looking back in *1805*, Wordsworth is very satirical and very clear about the attractions that Godwin had once held for him. He distinguishes between an early period of optimism in which thorough assimilation of Jacobin writings had hardly been called for—

> Meantime,
> As from the first, wild theories were afloat,
> Unto the subtleties of which at least,
> I had but lent a careless ear—assured
> Of this, that time would soon set all things right,
> Prove that the multitude had been oppressed,
> And would be so no more.

—and a later, more harassed time,

> when events
> Brought less encouragement, and unto these
> The immediate proof of principles no more
> Could be entrusted . . .
>
> (x. 773–82)

Robespierre's death in August 1794 was the last event to bring encouragement; the Terror ceased at once, but new policies failed to put a stop to the French invasions of foreign territory that seemed to Wordsworth and other radicals such a betrayal of the Revolution.[38] 'This was the time', he writes,

> when, all things tending fast
> To depravation, the philosophy
> That promised to abstract the hopes of man
> Out of his feelings, to be fixed thenceforth
> For ever in a purer element,
> Found ready welcome.
>
> (x. 805–10)

The mockery is very light, and directed quite as much against his former self as at Godwin:

> Tempting region that
> For zeal to enter and refresh herself,
> Where passions had the privilege to work,
> And never hear the sound of their own names . . .
>
> (x. 810–14)

Wordsworth's tones are disillusioned yet amused. Reason is a 'purer element', a 'tempting region', a paradise of self-deception where the emotions work unnamed, and therefore unimpeded. The lines that follow, though claiming to be spoken more in charity, become increasingly sharp in their ridicule of Godwin's positions:

> What delight!—
> How glorious!—in self-knowledge and self-rule
> To look through all the frailties of the world,
> And, with a resolute mastery shaking off
> The accidents of nature, time, and place,
> That make up the weak being of the past,
> Build social freedom on its only basis:
> The freedom of the individual mind,
> Which, to the blind constraint of general laws
> Superior, magisterially adopts
> One guide—the light of circumstances, flashed
> Upon an independent intellect.
>
> (x. 818–29)

After the poet's initial hamming, the satire is beautifully controlled—and it needs to be, if the writing is to deflect obvious comparisons between Godwinian arrogance and Wordsworthian egotistical solitude. The passage stresses again and again the folly of the individual, the disparity between his assumption of power and powerless actuality. 'Self-knowledge' he clearly does not possess (no one would expect him to do so after the ironic 'How glorious!'); 'self-*rule*' is another matter, but confers no right to survey and judge the kingdoms of the world; 'resolute mastery' might be fine in itself, but has no control over nature, time, or place, and cannot change the past; it is true in a way (and a Wordsworthian one) that the basis of social freedom is 'the individual mind', but not when it adopts a posture of superiority, regarding general laws as 'blind constraint', and 'magisterially' assuming that nothing need be taken into account bar such circumstances as happen to penetrate its unwarranted seclusion. As has frequently been pointed out, the final lines of the passage come from *The Borderers* (1796–7). Rivers, who derives his ideas from Godwin and his function from Iago, is congratulating Mortimer, who, responding merely to the light of circumstances, has left an innocent, aged, blind, loving, and saintly man to die alone on a heath:

> You have obeyed the only law that wisdom
> Can ever recognize: the immediate law
> Flashed from the light of circumstances
> Upon an independent intellect.
>
> (III. v. 30–3)

Wordsworth committed no murders, but the situation to which he seems to have awakened during the crisis period of spring 1796 was analogous to Mortimer's when duped by abstraction and apparent rationality. In his desperate soul-searching, 'passions, notions, shapes of faith' are dragged to the bar, and the court-room image takes one back to the recurrent dreams in which the poet himself (or the poet *as a whole*) had been on trial:

> Through months, through years, long after the last beat
> Of those atrocities . . .
> I scarcely had one night of quiet sleep,
> Such ghastly visions had I of despair,
> And tyranny, and implements of death,
> And long orations which in dreams I pleaded
> Before unjust tribunals, with a voice
> Labouring, a brain confounded, and a sense
> Of treachery and desertion in the place
> The holiest that I knew of—my own soul.
>
> (x. 370–80)

It is not at all difficult to believe that Wordsworth is recalling an actual nightmare. Consciousness that the tribunals are unjust is irrelevant because the dreamer is self-betrayed, convicted in his own eyes of some deeper unspecified guilt. Something of this frightening dream illogic is carried over into the image in which the poet presents conflict in his waking self. Insofar as he is the prisoner, he is again in the right; but now he is his own prosecutor, Godwinian reason taking in this psychomachy the part of Robespierre's tribunals. Innocence cannot avail the 'passions, notions, shapes of faith', because obviously they have no rational language in which to demonstrate, '*establish in plain day*', proof of their right to exert an influence within the republic of the mind. The result must be nightmare, the madness of self-division. Just as Wordsworth's identification with the popular cause in France makes it impossible for him to defend himself, however unjust the tribunal which in the name of the people accuses him, so his passionate wish that what Godwin says shall be true gives reason its power to call emotion to the bar.[39]

There seems to be little doubt that the *Prelude* lines evoke a time of painful re-assessment, perhaps of nervous breakdown, occasioned by Wordsworth's reading of the second edition of *Political Justice*. It could well be that he had not read the book properly before, and had not experienced the full force of its denial of the emotional values on which his own stability was based. But whether he had or not, he was now confronted in a way that he felt unable to ignore by the fact that 'passions', 'notions' (ideas, perhaps in this context sentiments, opinions), 'shapes of faith' (both external 'forms of beauty' and their images within the mind), were outlawed by Godwin's system. It would be most interesting to know whether the two men argued when they met on 7 June, and whether the four meetings of 1796 were different in character from those of the previous year.[40] *The Prelude*, of course, does not deal in such matters; what it does tell us is, characteristically, that though Wordsworth's imagination had seemed to be much impaired, the change had only been temporary—Dorothy and Nature had 'Maintained for [him] a saving intercourse/With [his] true self':

> then it was
> That the belovèd woman in whose sight
> Those days were passed—now speaking in a voice
> Of sudden admonition, like a brook
> That does but cross a lonely road; and now
> Seen, heard and felt, and caught at every turn,
> Companion never lost through many a league—
> Maintained for me a saving intercourse
> With my true self (for, though impaired, and changed
> Much, as it seemed, I was no further changed
> Than as a clouded not a waning moon);
> She, in the midst of all, preserved me still
> A poet, made me seek beneath that name
> My office upon earth, and nowhere else.
>
> (x. 907–20)

Dorothy's intervention was quite a positive one: she *made*, not bade, her brother pursue his role as poet rather than activist, political journalist, or whatever else as a Godwinian he might have become; and her 'voice/Of sudden admonition' connects her to other admonishing figures, notably the Leech Gatherer and London beggar, who have a border wisdom to offer. It is important too that her presence at this moment when Wordsworth himself is 'bewildered and engulphed' is conveyed in terms of the river of imagination of Book XIII. As the brook that is 'Seen, heard and felt, and caught at every turn' she not only reminds her brother of his true self (the promised effect of her wild eyes in *Tintern Abbey*), but momentarily takes on that selfhood, enabling the fallen consciousness of the poet to be in contact with its own unfallen state. As a result he himself again becomes the river:

> And lastly, Nature's self, by human love
> Assisted, through the weary labyrinth
> *Conducted me again to open day*,
> Revived the feelings of my earlier life,
> Gave me that strength and knowledge full of peace,
> Enlarged, and never more to be disturbed . . .
>
> (x. 921–6)

The strongest verbal link is with xiii. 175–6, 'followed it to light/ And open day', but Wordsworth is of course *re*surfacing ('Conducted me *again* to open day'), and the passage corresponds in the final retrospect with the moment when the river of imagination, no longer 'bewildered and engulphed', rises

> once more
> With strength, reflecting in its solemn breast
> The works of man, and face of human life . . .
>
> (xiii. 179–81)

There can be little doubt that this tribute to Dorothy as the brook was in fact inserted in Book X *after* the writing of XIII;[41] its implications are therefore of special interest as they show what the poet assumed the shape of his poem to be, on looking back.

One question stands out as peculiarly difficult to answer. If the crisis of spring 1796 is the central Fall of the full-length *Prelude*, and if the poet's imagination (impaired only as a clouded moon) recovers so fully through the ministrations of Dorothy and Nature that we are told at this stage in the poem that he has been given 'knowledge full of peace . . . *never more to be disturbed*', what is to be the function of the 'spots of time'? In *1799* the 'spots' had provided the rationale of the poem; in the five-Book *Prelude* the extended sequence had formed the climax, placed after the Ascent of Snowdon, not before, and bringing the poem full circle in a return to childhood experience to explain the adult power that Snowdon exemplified; in *1805* the positioning is once again impressive, but the effect is rather muted. If the 'renovating virtue' of the 'spots' was to be given its full weight, they had to be portrayed as responsible for the poet's emergence from the crisis of X(b). Wordsworth's tribute to his sister as the companionable brook who had 'Maintained for [him] a saving intercourse/With [his] true self' is not perhaps incompatible with their being so; after all she worked in conjuction with Nature, and her very presence would turn the mind to childhood memories. But the 'spots' are not introduced until half-way through Book XI, and from a structural point of view it is no help to have a statement 350 lines earlier that Dorothy and Nature have between them already given the poet strength that has lasted till the time of writing.

The introduction to Book XI, though it takes the reader back to the crisis period of 1796, does little to make connections. Wordsworth is brooding over past despondence—'I saw the spring return when I was dead/To deeper hope'—not structuring his poem. His present pleasure in Nature leads him to reflect that he had found

> a counterpoise in her
> Which, when the spirit of evil was at height,
> Maintained for [him] a secret happiness . . .
> (xi. 32–4)

The 'spots' and their restorative virtue are not yet in sight, but the crisis is dwindling in the poet's mind: Nature had apparently kept him secretly balanced all the time. As always, there are second thoughts:

> Her I resorted to, and loved so much
> I seemed to love as much as heretofore—

And yet this passion, fervent as it was,
Had suffered change; how could there fail to be
Some change, if merely hence . . .

(xi. 35–9)

Surely, one feels, Wordsworth must at this stage bring himself to say that rationalist conditioning had made him less receptive. But he cannot do it. The verse totters into bathos as once more he refuses to concede that his imagination has ever been actively impaired:

if merely hence, that years of life
Were going on, and with them loss or gain
Inevitable, sure alternative?

(xi. 39–41)

The shilly-shallying is quite unnecessary—doubly so in fact, as the whole introduction is a late addition.[42] The original opening had been at line 42 where Wordsworth turns, with obvious appropriateness, to consider the internal conflict he had felt as Godwin's disciple:

This history, my friend, hath chiefly told
Of intellectual power from stage to stage
Advancing hand in hand with love and joy,
And of imagination teaching truth
Until that natural graciousness of mind
Gave way to over-pressure of the times
And their disastrous issues.

(xi. 42–8)

The law-court metaphor of X(b), in which passions were dragged like culprits to the bar, had evoked with fitting violence the moment of crisis, as Godwinian reason—the prosecutor—lost control. For the preceding period, in which emotion had been wrongly but firmly suppressed, Wordsworth chooses a calmer image, with lulling literary associations which the eye and mind slide over rather too readily:

What availed,
When spells forbade the voyager to land,
The fragrance which did ever and anon
Give notice of the shore, from arbours breathed

Of blessed sentiment and fearless love?
What did such sweet remembrances avail—
Perfidious then, as seemed—what served they then?
My business was upon the barren seas,
My errand was to sail to other coasts.
Shall I avow that I had hope to see
(I mean that future times would surely see)
The man to come parted as by a gulph
From him who had been?—

(xi. 48–60)

Afloat on the barren sea of Godwinian philosophy, resolutely ignoring signals from the shores of loving relationship (letters, perhaps, from Annette and Dorothy), the poet is a would-be political borderer, crossing the gulf of time to the coasts of futurity. The parenthesis, 'I mean that future times would surely see', is an interesting self-correction. In fact it mirrors exactly a change to be seen in Godwin himself, as he moved away from a confidence (found chiefly in the earlier parts of the first edition of *Political Justice*) that there would be a speedy and successful revolution in England, to a more cautious view in later editions that truth would finally prevail.[43] Given his commitment to French revolutionary politics, Wordsworth could have no doubt of the need for change, but 'the herculean mace of Reason' was not a weapon that he could take up without sacrifice. In the name of a cause to which he was emotionally committed, he had to cut himself off from emotion. Personal attachment must go; and with it, rootedness in 'the great family' of the past, and even his admiration for the poets (whose portrayal of man had been of course anything but reasonable):

Thus strangely did I war against myself;
A bigot to a new idolatry,
Did like a monk who hath forsworn the world
Zealously labour to cut off my heart
From all the sources of her former strength . . .

(xi. 74–8)

The Wordsworth of 1793–6 becomes in the lines that follow a destructive rationalist Prospero, and the poet of 1805 places defiantly beside Godwin's his own alternative creed:

> And as, by simple waving of a wand,
> The wizard instantaneously dissolves
> Palace or grove, even so did I unsoul
> As readily by syllogistic words
> (Some charm of logic, ever within reach)
> Those mysteries of passion which have made,
> And shall continue evermore to make—
> In spite of all that reason hath performed,
> And shall perform, to exalt and to refine—
> One brotherhood of all the human race . . .
>
> (xi. 79–88)

In the poet's carefully parallel structures reason is given her due, but finally affronted, when the brotherhood that Godwin had ascribed to man as rational being is derived instead from 'mysteries of passion'.

With the 'spots of time' sequence Wordsworth brought over from the conclusion to the five-Book *Prelude* a version of xi. 96–256, in which he had attempted a year earlier to show the impoverishment of imaginative response in a pre-Godwinian context. One passage reads a little incongruously in its new surroundings, as it opposes two kinds of reason (in fact the Kantian *Vernunft* and *Verstand*), neither of them to be equated with the reason of *Political Justice*;[44] but on the whole the transfer is made rather successfully. In the five-Book poem Wordsworth, though conscious of the need to show imagination as impaired before its restoration through the 'spots', had never adequately explained why it should have been so. Self-accusations of judging Nature according to the picturesque, or looking for meagre novelty, had carried no conviction because no cause had been suggested for such unWordsworthian behaviour. The tyranny of the eye, and application of 'critic rules/Or barren intermeddling subtleties', become quite credible, however, when seen as an extension of the Godwinian denial of feelings. Mary Hutchinson's appearance under an implied date of 1793–6 is anachronistic,[45] but useful in that she stands for the possibility of a mind never seduced away from the paths of Nature. Not, of course, that Wordsworth in this sequence shows his own mind at all consistently as having been seduced. As in their original context, the lines have their hasty retractions: 'this,/Although a strong infection of the age,/Was never much *my* habit' (xi. 155–7);

'Gladly here'

> Would I endeavour to unfold the means
> Which Nature studiously employs to thwart
> This tyranny . . .
>
> (xi. 175–9)

That Wordsworth should preserve his earlier vacillations is not very surprising, that he should have written new ones into the immediate introduction to the 'spots of time' does seem rather odd. *MS W* shows the five-Book *Prelude* to have been quite brisk at this point:

> In truth this malady of which I speak
> Though aided by the times, whose deeper sound
> Without my knowledge sometimes might perchance
> Make rural Nature's milder minstrelsies
> Inaudible, did never take in me
> Deep root . . .
>
> (*1805*, xi. 256n.)

In *1805*, though he is now in a position to offer a single, clear-cut reason why his imagination should have needed renovation, he becomes suddenly terrified of appearing too specific:

> In truth this degradation—howsoe'er
> Induced, effect in whatsoe'er degree
> Of custom, that prepares such wantonness
> As makes the greatest things give way to least,
> Or any other cause that hath been named,
> Or, lastly, aggravated by the times,
> Which with their passionate sounds might often make
> The milder minstrelsies of rural scenes
> Inaudible—was transient.

The poetry is dithering. Fortunately the rest of the passage says what it means, and says it clearly—

> I had felt
> Too forcibly, too early in my life,
> Visitings of imaginative power
> For this to last: I shook the habit off
> Entirely and for ever, and again

In Nature's presence stood, as I stand now,
A sensitive and a *creative* soul.
(xi. 242–56; W.'s italics)

—but it is extraordinary that a great poet, leading into the great central statement of his work, which had been carefully set aside for a particular structural purpose, should fall back upon 'Or any other cause that hath been named', and cap it with 'Or, lastly . . .'.

When all is said and done, the paradise-lost-and-regained structure of *The Prelude* is never very marked. One is left wondering why after trying so hard to manufacture a Fall in the five-Book poem Wordsworth should have made so little of it in *1805* when he had one ready to hand. Is the answer perhaps that as a matter of biographical fact his imagination never had been seriously impaired? The malady, we are assured, never took deep hold, the degradation was transient; the poet could well have become a bigot to the new idolatry of reason, and ceased for a time to value responsiveness, without ever losing the capacity to respond. That he in deference to Godwin's views at any stage wilfully ignored the 'fragrance' of human relationship (xi. 48–56) is barely credible; the most that can easily be believed is that the ideal of Nature was temporarily displaced by his need, for political and personal reasons, to accept a rationalist optimism. Such acceptance was in its way a Fall, but Wordsworth was conscious of having emerged from the crisis to which it led, in spring 1796, as a result of Dorothy and the Dorset countryside near Racedown, not the 'spots of time'—which after all we know to have provided their help in a quite different situation nearly three years later.[46] Finally the poem depends more on Wordsworth's sense of having been, *and stayed*, a chosen son, than it does on the Miltonic structure that he tries—sometimes quite hard—to impose:

I shook the habit off
Entirely and for ever, and again
In Nature's presence stood, *as I stand now*,
A sensitive and a *creative* soul.

And yet of course there had been losses, and in one sense *The Prelude* does concern an imagination impaired—or rather, one that fears that it may be so. The Wordsworth who completed the poem in 1804–5 was preoccupied with loss: loss of unmediated pleasure, loss of primal vision, loss of the inspired secondary vision of Alfoxden. It is interesting to ask why, aside from the vying with Milton, he wanted to impose on his work a pattern of Fall and redemption. In part the answer may be that he was acting out his wish that present loss too should lead to renewal, but in addition there was the curiously dominant background presence of *Tintern Abbey*. Looking back in July 1798 Wordsworth had seen his life as a pattern in which enviable unthinking innocence was followed by experience and concomitant loss, and finally by a sadder, wiser vision that took into account the music of humanity. He had made no reference to rationalism or to other versions of the Fall, and if one wishes to be pedantic one can see that he had blurred his time-scheme, but the pattern he offers is broadly accurate. At that moment, though his belief in the One Life was perhaps already slackening, he could feel that he had won through.[47] But soon the confidence of spring 1798 came itself to seem a thing of the past, and *Tintern Abbey* became a standard against which new positions had to be measured. In these circumstances it is not surprising that Wordsworth should wish to impose its no longer relevant structure upon his life, not surprising that he should fail to do so, and not surprising either that loss should find its true expression not within the narrative of *The Prelude*, but in moments of border vision. The poem's subject, or material, may be the past growth of the poet's mind, but its greatness lies in a refraction of the needs, strains, inspirations of that mind at the time of writing—above all perhaps of the tension between Wordsworth's sense of loss and his obstinate sense of election:

> Oh mystery of man, from what a depth
> Proceed thy honours! I am lost, but see
> In simple childhood something of the base
> On which thy greatness stands . . .
> The days gone by
> Come back upon me from the dawn almost
> Of life; the hiding-places of my power
> Seem open, I approach, and then they close . . .
> (xi. 328–37)

Thus far the lines belong to February 1804 (and the five-Book *Prelude*); a year later Wordsworth was to add,

> I see by glimpses now, when age comes on
> May scarcely see at all; and I would give
> While yet we may, as far as words can give,
> A substance and a life to what I feel:
> I would enshrine the spirit of the past
> For future restoration.
>
> (xi. 337–42)

The need to shore up the future against the assaults of time was becoming increasingly urgent.[48] Loss could still be turned to gain, enshrined in poetry of unimpaired imaginative power, but the poet was by now distressingly aware of the shape of things to come.

Chapter 9

If Upon Mankind He Looks (*1805*, Books VIII and VII)

The lighted shops of the Strand and Fleet Street, the innumerable trades, tradesmen and customers, coaches, wagons, playhouses, all the bustle and wickedness round about Covent Garden . . . the sun shining upon the houses and pavements, the print shops, the *old book* stalls, parsons cheap'ning books, coffee houses, steams of soups from kitchens, the pantomimes—London itself, a pantomime and a masquerade—all these things work themselves into my mind and feed me without the power of satiating me. The wonder of these sights impells me into night-walks about her crowded streets, and I often shed tears in the motley Strand . . .

(Lamb to Wordsworth, 1801)

Wordsworth, who for some reason never wrote much in the summer, took four months' rest from *The Prelude* between early June and October 1804. Dorothy claimed that he was inspired to start work again by a Cowper poem sent him by the Beaumonts;[1] he himself puts the inspiration down, more whimsically, to a choir of robins sent to announce the arrival of 'their rough lord', a Spenserian personified Winter. Either way, he begins by taking stock. The passage in which he does so needs rather careful reading:

> Five years are vanished since I first poured out,
> Saluted by that animating breeze
> Which met me issuing from the city's walls,
> A glad preamble to this verse. I sang
> Aloud in dithyrambic fervour, deep
> But short-lived uproar, like a torrent sent
> Out of the bowels of a bursting cloud

Down Scawfell or Blencathara's rugged sides,
A waterspout from heaven. But 'twas not long
Ere the interrupted strain broke forth once more,
And flowed awhile in strength; then stopped for years—
Not heard again until a little space
Before last primrose-time.

(vii. 1–13)

Wordsworth is misrepresenting the course of *Prelude* composition, as he has to do if the Preamble (*1805*, i. 1–54) is to be offered as the poem's starting-point; but within the framework of this misrepresentation he is sticking very close to the truth. Thus, he accurately dates the Preamble back five years (from October 1804 to November 1799), he rightly distinguishes between an original torrent (*1799*, Part I, written October 1798–January 1799) and the second burst of composition (Part II; September–December 1799), and he marks the period of silence, or virtual silence, between the completion of *1799* and the beginning of work on the five-Book *Prelude* in January 1804. On the other hand, in order to portray the Preamble as belonging to the original period of composition he has to shorten his time-sequence by almost a quarter, the two Parts of *1799* (with the gap between them) being fitted by implication into 1800–3, together with the interval when the poet's strain was 'stopped for years'.

Wordsworth is writing in order to get himself started again, looking back over past phases of work in order to gain impetus that will take him into a new one.[2] It is interesting to ask where at this moment in autumn 1804 he thought his poem was going. The lines quoted above form part of an introduction that was designed at first not for Book VII, 'Residence in London', but for VIII, the 'Retrospect' of childhood. As the introduction stands in the original drafts of *MS Y* it ends in lines finally used in Book XIII that contain some very important implications. 'The last night's genial feeling', Wordsworth writes, 'overflows upon this morning',

efficacious more
By reason that my song must now return,
If she desert not her appointed path,
Back into Nature's bosom. Since the time
When with reluctance I withdrew from France

The story hath demanded less regard
To time and place; and where I lived, and how,
Hath been no longer scrupulously traced.[3]

Many questions go unanswered: how far had Wordsworth planned his song's appointed path? where was it to go after returning to Nature's bosom in Book VIII? how, and how soon, did he at this stage expect to link through to Snowdon and the 'spots of time' (set aside in March, after forming the conclusion to the five-Book *Prelude*)? On the other hand, certain details become clear. The line 'When with reluctance I withdrew from France' refers to x. 188–9, 'In this frame of mind/Reluctantly to England I returned', and establishes that before the summer's break Wordsworth had written versions of Book IX and the first half of X (revolutionary France in 1792, and the non-sequential account of his life back in England in the next year and a half). By the same token it appears not just that VIII must have been the first Book to be written in the autumn, but that it was intended to *follow* the French experiences. Finally, it seems almost certain that VII, with its full-scale treatment of London, was not at this stage a part of Wordsworth's thinking.

In the event, however, there was a change of plan, and Book VII was written immediately after VIII. At first glance the two Books have nothing in common—VIII concerning childhood in the Lake District, VII London at the age of 21. They are connected, however, by the fact that each in its different way is static, a pause in the forward movement of the poem,[4] and because they both examine, or reveal, the poet's none-too-easy relationship to his fellow human-beings. Wordsworth presumably started out on VIII because the political commitment he had been describing in the French Books reminded him that there had been little concern in the poem with men as individuals. An effort had been made to show the dawning of human-heartedness during the Hawkshead summer vacation in Book IV, but Wordsworth seems now to have felt a need to trace the origins of love of man as well as love of Nature in his childhood. In effect VIII was to be the counterpart of Book I, establishing the primacy of relationship as Book I had established (and XI would reiterate) that of creative response to the outside world. These twin positives would then be led through to a climax in which the higher, 'intellectual' or spiritual, love was shown to be inseparable from imagination.

Judged by Wordsworth's own frequently stated intentions, VIII is not a success. The shepherds chosen to show how the poet came to feel 'Love human to the creature in himself' (viii. 77) do nothing of the kind. They are symbolic figures stalking giant-like through the mist, or glorified by radiance from the setting sun. Wordsworth may claim

> thus my heart at first was introduced
> To an unconscious love and reverence
> Of human nature . . .
>
> (viii. 412–14)

but there is no reason why we should believe this when it follows the accurate statement, 'Thus was man/*Ennobled outwardly* before mine eyes'. The shepherds take hold of the imagination because they are so removed from the human normality they are supposed to exemplify. They are not 'brother[s] of this world', but borderers on the verge of another:

> Along a narrow valley and profound
> I journeyed, when aloft above my head
> Emerging from the silvery vapours lo,
> A shepherd and his dog, in open day.
> Girt round with mists they stood, and looked about
> From that enclosure small, inhabitants
> Of an aërial island floating on,
> As seemed, with that abode in which they were,
> A little pendant area of grey rocks,
> By the soft wind breathed forward.
>
> (viii. 92–101)

The journey, deep narrow valley, isolating mist, breathing wind, all carry border associations.[5] There is no developed 'spot of time'; but a memory, pointless enough in itself, has been transformed into great poetry—poetry that is not felt to be about shepherds at all, but about timelessness, art, imagination.

It is extraordinary the extent to which man in these recollections is a visual experience. In order to show 'Love of Nature Leading to Love of Mankind' Wordsworth chooses what must surely have been the most remote, least approachable, visible object that he could think of—a cross on an alpine peak:

> Or him have I descried in distant sky,
> A solitary object and sublime,
> Above all height, like an aërial cross
> As it is stationed on some spiry rock
> Of the Chartreuse, for worship.
>
> (viii. 406–10)

If in some special weather conditions, or by some trick of light, man can seem as impressive as a natural object, perhaps he can be loved as Nature is. At all costs, however, he must be kept at a distance. Yet it is the dawning of human-heartedness that Book VIII is designed to show. As in the see-saw alternations of III, the poet has again and again to recall himself to his intended theme:

> Meanwhile, this creature—spiritual almost
> As those of books, but more exalted far,
> Far more of an imaginative form—
> Was not a Corin of the groves, who lives
> For his own fancies, or to dance by the hour
> In coronal, with Phyllis in the midst,
> But . . . a man
> With the most common—husband, father—learned,
> Could teach, admonish, suffered with the rest
> From vice and folly, wretchedness and fear.
>
> (viii. 417–26)

For a moment it looks as if a positive assertion has been reached that can be built upon, but Wordsworth makes nothing of it, concluding abruptly and with unuseful honesty:

> Of this I little saw, cared less for it,
> But something must have felt.
>
> (viii. 427–8)

The grumpy concession of this final line is followed by defiance, as the poet goes back to justify the symbolic presentation from which he had briefly seemed to escape:

> Call ye these appearances
> Which I beheld of shepherds in my youth,
> This sanctity of Nature given to man,
> A shadow, a delusion?
>
> (viii. 428–31)

In his side-reference to 'Corin of the groves' and literary pastoral, Wordsworth claims to be defining the shepherds of his childhood by showing what they were not; but the trick is played so often and at such length in Book VIII that it comes to be seen clearly as a means of avoiding full-face treatment of humanity. The paradise of Grasmere is compared in Miltonic verse to 'Gehol's famous gardens', Shakespeare and Spenser are called upon to illustrate an English golden age, Horace and Pan are visited on 'Adria's myrtle shores', and from Wordsworth's own observations in Germany we learn of pastoral life with flute or flageolet in the Hartz mountains. Mid all this semi-relevance is set the Matron's Tale (viii. 222–311), composed originally for *Michael* in 1800. It is a fairly blatant case of using up old material, but does at least have some bearing on the poet's central theme: the devotion of Lake District shepherds to their sheep and their sons is surely more likely to lead a child to loving admiration than their distance from Arcadia or their tendency to the sublime.

Though Wordsworth claims that its presence was inevitable, the section of Book VIII most at odds with his intentions is probably the long discussion of fancy:

> My present theme
> Is to retrace the way that led me on
> Through Nature to the love of human-kind;
> Nor could I with such object overlook
> The influence of this power which turned itself
> Instinctively to human passions . . .
>
> (viii. 586–91)

The child we are told saw people and their natural surroundings in terms of literary fantasy: 'common death was none, common mishap'; tragedy had to be 'super-tragic' or he felt cheated; the yew-tree 'had its ghost/That took its station there for ornament' (viii. 528–9). Yet there can be little virtue in a power that directs attention to human emotions only to misrepresent, play games with them. Presumably one is to assume that this was a phase, and that fancy led on to imaginative sympathy; but we are not told that this *was* the case—let alone why it should be so. Nor is it reassuring when Wordsworth offers us his present, by implication unfanciful, interpretation alongside that of the past:

Where the harm
If when the woodman languished with disease
From sleeping night by night among the woods
Within his sod-built cabin, Indian-wise,
I called the pangs of disappointed love
And all the long etcetera of such thought
To help him to his grave? Meanwhile the man,
If not already from the woods retired
To die at home, was haply, as I knew,
Pining alone among the gentle airs,
Birds, running streams, and hills so beautiful
On golden evenings . . .

(viii. 610–21)

The child's game, harmless or otherwise, is seen merging as the passage progresses into far less acceptable adult sentimentality, and the poet's concluding fancy is quite as insensitive as those he has been mocking:

while the charcoal pile
Breathed up its smoke, an image of his ghost
Or spirit that was soon to take its flight.

(viii. 621–3)

It is Wordsworth's reflections, not his memories, that are inexcusable. The child's fantasies provide an opportunity for lightening of tone in VIII rather as the mock-heroic card-games had lightened the tone in Part I of *1799*; but fancy in the image of the charcoal-pile ghost is being used as a defence against emotional commitment at a moment when for once the poetry is touching on ordinary painful human experience.

It is difficult not to think that Wordsworth was trying to portray in his former self a kind of love that he didn't feel at the time of writing. Also composed for Book VIII, though not surprisingly discarded, is the fragment *We live by admiration*. Here the chosen spirit finds in Nature 'all things good,/Pure and consistent'—not so in man:

If upon mankind
He looks, and on the human maladies
Before his eyes, what finds he there to this
Framed answerably?—what but sordid men,

> And transient occupations, and desires
> Ignoble and depraved.

Love of Nature seems in this case to lead to outright rejection of humanity:

> Therefore he cleaves
> Exclusively to Nature, as in her
> Finding his image, what he has, what lacks,
> His rest and his perfection. From mankind,
> Like earlier monk or priest, as if by birth
> He is sequestered . . .
>
> (Norton *Prelude*, 504, ll. 191–201)

Wordsworth's use of the plural, 'men' ('what but sordid men') is important. His position is perhaps rather similar to that of Keats in his letter to Haydon of December 1818: 'I admire human nature but I do not like *men*.' 'I should like', Keats goes on, 'to compose things honourable to man—but not fingerable over by *men*.'[6] What both poets admired when it came to the point was human potential—or what they needed and chose to believe was human potential—not the fingering human natures they saw round about them.

To be crude, one could say that Wordsworth's ideal in autumn 1804 was the Christian twofold love of God and one's neighbour, to be attained through a life perfectly attuned to the rhythms of Nature. Whether as a direct perception of the One Life, or merely as 'an obscure sense/Of possible sublimity', he had himself at different times experienced (or created) the God in Nature; his fellow human-beings were the problem. Their occupations, he observed, were transient, their desires ignoble and depraved. Though announcing firmly and frequently that love of Nature led to love of man, he must surely while writing Book VIII have become aware of not having proved it on his pulses—and this despite his privileged position as a 'chosen son'. Had it been possible to show general human-heartedness as growing outwards from deeply felt personal relationship as he had hoped to do in *Home at Grasmere* (1800), the task might have been easier. Something of the sort had been achieved in Book IV, where love for Colthouse and Ann Tyson spreads very credibly to school-friends and villagers:

I read, without design, the opinions, thoughts
Of those plain-living people, in a sense
Of love and knowledge: with another eye
I saw the quiet woodman in the woods,
The shepherd on the hills.

(iv. 203–7)

A similar pattern in Book VIII would at least have presented Wordsworth's symbolic shepherds in a human context, even if it had failed to get beyond them to more general humanity. But VIII was designed to go back further than the student days of IV. Its purpose was to search for causes and origins; and inevitably these led to Nature and the solitary child of the Goslar *Prelude* episodes, whose imaginative isolation no doubt fitted very well with the poet's mood, but was inappropriate to his theme.

Wordsworth's hope that love of man might be derived from love of Nature of course goes back beyond *Home at Grasmere* to Alfoxden. In *Not useless do I deem*, drafted for *The Ruined Cottage* in early March 1798, it had seemed axiomatic that a man once taught to love natural objects, 'things that hold/An inarticulate language',

needs must feel
The joy of that pure principle of love
So deeply that, unsatisfied with aught
Less pure and exquisite, he cannot choose
But seek for objects of a kindred love
In fellow-natures, and a kindred joy.

'Accordingly', Wordsworth had continued,

he by degrees perceives
His feelings of aversion softened down,
A holy tenderness pervade his frame . . .

(Butler, 260–1)

It had all been a little theoretical even at Alfoxden, but the theory had been sound as long as one could accept its pantheist premisses. If God was present as a life-force in the round ocean and the blue sky, '*and* in the mind of man' (*Tintern Abbey*, 99–100), perception of His presence in the natural world would surely alter one's relationship to other people. As Coleridge had put it in 1795:

'Tis the sublime of man,
Our noontide majesty, to know ourselves
Parts and proportions of one wond'rous whole:
This fraternises man, this constitutes
Our charities and bearings.

(*Religious Musings*, 135–9)

By 1804 such views were a long way in Wordsworth's past. Far from being loved for his shared sense 'Of something far more deeply interfused' (*Tintern Abbey*, 97), man was now admired for a seldom achieved border potential that made his distinctiveness both from his fellows and from the other world of truth very apparent. Yet, prompted as ever by the wish that it might be so, Wordsworth went on making the claims. He even towards the end of Book VIII recollects the belief of 1798 that had so conveniently fraternized man, and inserts a paragraph that links the border perception of sublimity back specifically to the One Life:

There came a time of greater dignity,
Which had been gradually prepared, and now
Rushed in as if on wings—*the time in which*
The pulse of being everywhere was felt,
When all the several frames of things, like stars
Through every magnitude distinguishable,
Were half confounded in each other's blaze,
One galaxy of life and joy. Then rose
Man, inwardly contemplated, and present
In my own being, to a loftier height—
As of all visible natures crown, and first
In capability of feeling what
Was to be felt, in being rapt away
By the divine effect of power and love—
As, more than any thing we know, instinct
With godhead, and by reason and by will
Acknowledging dependency sublime.

(viii. 624–40)

As in *1799*, Part II, and its continuation in Book III, Wordsworth is ascribing his pantheism of spring '98 to a period of late adolescence; but there he had been able to incorporate sequences written for *The Pedlar* at Alfoxden when his faith was at its strongest ('in all things/I saw one life, and felt that it was joy'),[7] whereas now he has to re-create the earlier mood unaided. His Miltonic conclusion, high-sounding yet precise, shows most clearly how far he has travelled, but the distance is perceptible throughout in the language and terms of reference. 'The pulse of being everywhere was felt' catches exactly the tones of Wordsworth's original response, but the One Life now unites things not in 'the deep power of joy' shared by the individual with his natural surroundings, but in a remoter galactic blaze. Man, 'inwardly contemplated' (not met with, talked to, loved) rises 'to a loftier height', set apart from other forms of existence because his capacity for being rapt away shows him to be more 'instinct with godhead'.[8] He is the ultimate borderer, ideal, unapproachable, as distant in his moral loftiness as the shepherds on their mountain-tops.

One can hardly expect to define it, but obviously there is a sense in which these borderers are Wordsworth himself. They resemble him in their remoteness from common humanity, and they reflect the grandeur of his aspiration. They typify an imagination untrammelled, freed from all the anxieties to which the poet is subject—fears of death, transience, human (and thus his own) littleness. Faith in the godhead of man in autumn 1804 is very precarious. The point becomes especially clear in Book VII, but is nicely made in VIII by the echo of *Measure for Measure* that is to be heard in the account of the shepherd and his dog, and their island in the mist—

> A little pendant area of grey rocks
> By the soft wind breathed forward.
>
> (viii. 100–1)

The inhabitants of Wordsworth's aërial island achieve a stillness and a peace that is the opposite of Claudio's horrifying fantasy of being

> imprisoned in the viewless winds,
> And blown with restless violence round about
> The pendent world . . .
>
> (*Measure for Measure*, III. i. 125–7)

Shakespeare's vision (in this case) is of death as perpetual restless violence, Wordsworth's (characteristically) is of life stopped in a moment of transcendent calm. Terror has been replaced by comforting beauty; but the echo is there, and though presumably not intended to do so, it tells us how badly comfort is needed.

The one example in Book VIII of true human-heartedness, the workman who is introduced right at the end eyeing his sickly child with unutterable love, is rather surprisingly a Londoner. Wordsworth, having still no intention of writing a full-scale treatment of the city, was no doubt turning to London because this was the one major section of his autobiography that had been left out. But he did not have to portray the city in terms of unity and tenderness (and of course he did not later do so in VII):

> Add also, that among the multitudes
> Of that great city oftentimes was seen
> Affectingly set forth, more than elsewhere
> Is possible, the unity of man . . .
> And is not, too, that vast abiding-place
> Of human creatures, turn where'er we may,
> Profusely sown with individual sights
> Of courage, and integrity, and truth,
> And tenderness . . . ?
>
> (viii. 824–7, 837–41)

It is almost as if Wordsworth felt a sense of relief at breaking out of the self-imposed restrictions of the first two-thirds of VIII. The return to childhood to show love of Nature leading to love of man had been a failure; but now, taking his narrative quickly and rather arbitrarily forward into adulthood at the end of the Book, he suddenly felt able to exemplify the love that had been absent in the earlier lines. ''Twas a man', he wrote, as the previous spring he had written ''Twas a horse', but for once it is not a borderer that is described:

> 'Twas a man,
> Whom I saw sitting in an open square
> Close to an iron paling that fenced in
> The spacious grass-plot: on the corner-stone
> Of the low wall in which the pales were fixed
> Sate this one man, and with a sickly babe
> Upon his knee, whom he had thither brought

For sunshine, and to breathe the fresher air.
Of those who passed, and me who looked at him,
He took no note; but in his brawny arms
(The artificer was to the elbow bare,
And from his work this moment had been stolen)
He held the child, and, bending over it
As if he were afraid both of the sun
And of the air which he had come to seek,
He eyed it with unutterable love.

(viii. 844–59)

Occurring as it does in the same manuscript as 'what but sordid men . . .?', the passage would stand out most oddly in the context of October 1804 were it not for the birth of Wordsworth's daughter Dora two months before. The artificer is forgiven his no doubt transient occupation, and no questions are asked as to whether his desires were ignoble and depraved, because this particular memory stirred in the poet his own paternal feelings. It is interesting that echoes of *The Old Cumberland Beggar*, and especially of *The Ruined Cottage*, should suggest that Wordsworth at some level associated the tenderness of his description with the moods of 1797–8.[9] Insofar as love of Nature ever did lead to love of man it must have been at Racedown after the moral despair of spring 1796. When he wrote *Tintern Abbey* (July 1798) the poet had only quite recently learned to hear 'The still, sad music of humanity'.

In the last of the *Prelude* manuscripts, *MS E* of 1839, Wordsworth transferred the artificer and his child from Book VIII to the main account of London in VII, but it is unlikely that he ever thought of moving the preceding lines on his first entry into the city. The passage in its own right is highly impressive, but it makes little impact at the end of VIII, and to most readers it must seem incongruous that the poet should enter London on the roof of his 'itinerant vehicle' in 1788 a Book later than his experiences there in 1791. Some of *The Prelude*'s odd positionings may be oversight, but not this one. Composition of VII in November 1804 immediately followed the drafting of VIII (and related material in *MS Y*), and Wordsworth's decision to give London a Book to itself was certainly prompted by what he had just been writing. Nothing would have been simpler at this stage than to use the already written account of his first response to the city as the opening of his new Book, and yet he chose not to do so. Lines written into VIII when VII had been completed suggest that in fact he thought of the two London sections as wholly different in kind:

> Preceptress stern, that didst instruct me next,
> London, to thee I willingly return.
> Erewhile my verse played only with the flowers
> Enwrought upon thy mantle, satisfied
> With this amusement, and a simple look
> Of childlike inquisition now and then
> Cast upwards on thine eye to puzzle out
> Some inner meanings which might harbour there.
> (viii. 678–85)

By implication Wordsworth not only thought of Book VII as comparatively light, but had wished to make it so. This despite the fact that he recalled, and had very recently described, his first impression of London as a moment of apocalyptic importance:

> Never shall I forget the hour,
> The moment rather say, when, having thridded
> The labyrinth of suburban villages,
> At length I did unto myself first seem
> To enter the great city . . .
> great God!
> That aught *external* to the living mind
> Should have such mighty sway, yet so it was:
> A weight of ages did at once descend
> Upon my heart—no thought embodied, no
> Distinct remembrances, but weight and power,
> Power growing with the weight.
> (viii. 689–93, 700–6; W.'s italics)

In no real sense is London, with its weight of ages, '*external* to the living mind'. The mind has created the imaginative quality, or situation, to which it responds, yet feels its own heightened responses as an access of power. To the poet looking back the experience is 'a thing divine'; in effect he is saying once more to his soul, 'I recognise thy glory'. Unexpected though it may be in such a context, this is another usurpation, a 'visiting/Of awful promise' (vi. 532–4), and it is interesting that Wordsworth should have chosen to define the experience by inserting and extending the great simile of the cave, written the previous spring just after the Crossing of the Alps. In its original position the simile had evoked the anticlimax of failing to recognize a long anticipated moment of achievement: now it is adapted with extraordinary skill to almost an opposite situation. The poet *does* know (or choose) the particular moment of entering London, *is* duly and deeply moved, and his responses, so far from being frustrated, are of a kind that can on later occasions be 'recalled/To yet a second and a second life'.[10]

In a Virgilian echo appropriate to one of *The Prelude*'s two most consciously epic similes, the traveller of Wordsworth's original lines 'sees, or thinks he sees'[11] the roof of the cave,

> Which instantly unsettles and recedes—
> Substance and shadow, light and darkness, all
> Commingled, making up a canopy
> Of shapes, and forms, and tendencies to shape,
> That shift and vanish, change and interchange,
> Like spectres—ferment quiet and sublime,
> Which after a short space, works less and less . . .
> (viii. 718–24)

One becomes aware in this final line that amid the change and interchange the roof has turned imperceptibly into the sea of the poet's mind.[12] In the episode of the stolen boat the mind had 'Worked with a dim and undetermined sense/Of unknown modes of being', and later in Part I, the child's creative agitation had made 'The surface of the universal earth' specifically '*Work like a sea*' (*1799*, i. 121–2, 198). Within this most compelling of Wordsworth's images of restless creativity one wonders if there is not a hint too of another sense of 'work'—a hint that would lead to imagination as the yeast-like power that activates the 'ferment quiet and sublime'. Be that as it may. In October 1804, six months after composing his simile, Wordsworth no longer has to constrict its border potential. As before, the 'shapes, and forms, and tendencies to shape' are brought to light, 'in perfect view/ Exposed, and lifeless as a written book' (viii. 726–7), but now there is the possibility of imaginative renewal:

> But let him pause awhile and look again,
> And a new quickening shall succeed, at first
> Beginning timidly, then creeping fast
> Through all which he beholds: the senseless mass,
> In its projections, wrinkles, cavities,
> Through all its surface, with all colours streaming,
> Like a magician's airy pageant, parts,
> Unites, embodying everywhere some pressure
> Or image, recognised or new, some type
> Or picture of the world—forests and lakes,
> Ships, rivers, towers, the warrior clad in mail . . .
> (viii. 728–38)

'No otherwise had I at first been moved', Wordsworth adds,

> With such a swell of feeling, followed soon
> By a blank sense of greatness passed away—
> *And afterwards continued to be moved,*
> In presence of that great metropolis . . .
> (viii. 743–6)

The sense of greatness passed away is no longer of importance—a mere nod in the direction of the poet's original emphasis. The cave has been adapted to evoke a process much like the creative re-enactment described in the Preface to *Lyrical Ballads*, 1800. The traveller who is prepared to pause awhile and look again, recollect his emotion in tranquillity, is rewarded with 'a new quickening . . . at first/Beginning timidly, then creeping fast':

> the emotion is contemplated till by a species of reaction the tranquillity gradually disappears, and an emotion, similar to that which was before the subject of contemplation, is gradually produced, and does itself actually exist in the mind. In this mood successful composition generally begins . . .
> (*Prose Works*, i. 148)

The original swell of feeling experienced in the moment of entering London (the sea-swell of the cave) can be recaptured, and gives to the poet the power of turning 'the senseless mass/In its projections, wrinkles, cavities' into the magician's airy pageant. Presumably Wordsworth chose not to open his new Book with the entry into London because the apocalyptic quality of his memory was out of keeping with the stance he wished to take up. But stances cannot always be sustained. Given the surprising extensions to the simile of the cave, the London section in VIII makes a very good way into the wondering, uncensorious, sometimes disturbing and deeply imaginative Book that VII turned out to be.

One thinks of the Book as satirical, but in fact it is only very lightly and intermittently so. *The Task*, which often seems to be Wordsworth's model, can be far more damning about 'proud and gay/And gain-devoted cities' than ever *The Prelude* is:

Thither flow,
As to a common and most noisome sewer,
The dregs and feculence of every land.
In cities foul example on most minds
Begets its likeness. Rank abundance breeds
In gross and pampered cities sloth and lust,
And wantonness and gluttonous excess.

(*Task*, i. 681–8)

London in VII could so easily have called up the unthinking prejudice of which Wordsworth too was capable, but, until a sudden arbitrary change of tone in the last few lines, his observations are presented with amusement and indulgence.[13] Instead of 'The dregs and feculence of every land', he sees colour and strangeness:

Now homeward through the thickening hubbub, where
See—among less distinguishable shapes—
The Italian, with his frame of images
Upon his head; with basket at his waist,
The Jew; the stately and slow-moving Turk,
With freight of slippers piled beneath his arm . . .
The Swede, the Russian; from the genial south,
The Frenchman and the Spaniard; from remote
America, the hunter Indian; Moors,
Malays, Lascars, the Tartar and Chinese,
And negro ladies in white muslin gowns.

(vii. 227–32, 239–43)

In Book VII the pictorial vision, seen elsewhere in Wordsworth's frequent metaphors ('I cannot paint/What then I was', *Tintern Abbey*, 76–7; 'I should need/Colours and words that are unknown to man/To paint the visionary dreariness', *1799*, i. 320–2), is given unusual scope.

We are treated to a panorama of London life, a word-painting that has much in common with the giant contemporary *Eidometropolis* of Thomas Girtin.[14] It is bustle that chiefly catches the poet's eye, and the scale of it all:

> the quick dance
> Of colours, lights and forms, the Babel din,
> The endless stream of men and moving things,
> From hour to hour the illimitable walk
> Still among streets . . .
>
> (vii. 156–60)

He is vividly aware of

> the solemnity
> Of Nature's intermediate hours of rest
> When the great tide of human life stands still,
> The business of the day to come unborn,
> Of that gone by locked up as in the grave . . .
>
> (vii. 629–33)

but such moments are inevitably rare. Only by night is Nature's presence felt; by day the onlooker's consciousness is deafened and bemused, driven (or inspired) to create its own pageants and patterns from the ceaseless and meaningless activity that goes on before the eyes.

As a type of the whole city Wordsworth offers Bartholomew Fair. His tone as the passage opens is unusually self-conscious—this is to be a set-piece:

> For once the Muse's help will we implore,
> And she shall lodge us—wafted on her wings
> Above the press and danger of the crowd—
> Upon some showman's platform. What a hell
> For eyes and ears, what anarchy and din
> Barbarian and infernal!—'tis a dream
> Monstrous in colour, motion, shape, sight, sound.
> Below, the open space, through every nook
> Of the wide area, twinkles, is alive
> With heads; the midway region and above
> Is thronged with staring pictures and huge scrolls,
> Dumb proclamations of the prodigies;
> And chattering monkeys dangling from their poles,

And children whirling in their roundabouts . . .
All out-o'-th'-way, far-fetched, perverted things,
All freaks of Nature, all Promethean thoughts
Of man—his dullness, madness, and their feats,
All jumbled up together to make up
This parliament of monsters. Tents and booths
Meanwhile—as if the whole were one vast mill—
Are vomiting, receiving, on all sides,
Men, women, three years' children, babes in arms.
(vii. 656–69, 88–95)

The connection that has been made between this passage and *The Simplon Pass* is important.[15] The different features of the landscape there—'woods decaying, never to be decayed', the blasting yet stationary waterfalls, the muttering rocks, black drizzling crags, unfettered clouds—are uninfluenced either by man or by time. Everything is permanent, sublime, ultimately harmonious,

like workings of one mind, the features
Of the same face, blossoms upon one tree,
Characters of the great apocalypse,
The types and symbols of eternity,
Of first, and last, and midst, and without end.
(vi. 568–72)

In the fair, by contrast, nothing adds up, nothing is natural, nothing has a purpose. The energy is impressive, but wasted, frenetic. Man, whose promethean creativity made this nightmare world, has no power to contain it, drawn in and vomited forth by the vast Blakean mill that has usurped his control. The poet's reference to 'far-fetched, perverted things' and 'freaks of Nature' confirms that he has Milton's Hell in mind, where 'Nature breeds,/Perverse, all monstrous, all prodigious things' (*PL* ii. 624–5).Yet this seemingly is an underworld without pain. Wordsworth's own enjoyment is evident:

the open space, through every nook
Of the wide area, twinkles, is alive
With heads . . .

Man's ingenuity and madness are laughable, and his dullness carries with it mock-heroic echoes from *The Dunciad* that are not likely to be taken too seriously. The fair is 'a work that's finished to our hands',

> lays,
> If any spectacle on earth can do,
> The whole creative powers of man asleep.
>
> (vii. 653–5)

and the poet's situation, lodged 'Above the press and danger of the crowd/Upon some showman's platform', is an emblem of his relationship to the whole experience of London.[16] He is distanced from it, placed above it, gaining at once enjoyment and safety from turning life into art.

One is bound to ask, safety from what? The answer is certainly not that 'In cities foul example on most minds/Begets its likeness' (Cowper). There is no possibility here of a personal Fall, barely even of considering the Book in terms of Experience—Wordsworth on his platform plays no part. Nor is there fear of isolation as such: it is not as if he *wanted* to play a part. To some extent the threat must be the 'sordid men,/And transient occupations' that are so carefully never singled out from 'the quick dance/Of colours, lights, and forms'. More important though is the poet's confrontation with anonymity. London is so big, so alive, so colourful, so noisy; its weight of ages presses so heavily upon him. Less dramatically than in his Paris room after the September Massacres, but in the long run perhaps even more disquietingly, he is confronted by his own littleness, transience, irrelevance. His genuine enjoyment of it all, and his role as pattern-maker, permit the situation to be contained—London is presented as

> A vivid pleasure of my youth, and now,
> Among the lonely places that I love,
> A frequent day-dream . . .
>
> (vii. 151–3)

—but as usual there are the borderers to tell of stresses at a deeper level. Mary of Buttermere, the first of these, had no obvious place in a London Book, but is an extraordinary example of the power of art to cushion and assuage. She and her short-lived infant would have no part in the Book were it not that her sensational story (she was bigamously married by a forger who posed as a Scottish M.P. and brother of an Earl) had been made into a play by Sadler's Wells in July 1803. Unlike Coleridge, who wrote five articles about her case for *The Morning Post*, Wordsworth is not concerned with details—

> how the spoiler came, 'a bold bad man',
> To God unfaithful, children, wife, and home,
> And wooed the artless daughter of the hills,
> And wedded her in cruel mockery
> Of love and marriage-bonds.[17]
>
> (vii. 323–7)

Instead, he reminds Coleridge of her modesty and virtue when first they met her serving at her father's inn, and in a recollection of *Lycidas* he goes on to muse that he and Mary had been nursed among the self-same mountains, picked flowers as children by the self-same stream. It is all very pastoral and seemingly pointless, but then comes one of those strange Wordsworthian moments in which 'the picture of the mind/Revives again', asserting the right to qualify present experience:

> These last words uttered, to my argument
> I was returning, when—with sundry forms
> Mingled, that in the way which I must tread
> Before me stand—thy image rose again,
> Mary of Buttermere!
>
> (vii. 347–51)

Imaginatively transformed, Mary enters a new world, a sort of death-in-life that resembles Lucy's living death in *Three years she grew*:

> She lives in peace
> Upon the spot where she was born and reared;
> Without contamination does she live
> In quietness, without anxiety.
> Beside the mountain-chapel sleeps in earth
> Her new-born infant, fearless as a lamb
> That thither comes from some unsheltered place
> To rest beneath the little rock-like pile
> When storms are blowing. Happy are they both,
> Mother and child!
>
> (vii. 351–60)

Mary has gone half-way to meet the child, and he, not merely sleeping (the customary euphemism) but also 'fearless', has come to meet her too. Though she is alive and he dead, they share one happiness.

This is not Wordsworth at his best. The lines become increasingly sentimental, and he becomes increasingly self-conscious, but it is interesting nonetheless to watch the process of idealization as Mary turns borderer. We hear first of the bigamous marriage, then her virtues are extolled (in the past tense because the poet is looking back), then comes a reference to 'this memorial verse', and when her image rises in the mind only the most alert reader is likely to think she may still be alive. The lines that follow are patently an elegy, yet imperceptibly worded to imply that life persists. Responding to tone and expectation the eye makes a silent readjustment: 'She *rests* in peace . . . where she was born and raised'. Doubtless she was leading a quieter life than with her forger husband, but 'Without contamination does she live/In quietness' seems exaggerated to say the least.[18] The imagination has embalmed her, saved her from violence and change, and the poet himself from having to contemplate in their threatening actuality the projections, wrinkles, cavities of experience. Just as Milton identifies with Edward King as fellow shepherd and poet, 'nursed upon the self-same hill' (*Lycidas*, 23), so there is a sense in which Wordsworth identifies with Mary, giving her not only his own favoured childhood, but the timeless uncontaminated life of the imagination that he craved.

To some extent perhaps Wordsworth is aware of what has been taking place in his account of Mary and her child, for the image of embalming is used specifically in the parallel scene that he goes on to portray. This time the mother is scarcely remembered, and gets little sympathy; it is her son who is present to the mind:

'Twas at a theatre
That I beheld this pair; the boy had been
The pride and pleasure of all lookers-on
In whatsoever place, but seemed in this
A sort of alien scattered from the clouds.
Of lusty vigour, more than infantine,
He was in limbs, in face a cottage rose
Just three parts blown—a cottage-child, but ne'er
Saw I by cottage or elsewhere a babe

By Nature's gifts so honored. Upon a board,
Whence an attendant of the theatre
Served out refreshments, had this child been placed,
And there he sate environed with a ring
Of chance spectators, chiefly dissolute men
And shameless women—treated and caressed—
Ate, drank, and with the fruit and glasses played,
While oaths, indecent speech, and ribaldry
Were rife about him as are songs of birds
In springtime after showers.

(vii. 374–92)

Wordsworth's moral emphasis is not very acceptable—sentimental in its implication that innocence turns ribaldry to birdsong, and uncaring about dissolute men and shameless women whose lives were no doubt miserable—but he is working up towards one of the great isolated moments of *The Prelude*. The boy is not just abnormally beautiful, one who in London excels the cottage rose, he is 'an alien' who trails his clouds of glory from elsewhere. 'Among the wretched and the falsely gay' he resembles Shadrach, Meshack, and Abednego untouched in the burning fiery furnace of Daniel. 'He hath since/Appeared to me ofttimes', Wordsworth writes,

as if embalmed
By Nature—through some special privilege
Stopped at the growth he had—destined to live,
To be, to have been, come, and go, a child
And nothing more, no partner in the years
That bear us forward to distress and guilt,
Pain and abasement . . .

(vii. 399–406)

The boy unsinged by the flames of London vice moves us very little; his otherness is enforced in too trite a context. But in these magnificent lines he acquires the full creative strength and pathos of the poet's own craving for permanence. No doubt Wordsworth is influenced by the wish that Dora should not have to face (be a *partner* in, and thus responsible for, as well as subjected to) the years of 'distress and guilt/Pain and abasement'; but the 'us' is very important—'that bear *us* forward'. The boy amid his fruit and glasses, oaths and indecent speech, has achieved what the child of the *Ode* cannot achieve, travelling as he does 'daily farther from the east'. Stopped in his perfection, as the Virgin of Michelangelo's *Pietà* is stopped in hers, he represents the power of imagination over time. It is curiously satisfying in the circumstances that his stillness should be an active one. He stops, but does not die, as Lucy had done, in order to become part of a wider, different, natural harmony. He is 'destined to live', and the patient monosyllables that give these lines so much of their quiet passion enact the living out of his life—'To be, to have been, come, and go, a child'.

The third borderer of Book VII, the blind and labelled beggar, is at the other end of life's pilgrimage, and tells us most about the urgency of Wordsworth's imaginative creations. He is 'the thing itself, unaccommodated man', making a silent, sightless plea for alms, but otherwise completely divested of relationship. In this case the poet describes the mood in which his original experience took place, and the passage is among the last of his fully developed 'spots of time'. 'How often in the overflowing streets', he writes

> Have I gone forwards with the crowd, and said
> Unto myself, 'The face of everyone
> That passes by me is a mystery.'
>
> (vii. 595–8)

'The face of every neighbour whom I met', he had written the previous spring of his return to Hawkshead in 1789, 'Was as a volume to me' (iv. 58–9). It is not merely an opposition of town and country; Wordsworth is talking about rootedness, security. In London he is carried along by the crowd but vividly aware of difference:

> Thus have I looked, nor ceased to look, oppressed
> By thoughts of what, and whither, when and how,
> Until the shapes before my eyes became
> A second-sight procession, such as glides
> Over still mountains, or appears in dreams,
> And all the ballast of familiar life—
> The present, and the past, hope, fear, all stays,
> All laws of acting, thinking, speaking man—
> Went from me, neither knowing me, nor known.
>
> (vii. 599–607)

It is a wonderful study of deracination; the meaningless activity before the poet's eyes had intruded upon his consciousness, depriving him of the stabilizing 'ballast of familiar life' as the mountain on Ullswater had deprived him when a boy:

> In my thoughts
> There was a darkness—call it solitude,
> Or blank desertion—no familiar shapes
> Of hourly objects, images of trees . . .
>
> (*1799*, i. 122–5)

But where, before, Wordsworth's mind had been taken over by an imaginative re-creation of what he had seen—shapes of terror ('huge and mighty forms that do not live/Like living men')—this time he has created in his own defence a distancing equivalent, the gliding, reconciling, second-sight procession of Cumbrian legend.[19] 'Once', the passage continues, 'far travelled in such mood' (far travelled, that is, both in, and into, such a mood),

> beyond
> The reach of common indications, lost
> Amid the moving pageant, 'twas my chance
> Abruptly to be smitten with the view
> Of a blind beggar, who, with upright face,
> Stood propped against a wall, upon his chest
> Wearing a written paper, to explain
> The story of the man, and who he was.
> My mind did at this spectacle turn round
> As with the might of waters, and it seemed
> To me that in this label was a type
> Or emblem of the utmost that we know
> Both of ourselves and of the universe,
> And on the shape of this unmoving man,
> His fixèd face and sightless eyes, I looked,
> As if admonished from another world.
>
> (vii. 608–23)

Amid the moving actual pageant of the street, and the moving imaginative pageant of his mind, Wordsworth is confronted suddenly by absolute stillness, man turned to an object, a spectacle. The beggar is motionless, sightless, speechless—at the opposite extreme from the noisy bustling crowd, yet seeming to epitomize the utmost that we know of existence. The shock (Wordsworth is '*smitten* with [his] view', his mind turned irresistibly like a water-wheel) is not at the suffering implied, but that a few simple words on a label could be sufficient to convey the story and identity of a human being. The first version of the lines, preserved in *MS X*, makes the point less skilfully but with moving directness:

> and I thought
> That even the very most of what we know
> Both of ourselves and of the universe,
> The whole of what is written to our view,
> Is but a label on a blind man's chest.
>
> (vii. 620n.)

It is for Wordsworth an unusually painful insight. The episode as a whole can be seen as reflecting once again the achievement of imagination, but the truth to which it penetrates is a truth about littleness. It is as if the sound and fury of London had momentarily convinced the poet that life might indeed be 'a tale/ Told by an idiot . . . Signifying nothing'. Where the Leech Gatherer had, so it seemed, given '*human strength*, and strong admonishment', the beggar leaves him gazing 'As if admonished from another world'—a distant world in whose view humanity dwindles very uncomfortably. Of all the borderers this beggar shows most clearly the terror that underlies Wordsworthian optimism, the fear of the child bewildered by his mother's death, desertion, fear that the years must truly bear *us*—not just others, the sordid men and their transient occupations, but man in all his grandeur, and the poet too—'forward to distress and guilt,/Pain and abasement'.

It comes as a surprise when the last forty-five lines of VII portray London suddenly and very crudely as an assault upon the imagination. A new harshness enters the verse. Violently biased lines written for *Michael* in 1800 are brought in to show city-dwellers as

> The slaves unrespited of low pursuits,
> Living amid the same perpetual flow
> Of trivial objects, melted and reduced
> To one identity . . . [20]

The poet himself it seems had survived this trial-by-triviality by virtue of his imaginative strength and favoured upbringing (what, one wonders, went wrong with Luke's?). Because 'The mountain's outline and its steady form' had early given grandeur to his soul he was able to see London as part of a natural totality:

> though the picture weary out the eye,
> By nature an unmanageable sight,
> It is not wholly so to him who looks
> In steadiness, who hath among least things
> An under-sense of greatest, sees the parts
> As parts, but with a feeling of the whole.
>
> (vii. 708–13)

None of it convinces, or at least none of it appears necessary in terms of the poetry that has come before. Wordsworth's conclusion especially seems inappropriate:

> The spirit of Nature was upon me here,
> The soul of beauty and enduring life
> Was present as a habit, and diffused—
> Through meagre lines and colours, and the press
> Of self-destroying, transitory things—
> Composure and ennobling harmony.
>
> (vii. 736–41)

'Meagre lines and colours' is falsely disparaging—the poet's own wonderment has precluded any sense of meagreness—and 'self-destroying, transitory things' assumes a moral stance that has been notably absent in the Book as a whole. Nor will the grand assertions really do, impressive as they are. Composure has very seldom been apparent, and the harmony that has been created has had far more to do with the artist on the showman's platform than with contemplation imbued with the spirit of Nature.

The wish to see London as part of a total natural harmony might be relevant in terms of *The Prelude* as a whole, but has very little to do with VII as it was actually written. So far from ennobling the city, bestowing on its meagreness and transience the abiding soul of beauty, Wordsworth for most of the Book responds with pleasure at its life and strangeness. The picture doesn't weary out his eye, it proves a stimulus; and almost to the last it also proves manageable. The 'perpetual flow/Of trivial objects' can be perceived imaginatively as 'the quick dance/Of colours, lights, and forms'. Mary of Buttermere and the boy at the theatre show the imagination as entirely capable of protecting itself, creating permanence from surrounding transience, stillness from the Babel din. At the deepest level, however, represented by the sightless beggar, there is a threat of quite another kind—a threat that no pattern-making can neutralize, because it is a recognition of what the patterns have been about, why they have been needed. Wordsworth's remark that Bartholomew Fair cannot be made into a work of art as it is one already is true in a far more meaningful sense of the beggar. It is no use embalming him in self-defence, because here he is, ready embalmed, living in actuality the half-life of the borderer to which for safety the imagination would consign him. Like Henchard, the poet looking into the waters (the restless sea of the cave-roof that is London and the mind) sees floating there his effigy, a nightmare vision of himself. There is no comfort this time in the admonishment; the world across the border is suddenly alien. The beggar is a daemonic presence who embodies the terrors he might be expected to control. In him all the fears that have been so carefully allayed—fears aroused by the age, scale, speed, impersonality of London—are suddenly confronted. Lulled by the second-sight procession that he has created to render tolerable the endless stream of passers-by, conserve his own identity as an artist, Wordsworth is taken completely by surprise. What if his own life and work—*The Prelude* is after all 'The story of the man, and who he was'—could be seen by some remote and dispassionate wisdom as 'but a label on a blind man's chest'?

The Wordsworth of *The Prelude* never does look upon mankind. He had done so in 1797–8 (*The Ruined Cottage, The Idiot Boy, Old Cumberland Beggar*), and in 1800 (*The Brothers, Home at Grasmere, Michael*), and would do so again in *The Waggoner* of 1806, but in the periods that produced the great poetry of imagination (late 1798 and 1799, 1802, 1804–5), true fellow-feeling is very rare. *The Prelude* has its moments—Ann Tyson asleep on her bible in IV, the hunger-bitten girl of IX, the London artificer—but neither VIII ('Love of Nature Leading to Love of Mankind') nor VII (designed presumably to represent Experience, a seeing how the others live) turns out to be about people at all. In 1798 the song of the One Life had coexisted with the still sad music of humanity because both were to be perceived outside the self; but the internal voice of imagination that replaced the One Life was too loud—too dominant when in full song, and at other times too threatened—for the poet to do much listening. At these times he was indeed the 'spectator ab extra' that Coleridge called him, seeing *man* outwardly ennobled, or *men* in patterns, pageants, processions, that pleased his creativity and did not intrude too much upon his consciousness.

Chapter 10

The Image of a Mighty Mind (*1805*, Book XIII)

The secret Strength of things
Which governs thought, and to the infinite dome
Of heaven is as a law, inhabits thee.
And what were thou, and earth, and stars, and sea,
If to the human mind's imaginings
Silence and solitude were vacancy?
(Shelley: *Mont Blanc*)

The Climbing of Snowdon

It was a summer's night, a close warm night,
Wan, dull, and glaring, with a dripping mist
Low-hung and thick that covered all the sky,
Half threatening storm and rain; but on we went
Unchecked, being full of heart and having faith
In our tried pilot. Little could we see,
Hemmed round on every side with fog and damp,
And, after ordinary travellers' chat
With our conductor, silently we sunk
Each into commerce with his private thoughts.
Thus did we breast the ascent, and by myself
Was nothing either seen or heard the while
Which took me from my musings, save that once
The shepherd's cur did to his own great joy
Unearth a hedgehog in the mountain-crags,
Round which he made a barking turbulent.
This small adventure—for even such it seemed
In that wild place and at the dead of night—

Being over and forgotten, on we wound
In silence as before. With forehead bent
Earthward, as if in opposition set
Against an enemy, I panted up
With eager pace, and no less eager thoughts.
Thus might we wear perhaps an hour away,
Ascending at loose distance each from each,
And I, as chanced, the foremost of the band—
When at my feet the ground appeared to brighten,
And with a step or two seemed brighter still;
Nor had I time to ask the cause of this,
For instantly a light upon the turf
Fell like a flash. I looked about, and lo,
The moon stood naked in the heavens at height
Immense above my head, and on the shore
I found myself of a huge sea of mist,
Which meek and silent rested at my feet.
A hundred hills their dusky backs upheaved
All over this still ocean, and beyond,
Far, far beyond, the vapours shot themselves
In headlands, tongues, and promontory shapes,
Into the sea, the real sea, that seemed
To dwindle and give up its majesty,
Usurped upon as far as sight could reach.
Meanwhile, the moon looked down upon this shew
In single glory, and we stood, the mist
Touching our very feet; and from the shore
At distance not the third part of a mile
Was a blue chasm, a fracture in the vapour,
A deep and gloomy breathing-place through which
Mounted the roar of waters, torrents, streams
Innumerable, roaring with one voice.
The universal spectacle throughout
Was shaped for admiration and delight,
Grand in itself alone, but in that breach
Through which the homeless voice of waters rose,
That dark deep thoroughfare, had Nature lodged
The soul, the imagination of the whole.

A meditation rose in me that night
Upon the lonely mountain when the scene
Had passed away, and it appeared to me
The perfect image of a mighty mind,
Of one that feeds upon infinity,

That is exalted by an under-presence,
The sense of God, or whatsoe'er is dim
Or vast in its own being—above all,
One function of such mind had Nature there
Exhibited by putting forth, and that
With circumstance most awful and sublime:
That domination which she oftentimes
Exerts upon the outward face of things,
So moulds them, and endues, abstracts, combines,
Or by abrupt and unhabitual influence
Doth make one object so impress itself
Upon all others, and pervade them so,
That even the grossest minds must see and hear,
And cannot chuse but feel. The power which these
Acknowledge when thus moved, which Nature thus
Thrusts forth upon the senses, is the express
Resemblance—in the fulness of its strength
Made visible—a genuine counterpart
And brother of the glorious faculty
Which higher minds bear with them as their own.

(*1805*, xiii. 10–90)

'A meditation rose in me *that* night/Upon the lonely mountain . . .' (ll. 66–7), writes the poet; but the claim should not be taken as a statement of fact. Wordsworth climbed Snowdon with Robert Jones in the summer of 1791, and whatever else he was thinking about, it is not likely to have been the creative imagination. It was only by a gradual process that the scene came to have its later implications. Wordsworth himself had to learn to see in Wordsworthian terms. His first attempts at landscape are as far from the great poetry of *The Prelude* as the dying woman and her babes of *An Evening Walk* are from Margaret of *The Ruined Cottage*. In each case the failure of the early poetry can be blamed on the poet's idiom, but one suspects that Wordsworth at the age of 20 did not in fact feel very strongly either about landscape or about suffering—that the development of response brought with it the ability to create an appropriate medium.

Of Wordsworth's immediate impressions on Snowdon nothing is known; but certain deductions can be made from comparing his first account of the scene, in *Descriptive Sketches* of summer 1792, with the stanza of Beattie's *Minstrel* that is his literary source:

1793 *Descriptive Sketches*, 492–511

'Tis morn—with gold the verdant mountain glows;
More high, the snowy peaks with hues of rose.
Far stretched beneath the many-tinted hills,
A mighty waste of mist the valley fills,
A solemn sea, whose vales and mountains round
Stand motionless, to awful silence bound.
A gulf of gloomy blue, that opens wide
And bottomless, divides the midway tide;
Like leaning masts of stranded ships appear
The pines that near the coast their summits rear;
Of cabins, woods, and lawns a pleasant shore
Bounds calm and clear the chaos still and hoar.
Loud through that midway gulf ascending, sound
Unnumbered streams with hollow roar profound:
Mounts through the nearer mist the chaunt of birds,
And talking voices, and the low of herds,
The bark of dogs, the drowsy tinkling bell,
And wild-wood mountain lutes of saddest swell.
Think not, suspended from the cliff on high,
He looks below with undelighted eye.

The Minstrel, Part I, stanza xxiii

And oft the craggy cliff he loved to climb,
When all in mist the world below was lost.
What dreadful pleasure, there to stand sublime,
Like shipwrecked mariner on desert coast,
And view th'enormous waste of vapour, tost
In billows, lengthening to th'horizon round,
Now scooped in gulfs, with mountains now embossed—
And hear the voice of mirth and song rebound,
Flocks, herds, and waterfalls, along the hoar profound![1]

The extent to which the first passage derives from the second is very surprising. Situation and setting, diction and imagery, are contentedly taken over. Resemblances go beyond paraphrase ('mighty waste of mist'/'enormous waste of vapour') to presumably unconscious repetition of sound ('with hollow roar profound'; 'along the hoar profound'). Even where Wordsworth adds a new detail—the pines on the edge of the mist, for instance—he does so in terms of the earlier poem: 'Like leaning masts of stranded ships appear/The pines that near the coast'; 'Like shipwrecked mariner on desert coast'.

To compose his picturesque scene Wordsworth, one feels, hardly needed to go near a mountain, let alone have a specific occasion in mind. And yet there is one element in his description that does suggest personal experience—the 'gulf of gloomy blue' that is to become the 'deep and gloomy breathing-place' of *The Prelude*. As usual, there is a hint from Beattie ('Now *scooped in gulfs*, with mountains now embossed'), but it is no warrant for the way in which this particular rift is singled out:

> A mighty waste of mist the valley fills,
> A solemn sea, whose vales and mountains round
> Stand motionless, to awful silence bound.
> A gulf of gloomy blue, that opens wide
> And bottomless, divides the midway tide . . .
> Loud through that midway gulf ascending, sound
> Unnumbered streams with hollow roar profound . . .

It is possible that the 'Unnumbered streams' derive from a passage in James Clarke's *Survey of the Lakes* (1787), which seems to have produced Wordsworth's 'chaunt of birds' and the 'talking voices' that rise through the mist.[2] But if this is so, it is interesting that the poet deliberately contradicted Clarke's central point:

> About half way up the mountain, or not quite so high, you will be above the mist, which lyes thick and white below . . . *the voice of extremely distant waterfalls is heard perfectly distinct, and not one confusing another*. The loud crowing cock at every cottage, joined to the warbling of the smaller-feathered choir, comes with an almost magical sweetness to the ear . . . *every sound is much more distinctly heard than at any other time*. The words of men conversing at two miles distance are perfectly intelligible.[3]

For Clarke, who incidentally quotes Beattie's stanza, every sound is distinct: for Wordsworth the nearer, domestic ones are, but not those heard through the gloomy midway gulf. Wordsworth does not seem to have singled the rift out for any special purpose—it is not yet 'The soul, the imagination of the whole'—but already it is there, set apart from the cabins, woods, and lawns of the 'pleasant shore', its 'hollow roar profound' distinguished from the cosy rural noises.[4]

Wordsworth wrote no landscape poetry, at least as such, for

five and a half years between the summer of 1792 and the end of 1797. There are the heightened descriptions that form the backgrounds of *Salisbury Plain* and *The Borderers*, and there is the far more important natural setting of *The Ruined Cottage*, but not until the beginning of 1798 at Alfoxden does the poet go back to writing about his personal response to Nature. Then, prompted by the entry in his sister's *Journal* for 25 January, he composes *A Night-Piece*. Like *The Discharged Soldier*, with which it is closely connected (and *In storm and tempest*, which is perhaps a week or two later), the poem shows Wordsworth's border intuitions in the moment just before his 'obscure sense of possible sublimity' is exchanged for pantheist communion:

The sky is overspread
With a close veil of one continuous cloud
All whitened by the moon, that just appears,
A dim-seen orb, yet chequers not the ground
With any shadow—plant, or tower, or tree.
At last a pleasant instantaneous light
Startles the musing man whose eyes are bent
To earth. He looks around, the clouds are split
Asunder, and above his head he views
The clear moon and the glory of the heavens.
There in a black-blue vault she sails along
Followed by multitudes of stars, that small,
And bright, and sharp, along the gloomy vault
Drive as she drives. How fast they wheel away!—
Yet vanish not. The wind is in the trees;
But they are silent.[5]

In its details, and in the quality of personal response, the poetry is very close to Dorothy's prose:

The sky spread over with one continuous cloud, whitened by the light of the moon, which, though her dim shape was seen, did not throw forth so strong a light as to chequer the earth with shadows. At once the clouds seemed to cleave asunder, and left her in the centre of a black-blue vault. She sailed along, followed by multitudes of stars, small, and bright, and sharp. Their brightness seemed concentrated (half-moon).

A matter of weeks later Wordsworth was to write of the Pedlar's universe of blessedness and joy,

> The clouds were touched,
> And in their silent faces did he read
> Unutterable love . . .
>
> (*Pedlar*, 99–101)

but at this point feeling is not yet identified with perception of the One Life. In a sense the landscape is alive, but it is noticeable that Wordsworth's animist description of the moon comes almost verbatim from Dorothy. It was the level of response to Nature, identification with her, that the two shared; though in Wordsworth's greatest poetry it is not much more than the surface.

But, early and indebted as it is, the *Night-Piece* does have certain touches that go beyond Dorothy's sensitive yet limited vision. The penseroso, whose presence is itself a hint of border perceptions, sees not just the clear moon but 'the glory of the heavens'; and though taking over Dorothy's very precise observation of the stars as 'small and bright and sharp', Wordsworth adds the numinous detail of their silence—a silence heightened by the border possibilities of the wind in the trees. Like the non-existent steps 'Almost as silent as the turf they trod', the stars could not logically make a noise; their silence is an extension of the poetry beyond description and into the mind. As Kenneth Johnston has enviably said,

> The cumulative effect of all these details is to intimate, almost invisibly, the *conjunctive* character of the vision. A man suddenly discovers himself to be standing between heaven and earth, standing, moreover, as a link between them. The traveller does not simply apprehend or suffer this dualism, he *is* the dualism—without him it does not exist. The two spheres are brought together not so much by, as in, man; recognizing his mediate position, he defines his being.[6]

To some extent (as Professor Johnston is aware) this interpretation depends on reading backwards from later accounts of visionary experience. The difference between *A Night-Piece* and the Climbing of Snowdon is that in 1804–5 Wordsworth had fully understood, and was consciously portraying, the border condition which in February 1798, though certainly to be implied from the poetry, had yet to be thought out.[7]

There was presumably nothing in Wordsworth's actual memories of Snowdon in 1791 impressive enough to be useful in building up towards his account of the blue chasm; when looking for additional material he remembered the 'pleasant instantaneous light' seen at Alfoxden, and the *Prelude* lines combine the two quite separate experiences.[8] His purpose as he begins the Climbing of Snowdon is to create in the reader a sense of expectancy, and show in his former self a withdrawal into the state of mind in which the expected surprise can have its fullest effect. The poetry works through a series of contrasts between the poet's situation and what goes on about him. At first he is part of a group, undaunted like the others by the discomfort of the close night and dripping mist, and capable of 'ordinary travellers' chat'; but this normal responsiveness to the outside world is then removed. Surrounded by mist and silence, in commerce only with his own private thoughts, the poet is clearly ready to be startled; but Wordsworth is not yet ready to startle him. At this stage the unearthing of the hedgehog is introduced by way of a deliberate non-adventure, its unimportance emphasized by the grandiloquence of 'barking turbulent' and the levity of Wordsworth's use of 'joy':

> The shepherd's cur did to his own great joy
> Unearth a hedgehog in the mountain-crags,
> Round which he made a barking turbulent.
>
> (ll. 23–5)

On the face of it the episode is meant to stress the loneliness and silence in which the dog's hunting could be taken for a 'small adventure', but Wordsworth is also teasing his audience, as he does overtly in *Simon Lee* and *The Idiot Boy*, for having the wrong kind of anticipations.[9] And, as in the earlier 'spots of time', he is mocking his former self. The stolen boat in Patterdale seemed to the child 'an elfin pinnace'; the vision of the Woman on the Hill opens with a knight-errant and his trustly squire ('I mounted, and we rode towards the hills'); and here the poet—now 21, not 6—is seen panting up the mountain full of a slightly ridiculous eagerness, and as unaware as the child of what is really to be important. Like the 'fell destroyer' of the Woodcock-snaring, he is bent on conquest, 'as if in opposition set/Against an enemy' (ll. 30–1).

There are serious reasons too for playing up the drama of the scene. The 'pleasant instantaneous light' of *A Night-Piece* in its new context falls 'like a flash'. It is a deliberate use of shock, and carefully prepared for by anticipations that heighten the sense of expectancy without destroying the suddenness:

> at my feet the ground appeared to brighten,
> And with a step or two seemed brighter still;
> Nor had I time to ask the cause of this,
> For instantly a light upon the turf
> Fell like a flash.
>
> (ll. 36–40)

Despite the context one is startled into assuming that something dramatic, even supernatural, is about to happen. It isn't, of course; this is a Wordsworthian adventure. What follows is some of the greatest poetry he ever wrote:

> I looked about, and lo,
> The moon stood naked in the heavens at height
> Immense above my head, and on the shore
> I found myself of a huge sea of mist,
> Which meek and silent rested at my feet.
> A hundred hills their dusky backs upheaved
> All over this still ocean, and beyond,
> Far, far beyond, the vapours shot themselves
> In headlands, tongues, and promontory shapes,
> Into the sea, the real sea, that seemed
> To dwindle and give up its majesty,
> Usurped upon as far as sight could reach.
> Meanwhile, the moon looked down upon this shew
> In single glory, and we stood, the mist
> Touching our very feet . . .
>
> (ll. 40–54)

Once more we have a landscape that is alive, but its animism is some way from the fairly simple pathetic fallacy of the *Night-Piece* and the moon that sails along followed by attendant multitudes of stars. Nor, of course, should the passage be read in terms of the slightly later Alfoxden poetry of the One Life: 'The clouds were touched . . .'. It is not difficult to see how the Snowdon landscape could have been described in these terms. In place of the animism would have been a consciousness of the pervasive, life-giving presence of God; the moon, the mist, and the mind of the onlooking poet would have shared and reflected equally the blessedness of love. But this is 1804 not 1798. Perhaps there is still an element of pathetic fallacy in the moon's looking down upon the shew in single glory, though Wordsworth's identification with her as spectator and solitary gives her a new and positive role.[10] The meek and silent mist has life of quite a different kind. Oddly, though they had all made the standard comparison with the sea, neither Beattie and Clarke, nor Wordsworth himself in *Descriptive Sketches*, had treated the mist as alive. By making this extension in the Climbing of Snowdon, Wordsworth—half-consciously, perhaps—introduces a border potential, creates the sense of latent power that was lacking in the static, pictorial earlier descriptions. The landscape is at rest, but it is the rest of suppressed activity. For the moment all may be still, but the ocean is composed of a hundred hills, 'their dusky backs *upheaved*', of vapours that may again shoot into new 'headlands, tongues, and promontory shapes'. And yet not everything is animated: *hills* and dusky backs are juxtaposed, *headlands* and tongues. The whole situation is fluid. There is a fusion of different states, a possibility of change and interchange that Wordsworth exploits as the figurative sea usurps upon the real.

It is with the blue chasm that one becomes aware of transcendental associations in the landscape of Snowdon. Wordsworth is drawing partly on his own earlier description, partly on recollections of *Kubla Khan*, but the poetry he writes is very different from either:

> and from the shore
> At distance not the third part of a mile
> Was a blue chasm, a fracture in the vapour,
> A deep and gloomy breathing-place through which
> Mounted the roar of waters, torrents, streams
> Innumerable, roaring with one voice.
> The universal spectacle throughout
> Was shaped for admiration and delight,
> Grand in itself alone, but in that breach
> Through which the homeless voice of waters rose,
> That dark deep thoroughfare, had Nature lodged
> The soul, the imagination of the whole.
>
> (ll. 54–65)

The passage falls clearly in two, the casual opening of each half giving special emphasis to the chasm and its implications. There is a sense of Wordsworth building up to his full rhetorical power ('waters, torrents, streams/Innumerable') then deliberately checking himself and lowering the tone ('The universal spectacle throughout . . . ') so as to be sure that he is carrying the reader with him. The poetry is so good that one does not for a moment doubt that some great assertion is being made. And yet, as so often when Wordsworth is writing at his best, there is a disparity between what one takes to be there, and what is actually claimed. Though one may not read it as such, 'The soul, the imagination of the whole' is as clearly metaphor as are the *roaring* streams and the 'dusky backs' *upheaved* in the mist. The 'gulf of gloomy blue' from *Descriptive Sketches* is shown now as the centre of a humanized universe, just as in the Simplon Pass the disparate elements are drawn together by analogy of the features of a face or thoughts in a single mind. But *en route* the analogies make their own claims—and they make them more powerfully for being metaphor rather than simile. Simile must to some extent restrict association, tie it down. However grand the language of the Simplon Pass, however compelling its rhythms, one is conscious that the 'tumult and peace' are merely '*like* workings of one mind', *like* 'The types and symbols of eternity' (vi. 568, 571). The underlying implication can never become dominant, the figurative never entirely displace the real. In the Climbing of Snowdon, by contrast, Nature positively *lodges* 'The soul, the imagination' in the cloud rift, and one takes the statement with an absurd literalness. Indeed one tends to go *beyond* the literal implications of Wordsworth's lines. Despite the controlling presence of Nature, one reacts to the chasm as if it were itself a power at the centre of the landscape.

It may be worth going back to examine the passage quoted in greater detail. Wordsworth's verse has a disarming straightforwardness. His tones are those of the returned traveller—Bartram, or Barrow, perhaps.[11] The prosaic attention to detail ('not the third part of a mile') and the unexpected harshness of 'fracture', serve to emphasize the chasm's actuality, creating confidence in the narrator's authority at a moment when the poetry is moving away from its basis of fact. Important as it is, the 'deep and gloomy breathing-place' easily passes unnoticed. At the back of his mind Wordsworth seems to have Coleridge's always fanciful, now unfortunately ludicrous, simile of the chasm

> with ceaseless turmoil seething,
> As if this earth in fast thick pants were breathing . . .
> (*Kubla Khan*, 17–18)

But if he is aware of his debt, he has removed all traces of extravagance. So measured are his tones that despite the border adjectives 'deep' and 'gloomy', and the very strong border associations of breath, the 'breathing-place' remains as ordinary, and as physical, as the fracture in the vapour. What is odd is that it should be felt to be so concrete and yet not raise the question—answered easily enough on the level of Coleridge's fantasy—as to who is doing the breathing. *Kubla Khan* is at once more and less evocative: more in that the dream-world it portrays is deliberately exotic, less because the logic and the magic of a dream are dead-ends. On the one side there are 'Ancestral voices prophesying war', on the other is the noise of 'waters, torrents, streams/Innumerable', roaring with one voice that may, or may not, be transcendental. Coleridge's voices are static, caught like the figures on Keats' urn: Wordsworth's roaring streams can develop, expand—their meaning is not restricted. And yet at this point he stands back to make an aesthetic judgement that is straight out of *Kubla Khan*. 'It was a miracle of rare device', Coleridge had written, and Wordsworth catches his tones exactly:

> The universal spectacle throughout
> Was shaped for admiration and delight . . .
> (ll. 60–1)

The lines are quite un-Wordsworthian, but in their context oddly impressive. Wordsworth is playing for a moment on his reader's sense of the marvellous. It is not *his* way of looking at landscape, but it adds to the total effect. He does not himself take an uninvolved view (that is left to the moon who looks down upon the 'shew'), but suggests that even for those who did there would be pleasure of a kind. But more important, Wordsworth is enabled to give to the originally rather tenderly described scene a new grandeur and universality; and at the same time to present it as an artifact—something that has been consciously 'shaped'.

The implications of 'breathing-place' had been deliberately passed over, but the shaping power Wordsworth proposes to identify. Before doing so, however, he returns to the blue chasm, emphasizing its centrality, and developing the imagery that has gone before. It is now a 'breach' (which merely takes up the word 'fracture') through which rises 'the *homeless* voice of waters'. The border effect of 'homeless' is important. At a first reading the word seems to be asking sympathy for the voice of waters, but more significiant is the fact that where before Wordsworth had stressed the power and actuality of the torrents roaring through the mist, he now shows their sound as mysteriously disembodied. First the 'streams/Innumerable' merge into one noise, lose their separate identity; then this combined voice becomes detached, not only without a home, but by implication without a specific source. It is tempting to present the lines that follow as a complex and highly sophisticated use of paradox: the alternative is that they are a jumble that happens to work. 'Lodged' (stationary, by implication) within the chasm that has become a *thoroughfare*, and in some sense responsible for the voice that is *homeless*, is a power that is both soul and imagination, a part of the landscape and not a part of it, autonomous and yet subordinate. Whatever view one might take of intentionalism, it would be nice to know what Wordsworth meant in all this, and especially what he meant by the introduction of Nature, and the bracketing of soul and imagination.

It may be that as one actually reads the Climbing of Snowdon Nature makes little impression—so much is happening by this stage, and Wordsworth's rhythms are so forceful, that one is carried quickly past. But poetry does not exist solely in its immediate impact. At a closer reading her presence has the deadening effect of forcing out into the open the distinction between symbol and fact. Only if it belongs to God, or Nature, can the soul/imagination have an actual existence. If God (Nature) stands outside, there is no longer the possibility of seeing the landscape in terms of the universal mind. Even the breathing-place becomes overtly metaphor. In restrospect it cannot be the breath of God that rises through the dark deep thoroughfare, because God is seen to be an external shaping force, not an immanent presence. The chasm is deprived at a blow of the transcendental power it has come to possess. It is almost as if

Wordsworth was worried that the poetry should come so near to asserting his earlier belief in the One Life, and introduced Nature to give a conventional and acceptable air.

One responds to the terms soul and imagination as radically opposed, as bringing together and momentarily equating the religious principle in man (with the implication of communion with an ultimate power outside the self) and human creativity. Wordsworth was perfectly capable of a slovenly use of language in which no such distinction would be intended. It is disconcerting, for instance, to discover his willingness in the manuscripts to cross out 'heart' and write 'soul', 'soul' and write 'mind', simply to avoid repetition. In this case, however, the equation seems to have been more considered.[12] On a surface level the two words are identified as metaphors stressing the centrality of the cloud-rift; but their connection goes beyond this mere similarity of function. The opposition and reconciliation implied has a history in Wordsworth's poetry that goes back to 1798. In *Tintern Abbey* a distinction is made (and made in the context of a transcendental presence in landscape) between what the mind *perceives* and what it half-*creates* (ll. 107–8). Wordsworth may, as his footnote claims, be thinking of Young's 'And half-create the wond'rous world they see'; but also in the background is his Racedown fragment on the River Derwent,[13] and, much more important, his treatment of perception and imaginative creation in *The Pedlar*. At this earlier period Wordsworth had presented, and presumably believed in, the One Life as fact. His conviction was distantly related (via Coleridge and Joseph Priestley) to quasi-scientific theories about the presence of God in matter; but his own speculations centred not on the form taken by the 'active principle alive/In all things' so much as on the nature of human response. At one stage in *The Pedlar* 'predominance of thought' is offered as a possible means, but for the most part the alternatives, as in *Tintern Abbey*, are straightforward perception on the one hand, and the creative imagination on the other. Wordsworth is fully aware of a logical opposition between the two, and yet seems to feel from the first that the contradiction is unreal. In the Climbing of Snowdon he has chosen to evoke the importance of the blue chasm in terms that imply a complete reconciliation. He is not, of course, talking directly about human perception at all, but his metaphors have the effect of making this extension of theme. At the start merely the description of a particular expedition, the poetry expands to take in an animist landscape, then to evoke the power lying beneath the animation, and finally to imply the kind of response that is taking place.

Wordsworth himself naturally makes no such hard and fast distinctions. As Coleridge wrote in his 1802 letter to Sotheby; 'A poet's *heart and intellect* should be *combined, intimately* combined *and unified*, with the great appearances in Nature . . . ' (Griggs, ii. 864). The passage is quoted in full, and related to the Climbing of Snowdon, by Herbert Lindenberger in the second of his chapters on 'The Rhetoric of Interaction'. Much of his discussion is admirable, but there is too great an emphasis on deliberateness, method—the poetry makes 'a *radical attempt* to fuse inner and outer', Wordsworth makes '*constant endeavors* to synthesize his concepts and percepts into *dazzlingly new rhetorical formations*'[14]—and too little stress on vision, the way that Wordsworth felt things, saw into their life. Wordsworth *is* a conscious artist, *is* working with materials that he has thought about, but he is certainly *not* achieving his greatest effects through manipulation. The border implications and questionings of response come in sideways with the metaphor because their relevance is intuitively perceived, not part of the poet's considered intention. The greatness of the poetry is quite unmethodical. It can be broken down, named, for critical purposes; but in breaking it down one is seeing how it works, not how it was made. 'Dazzlingly new rhetorical formations' gives a false impression of lines and images that derive their power from an instinctive and largely unrationalized union of the poet's heart and intellect with the external world. Coleridge certainly had Wordsworth in mind as he wrote, but he was evoking the nature and grandeur of his creativity, not revealing the tricks of a trade.

'A meditation rose in me *that night*/Upon the lonely mountain', writes Wordsworth. It might have been more accurate to say, as he had done in Book VI, 'Imagination . . . here that power/In all the might of its endowments/Came athwart me'; but there were great advantages to be gained from claiming that this central imaginative insight of May 1805 had been his immediate reflection fourteen years before. The moments of *The Prelude* where Wordsworth steps back to draw conclusions from his experience are not always a success, but here the reader is carried straight through from the narrative (which has itself changed in tone a number of times) into the gloss; and the gloss instead of being flat and expository is composed of poetry that brilliantly takes up the earlier terms and implications:

> A meditation rose in me that night
> Upon the lonely mountain when the scene
> Had passed away, and it appeared to me
> The perfect image of a mighty mind,
> Of one that feeds upon infinity,
> That is exalted by an under-presence,
> The sense of God, or whatsoe'er is dim
> Or vast in its own being . . .
>
> (ll. 66–73)

Though Wordsworth is now explaining things that before had been unstated, the poetry has lost none of its fluidity. The opposition between soul and imagination is beautifully taken up by the last two quoted lines, and in the spatial quality of 'under-presence', 'dim', and 'vast', one responds again to the power of the deep and gloomy breathing-place. But this is not all. The meditation is said to rise *within* the poet, well up of its own accord from those same interior depths from which had 'Mounted the roar of waters, torrents, streams/Innumerable'; and the meditation too is a sense of God, or of the godlike in man, produced by the soul/imagination. Then there are the different, and appropriately different, ways of reading 'it': 'and *it* appeared to me/ The perfect image of a mighty mind'. The dominant meaning is no doubt that the cloud-rift images the mind ('image' in the primary sense still of 'picture'), but grammatically 'it' would be expected to refer back to the meditation as subject of the sentence, and that too in this interchange of meanings makes very good sense: the poet's thoughts reflect the mighty mind that is the subject of his poem, show it in the process of feeding upon infinity. Not that the mind is initially taken to *be* the poet's: at first—and again the confusion is useful, enhancing—one assumes that it is God's. It is an amazing piece of poetry, poetry adequate to this climactic moment when the epiphany that Wordsworth has kept back to be a second time his conclusion has to be shown in its relevance to his new, longer, far more complex, poem.

Among the complexities, or the complicating factors, at all

stages in the poem has been the presence of Milton. Clear and undoubted echoes take the Climbing of Snowdon back to *Paradise Lost*, Book VII—back, that is, to the account of Creation. Mountains that in Milton's poem

> appear
> Emergent, and their broad bare backs upheave
> Into the clouds . . .
>
> (*PL* vii. 285–7)

find themselves in *The Prelude* replaced by hills of mist, whose 'dusky backs upheaved' imply not the achievement of an original creative moment, but the sense of possible future sublimity. The poet and Jones on the edge of the mist recall two earlier figures (one could say two persons, but not in this case, two 'people') who stand similarly on the shore of a sea that is not a sea, and whose role similarly is to impose form through the power of innate creativity. As he writes, Wordsworth surely has at the back of his mind

> The King of Glory, *in his powerful Word*
> *And Spirit*, coming to create new worlds.

'On heavenly ground they stood', Milton had written,

> and from the shore
> They viewed the vast immeasurable abyss
> Outrageous as a sea, dark, wasteful, wild,
> Up from the bottom turned by furious winds
> And surging waves . . .
>
> (*PL* vii. 208–14)

Wordsworth's tones seem at first to be very different—

> and from the shore
> At distance not the third part of a mile
> Was a blue chasm . . .

—and so of course is his immediate purpose, but the 'waters, torrents, streams/Innumerable', though mounting with a single voice, have about them much of the surging energy of Chaos.[15] More surprising perhaps is that there should be affinities between Wordsworth's 'mighty mind', feeding upon the infinity of its own inner turmoil, and Milton's Holy Spirit, brooding dove-like over an external abyss. The mind, however, does not feed directly upon the dim and vast that are the ultimate sources of its strength, it subjects them first to a kind of brooding transformation:

He had discoursed
Like one who in the slow and silent works,
The manifold conclusions of his thought,
Had brooded till imagination's power
Condensed them to a passion, whence she drew
Herself new energies, resistless force.[16]

The condensing of thought to a passion seems closely analogous to the process by which experience becomes intensified into a 'spot of time'. In each case the mind confers upon its inchoate material a sort of pre-formal form, and then draws from its own creation strength that enables the poet consciously to become creative.[17]

The Prelude has been the image of a mighty mind, and the mist on Snowdon is presented as Nature's parallel creation. The landscape is an artifact like the poem itself, and shows in Nature 'a counterpart . . . of the glorious faculty/Which higher minds bear with them as their own'—

That domination which she oftentimes
Exerts upon the outward face of things . . .
by abrupt and unhabitual influence
[Making] one object so impress itself
Upon all others, and pervade them so,
That even the grossest minds must see and hear,
And cannot chuse but feel.

(xiii. 77–84)

Nature has demonstrated the role and power of the poet (and given him, incidentally, the confidence to insult the rest of us). He is at once her counterpart and her perfect audience, for higher minds

build up greatest things
From least suggestions, ever on the watch,
Willing to work and to be wrought upon.

(xiii. 98–100)

It was this process that had been exemplified in the transformation of the statue horse to 'A borderer dwelling betwixt life and death'. Because they are fully imaginative—both perceptive and creative—the Wordsworthian elect

> need not extraordinary calls
> To rouze them—in a world of life they live,
> By sensible impressions not enthralled,
> But quickened, rouzed, and made thereby more fit
> To hold communion with the invisible world.
>
> (xiii. 101–5)

'Such minds', Wordsworth concludes, 'are truly from the Deity,/ For they are powers' (xiii. 106–7). The poetry of course is saying loudly and clearly, 'for *we* are powers'—'for *I* am a power'— and the egocentricity becomes still more impressive as the poet asks

> Oh, who is he that hath his whole life long
> Preserved, enlarged, this freedom in himself?
>
> (xiii. 120–1)

and answers firmly, me.

For the last time in the poem the imagery of the Fall returns, as an older, sadder Wordsworth calls upon the hills and groves to witness that he for one has never colluded:

> Oh, who is he that hath his whole life long
> Preserved, enlarged, this freedom in himself?—
> For this alone is genuine liberty.
> Witness, ye solitudes, where I received
> My earliest visitations (careless then
> Of what was given me), and where now I roam,
> A meditative, oft a suffering man,
> And yet I trust with undiminished powers;
> Witness—*whatever falls my better mind,*
> *Revolving with the accidents of life,*
> *May have sustained—that, howsoe'er misled,*
> *I never in the quest of right or wrong*
> *Did tamper with myself from private aims*;
> Nor was in any of my hopes the dupe
> Of selfish passions; nor did wilfully
> Yield ever to mean cares and low pursuits;
> But rather did with jealousy shrink back
> From every combination that might aid
> The tendency, too potent in itself,
> Of habit to enslave the mind . . .

The sentence has gone on too long, and for the poet to reach his main point it has to go on longer still—

> I mean
> Oppress it by the laws of vulgar sense,
> And substitute a universe of death,
> The falsest of all worlds, in place of that
> Which is divine and true.
>
> (xiii. 120–43)

—but though the writing is slack, what is being said is important. Once more we are told that the Fall that would have mattered has never taken place. On the populous plain of experience the poet had been caught up by Fortune's wheel, 'Revolving with the accidents of life' (and implicitly opposed to the harmonious natural round of Lucy and the skating boy); he had been tempted, and he had been misled; but he had never eaten of the tree of the knowledge of good and evil. M. H. Abrams has suggested that imagination for Wordsworth has the redemptive role of Milton's Christ,[18] but in reading *The Prelude* one is more likely to be reminded of the poet's amazing remark in 1812 to Crabb Robinson: 'I have no need of a Redeemer' (Morley, i, 158). Imagination is the power that has *at all times* enabled him to ward off the universe of death, escape at once the tyranny of the eye and the counter-spirit of language ill used.

Perhaps the achievement of the Climbing of Snowdon is finally that it brings together in a uniquely satisfying way the two aspects of imagination that have been present throughout the poem: the shaping force that is perceived as an external agency, and has been responsible for restorative—one might say, preventive—impressions upon the mind, and the power that is felt to well up from underlying sources within the individual. It is imagination in this second aspect, perfectly imaged in the mounting streams on Snowdon that roar with a single voice, which supports the poet's hope that his own work, '*Proceeding from the depth of untaught things*,/Enduring and creative' may 'become/ A power like one of Nature's'. Internal depth, an inner vastness where things are 'untaught' because they lie beneath, and beyond, the palimpsest layers of experience, is the guarantee of a mind that is truly 'Of substance and of fabric more divine' (xiii. 452). In its portrayal of an 'under-soul', an 'under-*presence*'—

within the landscape, within the mind, within the mind of God—Snowdon enacts the ultimate border possibility. The poetry, and with it the poem as a whole, becomes a creative self-naming, a finite work that is the incarnation of man's highest aspiring, and that lays claim to permanence because it is not different in kind from 'the infinite I AM'.

Almost all these implications are fudged or removed in the text of *1850*. Wordsworth does not merely destroy one of his greatest pieces of poetry, he weakens precisely those aspects which had made it the fitting climax to his poem. To watch him in full retreat is to be reminded of the grandeur of the claims that he no longer dares to make. It is difficult to know whether it is the episode itself, or the gloss, that suffers most in revision. From the moment when the light first falls upon the turf, only half a dozen isolated lines have not been changed for the worse:

> *Nor was time given to ask or learn the cause,*
> For instantly a light upon the turf
> Fell like a flash, *and lo! as I looked up,*
> The Moon *hung* naked *in a firmament*
> *Of azure without cloud, and at my feet*
> *Rested a silent sea of hoary mist.*
> A hundred hills their dusky backs upheaved
> All over this still ocean; and beyond,
> Far, far beyond, *the solid vapours stretched*,
> In headlands, tongues, and promontary shapes,
> *Into the main Atlantic, that appeared*
> To dwindle, and give up *his* majesty,
> Usurped upon as far as sight could reach.
> *Not so the etherial vault; encroachment none*
> *Was there, nor loss; only the inferior stars*
> *Had disappeared, or shed a fainter light*
> *In the clear presence of the full-orbed Moon,*
> *Who, from her sovereign elevation, gazed*
> *Upon the billowy ocean, as it lay*
> *All meek and silent, save that through a rift—*
> *Not distant from the shore whereon we stood,*
> *A fixed, abysmal, gloomy breathing-place—*
> Mounted the roar of waters, torrents, streams
> Innumerable, roaring with one voice

> *Heard over earth and sea, and, in that hour,*
> *For so it seems, felt by the starry heavens.*
> (*1850*, xiv. 37–63; new work in italics)

The last two nebulous, safe, apologetic lines are designed to replace the now too daring implications of the earlier conclusion:

> The universal spectacle throughout
> Was shaped for admiration and delight,
> Grand in itself alone, but in that breach
> Through which the homeless voice of waters rose,
> That dark deep thoroughfare, had Nature lodged
> The soul, the imagination of the whole.
> (*1805*, xiii. 60–5)

The cloud-rift could not be removed altogether without recasting the passage, but the voice of its 'waters, torrents, streams innumerable' is no longer permitted either the immediacy of personal experience, or the transcendental associations of border poetry. It is diffused 'over earth and sea', heard by no one in particular, and cannot even be said for certain to be 'felt' by the heavens. There has been a new usurpation, in fact. The moon, always enviable to the poet as a fellow solitary ('Meanwhile the moon looked down upon this shew/In single glory') has taken over from the cloud-rift as the central focus of the landscape. It is a cosier moon now, no longer aloof, looking down upon the earth and its concerns as on a 'shew', but seen in conventional terms as queen of the night, full-orbed, and gazing from 'her sovereign elevation' amid attendants ('inferior stars') respectfully dimmed in her presence. Isolation which in *1805* had hinted at the poet's own aloofness, the distance of his vision from a norm, has been replaced by a different kind of distancing, as the poetic moon comes to represent withdrawal into the safety of convention—the world of hoary mist, firmament of azure, etherial vault, and starry heavens.

Elements of the great poetry of *1805* of course remain in Wordsworth's account of the moonscape, offering an intermittent and incongruous power that can no longer be put to a purpose. The gloss, however, is completely rewritten:

> When into air had partially dissolved
> That vision, given to spirits of the night

And three chance human wanderers, in calm thought
Reflected, it appeared to me the type
Of a majestic intellect, its acts
And its possessions, what it has and craves,
What in itself it is, and would become.
There I beheld the emblem of a mind
That feeds upon infinity, that broods
Over the dark abyss, intent to hear
Its voices issuing forth to silent light
In one continuous stream; a mind sustained
By recognitions of transcendent power,
In sense conducting to ideal form,
In soul of more than mortal privilege.

(*1850*, xiv. 63–77)

The spirits of the night must be among the most intrusive and distracting of all Wordsworth's later additions to *The Prelude*. Presumably they are there for decoration.[19] But though they have no function, they do have an effect. Comparison of *1850* and *1805* shows a dwindling in the poet's own importance that goes along with the playing down of the cloud-rift. The vision on Snowdon is given in the first place to spirits, and then, on a lower level (as the self-abasing tones imply), impartially to the shepherd, the poet, and Jones—the 'three chance human wanderers' through this vale of tears. It is true that it is still the poet who perceives the landscape as an emblem, but the meditation no longer rises in him, linking gloss and landscape in a recollection of the mounting voice of waters:

A meditation rose in me that night
Upon the lonely mountain when the scene
Had passed away, and it appeared to me
The perfect image of a mighty mind,
Of one that feeds upon infinity,
That is exalted by an under-presence,
The sense of God, or whatsoe'er is dim
Or vast in its own being.

(*1805*, xiii. 66–73)

It is not that the Wordsworth of *1850* wishes to cut out the transcendental implications, just that his earlier clarity frightens him. Man is still 'more than anything we know, instinct/With godhead', but he is also 'born/Of dust, and kindred to the worm' (*1850*, viii. 492–3, 487–8), and must not forget it. And so we get the fudging that will make the great claims less unacceptable. First a sequence of lines nominally presenting the scene as 'the type/Of a majestic intellect', but in fact with no relation to the landscape at all; the poet is simply permitting himself to dwell on irrelevant aspects of the mind that he would like his poetry to conjure up—

its acts
And its possessions, what it has and craves,
What in itself it is, and would become.

Then, after this buffer has been placed between the original account and any attempt at detailed allegorization, comes a reading of the landscape that needs very careful attention. Few readers probably will notice that the imagery preserved from *1805* is now being viewed from quite another standpoint:

There I beheld the emblem of a mind
That feeds upon infinity, that broods
Over the dark abyss, intent to hear
Its voices issuing forth . . .

Where? What now is the emblem? Not surely the landscape at the poet's feet, centring on the cloud-rift that had been 'The soul, the imagination, of the whole', but the moon, gazing and brooding up above. The 'roar of waters, torrents, streams' that had been an internal voice, welling up from within to speak of inner vastness and infinite possibilities, is now caught by an external listener waiting to be sustained by recognitions of a power beyond the self. It is a very big change.[20]

In their different ways, however, or from their different standpoints, both versions of the Climbing of Snowdon portray the source of the river of imagination. 'We have traced the stream/From darkness', Wordsworth wrote very shortly after composing the gloss in its original form,

and the very place of birth
In its blind cavern, whence it faintly heard
The sound of waters; followed it to light
And open day, accompanied its course
Among the ways of Nature, afterwards

Lost sight of it bewildered and engulphed,
Then given it greeting as it rose once more
With strength, reflecting in its solemn breast
The works of man, and face of human life;
And lastly, from its progress have we drawn
The feeling of life endless, the one thought
By which we live, infinity and God.

(xiii. 172–84)

As countless border images show, there had always been a sense in which Wordsworth lived by the one thought of infinity and God, but in May 1805, when these lines were presumably written, it was true in a different way. Possessed by grief at the death of John two months before, he leads the stream of imagination right through from the *Kubla Khan* caves of the womb to the ocean of Christian rest and reward in which he now so urgently needs to believe. But he is of course hoping too to impose retrospectively a structure on his poem, using the recurrent river image to suggest that imagination has been not just 'the moving soul of [his] long labour', but the subject of a connected narrative. The river of *The Prelude* had flowed along the dreams of the sleeping child in the very opening lines of *1799*, and made its appearance as metaphor a year later, in Part II:

Who that shall point as with a wand, and say
'This portion of the river of my mind
Came from yon fountain'?

(*1799*, ii. 247–9)

It is doubtful whether at the time Wordsworth had intended to develop the image, but it recurs at points in Book III of *1805*,[21] and early in IV there is a set-piece that shows just how aware the poet is of its structural possibilities. The student, returned from his first year at Cambridge is taking stock among the scenes of his boyhood, and confronts the stream in his landlady's garden—

that unruly child of mountain birth,
The froward brook, which, soon as he was boxed
Within our garden, found himself at once
As if by trick insidious and unkind,

Stripped of his voice, and left to dimple down
Without an effort and without a will
A channel paved by the hand of man.
I looked at him and smiled, and smiled again,
And in the press of twenty thousand thoughts,
'Ha', quoth I, 'pretty prisoner, are you there!'
—And now, reviewing soberly that hour,
I marvel that a fancy did not flash
Upon me, and a strong desire, straitway,
At sight of such an emblem that shewed forth
So aptly my late course of even days
And all their smooth enthralment, to pen down
A satire on myself.

(*1805*, iv. 39–55)

The indulgent personification of the stream alerts us to the fact that Wordsworth is penning down a satire on himself long before he chooses to point it out. In explaining the emblem, however, he is drawing attention not to a particular moment in a cottage-garden, but to a way of looking at his life and his poem.

To the same late period as the Book XIII stream of imagination belong almost certainly two river-images inserted in earlier Books—the relatively unimportant brook of x. 905 (and implied river of x. 923) and the full-scale apology for his meandering narrative that the poet makes in the opening lines of IX: 'As oftentimes a river . . . Turns and will measure back his course . . . ' It is interesting that this last example of retrospective structuring should be clearly influenced by lines from *The Task*. The Derwent at the opening of *1799* links *The Prelude* back via *Tintern Abbey* and the Wye to Coleridge and the Otter, Bowles and the Itchen, Warton and the Loden, Akenside and 'Wensbeck's limpid stream';[22] but as well as these nostalgic revisited rivers there is in the background Coleridge's scheme for *The Brook*, forerunner to *The Recluse*, in which the river was designed specifically to give the cohesion lacking in Cowper. 'I had considered it as a defect', Coleridge writes in *Biographia Literaria*,

in the admirable poem of the *Task* that the subject which gives the title to the work was not, and indeed could not be, carried on beyond the three or four first pages, and that throughout the poem the connections are frequently awkward,

> and the transitions abrupt and arbitrary. I sought for a subject that should give equal room and freedom for description, incident and impassioned reflections on men, nature and society, yet supply in itself a natural connection to the parts, and unity to the whole. Such a subject I conceived myself to have found in a stream, traced from its source in the hills among the yellow-red moss . . . to the first cultivated plot of ground . . . to the hamlet, the villages, the manufactories and the sea-port.
>
> (*BL* x. 108)

We know from the ludicrous 'Spy Nozy' episode that the Wordsworths and Coleridge charted the brook at Alfoxden in the summer of 1797, and there is every reason to think that they discussed the poetic use of a river as a structural device. At different times in his work on *The Prelude* Wordsworth seems to have recollected Coleridge's rather literal-minded scheme, but there was no likelihood of his adapting it consistently to his own very different vision and purposes. The river never achieves any great structural importance; instead it becomes the poet's organic metaphor for form—or metaphor for organic form—just as the wind is his live (reanimated) image for the dead metaphor of inspiration. Metaphors in *The Prelude* proliferate and interconnect: imagination may finally become the stream of Wordsworth's consciousness, but in the full-length poem it rises as 'the mild creative breeze' of the Preamble, and *en route* it has been the 'unfathered vapour' of Book VI, the mist on Snowdon. As well as these, a host of minor images evoke or enact imagination's power, few of them one supposes deliberately implanted, but all drawing attention in some small way to the poem's central preoccupation, and all in that sense connective. A characteristic way of thought is itself a structural principle, and it is that much more so if it finds expression in images that recur, and bring to mind their predecessors and their cousins. The truest of Wordsworth's retrospects in *The Prelude* does not seek to present the poem as a sequential narrative at all; an image of still water (water this time that is going nowhere) enables him to muse over the heterogeneous material of his poetry, seen amid distortions of every kind in the hidden depths of memory:

> As one who hangs down-bending from the side
> Of a slow-moving boat upon the breast
> Of a still water, solacing himself
> With such discoveries as his eye can make

Beneath him in the bottom of the deeps,
Sees many beauteous sights—weeds, fishes, flowers,
Grots, pebbles, roots of trees—and fancies more,
Yet often is perplexed, and cannot part
The shadow from the substance, rocks and sky,
Mountains and clouds, from that which is indeed
The region, and the things which there abide
In their true dwelling; now is crossed by gleam
Of his own image, by a sunbeam now,
And motions that are sent he knows not whence,
Impediments that make his task more sweet;
Such pleasant office have we long pursued
Incumbent o'er the surface of past time—
With like success.

(iv. 247–64)

On its more obvious level, the passage works superbly. The man looking over the side of his boat is single-mindedly trying to see what is on the bottom; he does not value the products of fancy, and wishes to exclude the reflections of surrounding Nature—rocks and sky, mountains and clouds. His own reflection and the sunbeams are both intrusions, and movements of the boat and water are hindrances (though they make his task more challenging as well as more difficult). But the 'solemn imagery' of Nature 'received / Into the bosom of [a] steady lake' was not irrelevant to Wordsworth. And isn't the whole poem about the gleam of his image, about sunbeams on water, and motions sent one knows not whence? A passage that appears to state the difficulties of getting at objective memory suggests on closer reading that there could be no point in trying. The growth of a poet's mind concerns not just the details of the period that is nominally his subject, but all those elements and experiences of the present and more recent past that confuse or refract them (for the I altering, alters all).

It is no wonder really that Wordsworth did not attempt to sustain a connective image such as Coleridge found to be lacking in *The Task*: he was too like Cowper, and he was too like Coleridge himself.[23] At the centre of *The Task* are the speaking voice and the personality of the writer, neither of them forceful or compelling, yet both attractive, and together strong enough to hold attention if we choose to give it. It is a poem of many moods, informative, indignant, satirical, reflective, and merely self-indulgent:

> Not undelightful is an hour to me
> So spent in parlour twilight: such a gloom
> Suits well the thoughtful or unthinking mind,
> The mind contemplative, with some new theme
> Pregnant, or indisposed alike to all.
>
> (*Task*, iv. 277–81)

Wordsworth of course knew Cowper too, and there is an obvious route from *The Task* through *Frost at Midnight* to *Tintern Abbey*, the two-Part *Prelude*, and on into *1805*. What Coleridge had for his own purposes cut down, Wordsworth built up again, but he did so retaining the features that had given new strength to the genre—in fact he made a bond between the two. Normally in the conversation-poem the writer's preoccupation had been foisted on the listener;[24] it is the greatness of *The Prelude* that the poetry is truly part of a relationship, part of a continuing discussion.

From the reference to *Frost at Midnight* in the eighth line of *1799* right through to the euphoric conclusion to *1805*—

> Prophets of Nature, we to them will speak
> A lasting inspiration . . .
>
> (xiii. 442 ff.)

—*The Prelude* is 'The Poem to Coleridge'. Part I of *1799* begins in response to Coleridge's pressure to write *The Recluse*; Part II cannot begin until Coleridge's approval has been gained, and comes to its conclusion in a touching farewell as he leaves for the south, seeking the haunts of men; the five-Book *Prelude* is undertaken in January 1804 as a gift for Coleridge to take abroad, and then redeveloped to beguile the poet of heavy thoughts before he even sets sail; the new work on *1805* later in the year begins in a progress-report for the poet's 'Beloved friend'; and in bringing his poem to an end, Wordsworth describes it as 'this offering of my love'. Coleridge is addressed again and again, and though *we* may at times forget his presence, Wordsworth never does. It is he who validates the whole undertaking, often providing the sustaining thought, and always providing the sustaining confidence that 'the discipline/And consummation of the poet's mind' is in truth heroic argument:

> O heavens, how awful is the might of souls,
> And what they do within themselves while yet
> The yoke of earth is new to them . . .
>
> (iii. 178–80)

Beneath the *Prelude's* defiance of Milton, and the attempt to impose Miltonic structures on the narrative, lie more personal Falls and fallings-away—Wordsworth's sense that *nothing*

> can bring back the hour
> Of splendour in the grass, of glory in the flower . . . [25]

—and, more important still, the sense that he and Coleridge have in common of a falling-off from the shared idealism and shared certainties of spring 1798.

Coleridge, looking back in the greatest of his conversation-poems, *Dejection* (April 1802), picks up the *Intimations* reference to loss of childhood vision ('There was a time when meadow, grove and stream . . . ') and applies it with a pathos that Wordsworth would very well understand to the creative joy that both had felt at Alfoxden:

> Yes, dearest Sara! Yes!
> There *was* a time when tho' my path was rough,
> The joy within me dallied with distress . . .
>
> (*Dejection*, 231–3)

Imagination for Coleridge has been sapped. He can form a concluding reconciliation from Sara's joy, but no longer believe in a regeneration of his own. Wordsworth as he works on the *Preludes* of 1804 and 1805 is just as aware that 'the power/Of harmony and the deep power of joy' will no longer enable him to 'see into the life of things'; but his domestic situation is tranquil, and his creativity for the moment is plainly unimpaired. Finally, though, it is his continuing sense of election that distinguishes his position from Coleridge's. As in *The Leech Gatherer*, he writes to supply both their needs, seeking constantly to find an alternative basis for optimism now that earlier certainties and sources of power seem closed. In a conversation with Coleridge it is naturally to the imagination that he turns most frequently. The thought that had been at the centre of his friend's despair—

> I may not hope from outward forms to win
> The passion and the life, whose fountains are within . . .
>
> O Sara! we receive but what we give,
> And in *our* life alone does Nature live.
>
> (*Dejection*, 50–1, 296–7)

—is transformed in *1805* to positive assertion. Dominance of mind becomes the criterion of excellence. Imagination has been the moving soul of *their* (the two poets') long labour, and as prophets of Nature they will instruct men

> how the mind of man becomes
> A thousand times more beautiful than the earth
> On which he dwells . . .

The poetry of this great final paragraph (xiii. 428–52) rises to the occasion, but the poet's *bravura* is to be valued chiefly in its poignancy. The millennarian assertions, carried over from the conclusion to *1799*, are hollow now, and if Coleridge could ever have been classed as a 'prophet of Nature', the time is long past. In Wordsworth's grandiloquence, however, one reads the depth and importance of the relationship that has sustained him through his poem.

It is Coleridge's presence that licenses *The Prelude*'s organic form. Sterne and Byron use apparent uncontrol as a structural method. Their voices tell the reader constantly that his formal expectations are being ignored, that they don't give a damn for his views; but their eyes are fixed constantly on audience-reaction. Their act depends on the projection of the writer's personality: they may lay claim to privacy, but if there are moments that are truly revealing, they happen by mistake. Wordsworth, though he too is his own subject, invents himself no character. Some of his voices of course are more public, and there is no doubt that from time to time he composes his gait, and shapes himself

> To give and take a greeting that might save
> [His] name from piteous rumours . . . .
>
> (iv. 118–19)

but he has no wish to be watched, and for the most part he is safe from the constrictions of formal behaviour. He is with a friend who values his monologue as a conversation that may be resumed or dropped at will—a conversation that cannot be formless because it grows out of relationship and preoccupation, and perfectly images the mind that is its subject.[26] Adopting a broadly chronological pattern, but feeling free to measure back his course, and to switch round blocks of poetry that do not in an ordinary sense belong to any single place, Wordsworth dawdles through his work 'like a river, murmuring/And talking to itself' (iv. 110–11). Often the current is slack, the narrative floats into a back-water of self-regard, is sucked into an eddy of irrelevance, but such leisureliness is the condition of the poetry:

> The writer must introduce the truth with such accompaniment as shall imply that he has mounted to the sources of things—penetrated the dark cavern from which the river that murmurs in every one's ear has flowed from generation to generation.
>
> (*Prose Works*, ii. 78–9)

If Wordsworth had imposed (or been able to impose) a tighter structure on *The Prelude*, it would surely have been restrictive. We should have been left wishing 'The river to have had an ampler range/And freer pace'(iii. 509–10).

Epilogue
The Light That Never Was
(*The Recluse*)

> 'Nay, nay, no compliments; I will not be interrupted. Dare you think that riches, rank, and power, are usurpations; and that wisdom and virtue only can claim distinction? Dare you make it the business of your whole life to overturn these prejudices, and to promote among mankind that spirit of universal benevolence which shall render them all equals, all brothers, all stripped of their artificial and false wants, all participating the labour requisite to produce the necessaries of life, and all combining in one universal effort of mind, for the progress of knowledge, the destruction of error, and the spreading of eternal truth?'
>
> (Holcroft: *Anna St. Ives*)

Wordsworth's mood when he prayed early in 1800 that his verse might

> live, and be
> Even as a lamp hung up in heaven to chear
> The world in times to come
>
> (Prospectus, 61–3)

was one of unusual and exalted confidence. Though his lines were printed with *The Excursion* (1814) 'as a kind of *Prospectus* of the design and scope' of *The Recluse*, their aspirations were never to be fulfilled—at least, not in the way that the poet himself had hoped. Yet as late as 1838 Mary Wordsworth still thought it worth setting the Boston publisher, George Ticknor, on to talk to her husband about the unwritten portions of *The Recluse*, because, as she said, she 'could not bear to have him occupied constantly in writing sonnets and other trifles, while this great work lay by him untouched'.[1] By this stage, to judge from the conversation with the poet that Ticknor goes on to report, Wordsworth himself seems at last to have admitted defeat, but for forty years *The Recluse* had been the centre of his thinking. The fact that its nature and history have been so little understood is due partly to a failure to see the poem in its original context, partly to the complicated and changing relationship of *The Recluse* to *The Prelude* and *Excursion*.

'It may be proper to state whence the poem, of which *The Excursion* is a part, derives its title of THE RECLUSE', Wordsworth writes in 1814—

> Several years ago, when the author retired to his native mountains, with the hope of being enabled to construct a literary work that might live, it was a reasonable thing that he should take a review of his own mind, and examine how far Nature and education had qualified him for such employment. . . . The result of the investigation . . . was a determination to compose a philosophical poem, containing views of man, Nature and society, and to be entitled, *The Recluse*, as having for its principal subject the sensations and opinions of a poet living in retirement.
>
> (*Oxford Wordsworth*, v. 1–2)

There follows the celebrated analogy of *The Prelude* as antechapel to the Gothic church of *The Recluse*. The origins of the two works as Wordsworth here presents them are indeed 'a reasonable thing', but they have little to do with the facts. The poet is quietly and deliberately reordering the past. *The Recluse* had been projected, and started, and named, in March 1798—six months before the earliest 'review' of the author's mind (Part I of *1799*), nearly two years before he retired to his native mountains, and more than eight before the full 'result of his investigation' (*1805*) could theoretically have determined him to compose a philosophical poem. Far from deciding on the project in a tidy, rational manner after rigorous self-inquiry, Wordsworth had entered into it in a brief moment of enthusiasm, when Coleridge had inspired him both with confidence in himself, and with faith in the most optimistic of philosophies—'the one life within us and abroad'.

The Recluse, however idiosyncratic it may seem, and be, is one of a great number of millenarian schemes of the late eighteenth and early nineteenth centuries. As Hazlitt puts it, writing with exquisite derision of Robert Owen's *A New View of Society* (1816):

> It may be true, but it is not new. . . . It is as old as the *Political Justice* of Mr Godwin, as the *Oceana* of Harrington, as the *Utopia* of Sir Thomas More, as the

> *Republic* of Plato; it is as old as society itself, and as the attempts to reform it by shewing what it ought to be, or by teaching that the good of the whole is the good of the individual—an opinion by which fools and honest men have been sometimes deceived, but which has never yet taken in the knaves and the knowing ones. The doctrine of universal benevolence, the belief in the omnipotence of truth, and in the perfectibility of human nature, are not new, but 'old, old', Master Robert Owen—why then do you say that they are new? (Howe, vii. 97–8)

The author of *The Recluse* is an honest man who is trying to believe in universal benevolence and the omnipotence of truth, and who to a large extent does believe in the perfectibility of human nature; like Master Robert Owen, he is old, old, in his ideals. He is also, according to Hazlitt's own later view, the purest emanation of the spirit of his age—an age new in many respects, not least in the advent and spiritual importance of the French Revolution.

The strangest thing about *The Recluse* for a modern reader must surely be the certainty of its millenarian assumptions. Wordsworth may lose confidence in his ability to explain how 'the blessed day', 'the fairer day than this', will come about, but he never doubts that it will. When he drops, or shelves, *The Recluse*, he does so not because a redemptive poem cannot be written, but because for the moment he cannot write it. There is something almost back-to-front about the whole business. Instead of perceiving a cause for hope, and going on to deduce from it that mankind will finally achieve happiness, he takes the happiness of the future for granted, and looks about for a way to account for it. It is a kind of thinking which has almost disappeared, and which Hazlitt in his comments on Robert Owen chooses already to ignore. Behind it lies the Book of Revelation. According to a tradition in which some believed quite literally, and from which many others drew unconsciously a measure of support, the created world will last for 6,000 years (effectively, the six days of God's working week), to be followed first by Judgement Day, then by a thousand further years of Christ's direct rule upon earth, and finally by apocalypse—the Last Day, when the dead shall arise incorruptible. 'The groans of Nature in this nether world', writes Cowper in 1784,

> Which Heaven has heard for ages, have an end.
> Foretold by prophets, and by poets sung

Whose fire was kindled at the prophets' lamp,
The time of rest, the promised sabbath, comes.
Six thousand years of sorrow have well-nigh
Fulfilled their tardy and disastrous course
Over a sinful world . . .

(*Task*, vi. 729–36)

The tones that Blake chooses to adopt six years later in *The Marriage of Heaven and Hell* are less easy to gauge, but he is making the same entirely serious point:

The ancient tradition that the world will be consumed by fire at the end of six thousand years is true, as I have heard from Hell.

For the cherub with his flaming sword is hereby commanded to leave his guard at the Tree of Life; and when he does, the whole creation will be consumed, and appear infinite and holy, whereas it now appears finite and corrupt.

(Plate 14; Erdman, 38)

Cowper is waiting patiently for the fulfilment of a prophecy that will take place a hundred years after the death of his material body (in 1996, according to the widely accepted views of Archbishop Ussher),[2] and Blake's thinking is naturally apocalyptic, but belief in the millennium did not have to be so literal-minded. Joseph Priestley, who, as Unitarian philosopher, scientist, radical, probably exercised as great an intellectual influence in his day as anyone save Edmund Burke, wrote in 1772:

Some have supposed that Christ himself will reign in person upon earth, and that the martyrs will actually rise from the dead, and live with him; but considering the figurative language of prophecy, it is more probable that the revival of the *cause* for which they suffered [i.e. the spirit of pure Christianity] is, in reality, the thing denoted by it.[3]

Hartley, whom Priestley was to edit three years later, and who is so frequently the origin of his theological views (and thus of the central tenets of modern Unitarianism), had devoted his concluding section to 'The Final Happiness of all Mankind'. Of the Second Coming he had written: 'We may perhaps say that some glimmerings of the day begin already to shine in the hearts of all those who study and delight in the word and works of God'.[4] It is this necessitarian optimism—based on the Scriptures, yet capable of taking into account human achievement and even the glimmerings of the heart—which in a later, more secular, form provides the underlying certainties of *The Recluse*. To Priestley, the purifying of Christianity (through the work of Hartley, and through Unitarianism), the progress of science (in which, again, he was much involved),[5] and even the far less evident improvements in government, appear to be sure signs that the millennium is approaching. As a result of the extension, and greater precision, of knowledge, human powers will be increased; men will become daily happier, and also more capable of communicating their happiness. 'Thus', he concludes—this time in his *Essay on the First Principles of Government* (1768)—'whatever was the beginning of this world, the end will be glorious and paradisiacal, beyond what our imaginations can now conceive.'[6]

To those who thought in such terms, the great political events of the day had the force of prophecy fulfilled. Priestley's fellow dissenter, Richard Price, whose sermon at the Old Jewry on 4 November 1789 is famous for having provoked Burke to his intemperate *Reflections upon the Revolution in France*, had four years earlier declared that 'next to the introduction of Christianity among mankind, the American revolution may prove the most important step in the progressive course of human improvement.'[7] At the climax of his sermon of 1789 he uses the words of Simeon in the Temple—the Nunc Dimittis—to associate the new political situation still more clearly with the Second Coming. Burke re-enacts the scene in a moment of brilliant sarcasm:

> Plots, massacres, assassinations, seem to some people a trivial price for obtaining a revolution. . . . There must be a great change of scene; there must be a magnificent stage effect; there must be a grand spectacle to rouze the imagination. . . . The Preacher found them all in the French Revolution. This inspires a juvenile warmth through his whole frame. His enthusiasm kindles as he advances, and when he arrives at his peroration, it is in full blaze. Then viewing, from the Pisgah of his pulpit, the free, moral, happy, flourishing, and glorious state of France, as in a bird-eye landscape of a promised land, he breaks out into the following rapture:
>
> 'What an eventful period this is! I am *thankful* that I have lived to it; I could almost say, *Lord, now lettest thou thy servant depart in peace, for mine eyes have seen thy salvation*. I have lived to see a *diffusion* of knowledge, which has undermined superstition and error. I have lived to see *the rights of men* better understood than ever; and nations panting for liberty which seemed to have lost the idea of it. I have lived to see *thirty millions of people*, indignant and resolute, spurning at slavery, and demanding liberty with an irresistible voice.'[8]

Burke might ridicule the aged Price, turning him with a wand from Simeon to Moses, but for a time his views were widely shared. Answers to the *Reflections* come from people of very different backgrounds and very different beliefs, yet all see positive cause for hope. To Priestley, as one might expect, the American and French Revolutions seem a beginning of 'the reign of peace', 'distinctly and repeatedly foretold in many prophecies, delivered more than two thousand years ago'.[9] The Earl of Stanhope, Pitt's brother-in-law (and for a long time his friend and supporter) offers a statesmanlike view that 'The Revolution in France is one of the most striking and memorable pages in history; and no political event was, perhaps, ever more pregnant with good consequences to future ages.'[10] Conscious of Burke's sarcasm, Mary Wollstonecraft specifically refuses to 'hail a millennium', but as well as drawing attention to his distortion of evidence, his 'mock dignity and haughty talk', she allows herself just one moment of vision: 'What salutary dews might not be shed to refresh this thirsty land, if men were more *enlightened*! . . . A garden more inviting than Eden would then meet the eye.'[11] Even Tom Paine, whose views are so practical, and whose deist horror of the Bible knows no bounds, can take up a millenarian image to show the extent of his faith in the new era of political change:

> Never did so great an opportunity offer itself to England, and to all Europe, as is produced by the two Revolutions of America and France. . . . The present age will hereafter merit to be called the Age of Reason, and the present generation will appear to the future as the Adam of a new world.[12]

'Few persons', Southey wrote in 1824, 'but those who have lived in it, can conceive or comprehend what the memory of the French Revolution was, nor what a visionary world seemed to open upon those who were just entering it. Old things seemed passing away, and nothing was dreamt of but the regeneration of the human race.'[13] Despite Burke's talk of plots, massacres, and assassinations, the Revolution for its first three years was dedicated to constitutional reform, and very seldom violent.[14] Not till the suspension of the King in August 1792, and the September Massacres three weeks later, was there cause to fear that moderates in the National Assembly would be unable to maintain control. And not until this stage was there any cause for

British radicals who believed in the regeneration of the human race to ask themselves how and why it should ever come about. Progress seemed to be inevitable because it could be seen to be happening. The heroine of Thomas Holcroft's novel, *Anna St. Ives*,

> has no doubt, some revolution in the planetary system excepted, that man will attain a much higher degree of innocence, length of life, happiness, and wisdom than have ever yet been dreamed of, either by historian, fabulist, or poet . . .

Her reason for these assumptions is that, '*By the laws of necessity*, mind, unless counteracted by accidents beyond its control, is continually progressive in improvement.'[15] Holcroft was an atheist and had no theological or philosophical support for adopting a necessitarian position; for a time, though, it was very easy for radicals to fall into such ways of thinking.

It was of course William Godwin who founded a system on the progressive improvement of mind. Though at the time of *Political Justice* he was an atheist, or at least an agnostic, his early career had been as a dissenting minister—first as a Sandemanian Calvinist, then for a short while as a follower of Priestley. Unlike Holcroft, he is necessitarian through and through.[16] The success of *Political Justice* in February 1793 was partly a matter of fortunate timing—Louis XVI had been executed two weeks before, and radical opinion was badly in need of encouragement—but there never was a philosophy that asserted with such assurance exactly what everyone would most like to believe. Godwin is a rationalist, but his hopes depend—as all Romantic hopes depend—upon an act of faith: 'every perfection or excellence that human beings are competent to conceive, human beings . . . are competent to attain.' 'This is an inference', he continues,

> which immediately follows from the omnipotence of truth. Every truth that is capable of being communicated, is capable of being brought home to the conviction of the mind. Every principle which can be brought home to the conviction of the mind, will infallibly produce a correspondent effect upon the conduct.[17]

It is all marvellously pat. Truth is omnipotent and discernible; man is perfectible; those to whom truth is communicated will act upon it; the mere exercise of reason will *of necessity* lead to the creation of a just and contented society.

Godwin himself was to be the educator, the bringer home of convictions to the mind: 'Infuse just views of society into a certain number of the liberally educated and reflecting members; give to the people guides and instructors; and the business is done' (*PJ* i. 69). The business, however, took more doing than he expected. The Government did not encourage reflecting members of society to think in revolutionary terms, and by the time of the second edition of *Political Justice* (1796) it must have been clear that truth if it was to prove omnipotent would need a good deal of help. A year later, one of Godwin's wealthier admirers, Tom Wedgwood, sent him an account of the 'master stroke' which he had hit upon for producing the leaders of the future:

> Fortune has placed a considerable trust in my hands. I have lately been considering how it may best be employed—perhaps I have hit upon the most profitable mode of beneficial expenditure.
>
> My aim is high—I have been endeavouring some master stroke which should anticipate a century or two upon the large-paced progress of human improvement. Almost every prior step of its advance may be traced to the influence of superior characters. Now, it is my opinion, that in the education of the greatest of these characters, not more than one hour in ten has been made to contribute to the formation of those qualities upon which this influence has depended . . .[18]

Wedgwood goes on to outline a scheme for the production of genius, and not just any genius, but the character which 'the actual state of society most demand[s]'. His plan will be drawn up by philosophers (including Godwin himself, Beddoes, Holcroft, and Horne Tooke), and implemented by superintendents. For this post the only likely candidates he can think of are Coleridge and Wordsworth—this despite the fact that the prospective genius is to have sense-impressions administered to him in regular sequence, to live in a nursery with plain grey walls and hard bodies hung about to stimulate the sense of touch, and to be deprived completely of the natural world until he is strong enough to take it:

> The gradual explication of Nature would be attended with great difficulty; *the child must never go out of doors* or leave his own apartment.
>
> (*BNYPL* lx, 431)

Wedgwood followed up his letter in September 1797 by going down to stay at Alfoxden. By implication he lost interest in Wordsworth, but was impressed by Coleridge, to whom in

December he and his brother first offered a substantial present, and then gave an annuity (Griggs, i. 373–4). It is interesting that when writing to Godwin he had thought that Coleridge might be 'too much a poet and religionist to suit [their] views'. As poet and religionist, Coleridge had just reprinted his own millenarian hopes in *Religious Musings:*

> Believe thou, oh my soul,
> Life is a vision shadowy of truth,
> And vice, and anguish, and the wormy grave,
> Shapes of a dream! The veiling clouds retire,
> And lo! the throne of the redeeming God,
> Forth flashing unimaginable day,
> Wraps in one blaze earth, heaven, and deepest hell.
> (ll. 413–19)

It is no longer easy to respond to prophetic vision and grand apocalyptic style, but Coleridge took what he was saying with an absolute seriousness, and expected others to do so too.[19] To his fellow Unitarian, Lamb, *Religious Musings* seemed 'the noblest poem in the language, next after the *Paradise Lost*'. 'And even that', he adds, 'was not made the vehicle of such grand truths' (Marrs, i. 95). His judgement has the same fervent partiality that led Priestley to think Hartley's *Observations* 'without exception the most valuable production of the human mind'.[20] It has also the same intellectual basis: 'I thank you for these lines', Lamb wrote when Coleridge first sent him the final section of *Religious Musings*, 'in the name of a *necessarian*' (Marrs, i. 18; Lamb's italics).

Priestleyan necessitarians did not believe that 'The Final Happiness of All Men' would come without effort; *Religious Musings* was part of a crusade which in spring 1796 Coleridge felt himself to be fighting single-handed. 'Was it right', he asks in *Reflections on Having left a Place of Retirement*,

> While my unnumbered brethren toiled and bled,
> That I should dream away the entrusted hours
> On rose-leaf beds, pampering the coward heart
> With feelings all too delicate for use?
> (ll. 44–8)

The question is rhetorical, and brings an answer that seems to be no less so:

> I therefore go, and join head, heart, and hand,
> Active and firm, to fight the bloodless fight
> Of science, freedom, and the truth in Christ.
>
> (ll. 60–2)

In his protest over the Two Bills the previous November Coleridge had shown himself as still committed to a political struggle; unlike the Wordsworth of *Descriptive Sketches*, however, he had never seen the millennium as an immediate possibility. He was two years younger than Wordsworth, and had not to the same extent been inspired by the French Revolution; he was alarmed by the thought of violent change and power misplaced; above all, he was by nature 'too much a religionist'. The ninety-eight lines of *Religious Musings* printed in *The Watchman* in March 1796, though entitled *The Present State of Society*, show inequality and suffering in the terms of Revelation:

> Rest awhile,
> Children of Wretchedness! More groans must rise,
> More blood must stream, or ere your wrongs be full.
> Yet is the day of retribution nigh:
> The Lamb of God hath opened the fifth seal:
> And upwards spring on swiftest plume of fire
> The innumerable multitude of wrongs
> By man on man inflicted! Rest awhile,
> Children of Wretchedness! The hour is nigh:
> And lo! the great, the rich, the mighty men,
> The kings and the chief captains of the world,
> With all, that fixed on high, like stars of heaven,
> Shot baleful influence, shall be cast to earth. . . .
>
> O return!
> Pure FAITH! meek PIETY! The abhorred form
> Whose scarlet robe was stiff with earthly pomp,
> Who drank iniquity in cups of gold;
> Whose names were many and all blasphemous;
> Hath met the horrible judgement! . . .

> Return pure FAITH! return meek PIETY!
> The kingdoms of the world are your's: each heart
> Self-governed, the vast family of love,
> Raised from the common earth by common toil,
> Enjoy the equal produce.
>
> (*Religious Musings*, 313ff.; *CC* ii. 64–7)

It is important to be clear what the Unitarian 'truth in Christ' consisted of. Priestley was, in Lamb's phrase, a 'one-Goddite', but in denying the divinity of Christ he created for him a special importance. Christ's unique achievement was that, *though a man*, he rose from the dead, thus showing what the rest (or the best) of us will one day be able to do. The return of 'pure Faith', 'meek Piety', the bonding of kingdoms into a 'vast family of love', will herald the Second Coming that is to precede the general resurrection. Suffering was not a matter of unconcern to Coleridge, but he could write, 'More groans must rise,/more blood must flow', with equanimity because the distant future happiness was not in doubt.

Wordsworth's position was very different. Beaupuy had taught him in 1792 that poverty 'would in a little time/Be found no more' (*1805*, ix. 523–4); and Godwin, with his secular necessitarianism, had supported him as political hopes became less credible. He had at no time been attracted by religious solutions. The appearance of *Religious Musings*, however, must have coincided exactly with the yielding up of moral questions in despair that is described in *1805*, Book X. Under these circumstances it is especially interesting that Wordsworth should have singled out for praise ('the best thing in the volume—worth all the rest'; Griggs, i. 216) the passage of Coleridge's poem that comes to a climax in the 'vision shadowy of truth'. No doubt he was excited by the grandeur of the writing, but he must also surely have been envious of the certainties that were being expressed. It would be convenient to claim that at this time he was actively drawn to Coleridge's way of thinking, but there is no evidence. What is certain is that when two years later, in March 1798, Wordsworth announced his scheme for *The Recluse* ('My object is to give pictures of Nature, man, and society. Indeed I know not any thing which will not come within the scope of my plan'; *EY* 212), he did so as a convert to the philosophical system of the One Life that had made its appearance in *Religious Musings*:

> There is one mind, one omnipresent mind,
> Omnific. His most holy name is LOVE. . . .
>
> 'Tis the sublime of man,
> Our noontide majesty, to know ourselves
> Parts and proportions of one wond'rous whole:
> This fraternizes man, this constitutes
> Our charities and bearings. But 'tis God
> Diffused through all, that doth make all one whole . . .
> (ll. 114–15, 135–40)

It is of course *Tintern Abbey* that contains the most famous statement of this belief made by either poet:

> And I have felt
> A presence that disturbs me with the joy
> Of elevated thoughts, a sense sublime
> Of something far more deeply interfused . . .
> A motion and a spirit, that impels
> All thinking things, all objects of all thought,
> And rolls through all things.
> (ll. 94–7, 101–3)

Behind these great lines, however, lie two specific Coleridge passages, the first a reference at the end of *Religious Musings* to spirits of 'plastic', or creative, power (particles of the infinite mind, as Coleridge suggests),

> *that interfused*
> *Roll through the grosser and material mass*
> With organizing surge . . .
> (ll. 423–5)

the second from a section written by Coleridge the previous year for Southey's *Joan of Arc*:

> Glory to Thee, Father of earth and heaven!
> All-conscious *presence* of the universe!
> Nature's vast ever-acting energy!
> In will, in deed, *impulse of all to all!*
> (*Destiny of Nations*, 459–62; *Joan of Arc*, ii. 442–5)

If Wordsworth had gone ahead with *The Recluse* in March 1798, instead of turning his hand to writing copy for *Lyrical Ballads*, his philosophical position would certainly have been pantheist. The 1,300 lines that he claimed already to have written consisted chiefly of *The Ruined Cottage*, for which *The Pedlar*, with its proselytizing tones—

> Wonder not
> If such his transports were; for in all things
> He saw one life, and felt that it was joy.
>
> (ll. 216–18)

—had very recently been composed.[21] The 'knowledge' of which Wordsworth felt himself at this moment 'to stand possessed' was of man's ability to perceive, as well as share, the omnipresence of God. Though later on his hard-won Trinitarian views would not have permitted him to put it so bluntly, this for Coleridge continued to be the central redemptive fact of *The Recluse*. His account of the scheme in *Table Talk* (1832) ends with the words, 'It is, in substance, what I have all my life been doing in my system of philosophy'; and the terms he uses are quite consistent with the ideals that Wordsworth had assimilated from him at Alfoxden:

> the plan laid out, and, I believe, partly suggested by me, was, that Wordsworth should assume the station of a man in mental repose, one whose principles were made up, and so prepared to deliver upon authority a system of philosophy. He was to treat man as man—a subject of eye, ear, touch, and taste, in contact with external nature, and informing the senses from the mind, and not compounding a mind out of the senses; then he was to describe the pastoral and other states of society, assuming something of the Juvenalian spirit as he approached the high civilizations of cities and towns, and opening a melancholy picture of the present state of degeneracy and vice; thence he was to infer and reveal the proof of, and necessity for, the whole state of man and society being subject to, and illustrative of, a redemptive process in operation, showing how this idea reconciled all the anomalies, and promised future glory and restoration.[22]

Clearly the scheme was an updating and expansion of *Religious Musings*. Wordsworth, who had worked on an imitation of Juvenal in 1795–6, was to produce a poem of mixed genres, turning satirist as Coleridge had done to show contemporary degradation before the approaching millennium.

The most detailed, though not necessarily the most reliable, account of *The Recluse* is provided by Coleridge's letter to Wordsworth of 30 May 1815. He is at work on *Biographia*

Literaria, and there are striking links between his own project and what he remembers of Wordsworth's intentions. The *Recluse* that he had been expecting was a single poem of four more-or-less distinct phases. Wordsworth should first

> have meditated the faculties of man in the abstract . . . laid a solid and immoveable foundation for the edifice by removing the sandy sophisms of Locke, and the mechanic dogmatists, and demonstrating that the senses were living growths and developments of the mind and spirit in a much juster as well as higher sense, than the mind can be said to be formed by the senses.
>
> (Griggs, iv. 574)

Next, more surprisingly, he should have exploded the absurd notion 'of man's having progressed from an ouran outang state—so contrary to all history, to all religion, nay, to all possibility', replacing it by what he describes as 'a Fall in some sense', of which the reality 'is attested by experience and conscience'. Fallen man should then 'have been contemplated in the different ages of the world . . . not disguising the sore evils, under which the whole creation groans'. And satire, in the final stage, should once again have led straight into 'a manifest scheme of redemption'. Leaving aside the crazy fight against evolution,[23] this is *The Recluse* as later set out in *Table Talk*; but it is far clearer here that Coleridge thinks of the scheme as having been founded upon the primary imagination. The poem should have concluded in

> a grand didactic swell on the necessary identity of a true philosophy with true religion, agreeing in the results and differing only as the analytic and synthetic process, as discursive from intuitive, the former chiefly useful as perfecting the latter . . .
>
> (Griggs, iv. 575)

The distinction is that made by Coleridge with the help of Kant and Milton in *Biographia*, chapter X. On the one hand is philosophy, analysis, understanding, or discursive reason; on the other, synthesis, and pure, or intuitive, reason. The first, as Raphael suggests to Adam, is the common human faculty, the second is of a higher order.[24] And to complete the picture, it is Wordsworth who points out, doubtless with Coleridge's backing, that 'reason in her most exalted mood' is imagination (*1805*, xiii. 170).

Wordsworth in the *Excursion* Preface is reordering the past so as to present a tidy public appearance, and Coleridge in his 1815 letter is thinking of *The Recluse* in terms of *Biographia*. It was not an unreasonable thing to do: the origins of *Biographia* go back into the period when Wordsworth had been relying upon him to produce material, and the two schemes could not fail to be entwined. Letters to Humphry Davy of October 1800 and February 1801 show Coleridge not only planning to write a life of Lessing, but also girding himself to attack 'An Essay on the Elements of Poetry' which 'would in reality be a disguised system of morals and politics'.[25] And a *Notebook* entry of autumn 1803 shows that the scheme has taken on a shape extraordinarily close to that of *Biographia*:

> Seem to have made up my mind to write my metaphysical *works* as *my life*, and *in* my life–intermixed with all the other events or history of the mind and fortunes of S. T. Coleridge.
>
> (*Notebooks*, i, no. 1515)

Clearly the true counterpart of *Biographia* is not *The Recluse*, but *The Prelude*; *The Recluse* has as its natural partner Coleridge's projected but never written *Logosophia*. Like *The Prelude*, *Biographia* makes its philosophical points, and *needs* to make its philosophical points, in a personal and literary context. Its announcements of the *Logosophia* that should 'give (*deo volente*) the demonstrations and constructions of the dynamic philosophy scientifically arranged' (*BL* xiii. 149) are no more credible than Wordsworth's trailers for *The Recluse*. The dynamic philosophy can only be the primary imagination, and that will emerge in *Biographia* itself, 'intermixed with all the other events or history of the mind and fortunes of S. T. Coleridge':

> The theory of natural philosophy would then be completed when all Nature was demonstrated to be identical in essence with that which in its highest known power exists in man as intelligence and self-consciousness; when the heavens and the earth shall declare not only the power of their maker but the glory and the presence of their God, even as He appeared to the great prophet during the vision of the mount . . .
>
> (*BL* xii. 146)

As He appeared, that is, to Moses in the moment of His first and eternal self-naming, I AM.

René Wellek has commented that:

> Coleridge has little insight into the incompatibility of different trends of thought. He lacks a sense for the subtle shades of terminological differences in

different thinkers, he seems sometimes almost blind to the wide implications in this or that idea.[26]

None of this is untrue (except perhaps the final clause, which is trying too hard to be kind), but can one usefully blame a man who is searching for the one and indivisible, if he fails to see distinctions? *Biographia* is the last of Coleridge's great creative works; like *The Prelude* it is a justification of the writer's life and aspirations, and offers to the sympathetic reader not bad philosophy but 'the philosophic imagination, the sacred power of self-intuition'. What need was there for a *Logosophia* in a thinker who took Wordsworth as his hero, regarded the carrying on of childhood wonder as 'the character and privilege of genius', and could say in full seriousness:

They and they only can acquire the philosophic imagination, the sacred power of self-intuition, who within themselves can interpret and understand the symbol that the wings of the air-sylph are forming within the skin of the caterpillar . . .[27]

(*BL* xii. 139)

Coleridge had read a great deal in the intervening period, yet his apprehensions in 1815 had changed very little from those of the early Berkleyan days. Life was still for him 'a vision shadowy of truth', and imagination still the power that read 'The lovely shapes and sounds intelligible' of Nature as the eternal language of God.[28]

But though Berkeley is presumably to be seen as the background to Coleridge's final views of imagination, there is no evidence that his influence in the early period led to positive definitions, or to a system that could have formed a basis for *The Recluse*. It is easier to think of this as deriving initially from the German visit of 1798–9, and as being reinforced—perhaps in fact, converted into a system—by opposition to 'the sandy sophisms of Locke':

the philosophy of mechanism which in every thing that is most worthy of the human intellect strikes *death* . . . and which idly demands conceptions where intuitions alone are possible or adequate to the majesty of truth.

(Griggs, iv. 575)

Coleridge's systematic refutation of Locke and Descartes took place at the beginning of 1801. On 23 March Locke is described as 'a perfect little-ist', and Coleridge adds: 'My opinion is this—that deep thinking is attainable only by a man of deep feeling, and that all truth is a species of revelation (Griggs, ii. 709). The mechanist universe is unacceptable because man is capable of 'a repetition in the finite mind of the eternal act of creation'. As 'creator and receiver both', the Infant Babe presumably suggests that Coleridge had been working towards such a position at Göttingen early in 1799;[29] but the fact that *Home at Grasmere*—Wordsworth's first serious attempt to write the central section of *The Recluse*—puts no reliance on imagination is evidence that as late as spring 1800 the scheme described in the different retrospects has not yet been drawn up.

Home at Grasmere shows the poet working very much on his own, supported neither by imagination, as *The Prelude* of 1804–5 will be, nor by the One Life, as *The Pedlar* had been in 1798. Though Coleridge had been pestering Wordsworth to get on with *The Recluse* ever since his return from Germany, his views have curiously little part in this attempt to do so. Or so it seems. It could be, however, that a link is provided by Cowper. Coleridge had urged *The Recluse* on Wordsworth at Alfoxden because he felt unable to write *The Brook*, and *The Brook* we are told had been designed specifically to overcome the structural weakness of *The Task*.[30] Surprisingly, Cowper nowhere describes himself as a recluse, but he had set himself up, consciously and self-consciously, as the poet living in retirement. And, though his millenarian views are very mildly expressed by comparison, they amount almost exactly to those of *Religious Musings*. In fact Coleridge's solemn warning, 'But 'tis God/Diffused through all, that doth make all one whole' (*Religious Musings*, 139–40), seems to be an echo of Cowper's

> The Lord of all, himself through all diffused,
> Sustains, and is the life of all that lives.
>
> (*Task*, vi. 221–2)

If Cowper was to have been a model for *The Recluse* in 1798, Wordsworth in *Home at Grasmere* may be seen as carrying out his original intentions, or instructions—or at least as trying to do so. He is writing dutifully, often with great beauty and tenderness, but he is a millenarian poet with no system to offer. He thinks as a necessitarian, but his assumption of future well-being for mankind rests on the quality of his personal happiness with Dorothy. He could easily have written, as Cowper does write early in *The Task*.

> Domestic happiness, thou only bliss
> Of Paradise that has survived the Fall!
>
> (iii. 41–2)

And there is every reason to think that he not only borrowed, but took comfort in, the muted certainties with which Cowper's poem ends:

> Thus heaven-ward all things tend. For all were once
> Perfect, and all must be at length restored.
> So God has greatly purposed. . . .
>
> He is the happy man, whose life ev'n now
> Shows somewhat of that happier life to come . . . [31]
>
> (vi. 818–20, 906–7)

But Cowper's is a Christian millennium, the predicted Second Coming, when Christ will rule on earth for a thousand years before the final apocalypse:

> One song employs all the nations; and all cry,
> 'Worthy the Lamb, for he was slain for us!'
> The dwellers in the vales, and on the rocks
> Shout to each other, and the mountain tops
> From distant mountains catch the flying joy . . .
>
> (vi. 791–5)

Beside such faith the Wordsworth of *Home at Grasmere* has only the sense that what is happening to him here and now, others must one day be able to attain.[32] Cowper writes of the Second Coming as 'scenes surpassing fable, and yet true' (vi. 759), and Wordsworth asks poignantly:

> Paradise and groves
> Elysian, blessed islands in the deep,
> Of choice seclusion—wherefore need they be
> A history, or but a dream, when minds
> Once wedded to this outward frame of things
> In love, find these the growth of common day?
>
> (Prospectus, 35–40)

His personal love for Dorothy and their surroundings tells him that ordinariness can become paradise, and he briefly allows himself to feel, and say, that paradise could become ordinary.

The mood of the Prospectus and the early parts of *Home at Grasmere* is no less exalted than that of 1798, but there is far less to support the optimism it inspires. At Alfoxden it had been possible to believe that love was general—

The clouds were touched,
And in their silent faces did he read
Unutterable love.

—that creation was singing the song of the One Life, and singing it for all to hear (*Pedlar*, 99–101, 219). But now Cowper's moral, sentimental, personal God—the God of Victorian children and their pets—is called in not merely to convey the poet's sense of the outrage committed at Hart-leap Well, but as the means of justifying his decision to become a recluse. Cowper had warned of the Judgement to come for maltreatment of 'creatures that exist but for our sake',

and God, some future day,
Will reckon with us roundly for the abuse
Of what he deems no mean or trivial trust . . .
(vi. 605–7)

and Wordsworth's tones are uncomfortably similar as he describes

The vision of humanity and of God
The mourner, God the sufferer, when the heart
Of his poor creatures suffers wrongfully . . . [33]
(*Home at Grasmere*, 244–6)

The lines that follow in *Home at Grasmere* have a much greater seriousness of purpose than anything achieved, or attempted, in *The Task*, but the faith that sustains them is private:

Both in the sadness and the joy we found
A promise and an earnest that we twain,
A pair seceding from the common world,
Might in that hallowed spot to which our steps
Were tending, in that individual nook,
Might even thus early for ourselves secure,
And in the midst of these unhappy times,
A portion of the blessedness which love

And knowledge will, we trust, hereafter give
To all the vales of earth and all mankind.
(*Home at Grasmere*, 247–56)

Matching himself against Milton in the Prospectus, Wordsworth could briefly assume a prophetic voice—in Cowper's phrase, his 'fire was kindled at the prophet's lamp'—but not even to please Coleridge could he 'deliver upon authority a system of philosophy'. Love of whom, knowledge of what? In the distant background are Beaupuy and the ideals of French republicanism—

France standing on the top of golden hours,
And human nature seeming born again.
(*1805*, vi. 353–4)

—and in the more recent past lie the pantheist views that Wordsworth had shared with Coleridge at Alfoxden,[34] but in 1800 'love' and 'knowledge' can have had very little meaning outside the personal context of the poet's love for Dorothy. He might retain his necessitarian ways of thought, his Godwinian faith in education and perfectibility, but his neighbours at Dove Cottage were no support to him. After the initial confidence, *Home at Grasmere* shows him to be more and more aware that future blessedness, if it depends on human beings, may be a very long way off. The fact that he was using for his drafts an interleaved copy of *Religious Musings* must have come to seem increasingly wry. As Coleridge mounted to his triumphant millenarian conclusion, Wordsworth's own poem—though grander still in its aspirations—faltered to a halt. 'Dismissing therefore all Arcadian dreams', he wrote, 'All golden fancies of the golden age',

Give entrance to the sober truth, avow
That Nature to this favoured spot of ours
Yields no exemption, but her awful rights
Enforces to the utmost and exacts
Her tribute of inevitable pain—
And that the sting is added, man himself
For ever busy to afflict himself . . .

On the opposite page stood lines that might have been chosen for their power to discomfort:

For in his own and in his Father's might
The SAVIOUR comes! While as to solemn strains
The THOUSAND YEARS lead up their mystic dance,
Old OCEAN claps his hands! the DESERT shouts!
And soft gales wafted from the haunts of Spring
Melt the primaeval North! The mighty Dead
Rise to new life, whoe'er from earliest time
With conscious zeal had urg'd Love's wond'rous plan,
Coadjutors of God. To MILTON's trump
The odorous groves of earth reparadis'd
Unbosom their glad echoes: inly hush'd
Adoring NEWTON his serener eye
Raises to heaven: and he of mortal kind
Wisest, he* first who mark'd the ideal tribes
Down the fine fibres from the sentient brain

*David Hartley

(Darlington, 236–9)

Milton, announcing the millennium to groves reparadised, had in Coleridge's fantasy performed exactly the function that *The Recluse* was designed to perform. Newton and Hartley, as 'coadjutors of God', had in their different ways 'urged Love's wond'rous plan', brought an advancement of knowledge. Coleridge himself, though his bringing up to date of the Book of Revelation might seem very different from Wordsworth's 'coming of the milder day', was to be seen writing with enviable confidence—and of course also writing with an enviable body of tradition to back him up. Looking across to the printed lines, Wordsworth must have been very conscious of his lack of comparable authority. In the pleasure of his return to Grasmere, the groves of earth had seemed indeed to be reparadised, but the intuition of man the serpent left him with little to be said. At an earlier stage in the writing of his poem it had seemed that Coleridge would play Milton's part—that on the arrival at Dove Cottage of this herald of the millennium the mountains would 'rejoice with open joy'[35]—but when in fact Coleridge did come, the drafts of *MS R* had almost certainly been abandoned. How, one wonders, did he react to the failure of *Home at Grasmere*? The previous September he had written 'of nothing but *The Recluse* can I hear patiently', but to judge from his letter to Southey of *c.* 10 April 1800 he seems now to have condoned Wordsworth's shelving of the poem in favour of a second volume of *Lyrical Ballads* (Griggs, i. 538, 585). Perhaps the disappointment was lost in the excitement of the first visit to Dove Cottage; perhaps the failure seemed less important than it does to us in retrospect. Coleridge could not know that Wordsworth would return again and again over the years to this false start, but never be able to make a radical new beginning. Neither of them seems to have admitted, at least for a very long time, that it was not in Wordsworth's nature to write 'the *first* and *only* true phil[osophical] poem in existence'.

With Coleridge coming to live at Greta Hall in July 1800, and in the following year carrying out the reading of Kant and Fichte (and reassessment of Locke) that lies behind the definitions of *Biographia*, Wordsworth should in theory quite soon have been in a position to make another attempt on *The Recluse*, along the lines that Coleridge claims to have expected. The definition of imagination reached in Coleridge's letter to Poole of 23 March 1801 is made precisely in opposition to 'Locke and the mechanic dogmatists':

> Be not afraid that I shall join the party of the *little-ists*—I believe that I shall delight you by the detection of their artifices. Now Mr Locke was the founder of this sect, himself a perfect little-ist. My opinion is this—that deep thinking is attainable only by a man of deep feeling, and that all truth is a species of revelation . . .

Newton, singled out in *Religious Musings* as the bringer of progress, now appears 'a mere materialist':

> *Mind* in his system is always passive—a lazy looker-on on an external world. If the mind be not *passive*, if it be indeed made in God's image, and that too in the sublimest sense—the image of the *Creator*—there is ground for suspicion that any system built on the passiveness of the mind must be false, as a system.
> (Griggs, ii. 708–9)

There was also, it might seem, ground for *The Recluse* to be written announcing a new system built on the mind's activity. But Wordsworth shows no signs of wishing to write it. Almost from the first there seems to have been deadlock: Coleridge pestering Wordsworth to make a start, and occasionally believing him to have done so;[36] Wordsworth countering with demands for material that become more and more desperate. 'I am very anxious', he writes on 6 March 1804, to have your notes for *The Recluse*. I cannot say how much importance I attach to this; if it should please God that I survive you, I should reproach myself for ever in writing the work if I had neglected to procure this help.

(*EY* 452)

Three weeks later he is more anxious still. Coleridge is *en route* for Malta, and the thought that he really might die with the all-important notes unwritten has been borne in on Wordsworth by news of his illness while waiting to set sail:

Your last letter but one informing us of your late attack was the severest shock to me, I think, I have ever received. . . . I will not speak of other thoughts that passed through me; but I cannot help saying that I would gladly have given 3 fourths of my possessions for your letter on *The Recluse* at that time. I cannot say what a load it would be to me, should I survive you and you die without this memorial left behind. Do for heaven's sake, put this out of the reach of accident immediately. . . . Heaven bless you for ever and ever. No words can express what I feel at this moment. Farewell, farewell, farewell.

(*EY* 464)

Spring 1804 is of course the period not just of Coleridge's departure, but of Wordsworth's greatest philosophical poetry. February had seen the Climbing of Snowdon with its celebration of the creative human mind, 'made in God's image'; and sandwiched between the two letters of March demanding material come the great central passages of *Prelude*, Book VI. Imagination, which Coleridge in 1815 regards as the basis of *The Recluse*, becomes the dominant force in *The Prelude* at a moment when Wordsworth seems to be especially conscious of lacking help for his major work.

No doubt what Wordsworth really wanted from Coleridge's notes was magic, sudden illumination, spontaneous awareness as to how one should set about delivering *upon authority* a system of philosophy. It was not that he had difficulty in assimilating Coleridge's thinking on imagination into his poetry; like the related earlier dogma of the One Life, it gave its support to truths that had been intuitively perceived. To present such truths within a system was another matter. Coleridge never succeeded in doing it for himself, and it is very doubtful whether his notes would have been any use to Wordsworth even if he had been able to write them.[37] In content they would have resembled the philosophical sections of *Biographia*; but these are successful (or acceptable) only because, like the comparable sequences of *The*

Prelude, they grow out of the surrounding personal and literary context. A more systematic removal of 'the sandy sophisms of Locke' could never have been poetic material. Wordsworth's faith in Coleridge is touching, but hopeless. Though he could not have known it, in *The Prelude* he was writing the great philosophical poem that *The Recluse* was intended to be, and writing it—as Coleridge was to write his 'Literary Life and Opinions', not the *Logosophia*—in the form and idiom that corresponded especially to the patterns of his thought. When *The Prelude* was completed in the full-length version of May 1805 there was never a hope of further progress. The flanking *Excursion* could still be written, but the scheme of *The Recluse* would have finally to do without its centrepiece.

The most poignant moments in the history of *The Recluse* are those when, as on Boxing Day 1805, Dorothy refers to her brother as 'very anxious to get forward', and 'reading for the nourishment of his mind, preparatory to beginning' (*EY* 664). Wordsworth was once more free to get on with his major task; and the pressure on him was now greater than ever, because writing had come to seem the fulfilment of a bond with the dead. John, as captain of the *Earl of Abergavenny*, had regarded himself as working so that his brother, in seclusion, could 'do something for the world'. 'This is the end of his part of the agreement, of his efforts for my welfare', Wordsworth had written on 23 February 1805, twelve days after the news of John's death, 'God grant me life and strength to fulfill mine . . . there is a bond between us yet, the same as if he were living, nay far more sacred' (*EY* 547). Sense of this obligation had no doubt helped him to finish *The Prelude* in May, but failed to carry him on into the main part of *The Recluse* as he must have hoped would be the case. Dorothy's reference to the poet's reading for the nourishment of his mind implies presumably that in Coleridge's absence he was trying by himself to find something appropriately philosophical to write about. How long he went on trying, or even what he read, we do not know, but sometime in the late spring or early summer of 1806, when the *Prelude* fair copies had been completed, Wordsworth seems to have returned to *Home at Grasmere*. The drafts of 1800 were revised, a little new material was added, and this poem too was made into fair copy—under the seemingly confident heading of 'Book First, *The Recluse*'. With the moving of the Prospectus to the end to form a climax, *Home at Grasmere* as a whole had become an introduction—and not a very modest introduction—to the larger work that could never be written.[38] Rather than attempting to continue at once his celebration of the millennium one day to come from a wedding of mind and Nature, Wordsworth seems at this point to have side-slipped quietly into *The Excursion*.

The earliest surviving reference to *The Excursion*, in Wordsworth's letter to De Quincey of 6 March 1804, is to an entirely separate work: after discussing first the half-completed *Prelude*, then the projected *Recluse*, the poet adds, apparently as an afterthought, 'I have also arranged the plan of a narrative poem' (*EY* 454). By the following December, however, *The Ruined Cottage*, which must surely have been the basis of this plan, is spoken of as part of *The Recluse* itself.[39] The same month, lines written for *Prelude*, Book X, suggest for the first time what it is that Wordsworth wishes to develop in his narrative poem, and also why *The Excursion* should have come to be thought of as within the poet's over-all redemptive scheme. 'Time may come', Wordsworth writes, as ever addressing Coleridge, and with his thoughts on the French Revolution:

> When some dramatic story may afford
> Shapes livelier to convey to thee, my friend,
> What then I learned—or think I learned—of truth,
> And the errors into which I was betrayed
> By present objects, and by reasonings false
> From the beginning, inasmuch as drawn
> Out of a heart which had been turned aside
> From Nature by external accidents . . .
>
> (*1805*, x. 879–86)

Wordsworth seems already to have mapped out, at least in his mind, the three Books of *The Excursion* (II–IV) that were drafted as a separate unit in the late summer of 1806, and centre on the character and story of the Solitary.[40] His intention was to explore not just his own personal experience of the Revolution, but the way in which the millenarian hopes felt by so many of his contemporaries should now properly be understood. Like the other characters in the poem, the Solitary is largely Wordsworth himself, but instead of being idealized as are the Wanderer, Poet, and Pastor, he is an embodiment of confusion that has been prolonged, disappointment that should long ago have been checked. His dramatic story is a cautionary tale—or at least, it is intended to be. He is the wrong kind of recluse. Instead of seceding from the common world to anticipate, and to further, the coming of the milder day of love and knowledge, he has chosen a selfish isolation. Yet when it comes to the point there often seems to be a very thin line between the despondency for which the Solitary is to be 'corrected', and the moods of the writer—himself 'A meditative, oft a suffering man' (*1805*, xiii. 126). His fault is loss of hope, yet he is not bitter, or misanthropic (like Rivers, or the figure in *Lines Left Upon a Seat in a Yew-tree*), or even unduly sceptical; and he is perfectly aware of the beauty of the hidden Cumbrian valley were Wordsworth has placed him, above Blea Tarn and beneath the Langdale Pikes. Even the detail of his past life that seems most clearly to distinguish him from the poet turns out on second thoughts to be a disconcerting parallel. Disillusioned with Europe, the Solitary sails for America, and there, rejecting the life of the cities, goes to seek in the wilds 'that pure archetype of human greatness', 'Primeval Nature's child'—only to find in his place

> A creature, squalid, vengeful, and impure;
> Remorseless, and submissive to no law
> But superstitious fear, and abject sloth.
>
> (*Ex* iii. 951, 919, 953–5)

The serpent in Wordsworth's Eden—'man himself,/For ever busy to afflict himself'—reappears, transformed from peasant to Red Indian, but once again destructive of any hope for mankind based on primitive goodness or beneficent Nature. The Wanderer has his answer of course—'faith absolute in God'—but it is the Solitary's 'vital anxiousness' that stays in the mind.

The irony with which the Solitary's quest for human goodness is described, and the vehemence with which the poor Caliban whom he discovers is denounced, are surely evidence that the poet could not find the Wanderer's view entirely satisfying. He was too committed to

> the very world which is the world
> Of all of us, the place in which, in the end,
> We find our happiness, or not at all.
>
> (*1805*, x. 726–8)

The Convention of Cintra shows that in summer 1808 the unlikely cause of Spanish liberty was able to awaken in him all his old political idealism. 'From the moment of the rising of the people of the Pyrenean peninsula', he writes,

> there was a mighty change; we were instantaneously animated; and, from that moment, the contest [the Peninsular War] assumed the dignity which it is not in the power of any thing but hope to bestow. . . . we looked backward upon the records of the human race with pride, and, instead of being afraid, we delighted to look forward into futurity. It was imagined that this new-born spirit of resistance, rising from the most sacred feelings of the human heart, would diffuse itself through many countries; and not merely for the distant future, but for the present, hopes were entertained as bold as they were disinterested and generous.
>
> (*Prose Works*, i. 227–8)

The Tuft of Primroses, Wordsworth's only known attempt to write a second Book for the central *Recluse*, must fall neatly between the Spanish rising itself, in May 1808, and the beginning of work on *The Convention* in November; yet not a hint of all this fervour and hope, and commitment to an ideal of general future happiness, gets into the poetry. At its best *The Tuft* has a quiet beauty, but it is very personal, very low-toned. Wordsworth's thoughts are of transience. He and the family have been away at Coleorton, and returned to find change (unthinkable on his and Dorothy's first arrival in 1799)—destruction at the very heart of Grasmere. The trees about the church, symbols of peace and the fitness of things, have been needlessly cut down:

> Ah, what a welcome—when from absence long
> Returning, on the centre of the vale
> I looked a first glad look, and saw them not!
> Was it a dream? Th'aerial grove, no more
> Right in the centre of the lovely vale
> Suspended like a stationary cloud,
> Had vanished like a cloud...

'Yet say not so', the poet continues, sadness and indignation leading him now to identify with the few survivors of the grove,

> For here and there a straggling tree was left
> To mourn in blanc and monumental grief,
> To pine and wither for its fellows gone.
>
> (ll. 95–104)[41]

The trees that remain stand as monuments to those that are fallen ('felled' seems too unemotive a word), but in their mourning they have taken on humanity, the ability to pine and wither *on behalf* of the dead. The poetry seems to be saying again and again, 'very soon/Even of the good is no memorial left' (*Ruined Cottage*, 71–2). At the foot of the church-tower, itself bereft—'Now stands the steeple naked and forlorn' (l. 127)—lie the graves of Joseph Sympson and his family; and across the vale is their cottage, empty now, and falling like Margaret's into decay. 'I own', the poet writes,

> Though I can look on their associate graves
> With nothing but still thoughts, that I repine—
> It costs me something like a pain to feel
> That after them so many of their works,
> Which round that dwelling covertly preserved
> The history of their unambitious lives,
> Have perished, and so soon.
>
> (ll. 184–91)

What then of the history of an ambitious life such as the poet's own? How different will it be? Gray had pleaded, from the distance of his station and his learning:

> Let not Ambition mock their useful toil,
> Their homely joys, and destiny obscure,
> Nor Grandeur hear with a disdainful smile
> The short and simple annals of the poor.
>
> (*Elegy*, 29–32)

Wordsworth is distanced too, but very much less so; while sharing the compassion, he can feel an identification impossible to Gray. Old Sympson, 'patriarch of the vale' and last surviving member of his family, has been 'A man of hope, a forward-looking mind/ Even to the last' (ll. 177–8). Like the Pedlar (who was in turn like Wordsworth) he had

> a flashing eye,
> A restless foot, a head that beat at nights
> Upon his pillow with a thousand schemes . . .
>
> (ll. 172–4)

He has lived as good, and as active, a life as could be lived, and he is dead. Worse than that, his works are dying too. The poet seems half-conscious of writing his own epitaph—a lament to be heard especially in the echoes that come thronging into the poetry. Near the Sympsons' cottage

> his daughter's bower
> Is creeping into shapelessness, self lost
> In the wild wood, like a neglected image
> Or fancy which hath ceased to be recalled.
>
> (ll. 202–5)

The poet mourns

> that these works
> Of love and diligence and innocent care
> Are sullied and disgraced; or that a gulf
> Hath swallowed them which renders nothing back;
> That they so quickly in a cave are hidden
> Which cannot be unlocked; upon their bloom
> That a perpetual winter should have fallen.
>
> (ll. 212–18)

Like Margaret's garden, the bower of Sympson's daughter is the product, and symbol, and finally, the memorial, of a short-lived moment of harmony. The stones of Michael's sheepfold are said in one discarded draft to lie

> some in heaps, and some
> In lines, that seem to keep themselves alive
> In the last dotage of a dying form.
>
> (*Oxford Wordsworth*, ii. 482)

but the bower is positively 'creeping into shapelessness'—aiding the process of decay. Form has been the result of a balancing of forces that could never be permanent. With the balance disturbed, identity itself will disappear, merging in a 'wild wood' that has far more to do with *Paradise Lost* and Adam's vision of living 'again in these wild woods forlorn' (ix. 910) than it does with the bare Cumbrian fell-side above the Sympsons' cottage. At the same time another merging is taking place in the poetry, as the neglected bower becomes neglected *image*. One is moved, not inappropriately, at the thought of Wordsworth cherishing, fostering, his stored-up mental pictures, as others do their gardens; but the important implication is that the bower, which in its time was Eden to the person who tended it, now exists only to the mind. Its life is preserved, and its shape sustained, by the visitings of memory. But how long will it continue to attract such attention? How soon will it—or the qualities and connections with which the mind has gifted it—become indeed a 'fancy that hath ceased to be recalled'?

Writing of *The Recluse* in the Preface to *The Excursion*, Wordsworth refers to 'the hope of being able to construct a literary work that might live'; *The Tuft of Primroses* shows the fear that he is in fact making one that will die. Back in 1800, at a moment when *Home at Grasmere* was not going too well, he had written with uncharacteristic humbleness:

> I would not wholly perish...
> Lie down and be forgotten in the dust,
> I and the modest partners of my days
> Making a silent company in death.

At that time it had been possible to add,

> *It must not be*, if I, divinely taught,
> Am privileged to speak as I have felt
> Of what in man is human or divine.
>
> (ll. 903–9)

but *The Tuft* has no such underlying confidence, no arrogance with which to assert either the divinity, or the godlike humanity, of man. There seems to be nothing to protect 'these works' (the poet's among them) 'Of love and diligence and innocent care' from the alliance of time and an active, oblivious Nature. All will be 'sullied and disgraced'—deprived of the grace that their human makers have been able briefly to confer.[42] The echoes of *Nutting* serve to emphasize the poet's now passive acceptance. Before, it had been he who was the aggressor, ravaging a natural bower:

> Then up I rose
> And dragged to earth both branch and bough, with crash
> And merciless ravage; and the green and shady nook
> Of hazels, and the green and mossy bower,
> Deformed and sullied, patiently gave up
> Their quiet being...
>
> (ll. 42–7)

The act had been wrong, but positive: an imposition of self, rather than the waiting for self to be lost in the wild wood—*or* swallowed in the gulf, *or* hidden in the cave, *or* subjected to a perpetual winter. The poet's succession of images is nearly ludicrous, but each in turn now tells the story of his personal fear of oblivion. At the centre is the gulf that swallows, and that renders nothing back. The Snowdon gulf, as source of strength, Romantic lodging-place of both soul and imagination, has been replaced by something much more primitive, much closer to the medieval vision of the greedy jaws of death. Before, the gulf had been a thoroughfare through which power mounted from an underpresence dim and vast within the self; now it is a hell, an under*world*, from which no traveller returns. Even the reason for the change is contained in the image that Wordsworth uses. Inability to go ahead with *The Recluse* had caused him in January 1804 to see himself

> Unprofitably travelling towards the grave,
> Like a false steward who hath much received
> And renders nothing back.
>
> (*1805*, i. 269–71)

At the time it had been a passing self-reproach, but now the gulf that 'renders nothing back' opens to receive the steward who has done the same.[43]

Given the exact repetition of phrase, and the number of times Wordsworth must recently have been over the *Prelude* lines with their discomfortable self-accusation,[44] it seems almost certain that this would have been an echo that he was aware of. Not that it greatly matters; conscious or otherwise, the link is especially interesting in that it casts back not just to the beginnings of the poet's work on the extended *Prelude*, but beyond these to the opening lines of *1799*. The words 'and renders nothing back' lead in *1805* directly into the self-reproachful questions with which the drafts of *MS JJ* had originally begun: 'was it for this/That one, the fairest of all rivers...'. Guilt in each of these cases is of course to be associated with *The Recluse*, but in October 1798 and January 1804 it had been merely over slowness in getting under way; there had been no real doubt that the mission would one day be fulfilled. In summer 1808 there is the thought—almost the acceptance—of over-all failure. Wordsworth in *The Tuft of*

Primroses is to be seen questioning his very role as the recluse. 'What impulse', he asks himself,

> drove the hermit to his cell,
> And what detained him there till life was spent,
> Fast anchored in the desart?
>
> (ll. 264–6)

Margaret in *The Ruined Cottage* had been detained in her similarly wretched spot by 'torturing hope...*fast rooted* at her heart'. The hermit (anchorite that he is) is held in his desert by the wish for peace, which is now regarded as 'The central feeling of all happiness'. The peace is valued 'Not as a refuge from distress or pain',[45]

> *But for its absolute self*, a life of peace,
> Stability without regret or fear,
> That hath been, is, and shall be ever more.
>
> (ll. 275–80)

The border craving for 'something evermore about to be' that has been at the centre of Wordsworth's greatest poetry is denied now in favour of unchanging calm. Earlier the poet had been vexed and *driven* by creativity—

> verse was what he had been wedded to;
> And his own mind did like a tempest strong
> Come to him thus, and drove the weary man along.
>
> (*Castle of Indolence Stanzas*, 34–6)

—now, it seems, he feels compelled towards a seclusion that is merely, or purely, meditative. In reply to his question, 'What impulse drove the hermit to his cell?' we have the sad, considered answer:

> What but this,
> The universal instinct of repose,
> The longing for confirmed tranquillity
> In small and great, in humble or sublime,
> The life where hope and memory are as one,
> Earth quiet and unchanged, the human soul
> Consistent in self-rule, and heaven revealed
> To meditation in that quietness.
>
> (ll. 264, 288–95)

Wordsworth had come to Grasmere to do a job, and to do it on behalf of mankind—

> No, we are not alone . . . .
> We do not tend a lamp
> Whose lustre we alone participate . . .
> (*Home at Grasmere*, 646, 655–6)

The light of *The Recluse* was to have shone out, chearing the world in times to come, and announcing a general future happiness. *The Tuft* shows him still as looking forward to an ideal future, but it is now utterly private—all that is universal is the instinct for repose. *The Recluse*, and with it all the poetry of the aspiring human mind, seems quite needless in this world where heaven is to be revealed in the quietness of personal meditation, and where there is no distinction to be made between future and past. That Wordsworth of all people should have been able to write, and to envy, 'The life where hope and memory are as one'![46]

It is a strange thought, coming from one who had dared to see 'The man to come parted as by a gulph/From him who had been' (*1805*, xi. 59–60); and doubly strange when one recalls that at the time when the line was written, the Spanish rising had enabled him once more to look 'backward upon the records of the human race with pride' and to take delight in looking forward into futurity. Political enthusiasm was being quietly and successfully kept out of work on *The Recluse*. Wordsworth's use of St. Basil as a surrogate in the last half of *The Tuft*, though perhaps suggesting that he knew the poem had to be wrenched away from Grasmere, is not a success, and the final turning to autobiography and the Grande Chartreuse has about it a despairing irrelevance.[47] News of the disgraceful treaty with the French at Cintra appeared in the British press on 16 September 1808, and would certainly have put an end to work on *The Tuft* if it hadn't already ceased. There is no doubt about Wordsworth's indignation at this betrayal of the Spanish freedom-fighters,[48] but it is not difficult to see in the energy, and the long months of hard labour that he devoted to writing and correcting *The Convention*, a sense of relief at once again having a palpable cause to devote himself to.

By May 1809 *The Convention* was in print, and Wordsworth was free either to go back to *The Tuft of Primroses*, or to make a new attempt at a centrepiece for *The Recluse*. He did neither. Instead at Allan Bank in the winter of 1809–10 he returned to *The*

Excursion. With Coleridge in the same house, and being for the moment very productive,[49] he must have been under a great deal of pressure, and it is noticeable that when in February Dorothy reports that three Books of *The Excursion* are nearly complete, she refers to the poem as '*The Recluse*' (*MY* i. 392). Repeated failures had not decreased Wordsworth's need to feel that he was making progress on his major work, fulfilling his bond with the dead. For a time he would be able to tell himself (as he had with *The Prelude*) that *The Excursion* was after all an integral part of his scheme.

It remains extraordinary that when *The Excursion* was completed Wordsworth should have decided to use the Preface as a means of advertising the poem that for sixteen years he had been unable to write. It was hardly necessary to mention *The Recluse* at all, and to offer his readers the Prospectus seems very like bravado. Perhaps he was trying to force his own hand; perhaps he just wished that the public should know of the grandeur of his aims. Either way, his gigantic boasts—

> Jehovah, with his thunder, and the choir
> Of shouting angels, and the empyreal thrones,
> I pass them unalarmed...
>
> (*Oxford Wordsworth*, v. 4, ll. 33–5)

—must have seemed utterly without substance.[50] The *Excursion* Preface as a whole has some of the pathos that attaches to Blake's *Descriptive Catalogue* and Exhibition of 1809:

> If Italy is enriched and made great by RAPHAEL, if MICHAEL ANGELO is its supreme glory, if art is the glory of a nation, if genius and inspiration are the great origin and bond of society, the distinction my works have obtained from those who best understand such things, calls for my Exhibition as the greatest of duties to my country.
>
> (Erdman, 518–19)

Both poets had gone on nourishing redemptive schemes born in the very different intellectual climate of the 1790s, and each laid himself wide open to ridicule. Blake, however, was being entirely consistent in his own terms. His 1810 'Additions' to the *Catalogue* state a position that goes straight back to *The Marriage of Heaven and Hell* twenty years before:

> Mental things alone are real. . . . Error, or Creation, will be burned up; and then, and not till then, truth or eternity will appear. It is burnt up the moment men cease to behold it.
>
> (Erdman, 555)

Wordsworth by contrast had changed very greatly. At precious and exalted moments imagination had been for him too a vision of truth and eternity, but in place of the prophet's enviable certainties there had been glimpses, the sense of a merely possible sublimity. Blake did not presumably think that the doors of perception could easily be cleansed, but in the world of his writing he lives untroubled by practicality. Wordsworth is not so privileged. His rootedness is both a strength and a limitation. He can take us with him—make use of his sense (and our sense) of a border, to stress the difficulty and achievement of crossing it—but he has no means of protecting himself from either the doubts, or the comforts, of normality. Perhaps it was inevitable that, taking more into account, his vision should also be harder to sustain. At all events, after finishing *1805* he never again writes a poetry of the transcendent imagination. Coleridge apparently goes on assuming that imagination will be the philosophical basis of *The Recluse*, but for Wordsworth himself by 1814 the apocalyptic thinking of *The Prelude* is far in the past. After the flurry over the Convention of Cintra, the longing for confirmed tranquillity has become itself confirmed. The poet who once had challenged Milton, and affronted Jehovah with gigantic boasts, now writes placidly to say that in epic poetry 'no subject but a religious one can answer the demand of the soul' (*MY* ii. 268).

From the point of view of *The Recluse* it is a very bad sign that within a month of publishing *The Excursion* in August 1814 Wordsworth should be making *Poems* 1815 ready for the press. As cells and oratories, the shorter poems could be given a place within the Gothic church, but for the fourth time running he was bringing out a collection precisely when he might have been expected to be getting on with the central part of the building: the first volume of *Lyrical Ballads* had followed his original announcement of *The Recluse* in March 1798, and work on the second had begun when *Home at Grasmere* was abandoned in April 1800; *Poems* 1807 had been put together when it became obvious at Coleorton that Coleridge was not going to be able to provide the material that was so urgently needed; and now Wordsworth was surely putting off the day when the consequences of his recent Preface would have to be faced. As in the period following the completion of *1805*, we begin to hear of family anxieties. By February 1815 there is the same ominous talk of the poet's reading for the nourishment of his mind: 'William has had one of his weeks of rest', Dorothy writes on the eighteenth,

> and we now begin to wish that he was at work again, but as he intends completely to plan the first part of *The Recluse* before he begins the composition, he must read many books before he will fairly set to labour again.
>
> (*MY* ii. 200)

What Wordsworth actually read there is no means of knowing, but it is unlikely that he made any substantial progress with *The Recluse*. On the evidence of the manuscript, he seems first to have gone back to *Home at Grasmere* in the hopes of making a new start, and then to have turned his attention to *The Prelude*.[51]

Each of the original *Prelude* versions—*1799*, the five-Book poem, and *1805*—had been associated with the poet's guilts over the central *Recluse*, and now revision too was to be a form of escape. The earliest corrections belong, as one might expect, to the period of Coleridge's return from Malta, and no doubt others were made from time to time that cannot be singled out and dated, but the first of the wholesale *Prelude* revisions takes place in the years 1816–19.[52] Wordsworth had not given up hope of writing his philosophical poem, but he was to be seen busily doing the other things that came more easily.[53] The pressure to get on was now chiefly from within the family. Dorothy comments briskly in 1821, 'After fifty years of age there is no time to spare, and unfinished works should not, if it be possible, be left behind' (*LY* i. 50); and, at the end of the Twenties, Mary cannot be got to enjoy the newly-written *Power of Sound* because 'it ought to have been in *The Recluse*'.[54] The *Prelude* revisions of 1832 seem to be a turning-point. For a brief moment the previous autumn it had really seemed that *The Recluse* was making progress, but all Wordsworth had done in fact was return for one last despairing time to his original starting place in *Home at Grasmere*.[55] The *Prelude* reworkings on this occasion are the most thorough and extensive of all; at some level the poet was now surely aware that the subordinate poem (still regarded as too egocentric to be published on its own) would finally have to take the place of the central *Recluse*. A letter from Dora to her future husband the following year significantly reports that although her mother is still reproaching the poet with writing 'tiresome small poems', and 'is vexed she cannot get him down to his long work', she herself does not 'believe that *The Recluse* will ever be finished'.[56] When three years later, in 1836, a new edition of *The Excursion* appears, the words 'Being a Portion of THE RECLUSE' have been removed from the title-page.

It was in May 1838, a month after the poet's sixty-eighth birthday, that the visit of George Ticknor to Rydal Mount took place. 'Mrs Wordsworth', he recalls in his *Journal*,

> asked me to talk to him about finishing . . . *The Recluse*; saying that she could not bear to have him occupied constantly in writing sonnets and other trifles, while this great work lay by him untouched, but that she had ceased to urge him on the subject, because she had done it so much in vain. I asked him about it, therefore. He said that the Introduction, which is a sort of autobiography, is completed. This I knew, for he read me large portions of it twenty years ago . . . . On my asking him why he does not finish it he turned to me very decidedly, and said, 'Why did not Gray finish the long poem he began on a similar subject? Because he found he had undertaken something beyond his powers to accomplish. And that is my case.' We controverted his position, of course; but I am not certain the event will not prove that he has acted upon his belief. At any rate, I have no hope it will ever be completed . . .[57]

Within weeks of this conversation we hear of Wordsworth reading *The Prelude* to Isabella Fenwick, and before long he is clearly revising it—making the printer's copy that would finally be used after his death. Forty years after his first confident announcement of *The Recluse* in March 1798, the poet had given up hope.

And so the lamp of *The Recluse* was never 'hung up in heaven to chear/The world in times to come'. When in 1805 Wordsworth had described to Beaumont his sacred bond with the dead, his thoughts had been on *Michael*, the poem about another such bond that had been written while John was staying at Dove Cottage in autumn 1800. Over the years it must have come to seem very bitter that he like Michael should be unable to keep his half of a covenant. But Michael's greatness lay in the strength of love, not the making of sheepfolds; and Wordsworth's genius could not be put to building Gothic churches, or other rigid structures. For him the imagination was not a philosophy to be established against Locke and the mechanic dogmatists. It was 'The light that never was on sea or land'—a light which could be at once 'the consecration, and the poet's dream', and which in the inspired days of February 1804 he had shed upon the statued horse, standing 'With a clear silver moonlight sky behind', and

> all his functions silently sealed up,
> Like an amphibious work of Nature's hand,
> A borderer dwelling betwixt life and death . . .

Appendix
Three Wordsworth Texts

(1) THE PEDLAR

The Pedlar has a complicated textual history. It was written in February-March 1798 to be inserted into *The Ruined Cottage* and provide a background for the narrator who tells the central story of Margaret—evidence as to why 'He could afford to suffer/With those whom he saw suffer' (ll. 283–4). A year later it was excerpted; and for a time it became a separate poem. Finally, it was put back into *The Ruined Cottage* at the period early in 1804 when *The Ruined Cottage* itself became in the poet's mind a part of the larger scheme of *The Excursion*. (To add to the confusion, at this stage the Wordsworth circle began to use the name '*Pedlar*' for the full-length *Ruined Cottage*—effectively, *Excursion*, Book I—and their practice has recently been followed by the Cornell editor; see Butler, 378–457.) Printed below is *The Pedlar* as first separated from *The Ruined Cottage* in *MS 18A* (*D.C. MS 16*). It was entered in the notebook in 1799, but contains no work that is later than March 1798. Despite its third-person narrative it is Wordsworth's earliest sustained piece of autobiographical and philosophical writing.

At what stage *The Pedlar* came to be thought of as a poem in its own right we cannot know. The reason for taking it out of *The Ruined Cottage* was presumably that it unbalanced the structure; and in transcribing it, Dorothy gave it no separate title. By October 1800, however, there are plans for publishing *The Pedlar* with *Christabel*; both Dorothy and Coleridge refer to the poem by name, and there can be no doubt that the text they have in mind is *18A*. For Coleridge it is specifically 'a long blank verse poem of Wordsworth's entitled *The Pedlar*' (Griggs, i. 631). No *Pedlar* revisions belong to this period, but on 21 December 1801 Dorothy records in her Journal: 'Wm sate beside me and read *The Pedlar*; he was in good spirits, and full of hope of what he should do with it.'

Though Wordsworth felt the need to do something with *The Pedlar*, and it is clear from the *Journals* that he spent a lot of time and trouble on revision during the early months of 1802, it is not at all likely that he improved on the poem as it stands in *18A*. In late 1799 a major pantheist sequence (ll. 204–22) had been taken into *The Prelude* (as *1799*, ii. 446–64), and in December 1801 another of *The Pedlar's* greatest passages (ll. 324–56) was removed as Wordsworth tried to expand *1799* into a third Part (see *1805*, iii. 82–167, *passim*). The *Pedlar* manuscripts of 1802 are lost, but to judge from *D.C. MS 37* (*Excursion, MS E*) of early 1804, no new material of comparable quality can have been added in revision. For photographs and transcripts of the relevant MSS, and a full discussion of the revisions of 1802, see Butler, 24–35 (who does not, however, provide a reading-text of *The Pedlar*). The text printed below was first published in *The Music of Humanity* (1969). It can be confidently said that it is not just the earliest version of the separate *Pedlar*, but the best.

Him had I seen the day before, alone
And in the middle of the public way
Standing to rest himself. His eyes were turned
Towards the setting sun, while, with that staff
Behind him fixed, he propped a long white pack
Which crossed his shoulders, wares for maids who live
In lonely villages or straggling huts.
I knew him—he was born of lowly race
On Cumbrian hills, and I have seen the tear
Stand in his luminous eye when he described
The house in which his early youth was passed,
And found I was no stranger to the spot.
I loved to hear him talk of former days
And tell how when a child, ere yet of age
To be a shepherd, he had learned to read
His bible in a school that stood alone,
Sole building on a mountain's dreary edge,
Far from the sight of city spire, or sound
Of minster clock. From that bleak tenement
He many an evening to his distant home
In solitude returning saw the hills
Grow larger in the darkness, all alone
Beheld the stars come out above his head,
And travelled through the wood, no comrade near,
To whom he might confess the things he saw.

  So the foundations of his mind were laid.
In such communion, not from terror free,
While yet a child and long before his time,
He had perceived the presence and the power
Of greatness, and deep feelings had impressed

Great objects on his mind with portraiture
And colour so distinct that on his mind
They lay like substances, and almost seemed
To haunt the bodily sense. He had received
A precious gift, for as he grew in years
With these impressions would he still compare
All his ideal stores, his shapes and forms,
And, being still unsatisfied with aught
Of dimmer character, he thence attained
An *active* power to fasten images
Upon his brain, and on their pictured lines
Intensely brooded, even till they acquired
The liveliness of dreams. Nor did he fail,
While yet a child, with a child's eagerness
Incessantly to turn his ear and eye
On all things which the rolling seasons brought
To feed such appetite. Nor this alone
Appeased his yearning—in the after day
Of boyhood, many an hour in caves forlorn
And in the hollow depths of naked crags
He sate, and even in their fixed lineaments,
Or from the power of a peculiar eye,
Or by creative feeling overborne,
Or by predominance of thought oppressed,
Even in their fixed and steady lineaments
He traced an ebbing and a flowing mind,
Expression ever varying.
Thus informed,
He had small need of books; for many a tale
Traditionary round the mountains hung,
And many a legend peopling the dark woods
Nourished imagination in her growth,
And gave the mind that apprehensive power
By which she is made quick to recognize
The moral properties and scope of things.
But greedily he read and read again
Whate'er the rustic vicar's shelf supplied:
The life and death of martyrs who sustained
Intolerable pangs, and here and there
A straggling volume, torn and incomplete,
Which left half-told the preternatural tale,
Romance of giants, chronicle of fiends,
Profuse in garniture of wooden cuts

Strange and uncouth, dire faces, figures dire,
Sharp-kneed, sharp-elbowed, and lean-ankled too,
With long and ghostly shanks, forms which once seen
Could never be forgotten—things though low,
Though low and humble, not to be despised
By such as have observed the curious links
With which the perishable hours of life
Are bound together, and the world of thought
Exists and is sustained. Within his heart
Love was not yet, nor the pure joy of love,
By sound diffused, or by the breathing air,
Or by the silent looks of happy things,
Or flowing from the universal face
Of earth and sky. But he had felt the power
Of Nature, and already was prepared
By his intense conceptions to receive
Deeply the lesson deep of love, which he
Whom Nature, by whatever means, has taught
To feel intensely, cannot but receive.

Ere his ninth year he had been sent abroad
To tend his father's sheep; such was his task
Henceforward till the later day of youth.
Oh then what soul was his, when on the tops
Of the high mountains he beheld the sun
Rise up and bathe the world in light. He looked,
The ocean and the earth beneath him lay
In gladness and deep joy. The clouds were touched,
And in their silent faces did he read
Unutterable love. Sound needed none,
Nor any voice of joy: his spirit drank
The spectacle. Sensation, soul, and form,
All melted into him; they swallowed up
His animal being. In them did he live,
And by them did he live— they were his life.
In such access of mind, in such high hour
Of visitation from the living God,
He did not feel the God, he felt his works.
Thought was not; in enjoyment it expired.
Such hour by prayer or praise was unprofaned;
He neither prayed, nor offered thanks or praise;
His mind was a thanksgiving to the power
That made him. It was blessedness and love.

A shepherd on the lonely mountain-tops,
Such intercourse was his, and in this sort
Was his existence oftentimes possessed.
Oh *then* how beautiful, how bright, appeared
The written promise. He had early learned
To reverence the volume which displays
The mystery, the life which cannot die,
But in the mountains did he FEEL his faith,
There did he see the writing. All things there
Breathed immortality, revolving life,
And greatness still revolving, infinite.
There littleness was not, the least of things
Seemed infinite, and there his spirit shaped
Her prospects—nor did he *believe*; he saw.
What wonder if his being thus became
Sublime and comprehensive? Low desires,
Low thoughts, had there no place; yet was his heart
Lowly, for he was meek in gratitude
Oft as he called to mind those exstacies,
And whence they flowed; and from them he acquired
Wisdom which works through patience—thence he learned
In many a calmer hour of sober thought
To look on Nature with an humble heart,
Self-questioned where it did not understand,
And with a superstitious eye of love.

Thus passed the time, yet to the neighbouring town
He often went with what small overplus
His earnings might supply, and brought away
The book which most had tempted his desires
While at the stall he read. Among the hills
He gazed upon that mighty orb of song,
The divine Milton. Lore of different kind,
The annual savings of a toilsome life,
The schoolmaster supplied—books that explain
The purer elements of truth involved
In lines and numbers, and by charm severe,
Especially perceived where Nature droops
And feeling is suppressed, preserve the mind
Busy in solitude and poverty.
And thus employed he many a time o'erlooked
The listless hours when in the hollow vale,
Hollow and green, he lay on the green turf

In lonesome idleness. What could he do?
Nature was at his heart, and he perceived,
Though yet he knew not how, a wasting power
In all things which from her sweet influence
Might tend to wean him. Therefore with her hues,
Her forms, and with the spirit of her forms,
He clothed the nakedness of austere truth.
While yet he lingered in the elements
Of science, and among her simplest laws,
His triangles they were the stars of heaven,
The silent stars; his altitudes the crag
Which is the eagle's birth-place, or some peak
Familiar with forgotten years which shews
Inscribed, as with the silence of the thought,
Upon its bleak and visionary sides
The history of many a winter storm,
Or obscure records of the path of fire.
Yet with these lonesome sciences he still
Continued to amuse the heavier hours
Of solitude. Yet not the less he found
In cold elation, and the lifelessness
Of truth by oversubtlety dislodged
From grandeur and from love, an idle toy,
The dullest of all toys. He saw in truth
A holy spirit and a breathing soul;
He reverenced her and trembled at her look,
When with a moral beauty in her face
She led him through the worlds.

But now, before his twentieth year was passed,
Accumulated feelings pressed his heart
With an encreasing weight; he was o'erpowered
By Nature, and his spirit was on fire
With restless thoughts. His eye became disturbed,
And many a time he wished the winds might rage
When they were silent. Far more fondly now
Than in his earlier season did he love
Tempestuous nights, the uproar and the sounds
That live in darkness. From his intellect,
And from the stillness of abstracted thought,
He sought repose in vain. I have heard him say
That at this time he scanned the laws of light
Amid the roar of torrents, where they send
From hollow clefts up to the clearer air

A cloud of mist, which in the shining sun
Varies its rainbow hues. But vainly thus,
And vainly by all other means he strove
To mitigate the fever of his heart.

From Nature and her overflowing soul
He had received so much that all his thoughts
Were steeped in feeling. He was only then
Contented when with bliss ineffable
He felt the sentiment of being spread
O'er all that moves, and all that seemeth still,
O'er all which, lost beyond the reach of thought
And human knowledge, to the human eye
Invisible, yet liveth to the heart;
O'er all that leaps, and runs, and shouts, and sings,
Or beats the gladsome air; o'er all that glides
Beneath the wave, yea, in the wave itself,
And mighty depth of waters. Wonder not
If such his transports were; for in all things
He saw one life, and felt that it was joy.
One song they sang, and it was audible—
Most audible then when the fleshly ear,
O'ercome by grosser prelude of that strain,
Forgot its functions, and slept undisturbed.

These things he had sustained in solitude
Even till his bodily strength began to yield
Beneath their weight. The mind within him burnt,
And he resolved to quit his native hills.
The father strove to make his son perceive
As clearly as the old man did himself
With what advantage he might teach a school
In the adjoining village. But the youth,
Who of this service made a short essay,
Found that the wanderings of his thought were then
A misery to him, that he must resign
A task he was unable to perform.
He asked his father's blessing, and assumed
This lowly occupation. The old man
Blessed him and prayed for him, yet with a heart
Forboding evil.
From his native hills
He wandered far. Much did he see of men,
Their manners, their enjoyments and pursuits,

Their passions and their feelings, chiefly those
Essential and eternal in the heart,
Which mid the simpler forms of rural life
Exist more simple in their elements,
And speak a plainer language. Many a year
Of lonesome meditation and impelled
By curious thought he was content to toil
In this poor calling, which he now pursued
From habit and necessity. He walked
Among the impure haunts of vulgar men
Unstained; the talisman of constant thought
And kind sensations in a gentle heart
Preserved him. Every shew of vice to him
Was a remembrancer of what he knew,
Or a fresh seed of wisdom, or produced
That tender interest which the virtuous feel
Among the wicked, which when truly felt
May bring the bad man nearer to the good,
But, innocent of evil, cannot
Sink the good man to the bad.
Among the woods
A lone enthusiast, and among the hills,
Itinerant in this labour he had passed
The better portion of his time, and there
From day to day had his affections breathed
The wholesome air of Nature; there he kept
In solitude and solitary thought,
So pleasant were those comprehensive views,
His mind in a just equipoise of love.
Serene it was, unclouded by the cares
Of ordinary life—unvexed, unwarped
By partial bondage. In his steady course
No piteous revolutions had he felt,
No wild varieties of joy or grief.
Unoccupied by sorrow of its own,
His heart lay open; and, by Nature tuned
And constant disposition of his thoughts
To sympathy with man, he was alive
To all that was enjoyed where'er he went,
And all that was endured; and, in himself
Happy, and quiet in his chearfulness,
He had no painful pressure from within
Which made him turn aside from wretchedness

With coward fears. He could afford to suffer
With those whom he saw suffer. Hence it was
That in our best experience he was rich,
And in the wisdom of our daily life.
For hence, minutely, in his various rounds
He had observed the progress and decay
Of many minds, of minds and bodies too—
The history of many families,
And how they prospered, how they were o'erthrown
By passion or mischance, or such misrule
Among the unthinking masters of the earth
As makes the nations groan. He was a man,
One whom you could not pass without remark—
If you had met him on a rainy day
You would have stopped to look at him. Robust,
Active, and nervous, was his gait; his limbs
And his whole figure breathed intelligence.
His body, tall and shapely, shewed in front
A faint line of the hollowness of age,
Or rather what appeared the curvature
Of toil; his head looked up steady and fixed.
Age had compressed the rose upon his cheek
Into a narrower circle of deep red,
But had not tamed his eye, which, under brows
Of hoary grey, had meanings which it brought
From years of youth, which, like a being made
Of many beings, he had wondrous skill
To blend with meanings of the years to come,
Human, or such as lie beyond the grave.
Long had I loved him. Oh, it was most sweet
To hear him teach in unambitious style
Reasoning and thought, by painting as he did
The manners and the passions. Many a time
He made a holiday and left his pack
Behind, and we two wandered through the hills
A pair of random travellers. His eye
Flashing poetic fire he would repeat
The songs of Burns, or many a ditty wild
Which he had fitted to the moorland harp—
His own sweet verse—and as we trudged along,
Together did we make the hollow grove
Ring with our transports.

Though he was untaught,

In the dead lore of schools undisciplined,
Why should he grieve? He was a chosen son.
He yet retained an ear which deeply felt
The voice of Nature in the obscure wind,
The sounding mountain, and the running stream.
From deep analogies by thought supplied,
Or consciousnesses not to be subdued,
To every natural form, rock, fruit, and flower,
Even the loose stones that cover the highway,
He gave a moral life; he saw them feel,
Or linked them to some feeling. In all shapes
He found a secret and mysterious soul,
A fragrance and a spirit of strange meaning.
Though poor in outward shew, he was most rich:
He had a world about him—'twas his own,
He made it—for it only lived to him,
And to the God who looked into his mind.
Such sympathies would often bear him far
In outward gesture, and in visible look,
Beyond the common seeming of mankind.
Some called it madness; such it might have been,
But that he had an eye which evermore
Looked deep into the shades of difference
As they lie hid in all exterior forms,
Near or remote, minute or vast—an eye
Which from a stone, a tree, a withered leaf,
To the broad ocean and the azure heavens
Spangled with kindred multitudes of stars,
Could find no surface where its power might sleep—
Which spake perpetual logic to his soul,
And by an unrelenting agency
Did bind his feelings even as in a chain.

(2) THE PROSPECTUS TO THE RECLUSE

The Prospectus gets its name from the fact that in 1814 it was published in the Preface to *The Excursion* as an advertisement to Wordsworth's overall scheme for *The Recluse*. The opening words are a restatement of the plan for *The Recluse* as set out in March 1798: 'I have written 1300 lines of a poem in which I contrive to convey most of the knowledge of which I am possessed. My object is to give pictures of Nature, man and society' (*EY* 212). Clearly the Prospectus was intended to be the beginning of the poet's work on the central philosophical section of *The Recluse*. It seems to have been composed soon after the Wordsworths' arrival at Dove Cottage in late December 1799, and was followed in March by the writing of *Home at Grasmere* (described by the poet in 1806 as the first Book of *The Recluse*, and in fact the only part of the central work to be completed; see headnote below). There is evidence to suggest that at first the Prospectus was regarded as an introduction to *Home at Grasmere*, but in *MS B* (*D.C. MS 59*) of 1806 it is used to form the climax. In the earliest surviving text, as printed below, it stands as a separate work. For photographs and transcripts of Prospectus *MS 1* (*D.C. MS 45*), see Darlington, 255–63; and for a discussion of the date and function of the poem, see Jonathan Wordsworth, 'On Man, on Nature, and on Human Life', *RES* New Series, xxxi, no. 121 (1980), 26–9. The words 'breathe in' at l. 17 in the text below are supplied from *MS B* to fill a gap left in the manuscript; at l. 63, 'with' was omitted in transcription.

On man, on Nature, and on human life,
Thinking in solitude, from time to time
I find sweet passions traversing my soul
Like music; unto these, where'er I may,
I would give utterance in numerous verse.
Of truth, of grandeur, beauty, love, and hope,
Of joy in various commonalty spread,
Of the individual mind that keeps its own
Inviolate retirement, and consists
With being limitless, the one great life,
I sing; fit audience let me find, though few!
  'Fit audience find, though few'—thus prayed the bard,
Holiest of men. Urania, I shall need
Thy guidance, or a greater muse, if such
Descend to earth or dwell in highest heaven;
For I must tread on shadowy ground, must sink
Deep, and ascend aloft, and breathe in worlds
To which the heaven of heavens is but a veil.
All strength, all terror, single or in bands,
That ever was put forth by personal forms—
Jehovah, with his thunder, and the choir
Of shouting angels, and the empyreal thrones—
I pass them unalarmed. The darkest pit
Of the profoundest hell, night, chaos, death,
Nor aught of blinder vacancy scooped out
By help of dreams, can breed such fear and awe
As fall upon me often when I look
Into my soul, into the soul of man,

My haunt, and the main region of my song.
Beauty, whose living home is the green earth,
Surpassing far what hath by special craft
Of delicate poets been culled forth and shaped
From earth's materials, waits upon my steps,
Pitches her tents before me as I move,
My hourly neighbour. Paradise and groves
Elysian, blessed islands in the deep,
Of choice seclusion—wherefore need they be
A history, or but a dream, when minds
Once wedded to this outward frame of things
In love, find these the growth of common day?

Such pleasant haunts foregoing, if my song
Must turn elsewhere, and travel near the tribes
And fellowships of men, and see ill sights
Of passions ravenous from each other's rage,
Insult and injury and wrong and strife,
Wisdom be thou my guide, and if so tasked
I hear humanity in fields and groves
Pipe solitary anguish, or must hang
Brooding above the fierce confederate storm
Of sorrow, barricadoed ever more
Within the walls of cities, to these sounds
Do thou give meaning more akin to that
Which to God's ear they carry, that even these
Hearing, I be not heartless, or forlorn.
Come thou, prophetic spirit, soul of man,
Thou human soul of the wide earth, that hast
Thy metropolitan temple in the hearts
Of mighty poets; unto me vouchsafe
Thy foresight, teach me to discern, and part
Inherent things from casual, what is fixed
From fleeting, that my song may live, and be
Even as a light hung up in heaven to chear
The world in times to come. And if with this
I mingle humbler matter, with the thing
Contemplated describe the mind and man
Contemplating, and who he was and what,
The transitory being that beheld
This vision, when and where and how he lived,
In part a fellow citizen, in part
An outlaw, and a borderer of this age—
Be not this labour useless. O great God,

To less than thee I cannot make this prayer:
Innocent mighty spirit, let my life
Express the image of a better time;
Desires more wise, and simpler manners, nurse
My heart in genuine freedom; all pure thoughts
Be with me, and uphold me to the end.

(3) HOME AT GRASMERE

Home at Grasmere was written in March–early April 1800, and tidied up in the late summer of 1806. Of the extant manuscripts, *MS A* (*D.C. MS 58*) is an 1806 fair copy of work belonging to 1800; it contains ll.192–457, and implies a missing previous leaf that held the Prospectus and ll. 1–191. *MS R* (*D.C. MS 28*), as well as containing material written for *Michael* and the Preface to *Lyrical Ballads*, preserves drafts of *Home at Grasmere*, 469–859. Though for a time regarded by scholars as belonging to 1806, it is a surviving section of what was probably Wordsworth's chief rough-notebook of 1800; see Jonathan Wordsworth, 'On Man, on Nature, and on Human Life', *RES* New Series, xxxi, no. 121 (1980), 17–29. *MS B* (*D.C. MS 59*), third of the manuscripts of *Home at Grasmere* that survive from the early period, is a fair copy of the complete poem as it stood in September 1806. The Prospectus has been transferred to the end (as ll. 959–1048), and contains a new passage of great importance, 'I, long before the blessèd hour arrives . . .' (ll. 1002–14). Of the hundred lines (859–958) following the material drafted in *MS R*, and leading up to the Prospectus, it can be said with certainty only that the opening paragraph (ll. 859–74) must from its internal reference be 1800, and the final lines (953–8) are a transition belonging to 1806; on grounds of style and content there is no reason why the remainder should not be early work revised by the poet during transcription.

The text *MS B* presented below is endebted to the Cornell editor's photographs and transcripts (Darlington, 269–409), and also to an unpublished text of *Home at Grasmere*, and some highly useful notes, prepared by James Butler. Four gaps in the manuscript have been filled, 'worthiest' in l. 680, and 'A term' in 749, being supplied from the final reading of *MS R*; 'blinder' in l. 986, and 'pleasant haunts' in 1015, from Prospectus *MS 1*. A fifth gap, at l. 1042, cannot be filled, as the line appears for the first time in *MS B*, and is entirely recast in the poet's later revisions.

Once on the brow of yonder hill I stopped,
While I was yet a schoolboy (of what age
I cannot well remember, but the hour

I well remember though the year be gone),
And with a sudden influx overcome
At sight of this seclusion, I forgot
My haste—for hasty had my footsteps been,
As boyish my pursuits—and sighing said,
'What happy fortune were it here to live!
And if I thought of dying, if a thought
Of mortal separation could come in
With paradise before me, here to die'.
I was no prophet, nor had even a hope,
Scarcely a wish, but one bright pleasing thought,
A fancy in the heart of what might be
The lot of others, never could be mine.

The place from which I looked was soft and green,
Not giddy yet aërial, with a depth
Of vale below, a height of hills above.
Long did I halt; I could have made it even
My business and my errand so to halt.
For rest of body 'twas a perfect place,
All that luxurious nature could desire,
But tempting to the spirit; who could look
And not feel motions there? I thought of clouds
That sail on winds; of breezes that delight
To play on water, or in endless chase
Pursue each other through the liquid depths
Of grass or corn, over and through and through
In billow after billow evermore;
Of sunbeams, shadows, butterflies and birds,
Angels, and wingèd creatures that are lords
Without restraint of all which they behold.
I sate, and, stirred in spirit as I looked,
I seemed to feel such liberty was mine,
Such power and joy—but only for this end,
To flit from field to rock, from rock to field,
From shore to island, and from isle to shore,
From open place to covert, from a bed
Of meadow-flowers into a tuft of wood,
From high to low, from low to high, yet still
Within the bounds of this huge concave; here
Should be my home, this valley be my world.

From that time forward was the place to me
As beautiful in thought as it had been

When present to my bodily eyes: a haunt
Of my affections, oftentimes in joy
A brighter joy, in sorrow (but of that
I have known little), in such gloom, at least,
Such damp of the gay mind as stood to me
In place of sorrow, 'twas a gleam of light—
And now 'tis mine for life! Dear vale,
One of thy lowly dwellings is my home.

Yes, the realities of life—so cold,
So cowardly, so ready to betray,
So stinted in the measure of their grace,
As we report them, doing them much wrong—
Have been to me more bountiful than hope,
Less timid than desire. Oh bold indeed
They have been, bold and bounteous unto me,
Who have myself been bold, not wanting trust,
Nor resolution, nor at last the hope
Which is of wisdom, for I feel it is.

And did it cost so much, and did it ask
Such length of discipline, and could it seem
An act of courage, and the thing itself
A conquest? Shame that this was ever so,
Not to the boy or youth, but shame to thee,
Sage man, thou sun in its meridian strength,
Thou flower in its full blow, thou king and crown
Of human nature—shame to thee, sage man.
Thy prudence, thy experience, thy desires,
Thy apprehensions, blush thou for them all!
But I am safe—yes, one at least is safe—
What once was deemed so difficult is now
Smooth, easy, without obstacle; what once
Did to my blindness seem a sacrifice,
The same is now a choice of the whole heart.
If e'er the acceptance of such dower was deemed
A condescension or a weak indulgence
To a sick fancy, it is now an act
Of reason that exultingly aspires.
This solitude is mine; the distant thought
Is fetched out of the heaven in which it was.
The unappropriated bliss hath found
An owner, and that owner I am he!—
The lord of this enjoyment is on earth

And in my breast. What wonder if I speak
With fervour, am exalted with the thought
Of my possessions, of my genuine wealth
Inward and outward—what I keep, have gained,
Shall gain, must gain—if sound be my belief,
From past and present rightly understood,
That in my day of childhood I was less
The mind of Nature, less, take all in all,
Whatever may be lost, than I am now?
For proof behold this valley—and behold
Yon cottage, where with me my Emma dwells.

Aye, think on that, my heart, and cease to stir;
Pause upon that, and let the breathing frame
No longer breathe, but all be satisfied.
Oh, if such silence be not thanks to God
For what hath been bestowed, then where, where then,
Shall gratitude find rest? Mine eyes did ne'er
Rest on a lovely object, nor my mind
Take pleasure in the midst of happy thoughts,
But either she whom now I have, who now
Divides with me this loved abode, was there
Or not far off. Where'er my footsteps turned,
Her voice was like a hidden bird that sang;
The thought of her was like a flash of light
Or an unseen companionship, a breath
Or fragrance independent of the wind
In all my goings, in the new and old
Of all my meditations—and in this
Favorite of all, in this the most of all.
What being, therefore, since the birth of man
Had ever more abundant cause to speak
Thanks, and if music and the power of song
Make him more thankful, then to call on these
To aid him, and with these resound his joy?
The boon is absolute: surpassing grace
To me hath been voutchsafed. Among the bowers
Of blissful Eden this was neither given,
Nor could be given—possession of the good
Which had been sighed for, antient thought fulfilled,
And dear imaginations realized
Up to their highest measure, yea, and more.

Embrace me then, ye hills, and close me in;
Now in the clear and open day I feel
Your guardianship, I take it to my heart—

'Tis like the solemn shelter of the night.
But I would call thee beautiful, for mild
And soft and gay and beautiful thou art,
Dear valley, having in thy face a smile,
Though peaceful, full of gladness. Thou art pleased,
Pleased with thy crags and woody steeps, thy lake,
Its one green island and its winding shores,
The multitude of little rocky hills,
Thy church and cottages of mountain stone—
Clustered like stars, some few, but single most,
And lurking dimly in their shy retreats,
Or glancing at each other chearful looks,
Like separated stars with clouds between.
What want we? Have we not perpetual streams,
Warm woods and sunny hills, and fresh green fields,
And mountains not less green, and flocks and herds,
And thickets full of songsters, and the voice
Of lordly birds—an unexpected sound
Heard now and then from morn to latest eve
Admonishing the man who walks below
Of solitude and silence in the sky?
These have we, and a thousand nooks of earth
Have also these; but nowhere else is found—
Nowhere (or is it fancy?) can be found—
The one sensation that is here; 'tis here,
Here as it found its way into my heart
In childhood, here as it abides by day,
By night, here only; or in chosen minds
That take it with them hence, where'er they go.
'Tis (but I cannot name it), 'tis the sense
Of majesty and beauty and repose,
A blended holiness of earth and sky,
Something that makes this individual spot,
This small abiding-place of many men,
A termination and a last retreat,
A centre, come from whereso'er you will,
A whole without dependence or defect,
Made for itself and happy in itself,
Perfect contentment, unity entire.

Long is it since we met to part no more,
Since I and Emma heard each other's call
And were companions once again, like birds
Which by the intruding fowler had been scared,
Two of a scattered brood that could not bear

To live in loneliness; 'tis long since we,
Remembering much and hoping more, found means
To walk abreast, though in a narrow path,
With undivided steps. Our home was sweet—
Could it be less? If we were forced to change,
Our home again was sweet; but still—for youth,
Strong as it seems and bold, is inly weak
And diffident—the destiny of life
Remained unfixed, and therefore we were still

[Seven lines missing]

We will be free, and, as we mean to live
In culture of divinity and truth,
Will chuse the noblest temple that we know.
Not in mistrust or ignorance of the mind,
And of the power she has within herself
To enoble all things, made we this resolve;
Far less from any momentary fit
Of inconsiderate fancy, light and vain;
But that we deemed it wise to take the help
Which lay within our reach; and here, we knew,
Help could be found of no mean sort—the spirit
Of singleness and unity and peace.
In this majestic, self-sufficing world,
This all in all of Nature, it will suit,
We said, no other [ ] on earth so well,
Simplicity of purpose, love intense,
Ambition not aspiring to the prize
Of outward things, but for the prize within—
Highest ambition. In the daily walks
Of business 'twill be harmony and grace
For the perpetual pleasure of the sense,
And for the soul—I do not say too much,
Though much be said—an image for the soul,
A habit of eternity and God.
  Nor have we been deceived; thus far the effect
Falls not below the loftiest of our hopes.
Bleak season was it, turbulent and bleak,
When hitherward we journeyed, and on foot,
Through bursts of sunshine and through flying snows,
Paced the long vales. How long they were, and yet
How fast that length of way was left behind—
Wensley's long vale and Sedbergh's naked heights.

The frosty wind, as if to make amends
For its keen breath, was aiding to our course
And drove us onward like two ships at sea.
Stern was the face of Nature; we rejoiced
In that stern countenance, for our souls had there
A feeling of their strength. The naked trees,
The icy brooks, as on we passed, appeared
To question us. 'Whence come ye? To what end?'
They seemed to say. 'What would ye?' said the shower,
'Wild wanderers, whither through my dark domain?'
The sunbeam said, 'Be happy'. They were moved—
All things were moved—they round us as we went,
We in the midst of them. And when the trance
Came to us as we stood by Hart-leap Well,
The intimation of the milder day
Which is to come, the fairer world than this,
And raised us up, dejected as we were
Among the records of that doleful place
By sorrow for the hunted beast who there
Had yielded up his breath—the awful trance,
The vision of humanity and of God
The mourner, God the sufferer, when the heart
Of his poor creatures suffers wrongfully—
Both in the sadness and the joy we found
A promise and an earnest that we twain,
A pair seceding from the common world,
Might in that hallowed spot to which our steps
Were tending, in that individual nook,
Might even thus early for ourselves secure,
And in the midst of these unhappy times,
A portion of the blessedness which love
And knowledge will, we trust, hereafter give
To all the vales of earth and all mankind.

Thrice hath the winter moon been filled with light
Since that dear day when Grasmere, our dear vale,
Received us. Bright and solemn was the sky
That faced us with a passionate welcoming
And led us to our threshold, to a home
Within a home, what was to be, and soon,
Our love within a love. Then darkness came,
Composing darkness, with its quiet load
Of full contentment, in a little shed,
Disturbed, uneasy in itself, as seemed,

And wondering at its new inhabitants.
It loves us now—this vale so beautiful
Begins to love us. By a sullen storm,
Two months unwearied of severest storm,
It put the temper of our minds to proof,
And found us faithful through the gloom, and heard
The poet mutter his prelusive songs
With chearful heart, an unknown voice of joy
Among the silence of the woods and hills,
Silent to any gladsomeness of sound
With all their shepherds. But the gates of Spring
Are opened; churlish Winter hath given leave
That she should entertain for this one day—
Perhaps for many genial days to come—
His guests and make them happy. They are pleased,
But most of all, the birds that haunt the flood,
With the mild summons, inmates though they be
Of Winter's household. They are jubilant
This day, who drooped, or seemed to droop, so long;
They shew their pleasure, and shall I do less?
Happier of happy though I be, like them
I cannot take possession of the sky,
Mount with a thoughtless impulse, and wheel there,
One of a mighty multitude whose way
And motion is a harmony and dance
Magnificent. Behold them, how they shape
Orb after orb their course still round and round
Above the area of the lake, their own
Adopted region, girding it about
In wanton repetition, yet therewith—
With that large circle evermore renewed—
Hundreds of curves and circlets, high and low,
Backwards and forwards, progress intricate,
As if one spirit was in all and swayed
Their indefatigable flight. 'Tis done!
Ten times or more I fancied it had ceased,
And lo, the vanished company again
Ascending—list, again I hear their wings—
Faint, faint at first, and then an eager sound,
Passed in a moment, and as faint again.
They tempt the sun to sport among their plumes;
They tempt the water and the gleaming ice
To shew them a fair image. 'Tis themselves,

Their own fair forms upon the glimmering plain,
Painted more soft and fair as they descend
Almost to touch, then up again aloft,
Up with a sally and a flash of speed
As if they scorned both resting-place and rest.
Spring—for this day belongs to thee—rejoice!
Not upon me alone hath been bestowed—
Me, blessed with many onward-looking thoughts—
The sunshine and mild air. Oh, surely these
Are grateful: not the happy quires of love,
Thine own peculiar family, sweet Spring,
That sport among green leaves, so blithe a train.

But two are missing—two, a lonely pair
Of milk-white swans. Ah, why are they not here?
These above all, ah, why are they not here
To share in this day's pleasure? From afar
They came, like Emma and myself, to live
Together here in peace and solitude,
Chusing this valley, they who had the choice
Of the whole world. We saw them day by day,
Through those two months of unrelenting storm,
Conspicuous in the centre of the lake,
Their safe retreat. We knew them well—I guess
That the whole valley knew them—but to us
They were more dear than may be well believed,
Not only for their beauty and their still
And placid way of life and faithful love
Inseparable, not for these alone,
But that their state so much resembled ours,
They also having chosen this abode—
They strangers, and we strangers—they a pair,
And we a solitary pair like them.
They should not have departed! Many days
I've looked for them in vain, nor on the wing
Have seen them, nor in that small open space
Of blue unfrozen water, where they lodged
And lived so long in quiet, side by side.
Companions, brethren, consecrated friends,
Shall we behold them yet another year
Surviving, they for us and we for them,
And neither pair be broken? Nay, perchance
It is too late already for such hope;

The shepherd may have seized the deadly tube
And parted them, incited by a prize
Which, for the sake of those he loves at home,
And for the lamb upon the mountain-tops,
He should have spared. Or haply both are gone—
One death—and that were mercy—given to both.

I cannot look upon this favoured vale
But that I seem, by harbouring this thought,
To wrong it, such unworthy recompence
Imagining, of confidence so pure.
Ah, if I wished to follow where the sight
Of all that is before my eyes, the voice
Which is as a presiding spirit here,
Would lead me, I should say unto myself,
'They who are dwellers in this holy place
Must needs themselves be hallowed'. They require
No benediction from the stranger's lips,
For they are blessed already. None would give
The greeting 'Peace be with you' unto them,
For peace they have—it cannot but be theirs—
And mercy and forbearance. Nay, not these,
There is no call for these—that office love
Performs, and charity beyond the bounds
Of charity—an overflowing love,
Not for the creature only, but for all
Which is around them; love for every thing
Which in this happy valley we behold.

Thus do we soothe ourselves, and when the thought
Is passed, we blame it not for having come.
What if I floated down a pleasant stream
And now am landed, and the motion gone,
Shall I reprove myself? Ah no, the stream
Is flowing and will never cease to flow,
And I shall float upon that stream again.
By such forgetfulness the soul becomes
Words cannot say how beautiful. Then hail,
Hail to the visible presence! Hail to thee,
Delightful valley, habitation fair,
And to whatever else of outward form
Can give us inward help, can purify
And elevate and harmonize and soothe,
And steal away and for a while deceive

And lap in pleasing rest, and bear us on
Without desire in full complacency,
Contemplating perfection absolute
And entertained as in a placid sleep.

But not betrayed by tenderness of mind
That feared, or wholly overlooked, the truth
Did we come hither, with romantic hope
To find in midst of so much loveliness
Love, perfect love, of so much majesty
A like majestic frame of mind in those
Who here abide—the persons like the place.
Nor from such hope, or aught of such belief,
Hath issued any portion of the joy
Which I have felt this day. An awful voice,
'Tis true, I in my walks have often heard,
Sent from the mountains or the sheltered fields,
Shout after shout, reiterated whoop
In manner of a bird that takes delight
In answering to itself, or like a hound
Single at chace among the lonely woods—
A human voice (how awful in the gloom
Of coming night, when sky is dark, and earth
Not dark, nor yet enlightened, but by snow
Made visible) amid the noise of winds
And bleatings manifold of sheep that know
Their summons and are gathering round for food—
That voice, the same, the very same, that breath
Which was an utterance awful as the wind,
Or any sound the mountains ever heard!

That shepherd's voice, it may have reached mine ear
Debased and under prophanation, made
An organ for the sounds articulate
Of ribaldry and blasphemy and wrath,
Where drunkenness hath kindled senseless frays.
I came not dreaming of unruffled life,
Untainted manners; born among the hills,
Bred also there, I wanted not a scale
To regulate my hopes; pleased with the good,
I shrink not from the evil in disgust,
Or with immoderate pain. I look for man,
The common creature of the brotherhood,
But little differing from the man elsewhere

For selfishness and envy and revenge
(Ill neighbourhood!—folly that this should be),
Flattery and double-dealing, strife and wrong.

Yet is it something gained—it is in truth
A mighty gain—that labour here preserves
His rosy face, a servant only here
Of the fireside or of the open field,
A freeman, therefore sound and unenslaved;
That extreme penury is here unknown,
And cold and hunger's abject wretchedness,
Mortal to body and the heaven-born mind;
That they who want, are not too great a weight
For those who can relieve. Here may the heart
Breathe in the air of fellow-suffering
Dreadless, as in a kind of fresher breeze
Of her own native element—the hand
Be ready and unwearied, without plea,
From tasks too frequent and beyond its powers,
For languor or indifference or despair.
And as these lofty barriers break the force
Of winds (this deep vale as it doth in part
Conceal us from the storm) so here there is
A power and a protection for the mind—
Dispensed indeed to other solitudes
Favoured by noble privilege like this,
Where kindred independence of estate
Is prevalent, where he who tills the field,
He, happy man, is master of the field
And treads the mountain which his father trod.
Hence, and from other local circumstance,
In this enclosure many of the old
Substantial virtues have a firmer tone
Than in the base and ordinary world.

Yon cottage, would that it could tell a part
Of its own story; thousands might give ear—
Might hear it, and blush deep. There few years past
In this his native valley dwelt a man,
The master of a little plot of ground,
A man of mild deportment and discourse,
A scholar also (as the phrase is here),
For he drew much delight from those few books
That lay within his reach, and for this cause

Was by his fellow-dalesmen honoured more.
A shepherd and a tiller of the ground,
Studious withal, and healthy in his frame
Of body, and of just and placid mind,
He with his consort and his children saw
Days that were seldom touched by petty strife,
Years safe from large misfortune—long maintained
That course which men the wisest and most pure
Might look on with entire complacency.
Yet in himself and near him were there faults
At work to undermine his happiness
By little and by little. Active, prompt,
And lively was the housewife—in the vale
None more industrious—but her industry
Was of that kind, 'tis said, which tended more
To splendid neatness, to a shewy, trim,
And overlaboured purity of house,
Than to substantial thrift. He, on his part,
Generous and easy-minded, was not free
From carelessness, and thus in course of time
These joint infirmities, combined perchance
With other cause less obvious, brought decay
Of worldly substance and distress of mind,
Which to a thoughtful man was hard to shun,
And which he could not cure. A blooming girl
Served them, an inmate of the house. Alas!
Poor now in tranquil pleasure, he gave way
To thoughts of troubled pleasure; he became
A lawless suitor of the maid, and she
Yielded unworthily. Unhappy man—
That which he had been weak enough to do
Was misery in remembrance; he was stung,
Stung by his inward thoughts, and by the smiles
Of wife and children stung to agony.
His temper urged him not to seek relief
Amid the noise of revellers, nor from draught
Of lonely stupefaction; he himself—
A rational and suffering man—himself
Was his own world, without a resting-place.
Wretched at home, he had no peace abroad,
Ranged through the mountains, slept upon the earth,
Asked comfort of the open air, and found
No quiet in the darkness of the night,

No pleasure in the beauty of the day.
His flock he slighted; his paternal fields
Were as a clog to him, whose spirit wished
To fly, but whither? And yon gracious church,
That has a look so full of peace and hope
And love—benignant mother of the vale,
How fair amid her brood of cottages!—
She was to him a sickness and reproach.
I speak, conjecturing from the little known
The much that to the last remained unknown,
But this is sure: he died of his own grief—
He could not bear the weight of his own shame.

That ridge, which elbowing from the mountain-side
Carries into the plain its rocks and woods,
Conceals a cottage where a father dwells
In widowhood, whose life's co-partner died
Long since, and left him solitary prop
Of many helpless children. I begin
With words which might be prelude to a tale
Of sorrow and dejection, but I feel—
Though in the midst of sadness, as might seem—
No sadness, when I think of what mine eyes
Have seen in that delightful family.
Bright garland make they for their father's brows,
Those six fair daughters, budding yet—not one,
Not one of all the band, a full-blown flower!
Go to the dwelling: there thou shalt have proof
That He who takes away, yet takes not half
Of what He seems to take, or gives it back
Not to our prayer, but far beyond our prayer;
He gives it, the boon-produce of a soil
Which Hope hath never watered. Thou shalt see
A house, which at small distance will appear
In no distinction to have passed beyond
Its fellows—will appear, like them, to have grown
Out of the native rock—but nearer view
Will shew it not so grave in outward mien
And soberly arrayed as for the most
Are these rude mountain-dwellings (Nature's care,
Mere friendless Nature's), but a studious work
Of many fancies and of many hands,
A plaything and a pride; for such the air
And aspect which the little spot maintains

In spite of lonely winter's nakedness.
They have their jasmine resting on the porch,
Their rose-trees, strong in health, that will be soon
Roof-high; and here and there the garden-wall
Is topped with single stones, a shewy file
Curious for shape or hue—some round, like balls,
Worn smooth and round by fretting of the brook
From which they have been gathered, others bright
And sparry, the rough scatterings of the hills.
These ornaments the cottage chiefly owes
To one, a hardy girl, who mounts the rocks
(Such is her choice; she fears not the bleak wind),
Companion of her father—does for him
Where'er he wanders in his pastoral course
The service of a boy, and with delight
More keen, and prouder daring. Yet hath she
Within the garden, like the rest, a bed
For her own flowers or favorite herbs, a space
Holden by sacred charter; and I guess
She also helped to frame that tiny plot
Of garden-ground which one day 'twas my chance
To find among the woody rocks that rise
Above the house, a slip of smoother earth
Planted with gooseberry-bushes—and in one,
Right in the centre of the prickly shrub,
A mimic bird's-nest, fashioned by the hand,
Was stuck, a staring thing of twisted hay,
And one quaint fir-tree towered above the whole.
But in the darkness of the night, then most
This dwelling charms me; covered by the gloom
Then, heedless of good manners, I stop short
And (who could help it?) feed by stealth my sight
With prospect of the company within,
Laid open through the blazing window. There
I see the eldest daugher at her wheel,
Spinning amain, as if to overtake
She knows not what, or teaching in her turn
Some little novice of the sisterhood
That skill or this, or other household work
Which from her father's honored hands, herself,
While she was yet a little one, had learned.
Mild man—he is not gay; but they are gay,
And the whole house is filled with gaiety.

From yonder grey stone that stands alone
Close to the foaming stream, look up and see,
Not less than half way up the mountain-side,
A dusky spot, a little grove of firs—
And seems still smaller than it is. The dame
Who dwells below, she told me that this grove,
Just six weeks younger than her eldest boy,
Was planted by her husband and herself
For a convenient shelter, which in storm
Their sheep might draw to. 'And they know it well',
Said she, 'for thither do we bear them food
In time of heavy snow'. She then began
In fond obedience to her private thoughts
To speak of her dead husband. Is there not
An art, a music, and a stream of words
That shall be life, the acknowledged voice of life—
Shall speak of what is done among the fields,
Done truly there, or felt, of solid good
And real evil, yet be sweet withal,
More grateful, more harmonious than the breath,
The idle breath of sweetest pipe attuned
To pastoral fancies? Is there such a stream,
Pure and unsullied, flowing from the heart
With motions of true dignity and grace—
Or must we seek these things where man is not?
Methinks I could repeat in tuneful verse,
Delicious as the gentlest breeze that sounds
Through that aërial fir-grove, could preserve
Some portion of its human history
As gathered from that matron's lips, and tell
Of tears that have been shed at sight of it,
And moving dialogues between this pair,
Who in the prime of wedlock with joint hands
Did plant this grove, now flourishing while they
No longer flourish—he entirely gone,
She withering in her loneliness. Be this
A task above my skill; the silent mind
Has its own treasures, and I think of these,
Love what I see, and honour humankind.

No, we are not alone; we do not stand,
My Emma, here misplaced and desolate,
Loving what no one cares for but ourselves.
We shall not scatter through the plains and rocks

Of this fair vale and o'er its spatious heights
Unprofitable kindliness, bestowed
On objects unaccustomed to the gifts
Of feeling, that were cheerless and forlorn
But few weeks past, and would be so again
If we were not. We do not tend a lamp
Whose lustre we alone participate,
Which is dependent upon us alone,
Mortal though bright, a dying, dying flame.
Look where we will, some human heart has been
Before us with its offering; not a tree
Sprinkles these little pastures, but the same
Hath furnished matter for a thought, perchance
To some one is as a familiar friend.
Joy spreads and sorrow spreads; and this whole vale,
Home of untutored shepherds as it is,
Swarms with sensation, as with gleams of sunshine,
Shadows or breezes, scents or sounds. Nor deem
These feelings—though subservient more than ours
To every day's demand for daily bread,
And borrowing more their spirit and their shape
From self-respecting interests—deem them not
Unworthy therefore and unhallowed. No,
They lift the animal being, do themselves
By Nature's kind and ever present aid
Refine the selfishness from which they spring,
Redeem by love the individual sense
Of anxiousness with which they are combined.
Many are pure, the best of them are pure;
The best, and these, remember, most abound,
Are fit associates of the worthiest joy,
Joy of the highest and the purest minds.
They blend with it congenially; meanwhile,
Calmly they breathe their own undying life,
Lowly and unassuming as it is,
Through this, their mountain sanctuary (long,
Oh long may it remain inviolate!),
Diffusing health and sober chearfulness,
And giving to the moments as they pass
Their little boons of animating thought,
That sweeten labour, make it seem and feel
To be no arbitrary weight imposed,
But a glad function natural to man.

Fair proof of this, newcomer though I be,
Already have I seen; the inward frame,
Though slowly opening, opens every day.
Nor am I less delighted with the show
As it unfolds itself, now here, now there,
Than is the passing traveller, when his way
Lies through some region then first trod by him
(Say this fair valley's self), when low-hung mists
Break up and are beginning to recede.
How pleased he is to hear the murmuring streams,
The many voices, from he knows not where,
To have about him, which way e'er he goes,
Something on every side concealed from view,
In every quarter some thing visible,
Half seen or wholly, lost and found again—
Alternate progress and impediment,
And yet a growing prospect in the main.

Such pleasure now is mine, and what if I—
Herein less happy than the traveller—
Am sometimes forced to cast a painful look
Upon unwelcome things, which unawares
Reveal themselves? Not therefore is my mind
Depressed, nor do I fear what is to come;
But confident, enriched at every glance,
The more I see the more is my delight.
Truth justifies herself; and as she dwells
With Hope, who would not follow where she leads?

Nor let me overlook those other loves
Where no fear is, those humbler sympathies
That have to me endeared the quietness
Of this sublime retirement. I begin
Already to inscribe upon my heart
A liking for the small grey horse that bears
The paralytic man; I know the ass
On which the cripple, in the quarry maimed,
Rides to and fro: I know them and their ways.
The famous sheep-dog, first in all the vale,
Though yet to me a stranger, will not be
A stranger long; nor will the blind man's guide,
Meek and neglected thing, of no renown.
Whoever lived a winter in one place,
Beneath the shelter of one cottage-roof,

And has not had his red-breast or his wren?
I have them both; and I shall have my thrush
In spring-time, and a hundred warblers more;
And if the banished eagle pair return,
Helvellyn's eagles, to their antient hold,
Then shall I see, shall claim with those two birds
Acquaintance, as they soar amid the heavens.
The owl that gives the name to Owlet-crag
Have I heard shouting, and he soon will be
A chosen one of my regards. See there,
The heifer in yon little croft belongs
To one who holds it dear; with duteous care
She reared it, and in speaking of her charge
I heard her scatter once a word or two,
A term domestic, yea, and motherly,
She being herself a mother. Happy beast,
If the caresses of a human voice
Can make it so, and care of human hands.

And ye, as happy under Nature's care,
Strangers to me and all men, or at least
Strangers to all particular amity,
All intercourse of knowledge or of love
That parts the individual from the kind;
Whether in large communities ye dwell
From year to year, not shunning man's abode,
A settled residence, or be from far,
Wild creatures, and of many homes, that come
The gift of winds, and whom the winds again
Take from us at your pleasure—yet shall ye
Not want for this, your own subordinate place,
According to your claim, an underplace
In my affections. Witness the delight
With which erewhile I saw that multitude
Wheel through the sky and see them now at rest,
Yet not at rest, upon the glassy lake.
They cannot rest—they gambol like young whelps,
Active as lambs and overcome with joy;
They try all frolic motions, flutter, plunge,
And beat the passive water with their wings.
Too distant are they for plain view, but lo!
Those little fountains, sparkling in the sun,
Which tell what they are doing, which rise up,
First one and then another silver spout,
As one or other takes the fit of glee—

Fountains and spouts, yet rather in the guise
Of plaything fire-works, which on festal nights
Hiss, hiss about the feet of wanton boys.
How vast the compass of this theatre,
Yet nothing to be seen but lovely pomp
And silent majesty. The birch-tree woods
Are hung with thousand thousand diamond drops
Of melted hoar-frost, every tiny knot
In the bare twigs, each little budding-place
Cased with its several bead; what myriads there
Upon one tree, while all the distant grove
That rises to the summit of the steep
Is like a mountain built of silver light!
See yonder the same pageant, and again
Behold the universal imagery
At what a depth, deep in the lake below.
Admonished of the days of love to come,
The raven croaks and fills the sunny air
With a strange sound of genial harmony;
And in and all about that playful band,
Incapable although they be of rest,
And in their fashion very rioters,
There is a stillness, and they seem to make
Calm revelry in that their calm abode.
I leave them to their pleasure, and I pass,
Pass with a thought the life of the whole year
That is to come—the throngs of mountain flowers
And lillies that will dance upon the lake.

Then boldly say that solitude is not
Where these things are: he truly is alone,
He of the multitude, whose eyes are doomed
To hold a vacant commerce day by day
With that which he can neither know nor love—
Dead things, to him thrice dead—or worse than this,
With swarms of life, and worse than all, of men,
His fellow men, that are to him no more
Than to the forest hermit are the leaves
That hang aloft in myriads—nay, far less,
Far less for aught that comforts or defends
Or lulls or chears. Society is here:
The true community, the noblest frame
Of many into one incorporate;
That must be looked for here; paternal sway,

One household under God for high and low,
One family and one mansion; to themselves
Appropriate, and divided from the world
As if it were a cave, a multitude
Human and brute, possessors undisturbed
Of this recess, their legislative hall,
Their temple, and their glorious dwelling-place.

Dismissing therefore all Arcadian dreams,
All golden fancies of the golden age,
The bright array of shadowy thoughts from times
That were before all time, or are to be
When time is not, the pageantry that stirs
And will be stirring when our eyes are fixed
On lovely objects and we wish to part
With all remembrance of a jarring world—
Give entrance to the sober truth; avow
That Nature to this favourite spot of ours
Yields no exemption, but her awful rights
Enforces to the utmost, and exacts
Her tribute of inevitable pain,
And that the sting is added, man himself
For ever busy to afflict himself.
Yet temper this with one sufficient hope—
What need of more?—that we shall neither droop
Nor pine for want of pleasure in the life
Which is about us, nor through dearth of aught
That keeps in health the insatiable mind;
That we shall have for knowledge and for love
Abundance; and that, feeling as we do,
How goodly, how exceeding fair, how pure
From all reproach is this aetherial frame
And this deep vale, its earthly counterpart,
By which and under which we are enclosed
To breathe in peace; we shall moreover find
(If sound, and what we ought to be ourselves,
If rightly we observe and justly weigh)
The inmates not unworthy of their home,
The dwellers of the dwelling. And if this
Were not, we have enough within ourselves,
Enough to fill the present day with joy
And overspread the future years with hope—
Our beautiful and quiet home, enriched
Already with a stranger whom we love

Deeply, a stranger of our father's house,
A never-resting pilgrim of the sea,
Who finds at last an hour to his content
Beneath our roof; and others whom we love
Will seek us also, sisters of our hearts,
And one, like them, a brother of our hearts,
Philosopher and poet, in whose sight
These mountains will rejoice with open joy.
Such is our wealth: O vale of peace, we are
And must be, with God's will, a happy band!

But 'tis not to enjoy, for this alone
That we exist; no, something must be done.
I must not walk in unreproved delight
These narrow bounds and think of nothing more,
No duty that looks further and no care.
Each being has his office, lowly some
And common, yet all worthy if fulfilled
With zeal, acknowledgement that with the gift
Keeps pace a harvest answering to the seed.
Of ill-advised ambition and of pride
I would stand clear, yet unto me I feel
That an internal brightness is vouchsafed
That must not die, that must not pass away.
Why does this inward lustre fondly seek
And gladly blend with outward fellowship?
Why shine they round me thus, whom thus I love?
Why do they teach me, whom I thus revere?
Strange question, yet it answers not itself.
That humble roof, embowered among the trees,
That calm fireside—it is not even in them,
Blessed as they are, to furnish a reply
That satisfies and ends in perfect rest.
Possessions have I, wholly, solely mine,
Something within, which yet is shared by none—
Not even the nearest to me and most dear—
Something which power and effort may impart.
I would impart it; I would spread it wide,
Immortal in the world which is to come.
I would not wholly perish even in this,
Lie down and be forgotten in the dust,
I and the modest partners of my days
Making a silent company in death.
It must not be, if I, divinely taught

Am privileged to speak as I have felt
Of what in man is human or divine.

While yet an innocent, a little one, a heart
That doubtless wanted not its tender moods,
I breathed (for this I better recollect)
Among wild appetites and blind desires,
Motions of savage instinct, my delight
And exaltation. No thing at that time
So welcome, no temptation half so dear
As that which [urged] me to a daring feat.
Deep pools, tall trees, black chasms, and dizzy crags—
I loved to look at them, to stand and read
Their looks forbidding, read and disobey,
Sometimes in act, and evermore in thought.
With impulses which only were by these
Surpassed in strength, I heard of danger met
Or sought with courage, enterprize forlorn,
By one, sole keeper of his own intent,
Or by a resolute few, who for the sake
Of glory fronted multitudes in arms.
Yea, to this day I swell with like desire;
I cannot at this moment read a tale
Of two brave vessels matched in deadly fight
And fighting to the death, but I am pleased
More than a wise man ought to be; I wish,
I burn, I struggle, and in soul am there.
But me hath Nature tamed and bade me seek
For other agitations or be calm,
Hath dealt with me as with a turbulent stream—
Some nurseling of the mountains which she leads
Through quiet meadows after it has learned
Its strength and had its triumph and its joy,
Its desperate course of tumult and of glee.
That which in stealth by Nature was performed
Hath reason sanctioned. Her deliberate voice
Hath said, 'Be mild and love all gentle things;
Thy glory and thy happiness be there.
Yet fear (though thou confide in me) no want
Of aspirations which have been—of foes
To wrestle with and victory to complete,
Bounds to be leapt and darkness to explore.
That which enflamed thy infant heart—the love,

The longing, the contempt, the undaunted quest—
These shall survive, though changed their office, these
Shall live; it is not in their power to die'.
Then farewell to the warrior's deeds, farewell
All hope, which once and long was mine, to fill
The heroic trumpet with the muse's breath!
Yet in this peaceful vale we will not spend
Unheard-of days, though loving peaceful thoughts;
A voice shall speak, and what will be the theme?

On man, on Nature, and on human life,
Thinking in solitude, from time to time
I feel sweet passions traversing my soul
Like music; unto these, where'er I may,
I would give utterance in numerous verse.
Of truth, of grandeur, beauty, love, and hope—
Hope for this earth and hope beyond the grave—
Of virtue and of intellectual power,
Of blessed consolations in distress,
Of joy in widest commonalty spread,
Of the individual mind that keeps its own
Inviolate retirement, and consists
With being limitless, the one great life,
I sing; fit audience let me find, though few!

'Fit audience find, though few'—thus prayed the bard,
Holiest of men. Urania, I shall need
Thy guidance, or a greater muse, if such
Descend to earth or dwell in highest heaven;
For I must tread on shadowy ground, must sink
Deep, and aloft ascending, breathe in worlds
To which the heaven of heavens is but a veil.
All strength, all terror, single or in bands,
That ever was put forth in personal forms—
Jehovah, with his thunder, and the quire
Of shouting angels and the empyreal thrones—
I pass them unalarmed. The darkest pit
Of the profoundest hell, chaos, night,
Nor aught of blinder vacancy scooped out
By help of dreams, can breed such fear and awe
As fall upon us often when we look
Into our minds, into the mind of man,
My haunt, and the main region of my song.
Beauty, whose living home is the green earth,

Surpassing the most fair ideal forms
The craft of delicate spirits hath composed
From earth's materials, waits upon my steps,
Pitches her tents before me where I move,
An hourly neighbour. Paradise and groves
Elysian, fortunate islands, fields like those of old
In the deep ocean—wherefore should they be
A history, or but a dream, when minds
Once wedded to this outward frame of things
In love, find these the growth of common day?
I, long before the blessèd hour arrives,
Would sing in solitude the spousal verse
Of this great consummation, would proclaim—
Speaking of nothing more than what we are—
How exquisitely the individual mind
(And the progressive powers perhaps no less
Of the whole species) to the external world
Is fitted; and how exquisitely too—
Theme this but little heard of among men—
The external world is fitted to the mind;
And the creation (by no lower name
Can it be called) which they with blended might
Accomplish: this is my great argument.

Such pleasant haunts foregoing, if I oft
Must turn elsewhere, and travel near the tribes
And fellowships of men, and see ill sights
Of passions ravenous from each other's rage,
Must hear humanity in fields and groves
Pipe solitary anguish, or must hang
Brooding above the fierce confederate storm
Of sorrow, barricadoed evermore
Within the walls of cities—may these sounds
Have their authentic comment, that even these
Hearing, I be not heartless or forlorn.
Come, thou prophetic spirit, soul of man,
Thou human soul of the wide earth that hast
Thy metropolitan temple in the hearts
Of mighty poets; unto me vouchsafe
Thy guidance, teach me to discern, and part
Inherent things from casual, what is fixed
From fleeting, that my verse may live, and be
Even as a light hung up in heaven to chear
Mankind in times to come. And if with this

I blend more lowly matter, with the thing
Contemplated describe the mind and man
Contemplating, and who and what he was,
The transitory being that beheld
This vision, when and where and how he lived,
With all his little realties of life—
Be not this labour useless. If such theme
With highest things may [ ], then great God,
Thou who art breath and being, way and guide,
And power and understanding, may my life
Express the image of a better time;
More wise desires and simpler manners nurse
My heart in genuine freedom; all pure thoughts
Be with me, and uphold me to the end!

Notes

CHAPTER 1: AN OBSCURE SENSE OF POSSIBLE SUBLIMITY

1. The Climbing of Snowdon (*1805*, xiii. 1–65, and a version of the subsequent lines) was originally written to form the opening of the last Book of the short-lived five-Book *Prelude* of January-March 1804. For an account of the structure and composition of this entirely separate version of *The Prelude*, see Chapter 8, section i, and for Wordsworth's discarded draft-material of the period, including the description of the horse, see Norton *Prelude*, 496–500.

2. J. Hillis Miller has described what he regards as a radical ambiguity of meaning in this poem in 'The Still Heart: Poetic Form in Wordsworth', *NLH* ii. 2 (winter 1971), 297–310.

3. *1779*, ii. 459–64/*1805*, ii. 429–34; the lines were incorporated in *The Prelude* in autumn 1799, but had been written (in the third person) for *The Pedlar* in spring 1798, four months before *Tintern Abbey*; see Appendix (i), ll. 217–22.

4. 'The Idiom of Vision', *New Perspectives on Coleridge and Wordsworth*, ed. Geoffrey H. Hartman (New York and London, 1972), 9. Professor Johnston's brilliant description of the poet as borderer is quoted in Chapter 10.

5. It is difficult to know what to make of Wordsworth's claim in a letter of 7 November 1805 not to have seen Marvell's poems 'these many years' (*EY* 642). Apart from anything else, he had late in 1802 copied *An Horatian Ode* into *MS W*. (significantly next in use in February 1804, when Wordsworth was working on his two great odes, *Intimations* and *To Duty*). Marvell is not in Anderson's *British Poets*, the collection in which Wordsworth in spring 1802 read widely in sixteenth-and seventeenth-century verse, and it could well be that at that period he borrowed a copy of Edward Thompson's edition of 1776 (the first to include the Cromwell Poems, cancelled in the posthumous edition of 1681).

6. See, for instance, Vaughan's *Retreat*,

> Happy those early days when I
> Shined in my angel-infancy,
> Before I understood this place
> Appointed for my second race . . .
> When on some gilded cloud or flower
> My gazing soul would dwell an hour,
> And in those weaker glories spy
> Some shadows of eternity.

(ll. 1–4, 11–14)

7. For definitions and discussion of the primary imagination, see Chapters 3 and 6. Again and again in Coleridge's poetry the highest imaginative act, that is the creative perception of harmony, takes the form of a prayer or blessing; see especially, *This Lime-Tree Bower My Prison*, *The Ancient Mariner*, *Frost at Midnight*, *Dejection*, and *To William Wordsworth*.

8. Clough, *Amours de Voyage*, iii. 159–62; Browning, *By the Fireside*, 181.

9. *The Idea of Order at Key West*, final line, and *Notes Towards a Supreme Fiction*, section VII.

10. In their original position in Act III, scene v of *The Borderers* they are spoken by the villain, Rivers, to his dupe, Mortimer, whom he believes he has deluded into murdering an innocent man, and thus repeating his (Rivers's) own earlier crime. The lines oppose not action and suffering in general, but the horrifying speed with which irrevocable deeds may be committed, and the permanence of subsequent guilt. In 1837 when Wordsworth excerpted them from his still unpublished play as an epigraph to *The White Doe of Rylstone* he did so as a Christian poet, and added lines that draw attention to the saintliness of Emily's lifetime of suffering after the deaths of her father and brothers.

11. At the back of Wordsworth's mind are lines in *Paradise Lost*, Book II that have, on a Romantic reading, all the attributes of border vision:

> Before their eyes in sudden view appear
> The secrets of the hoary deep, a dark
> Illimitable ocean without bound,
> Without dimension, where length, breadth, and highth,
> And time and place are lost.
>
> (*PL* ii. 890–4)

The connection is one of many pointed out to me by Lucy Newlyn during the final revision of this book.

12. The role of the beggar, and his disturbing power, are discussed at some length in Chapter 9.

13. My use of the earliest texts—justified, surely, in a book that seeks to present the poetry in its period—may on occasion create a sense of unfamiliarity. In the lines quoted, most readers will have in mind Wordsworth's revision for *Poems* 1807, '*by apt* admonishment'.

14. See Lewis Carroll, *Upon the Lonely Moor* (1856),

> I met an aged, aged man
> Upon the lonely moor:
> I knew I was a gentleman,
> And he was but a boor.
> So I stopped and roughly questioned him,
> 'Come, tell me how you live!'
> But his words impressed my ear no more
> Than if it were a sieve . . .

and Max Beerbohm, 'Mr Wordsworth in the Lake District at Cross Purposes', *Poets' Corner* (1904).

15. First printed as the separate poem that it originally was, by Beth Darlington, *Bicentenary Studies*, 433–7. A revised version of *The Discharged Soldier* was incorporated in the five-Book *Prelude* in February 1804, and became finally *1805*, iv. 363–504.

16. *Discharged Soldier*, 43–7 ('There was in his form . . . sustained') are rewritten in *1805*, and 55–60 ('His face was turned' . . . nature') are cut. Wordsworth's revisions are designed to remove the more personal touches.

17. See *Oxford Wordsworth*, i. 277–8, ll. 337–9, and *PL* ii. 666ff.

18. As I think it is by Jonathan Bishop in 'Wordsworth and the Spots of Time', who regards the immediate experience of the 'spots' in general as one of terror, and who, though writing better than anyone about their shared characteristics, does not seem to me to have assessed so accurately why the memories were precious to Wordsworth; see especially *Casebook*, 138–40.

19. 'Ghastly' is glossed by Johnson as 'Like a ghost, having horror in the countenance', and 'ghostly' as 'Spiritual, relating to the soul', but it is doubtful whether Wordsworth regarded the two words as quite so distinct.

20. *In storm and tempest*, 5–20, incorporated in *The Prelude* (with change of pronoun, 'he' to 'I') as *1779*, ii. 356–71/*1805*, ii. 326–41.

21. Wordsworth's account of the creative process is quoted and discussed in Chapter 9.

22. Compare the lines from *Frost at Midnight*, quoted p. 23.

23. It is not merely chance that the prefix 'un' occurs in three of the above quotations. Like the double negative, it is often misused by Wordsworth—especially in the Miltonic set-piece repetitions: 'Unburthened, unalarmed and unprofaned' (*1805*, iii. 245), for example—but it can similarly be effective: Lucy lived 'among the *un*trodden ways', and the Old Cumberland Beggar ate his food in solitude, 'Surrounded by those wild *un*peopled hills' (l. 14).

24. An attempt is made in Chapter 7 to relate the associative patterning of Wordsworth's language to the underlying sources of his poetry.

25. John Wordsworth, Commander of the *Earl of Abergavenny*, was drowned when the ship sank off Portland Bill on 5 February 1805.

26. 'Enwrought' implies an image of embroidery (or it could be the sculpting of a bas-relief—the point being in each case that a design is worked upon a surface). Human sweetness may be this surface, or 'ground', which the echo of the woman's voice embellishes with the thought of endless travelling. Or it may be the finished work, created with ('out of') the material that is the poet's thought.

27. In fact he points out that Schiller and Richter were 'simply re-phrasing Kant in a more popular manner', and quotes in support from Kant's *Critique of Aesthetic Judgement*, ed. Meredith (Oxford, 1911), 90:

> The beautiful in Nature is a question of the form of the object, and this consists in limitation, whereas the sublime is to be found in an object even devoid of form, so far as it immediately involves, or else by its presence provokes, a representation of limitlessness, yet with a super-added thought of its totality.
>
> (Raysor, ii, 138–9 n.)

28. *Enquiry*, 59; Burke in fact quotes eight lines of Milton (*PL* ii. 666–73).

29. Hugh Blair, whose *Lectures on Rhethoric and Belles Lettres* (1783) Coleridge had out of the Bristol Library in January–February 1798 (and who was a major influence on the Preface to *Lyrical Ballads*, 1800), commented at the end of his third lecture,

> I am inclined to think, that mighty force or power, whether accompanied with terror or not, whether employed in protecting, or in alarming us, has a better title, than any thing that has yet been mentioned, to be the fundamental quality of the sublime . . .
>
> (*Lectures*, i. 35–6)

30. *Enquiry*, 63, and n. Burke's rejection of clarity and distinctness of imagery aroused immediate opposition.

31. Wordsworth's commitment to the Revolution is discussed in Chapter 8.

32. Spring 1800 is the subject of Chapter 4; see especially pp. 114–32.

33. The blank-verse fragment *There is an active principle* belongs to February/March 1798. That it should have become in a revised form the opening of *Excursion*, Book IX, is an example not merely of Wordsworth's tendency to use up old material, but of the fact that he did not think of his views as having changed.

34. The aspirations and disappointments of Wordsworth's scheme for *The Recluse* are the subject of the Epilogue.

35. Which, be it said, is the opposite of what he claimed to have been the case. 'For a very long time indeed', he writes in *Biographia*, Chapter X, 'I could not reconcile personality with infinity; and my head was with Spinoza, though my whole heart remained with Paul and John' (p. 112). The truth was rather that he could not reconcile infinity, the 'something *one and indivisible*' which he ached to behold and know (Griggs, i. 349), with the three persons and one God of Anglican theology. *Biographia* has no shaping spirit until one realizes that it is a defence of early views to which the writer is still emotionally committed. For a discussion of the repressed pantheism of Coleridge's later positions, see Chapter 6, pp. 184–6.

36. For pantheist material in *MS JJ* and *Peter Bell MS 2*, belonging respectively to October 1798 and *c*. February 1799, see Norton *Prelude*, 489, ll. 104–14, and 496, ll. 9–20. 'Wisdom and spirit of the universe' (*1805*, i. 428ff.) is an interesting case of Wordsworth in January 1804 replacing the literary spirit-world of *1799*, Part I (discussed pp. 29–30 and Chapter 2, pp. 38–41) with a Platonic world-soul that is very close to the immanent life-force of *Tintern Abbey*.

37. *The Limits of Mortality* (Middletown, Conn., 1959), 79.

38. Hugh Sykes Davies has put forward the view that the poem is not about Lucy at all ('Another New Poem by Wordsworth', *EC* xv (1965), 135–61). No girl is named, of course, and the pronoun 'She' in line 3 could well refer back to the poet's spirit in line 1. There are objections to such a reading (Wordsworth might have attributed feeling, hearing, and sight to his spirit, but more probably he didn't), but what is interesting is that there should be so little opposition between what would appear at first to be two radically different ways of looking at the poem. As regards *meaning* they come to the same thing: one's concern is merely as to whether the poet is talking directly or in symbolic terms about his own experience. One possibility is that the eight lines of *A slumber* were originally stanzas four and five of *She dwelt among the untrodden ways*, the poem that precedes it in *Lyrical Ballads*, 1800. 'She' in line 3 of *A slumber* would then refer back naturally to Lucy in line 10 of *She dwelt*. The 1798 text of *Lines Written near Richmond* was split in a similar way in 1800, but in this case the division would have to have been almost immediate as *She dwelt* had been sent to Coleridge 'some months' before 6 April 1799 (Griggs, i. 479), and cannot have been composed, whatever its original shape, before *c*. early December 1798.

39. It is a fair guess that he first wrote the ballad *Lucy Gray*, with its more ordinary border image of survival:

> Yet some maintain that to this day
> She is a living child . . .
>
> (ll. 57–8)

To the same group belongs *The Danish Boy* (discussed in Chapter 3), also a solitary, singing, ghostly presence, but in fact rather more palpable.

40. From *Tait's Magazine*, 1839; reprinted Jordan, 443.

41. For landscape poetry of conscious sublimity see, for example, the Simplon Pass of 1804, quoted p. 32.

42. The implications of the spirit-world of *1799* are discussed more fully in Chapter 2, pp. 38–41.

43. As De Quincey puts it in *Suspiria De Profundis*, 'Suffering is a mightier agency in the hands of Nature, as a Demiurgus creating the intellect, than most people are aware of' (Ward, 187). De Quincey's insights and observations have quite frequently in this book been used as a way of understanding Wordsworth's relation to childhood and memory; see especially Chapter 2.

44. For an extensive discussion of the Infant Babe, see Chapter 3, pp. 76–82.

45. The poetry of spring 1802 and its very special moods is the subject of Chapter 5; in a more specific context the role of childhood in *Intimations* is discussed in Chapter 3, pp. 89–97.

46. An attempt is made in Chapter 6 to give an account of the great border poetry of spring 1804.

47. As in *The Prelude* itself, imagination in this book is a recurrent, almost a consistent, preoccupation; but see especially Chapter 3 (pp. 82–7) for its role in *1799*, Chapter 6 (pp. 184–6) for some basic definitions, Chapter 8 for Wordsworth's inability to portray his own imagination as ever having been impaired, Chapter 10 for his final position in *The Prelude*, and the Epilogue for the part played by imagination over the years in the scheme of *The Recluse*.

48. The phrase belongs to John Jones, the final chapter of whose *Egotistical Sublime* (1954) is still the most sympathetic and impressive account of Wordsworth's later poetry.

49. *Oxford Wordsworth*, iv. 374–5, ll. 15–16, 26–8.

50. *The River Duddon* (1820), xxxiii, *Conclusion*, 8–14.

CHAPTER 2: SPOTS OF TIME AND SOURCES OF POWER

1. An annotated transcription of *MS JJ* is provided in Norton *Prelude*, 485–95, but see also the photographs of the manuscript, Parrish, 72–119. These should be read backwards from 114–15 (for the status of 116–17, see Chapter 4, note 5).

2. The first line begins in the lower case in both early manuscripts, *MS JJ* and the *Christabel Notebook*. The fact that Wordsworth didn't write an introduction in December 1799, however, when carrying out other needful alterations before the poem was fair-copied, suggests very strongly that he had come to find the abruptness acceptable.

3. Details of the tradition emerged in a *TLS* correspondence of April–July 1975. Pope repeats 'Was it for this' four times in *Rape of the Lock*, iv. 97–102, and Thomson three in *Seasons*, iii. 1184–8, and there are further eighteenth-century examples in Jago and Shenstone (not to mention more recent ones in Byron, Hazlitt, Owen, Yeats). I am especially grateful to John Woolford for pointing out the Milton example, and for writing more recently to add to the list the opening of Quarles's *Hieroglyphic*, viii (1638). No striking classical source has come to light (in *Aeneid*, ii. 644, for instance, the questioning is not developed), but it seems likely that one exists.

4. The millenarian scheme for *The Recluse* had been drawn up six months before at Alfoxden, with Coleridge, for whom Wordsworth from the first is writing in the drafts that become *1799*; for an extended discussion of Wordsworth's aims, see the Epilogue.

5. In a succession of important and challenging books (notably, *The Anxiety of Influence*, 1973, *A Map of Misreading*, 1975, and *Poetry and Repression*, 1976), Harold Bloom has put forward a view of the creative writer as experiencing anxiety over the too dominant influence of his precursor(s). As ephebe he fights against both influence and his own belatedness, using a series of 'revisionary ratios' that are at once literary devices and psychic defences. The battle, however, can never be won, as the aim of the ephebe is to establish an anteriority that cannot be achieved.

6. For an alternative reading of the initial questions of *1799*, as confident in tone and implication, 'perhaps even quietly exultant', see Parrish, 6.

7. Norton *Prelude*, 489, ll. 98–9.

8. The echo in *MS JJ* was pointed out to me by Adrienne Atkinson.

9. *Wordsworth's Poetry, 1787–1814* (New Haven, 1964), 5.

10. Anxiety may perhaps be detected again in the allusion to *Paradise Lost* at ii. 262; see p. 76.

11. Kenneth Johnston puts what one might expect to be the case, referring to 'The pattern established in Book I of *The Prelude*, of intensely emotional concrete descriptions alternated with highly rhetorical abstract interpretations', and commenting that 'These interpretive passages were often composed separately from and later than the visionary descriptions to which they are attached' (*New Perspectives*, 5). It isn't so. The personal experiences and abstract interpretations typically belong to the same moment.

12. Norton *Prelude*, 489, ll. 98–115.

13. Lines 420–6; presumably one should try to think of the Polar Spirit of *The Ancient Mariner* as a monad. I am grateful to Ian Wylie for establishing that *Religious Musings*, 1–272 belongs to an original 300-line poem on the Nativity of December 1794–c. February 1795, and the remainder to February–March 1796, with perhaps some work in December 1795.

14. The same tends to be true of their appearance in other poets of the middle and late eighteenth century, Mark Akenside, for instance, whose *Pleasures of the Imagination* is a major stylistic influence on *1799*, Part I, and Wordsworth's near-contemporary, Erasmus Darwin. Darwin in fact mentions 'genii' specifically as 'proper machinery for a philosophic poem' (*Botanic Garden,* I. i. 73 n.). In addition to these recent sources, Wordsworth at *1799*, i. 186–9 clearly has in mind *Tempest*, V. i. 33, 'Ye elves of hills, brooks, standing lakes, and groves'.

15. The italicized lines are cut or changed in *1805*.

16. 'As pants the hart for cooling streams/When heated in the chase', Psalm 42 in the commonly sung version of Tate and Brady (1696).

17. Thomas Pennant, *Tour in Scotland; 1772*, i. 36–7, records the methods used to snare the birds on the open fells, and adds that they were 'sold on the spot for sixteen pence or twenty pence a couple' and sent by stage-coach to London (see Moorman, i. 33).

18. The border implications of *There was a boy* are discussed in Chapter 1, pp. 28–31, above.

19. *Nutting* appears first in the *Christabel Notebook* and the letter written by Wordsworth and Dorothy to Coleridge on 21 December 1798. Though not in *JJ*, it seems to have developed from *I would not strike a flower*, which has its beginnings there.

20. The first two-and-a-half lines quoted read in the earliest texts: 'They led me far,/ Those guardian-spirits, into some dear nook . . .' (*EY*, 241).

21. A few very tentative suggestions as to these sources are made at the end of the Chapter.

22. As Burke puts it, 'After whirling about; when we sit down, the objects about us still seem to whirl' (*Enquiry*, 73).

23. See Chapter 1, pp. 26–7, above.

24. There is no doubt as to the importance that both Wordsworth and Coleridge attributed to fairy-tales in the early development of imagination (see, for example, Griggs, i. 354), but the implication that fear would be precluded seems false to the poetry of *1799*.

25. The role of the 'spots of time' sequence in later versions of *The Prelude* is discussed in Chapter 8.

26. See Chapter 3, pp. 82–9.

27. A further case of spoiling through elaboration is found in the visit to Furness Abbey of Part, and Book, II. Compare *1799*, ii. 112–17 and *1805*, ii. 115–21, and note the parenthesis inserted at *1805*, ii. 129–30.

28. It stood by the road on Red Hill, a mile or so to the east of Penrith.

29. I first heard this information from Eileen Jay, author of *Wordsworth at Colthouse* (Kendal, 1970). In his *Unpublished Tour* Wordsworth recalls, 'Part of the irons and some of the wood work remained in my memory', and goes on to express his horror at the thought of 'a human figure tossing about in the air in one of these sweet valleys' (*Prose Works*, ii. 333).

30. If the letters had been part of Wordsworth's original experience, or he had known about them in 1799, he would surely have used them in his first account of the scene. They are not mentioned in a literary source until the anonymous *History of Penrith* of 1858, where they are said (not very convincingly) to have commemorated the victim not the murderer, and to have read 'TPM' for 'Thomas Parker Murdered'.

31. The echo, from lines contributed by Coleridge to Southey's *Joan of Arc* in 1795 (later printed as *Destiny of Nations*, 124–5) is confirmed by Coleridge's reference to Joan herself as 'tracing back her steps/Aside the beacon . . . Unconscious of the driving element' (*Destiny of Nations*, 263–6). Another passage (by Southey) in *Joan of Arc* had in summer 1797 formed the source of *The Ruined Cottage*, and there is ample evidence that this was poetry that Wordsworth knew well. A connection between Joan and the Woman on the Hill was first pointed out by Reeve Parker, *Coleridge's Meditative Art* (Ithaca, N.Y. and London, 1975), 116–18.

32. In De Quincey's words,

> An adult sympathizes with himself in childhood because he *is* the same, and because (being the same) yet he is *not* the same. He acknowledges the deep, mysterious identity between himself, as adult and as infant, for the ground of his sympathy; and yet, with this general agreement and necessity of agreement he feels the differences between his two selves as the main quickeners of his sympathy..He pities the infirmities, as they arise to light in his young forerunner . . . he looks indulgently upon the errors of the understanding or limitations of view which now he has long survived; and sometimes, also, he honors in the infant [a] rectitude of will . . .
>
> (*Suspiria De Profundis*; Ward, 118)

33. My position at this point differs in an important way from Jonathan Bishop's. He seems to me to have observed precisely the nature of Wordsworth's involutes in the Woman on the Hill:

> Can we read the extraordinary concentration upon the separate images of pool, beacon, and girl as a displacement of feeling from the evidences of crime and punishment to accidental concomitants of an experience too overwhelming to be faced directly? The three static impressions have become symbols which bear all the weight of a meaning not directly their own.
>
> (*Casebook*, 145)

But, taking the Waiting for the Horses into account, and the awareness that it implies in Wordsworth of the building up of memories within the mind (one might almost say, of the creation of screen-memories, though the poet can't have known in so many words that that was what they were), it can't surely be enough to write:

> Given a chance conjunction in Wordsworth's environment of certain elements which have an *a priori* significance for him, together with a state of mind under a sufficient condition of tension, waking experiences as vivid, symbolic, and mysterious as a dream could overwhelm him . . .
>
> (*Casebook*, 149)

It would be very difficult to deduce which experiences in *The Prelude* overwhelmed the poet at the time, or indeed which of them occurred in anything like the form in which they are described; and recurrent features of Wordsworth's mental (or poetic) landscape are not at all likely to have been chance conjunctions that he saw around him.

34. Compare the scene recalled by De Quincey, when he and the poet were waiting for the mail-coach on Dunmail Raise:

At intervals, Wordsworth had stretched himself at length on the high road, applying his ear to the ground, so as to catch any sound of wheels that might be groaning along at a distance. Once, when he was slowly rising from this effort, his eye caught a bright star that was glittering between the brow of Seat Sandal, and of the mighty Helvellyn. He gazed upon it for a minute or so; and then, upon turning away to descend into Grasmere, he made the following explanation:– 'I have remarked, from my earliest days, that if, under any circumstances, the attention is energetically braced up to an act of steady observation, or of steady expectation, then, if this intense condition of vigilance should suddenly relax, at that moment any beautiful, any impressively visual object, or collection of objects, falling upon the eye, is carried to the heart with a power not known under other circumstances.'

(Jordan, 442)

35. In one respect Wordsworth seems to have misread *Hamlet*. With support, incidentally, from Dr Johnson, he took 'questionable' to mean 'doubtful' or 'suspect' rather than 'that which can be questioned'; 'indisputable' thus has its normal meaning.

36. 'There's not a man/That lives who hath not had his godlike hours' (*1805*, iii. 191–2).

CHAPTER 3: THE CHILD AS FATHER

1. To be pedantic, Dorothy's *Journal* tells us only that Wordsworth wrote 'part of an ode' at breakfast on 27 March, but there can be very little doubt that the poem was *Intimations*. He was interrupted not by a man from Porlock, but by Mr Olliff with the dung, and went out to work in the garden.

2. The relationship between the One Life and *The Recluse* is discussed in the Epilogue.

3. Hartley is introduced at the end of *The Nightingale* because his border receptiveness is a validation of Coleridge's own responses, but remains very much the child they all knew:

> My dear babe,
> Who, capable of no articulate sound,
> Mars all things with his imitative lisp,
> How he would place his hand behind his ear,
> His little hand, the small forefinger up,
> And bid us listen!
>
> (ll. 91–6)

See also the lines that follow, and *Notebooks*, i, no. 219, on which they are based.

4. Place too has become numinously unspecific; through the leaving off of the 's', 'ancient mountain' becomes almost an abstraction. Hartley as the 'faery voyager' of *To H. C.: Six Years Old* is discussed at the end of the chapter.

5. Lamb, in *This Lime-Tree Bower*, has pined

> And hungered after Nature many a year,
> In the great city pent, winning [his] way
> With sad yet patient soul, through evil and pain
> And strange calamity . . .
>
> (ll. 28–32)

and this is very much Coleridge's own position, as opposed to Hartley's, in *Frost at Midnight*.

6. For an interesting discussion of *The Danish Boy* in just this context, see Geoffrey Hartman, *The Fate of Reading*, 182–5.

7. 'Though I felt strength unabated', Wordsworth wrote after seeing Coleridge in Göttingen, 'yet I seemed to need/Thy chearing voice or ere I could pursue/My voyage . . .' (*1799*, ii. 3n.).

8. See Chapter 2, pp. 38–9 above.

9. For the original pantheist context of Wordsworth's comment on the creation of 'puny boundaries' (lines 3–6 of the passage quoted), see Chapter 7, pp. 218–19. Lines 249–55, 'Thou, my friend . . . revealed' are a later insertion in the margin of *MS RV*; see the photograph, Parrish, 186–7.

10. 'Most apprehensive habitude' turns out to mean 'condition or relationship best suited to learning'.

11. For a discussion of this characteristic Wordsworthian process, see Chapter 6.

12. *The Character of the Poet* (Princeton, 1971), 69–70.

13. See Chapter 1, pp. 16–17 above.

14. *Biographia Literaria*, ed. J. Shawcross (2 vols., Oxford, 1907), i. 272.

15. I. A. Richards, *Coleridge on Imagination* (1934), 58.

16. 'Coleridge on Imagination and Fancy', *Proceedings of the British Academy*, xxxii. 177, and *Samuel Taylor Coleridge* (1972), 198–9.

17. 'Coleridge on the Function of Art', *Perspectives of Criticism*, xx (Cambridge, Mass., 1950), 145.

18. 'Coleridge on Imagination and Fancy', 175.

19. Compare Wordsworth's account of the creative process in the Preface to *Lyrical Ballads*, discussed in Chapter 9.

20. Following Professor Bate, and similarly to the point, J. A. Appleyard has written:

> The definition of the primary imagination represents perhaps the highest aspirations of [Coleridge's] desire for a mediating power in the act of knowledge: as a universal active power in all perception it repeats the creative informing act of God. It is Coleridge's boldest attempt to escape the Cartesian dualism.

(*Coleridge's Philosophy of Literature* (Cambridge, Mass., 1965, 205.) For a discussion of the pantheist implications of Coleridge's definitions, and a comparison of his later position with that of Wordsworth in 1804–5, see Chapter 6 and the Epilogue.

21. German thinking made no obvious impact on Coleridge until his reading of Fichte and Kant in February 1801 (Griggs, ii. 673, 676). The one recorded conversation about philosophy was with Klopstock, who in September 1798 told him and Wordsworth that Kant 'was a mountebank and the disgrace of Germany—an unintelligible jargonist' (Griggs, i. 444); but the same letter remarks, 'All are Kantians whom I have met with'. It would be interesting to know when he first encountered the work of Tetens, whose very strong influence has recently been demonstrated by Thomas McFarland, 'The Origin and Significance of Coleridge's Theory of the Secondary Imagination', *New Perspectives*, 195–246.

22. Quoted and discussed in Chapter 1, pp. 15–16 above.

23. The passage is discussed in connection with Wordsworth's fears of the autonomy of language in Chapter 7.

24. Griggs, i. 278; Wordsworth's comparable statement in the Fenwick Note to the Ode is quoted above p. 90.

25. See Lucy Newlyn, 'The Little Actor and his Mock Apparel' (forthcoming in *WC*).

26. For Coleridge's part in the Preface to *Lyrical Ballads*, see Chapter 7, note 15, below.

27. See Chapter 10, and for the urgency of Wordsworth's need, his letter to Beaumont of 12 March 1805:

> As I have said, your last letter affected me much: a thousand times have I asked myself, as your tender sympathy led me to do, 'why was he taken away?', and I have answered the question as you have done.

In fact, there is no other answer which can satisfy and lay the mind at rest. Why have we a choice and a will, and a notion of justice, and injustice, enabling us to be moral agents? Why have we sympathies that make the best of us so afraid of inflicting pain and sorrow, which yet we see dealt about so lavishly by the supreme Governor? Why should our notions of right towards each other, and to all sentient beings within our influence, differ so widely from what appears to be His notion and rule, if every thing were to end here? Would it be blasphemy to say that upon the supposition of the thinking principle being destroyed by death, however inferior we may be to the great Cause and Ruler of things, we have *more of love* in our nature than he has? The thought is monstrous; and yet how to get rid of it except upon the supposition of *another* and a *better world* I do not see. As to my departed brother who leads our minds at present to these reflections . . .

(*EY* 556; W.'s italics)

CHAPTER 4: VISIONS OF PARADISE: SPRING 1800

1. *Notebooks*, i, no. 555; the 'weiblich tetragrammaton' is literally a 'female four-letter-word'. It appears that on a later occasion Wordsworth and Dorothy laughed with Coleridge at 'that round *backside* hill' (*Notebooks*, i. no. 798).

2. J. F. W. Papers; quoted *Chronology*, i. 280–1 n.

3. *Notebooks*, i. no. 1575. The entry was written in October 1803, and reads in the original:

Stood up round the fire, et Sarae manum a tergo longum in tempus prensabam, and tunc temporis, tunc primum, amor me levi spiculo, venenato, eheu! et insanabili, etc

4. John Finch, 'Wordsworth's Two-Handed Engine', *Bicentenary Studies*, 1–13, established that in its original version the Preamble was begun on 18 November *en route* from Ullswater to Grasmere.

5. Drafts that contribute to these lines are found in *MS JJ* and must presumably go back to October/November 1798. There is no likelihood, however, either that Wordsworth at Goslar was working on an introduction for *1799* (see Norton *Prelude*, 485–6), or that when composing the Preamble he had associated it with *The Prelude*. Had he done so, it would appear in the *1799* fair copies: Part II was not completed until Wordsworth's return to Sockburn on 26 November, and *MSS V* and *U* were then transcribed.

6. From the Fenwick Note to *An Evening Walk:*

I will conclude my notice of this poem by observing that the plan of it has not been confined to a particular walk, or an individual place; a proof (of which I was unconscious at the time) of my unwillingness to submit the poetic spirit to the chains of fact and real circumstance.

(Grosart, iii. 5)

7. A sort of tender commentary on the Preamble lines, and the poet's own moods, and the first year at Dove Cottage, is provided by *A narrow girdle of rough stones and crags*, a poem so essentially Wordsworthian that it is full of echoes (and of anticipations too):

And in our vacant mood
Not seldom did we stop to watch some tuft
Of dandelion-seed or thistle's beard,
Which seeming lifeless half, and half impelled
By some internal feeling, skimmed along
Close to the surface of the lake that lay
Asleep in a dead calm . . .
now here, now there,
In all its sportive wanderings, all the while
Making report of an invisible breeze
That was its wings, its chariot, and its horse,
Its very playmate, and its moving soul.

(ll. 16–27)

8. In the terms of Harold Bloom there has surely been a complete transumption of the precursor. Wordsworth's anteriority is clearly established, as he steals behind Milton, creates himself the prelapsarian Adam, and enters Paradise.

9. Texts of the Prospectus in its earliest surviving form (*MS 1*), and of the first completed version of *Home at Grasmere* (*MS B*), will be found in the Appendix. Prospectus quotations are drawn from *MS 1* unless it is specified that they come from an extended later version which in *MS B* is used to form the climax of *Home at Grasmere*. For a discussion of the dating of both the Prospectus and *Home at Grasmere*, see Jonathan Wordsworth, 'On Man, on Nature, and on Human Life', *RES* New Series xxxi, no. 121 (1980), 17–29.

10. Marginalia to a transcript of the Prospectus made by Blake in 1826; Erdman, 656.

11. *Marriage of Heaven and Hell*, Plates 14 and 11 (Erdman, 39, 37).

12. Twelve much-quoted lines, 'I long before the blessed hour arrives . . .' (*Home at Grasmere*, 1002–14), are inserted at this point in *MS B*. The fact that they are not found in Prospectus *MS 1* shows them to have been written in summer 1806. They are quoted and discussed, pp. 111–13.

13. M. H. Abrams, *Natural Supernaturalism*, 51, draws attention to these passages, and to the 'serious conceit' of their parallelism with Satan's bringing with him into Eden 'the hot hell that always in him burns,/Though in mid heaven' (*PL* ix. 467–8).

14. Erdman, 656.

15. 'A very interesting chat with Wordsworth about his poetry. He repeated emphatically what he had said before to me, that he did not expect or desire from posterity any other fame than that which would be given him for the way in which his poems exhibit man in his essentially human character and relations—as child, parent, husband, the qualities which are common to all men as opposed to those which distinguish one man from another' (Crabb Robinson, 17 Aug. 1837; Morley, ii. 535).

16. See pp. 146–7, for evidence that the Prospectus, before becoming in *MS B* the climax to *Home at Grasmere*, was at one stage thought of as the introduction.

17. Compare *1799*, ii. 161–74, and their source in *Vale of Esthwaite* (1785–7), *Oxford Wordsworth*, i. 281, ll. 498–9, 504–7.

18. The 'forms of beauty' that have not been to the poet 'As is a landscape to a blind man's eye' (ll. 24–5), whatever the perplexity that results from comparing their images to the landscape itself, exert their continued influence not as products of imagination, but in and for themselves (see Chapter 6).

19. There can be no doubt that Grasmere did hold a special importance for Wordsworth from a very early stage. In *Septimi Gades* of 1790 or '91 he looks forward to bringing Mary Hutchinson 'to some lowly door' in 'Grasmere's quiet vale' (*Oxford Wordsworth*, i. 296–8). Mary was in fact one of the first visitors to Dove Cottage, in February 1800, and came to live there when she and the poet were married in October 1802.

20. It seems a fairly pointless form of speculation. Wordsworth was not Byron. The idea of incest has titillated some of his critics, but would have had no attraction to him. He and Dorothy enjoyed, as did others of their day, far more physical expression of tenderness than would now be usual; but they had quite conventional moral views, and if sexual feelings were at any time aroused it is not at all likely that they were acknowledged—much less fulfilled. Their relationship is well described in Moorman, i. 281–2.

21. The frost in *Frost at Midnight* is of course associated not with cold or discomfort, but with stillness, magic, imagination—as well as the secret ministry that parallels Dorothy's 'unseen companionship'.

22. Perhaps the link was strengthened in Wordsworth's mind by memory of a reference in

Dorothy's own *Journal* (1 Mar. 1798) to 'The unseen birds singing in the mist'.

23. Compare *Lines Left Upon a Seat*, 46–50:

> Stranger, henceforth be warned, and know that pride
> Howe'er disguised in its own majesty,
> Is littleness—that he who feels contempt
> For any living thing hath faculties
> Which he has never used.

24. See p. 104 above.

25. In the *1850* text of the Climbing of Snowdon the vision on the mountain is given to '*three* chance human wanderers'; for the conscientious fudging and rewriting of this great piece of poetry, see Chapter 10.

26. *Der Wilde Jäger* and *Lenore* had been translated by Walter Scott, and published anonymously as *The Chase and William and Helen* (Edinburgh, 1796).

27. Earl Walter's fate in *The Chase* will 'instruct the proud/God's meanest creature is his child' (p. 15).

28. In the background is the 'awful voice of thunder' that speaks 'High o'er the sinner's humbled head's in *The Chase* (pp. 14–15).

29. The relevant draft from the *Alfoxden Notebook* of February 1798 is quoted Chapter 6, note 6, below. It is important to emphasize that the stream of *Home at Grasmere* is not, like the rivers of *The Prelude* (discussed in Chapter 10), associated with imagination.

30. Spinning by the fire is as important to the economy of the region as outdoor work among the sheep, and both equally bring colour to the cheeks (see *Brothers*, 20–5, and *Michael*, 83–7). The fireside takes on for Wordsworth a special implication of domestic harmony, seen first in the Goslar poem *To a Sexton*, 12, 'Andrew's whole fireside is there', and then (in 1800) twice in *The Brothers*, twice in *To Joanna*, three times in *Michael*, as well as in the quoted *Home at Grasmere* reference.

31. See Wordsworth's comments about *The Brothers* and *Michael* when sending a copy of *Lyrical Ballads* to the Whig Leader Charles James Fox in January 1801. He has attempted, he says, 'to draw a picture of domestic affections' as they exist:

> amongst a class of men who are now almost confined to the north of England. They are small independent *proprietors* of land here called statesmen, men of respectable education who daily labour on their own little properties . . . the power which these affections will acquire amongst such men is inconceivable by those who have only had an opportunity of observing hired labourers, farmers, and the manufacturing poor.
>
> (*EY* 314; W.'s italics)

32. The two stories comprise *Home at Grasmere* 469–605, and become *Excursion*, vi. 1080–1191. *MS R* consists of three gatherings from an interleaved copy of Coleridge's *Poems* 1796, and contains drafts of *Home at Grasmere*, 471–859; photographs and transcriptions are to be found in Darlington, 139–253. My reasons for dating the drafts 1800, and not 1806—the date established by John Finch's posthumous essay, 'On the Dating of *Home at Grasmere*' (*Bicentenary Studies*, 14–28) and accepted by later scholars including Professor Darlington—are set out in 'On Man, on Nature, and on Human Life'. They receive, I think, a great deal of support from the critical account of *Home at Grasmere* given in this chapter. Though it appeared at one time to be conclusive, manuscript evidence for 1806 is not at all impressive, and it seems to me highly unlikely that Wordsworth could in the changed circumstances of that period have thought himself back into the manner and concerns of 1800—even if he had wished to do so. Tone, style, language, preoccupation, frequent references to the season and to being a new arrival, the relation to other poetry, and the poet's relation to Dorothy, all suggest that the drafts of *MS R*—and thus, by

implication, at least the first 859 lines of *Home at Grasmere* (as well as the Prospectus)—belong to 1800.

33. See ll. 573–91, especially 575–9:

> . . . she fears not the bleak wind),
> Companion of her father—does for him
> Where'er he wanders in his pastoral course
> The service of a boy, and with delight
> More keen, and prouder daring.

Though it may seem more surprising, Dorothy's companionship is presumably to be seen also in the contemporary portrait of Luke and Michael.

34. 'Several of my friends are anxious for the success of these poems', Wordsworth writes on the second page of the Preface, 'from a belief, that if the views, with which they were composed, were indeed realized, a class of poetry would be produced, well adapted to interest mankind permanently. . . .' In conclusion he repeats the words almost verbatim, but slides in a reference to 'genuine poetry' that makes them slightly more emphatic (*Prose Works*, i. 120, 158).

35. David Hartley, *Observations on Man* (1749), reissued with Notes by H. Pistorius (3 vols., 1791), i. 320.

36. *Observations*, i. 315–16.

37. 'And the whole earth was of one language and of one speech' (Genesis 11:1). In Genesis 11:5–9, the Lord confounds the language of the builders of the Tower of Babel as a means of destroying their unity, and thus restraining them in their aspirations to godhead: 'And the Lord said, behold, the people is one, and they have all one language; and this they begin to do: and now nothing will be restrained from them, which they have imagined to do.'

38. Hugh Blair, for instance, whose *Lectures on Rhetoric and Belles Lettres* so often lies behind the Preface, traces language back to a period when there was 'a natural relation between words and objects', and is confirmed in doing so by concluding (from the similarities of existing languages, and the circumstances of primitive society) that 'there seems to be no small reason for referring the first origin of all language to divine teaching or inspiration' (*Lectures*, i. 100–6); Blair's views are quoted and discussed in Chapter 7.

39. Hartley was so conscious of the necessitarian progress towards a millennium implied in his doctrine of associationism that he felt the need to apologize in his Preface: 'Some persons may perhaps think, that I ought not to have delivered my opinions so freely and openly, concerning the necessity of human actions, and the ultimate happiness of all mankind . . .' (*Observations*, I, v).

40. This aspect of Wordsworth is discussed in Chapter 6. Blake's line (*Marriage*, plate 10; Erdman, 37) is extremely unlikely to have been known to him.

41. The passage is quoted in full in Chapter 1, p. 23 above.

42. Wordsworth had been concerned to make the same point about the Swiss Herdsman in his earliest millenarian poem, *Descriptive Sketches*:

> Think not, suspended from the cliff on high
> He looks below with undelighted eye.
>
> (1793 text, ll. 510–11)

43. John was at Dove Cottage, January-September 1800.

44. From *MS 2* of *Michael*; see *Oxford Wordsworth*, ii. 482(b), ll. 1–5, 9–11.

45. *Oxford Wordsworth*, ii. 482(b), ll. 12–21.

46. Michael and Isabel are 'neither gay perhaps,/Nor chearful, yet with objects and with hopes/Leading a life of eager industry' (ll. 123–5), and the unnamed priest of *The Brothers* sits with his wife, Jane, and their youngest child, all three of them engaged in the carding and spinning of wool which gives their lives a Wordsworthian sense of purpose (ll. 15–33).

47. Darlington, 238–41.

48. There is an identical volume among the Coleridge notebooks at the British Library. Presumably they were bound up originally to help in revision, then used as notebooks because paper was expensive.

49. For discussion of *Religious Musings* in its relation to the scheme of *The Recluse*, see the Epilogue.

50. 'I have written 1300 lines of a poem in which I contrive to convey most of the knowledge of which I am possessed'; letter to James Tobin, 6 March 1798 (*EY* 212).

51. See Chapter 1, pp. 22–3 above, and Epilogue, pp. 350–2.

52. In feeling, the *Home at Grasmere* reference to the ducks that come and go the gift of winds is closest to the border language of *Michael*, 58–60—

he had been alone
Amid the heart of many thousand mists
That came to him and left him on the heights.

—and *Intimations*, 28, 'The winds come to me from the fields of sleep'; but it was only six months since Wordsworth had adapted for *1799*, Part II, the Alfoxden fragment *In storm and tempest*, with its allusion to 'sounds that . . . make their dim abode in distant winds', and the categorical statement: 'Thence did he drink the visionary power' (ll. 6–9, quoted in full, pp. 15–16 above).

53. Compare, for instance, *Seasons*, i. 821–4:

Nor undelighted by the boundless spring
Are the broad monsters of the foaming deep . . .
They flounce and tumble in unwieldy joy.

54. For comparably unbalanced views of London, all belonging to 1800, see *To Joanna*, 1–7, *Michael*, 451–6, and *1805*, vii. 696–707.

55. Wordsworth did not always bother to complete lines—or words, either, for that matter—when he was composing fast; he also crossed out a great deal. My text contains a number of conjectural readings, none of which could materially alter the sense if they were wrong. For a photograph of the original, and an attempted transcript, see Darlington, 252–3.

56 See the photographs and transcripts, Darlington, 238–41.

57. Darlington, 238–41.

58. Wordsworth is harking back to ll. 161–70, discussed at p. 124, above. At the earlier stage he had been aware that his perception of Grasmere as 'A blended holiness of earth and sky . . . unity entire' was to some extent fanciful, and perfectly clear about the temptation to believe that 'dwellers in [that] holy place/Must needs themselves be hallowed' (ll. 366–7).

59. Between the poet's reassessment (ll. 875–909) and the Prospectus (ll. 959–1049, in the version of *MS B*) comes a section concluding in the 'two brave vessels matched in deadly fight' (ll. 910–33) that looks on stylistic grounds more likely to be 1800 than 1806, but which could belong to either period. It is completely self-contained, and could in fact have been written as a separate fragment, or for some other poem, and embedded in *Home at*

Grasmere during the putting-together of *MS B*. Only the lead-in to the Prospectus (ll. 934–58) seems fairly certain to be 1806, though even here it is questionable whether the whole passage is late, or merely the last few lines, 'Then farewell to the warrior's deeds . . .'.

60. The Prospectus almost certainly stood before the opening of *Home at Grasmere* on the missing first leaf of *MS A*; it was not, however, numbered as part of the main text. See 'On Man, on Nature, and on Human Life', and Appendix (2).

61. Coleridge defines at great length the sense in which he had hoped *The Recluse* would be a philosophical poem—by 'removing the sandy sophisms of Locke, and the mechanic dogmatists', among other things—in his letter to Wordsworth of 30 May 1815 (Griggs, iv. 574–6); see Epilogue, pp. 352–3.

62. Wordsworth wished posterity to believe that *The Prelude* had been a stock-taking of this kind, made 'when the author retired to his native mountains . . . to construct a literary work that might live'; see the misleading claims of the Preface to *The Excursion* (1814), quoted in the Epilogue.

63. The detail of Michael and Isabel's lamp and the naming of the cottage depends on local Grasmere knowledge which Wordsworth seems already to have possessed when he wrote the Prospectus and *Home at Grasmere*. Behind all the references, of course, is the bible: 'Let your light so shine before men, that they may see your good works . . .' (Mathew 5:16).

CHAPTER 5: JOY AND JOLLITY: SPRING 1802

1. Some paper has been torn away with the seal, affecting the beginning of five lines. The words supplied are pure conjecture. Line 90 could, for instance, read: '[Above be]low . . .'.

2. The poem was discovered by Peter Clark in a letter of 22 September 1807 from the minor poet Charles Abraham Elton to his sister Julia, recently married to the histórian Henry Hallam. It was first published in *The New Statesman*, 31 July 1964, and its authenticity and date were established in 'The New Wordsworth Poem', *College English*, xxvii (1966), 455–65. The attribution to Wordsworth received support from Mark Reed (*College English*, xxviii (1967), 60–1), and Jared Curtis (who presents a text, *Experiments with Tradition*, 218–21); no doubts have been raised. It is impossible to know whether Wordsworth in fact kept a copy of the poem, as the drafts of his 1802 lyrics are lost, together with the manuscript of February-March 1804 in which unpublished poetry was entered for preservation at Grasmere (while *MS M* was being transcribed for Coleridge to take to Malta).

3. It is clear neither where the joke lies in Wordsworth's presumably comic reference to Peter Grimes, nor why he and Crabbe (in *The Borough*, 1810) should have chanced on the same not very common name. The direct influence of either poet on the other seems out of the question.

4. Anonymous review of *Lyrical Ballads*, *Critical Review*, xxiv (Oct 1798), 197–204.

5. Those who have lingering doubts about the authenticity of *The Barberry-Tree* should ask themselves whether they would have recognized *The Tinker* as being by Wordsworth if they had come upon it without attribution.

6. The timing of Wordsworth's visit to Annette was perhaps not quite as tidy-minded as it seems, in that the Peace of Amiens of March 1802 was the first truce since the beginning of the war with France nine years before.

7. The title *Dejection* is used in this book to describe Coleridge's verse-letter to Sara

Hutchinson, composed (or begun) on 4 April 1802, as opposed to the shortened and reconstructed poem, *Dejection: An Ode*, first published in the *Morning Post* on 4 October.

8.

My heart leaps up when I behold
A rainbow in the sky;
So was it when my life began,
So is it now I am a man,
So be it when I shall grow old,
Or let me die . . .

(*The Rainbow*, 1–6)

9. *Experiments with Tradition*, 18.

10. One certainly feels that the poet should have been worried, but there is no positive reason to think that he was.

11. Writing to Dorothy on 20 March 1793, but momentarily addressing William, Annette looks forward to a touching—if rather doting—future, in which she, Caroline, and Dorothy will equally minister to his needs: 'Quand tu sera environéz de ta soeur, ta femme, ta fille, qui ne respirerons que pour toi, nous naurons qu'un même sentiment, qu'un coeur, qu'une âme, et tout sera reportée à mon cher Williams [sic]'; Emile Legouis, *William Wordsworth and Annette Vallon* (London and Toronto, 1922), 129.

12. F. W. Bateson, *Wordsworth: A Reinterpretation* (1954) and William Heath, *Wordsworth and Coleridge: A Study of their Literary Relations in 1801–1802* (Oxford, 1970), have sought to play down Mary's role in favour of Annette's and Dorothy's. No letters survive from the early period, but the 1810–12 correspondence of William and Mary that came to light in 1977 refers back in very emotional terms to their closeness in 1797; see *The Love Letters of William and Mary Wordsworth*, ed. Beth Darlington (1981), 61–2. Over the fifteen years between the scenes of young love recorded in *1805*, vi. 233–45 and xi. 316–26, and their marriage in October 1802, they built up a relationship that was undramatic, yet important to them both. Looking back to 1799 Coleridge writes, 'I did not then know of Mary's and William's attachment' (*Notebooks*, i, no. 1575), but he doesn't doubt the attachment existed. The decision to get married seems to have been taken at the end of 1801, with no anguish and no fanfare of trumpets. No doubt there had been an understanding, voiced or otherwise, that when the poet came to settle down they would do so. It was all very much to be expected.

13. Betrayal of Annette is another matter: Wordsworth clearly did feel responsibility towards her and Caroline, and it would not have been impossible to get married during the Peace of Amiens despite ten years' separation. Annette's two surviving letters of 1793 are full of tender anticipation, and imply that everyone—Dorothy too—is looking forward to the marriage; at what stage each independently ceased to do so, we cannot know. All that can be said is that the case for guilt over Annette, though never as strong as some have thought, is far easier to make at the time of the two versions of *Salisbury Plain* (1793 and 1795) than it is in 1802.

14. Less certainly justified is the implication that through firmness of mind poets may continue to be so deified.

15. Because of his views on divorce.

16. The lines of *Frost at Midnight* that Wordsworth has especially in his thoughts are those in which Coleridge in his solitude had claimed a relationship with his inanimate surroundings:

Only that film, which fluttered on the grate,
Still flutters there, the sole unquiet thing.
Methinks its motion in this hush of Nature

Gives it dim sympathies with me who live,
Making it a companionable form . . .

(ll. 15–19)

17. To see (or feel) the difference one has only to put

Yet be thou ever as now,
Sweetness and breath, with the quiet of death . . .

beside:

And hers shall be the breathing balm,
And hers the silence and the calm
Of mute insensate things.

(*Three years she grew*, 16–18)

The personal quality that makes the first quotation so moving is also a limitation. For its grander effects Wordsworth's imagination required a more strenuous, more passionate engagement.

18. Dorothy's italics. Two years later, in his continuation of the Ode, Wordsworth gave to this fantasy a border implication that it did not originally possess:

Thou unto whom the grave
Is but a lonely bed, without the sense or sight
Of day or the warm light,
A living place *where we in waiting lie* . . .

(*Intimations*, 120–3)

19. To the list of Coleridge's troubles provided by *Dejection* itself one has of course to add the physical and mental sufferings of opium addiction.

20. Wordsworth and Coleridge both plainly enjoyed moods in which, to use Lamb's typically sensitive description, 'the mind knowingly passes a fiction upon herself . . . and, in the same breath detecting the fallacy, will not part with the wish' (Marrs, i, 265).

21. The first version of *Dejection: An Ode* was addressed to Wordsworth (under the pseudonym Edmund), and appeared in the *Morning Post* on his wedding-day, 4 October 1802. There is a sense in which the poem had been from the first written for him as much as, or as well as, for Sara; see David Pirie, 'A Letter to [Asra]', *Bicentenary Studies*, 294ff.

22. 'Nor, perchance if I were not thus taught', he says, turning to Dorothy, 'should I the more/Suffer my genial spirits to decay:/ For thou art with me' (ll. 112–15).

23. Again Wordsworth's own experience is invoked, this time by a direct reference to *Intimations*:

These mountains too, these vales, these woods, these lakes . . .
I were sunk low indeed, did they *no* solace give;
But oft I seem to feel, and evermore I fear,
They are not to me now the things, which once they were.

(*Dejection*, 290–5)

The lines are a reminder that in certain moods Wordsworth himself has been unable to summon up sufficient joy to subdue his sense of loss.

24. The dancing of the berberis reminds one, as it would surely have reminded Coleridge, of the bird, tuning 'his wanton song/Like tipsy Joy that reels with tossing head' (*Nightingale*, 85–6).

25. The lines that follow in fact contain an anticipation of *Daffodils* as well:

For as I went, in sober sooth,
It seemed to go along with me . . .
It seemed part of myself to be—
That in my inner self I had
Those whispering sounds that made me glad.

(ll. 67–72)

They flash upon that inward eye
Which is the bliss of solitude.

(*Daffodils*, 15–16).

26. Robert Woof produces evidence that the *Soliloquy*, for all its facetiousness, is a poem of 1802. Wordsworth was revising *Peter Bell* in February, and Coleridge's reference here to the sky-canoe of the Prologue is closely parallel to *Dejection*, 41; A Coleridge-Wordsworth Manuscript and "Sarah Hutchinson's Poets"', *SIB* xix (1966), 230.

27. Dr Curtis has written beautifully about the process; see *Experiments with Tradition*, 97–113.

CHAPTER 6: USURPATION AND REALITY: SPRING 1804

1. Erdman, 655; a brief attempt is made to compare Wordsworth's view of Nature to Blake's, pp. 191–2.

2. The stamping of images on the mind, and the weight with which they lie there, are discussed in Chapter 7, pp. 204–6.

3. From a conversation with Christopher Wordsworth Junior; Grosart, iii. 464.

4. It is interesting to compare the process with the nourishment and invisible repair which is said to take place within the mind as a result of the 'spots of time' (1799, i. 288–94).

5. 'Glory to thee', Coleridge had written in 1795 in lines first contributed to Southey's *Joan of Arc*,

Father of earth and heaven!
All-conscious presence of the universe!
Nature's vast ever-acting energy!
(*Destiny of Nations*, 459–61)

6. The point is made of course in *Expostulation and Reply*, 21–4

Nor less I deem that there are powers
Which of themselves our minds impress,
That we can feed this mind of ours
In a wise passiveness.

and better still in the *Pedlar* draft in the *Alfoxden Notebook* that lies behind it:

There is a holy indolence
Compared to which our best activity
Is oftimes deadly bane
They rest upon their oars,
Float down the mighty stream of tendency
In a calm mood of holy indolence,
A most wise passiveness in which the heart
Lies open *and is well content to feel*
As Nature feels, and to receive her shapes
As she has made them
The mountain's outline . . .

(Butler, 114–15)

7. Quoted from *MS W*; in a revised form the lines became *1805*, xiii. 103–5.

8. Added at line 26, in the Errata to *Sybilline Leaves* (1817).

9. It is disappointing that Thomas McFarland's impressively learned book *Coleridge and the Pantheist Tradition* (Oxford, 1969) makes so little attempt to show how Coleridge's views during the 1790s anticipate, and indeed form a basis for, his later positions. As a professional philosopher, Mary Warnock too is unable in her otherwise extremely useful study, *Imagination* (Oxford, 1976) to take seriously Coleridge's thinking of the pre-German period. The dominant early influence of Joseph Priestley was first given the attention it deserves by H. W. Piper, *The Active Universe* (1962). Because he was so closely identified with Unitarianism, Priestley is quite unacceptable to the later Coleridge; Boehme, however, receives a magnificent tribute in *Biographia*, Chapter IX—'Why need I be afraid? Say rather how dare I be ashamed of the Teutonic theosophist, Jacob Behman?' (p. 80)—and with Spinoza, Coleridge maintained an admiring but uneasy relationship. Boehme could be patronized, his mysticism treated with indulgence, but Spinoza embodied in a very direct way the pantheist views that Coleridge felt drawn to, and knew he must reject. For Coleridge's deeply ambivalent feelings see, e.g., *Biographia*, Chapter XXII (p. 261) and *CC* IV. i. 54n.: the fourth section of the projected *Logosophia* was to have been on Spinoza and Spinozism, and entitled significantly 'Logos Agonistes' (Griggs, iii. 533). The very important influence of Berkeley in the later 1790s is discussed most fully by J. A. Appleyard in *Coleridge's Philosophy of Literature*.

10. Though he sometimes gives the impression of hunting Coleridge down (rather than seeking to understand the workings, and failings, of a great writer), Norman Fruman in *The Damaged Archangel* (1971) has amassed a great deal of evidence that more dispassionate critics have to take into account. Coleridge was not an accidental plagiarist.

11. *BL* ix. 84. 'In spite therefore of his own declarations', he adds on the following page, 'I could never believe it was possible for him to have meant no more by his *Noumenon*, or Thing in itself, than his mere words express.'

12. As Thomas McFarland comments in 'The Origin and Significance of Coleridge's Theory of the Secondary Imagination',

> Coleridge's last statement [in Chapter XIII] before breaking off and writing himself his explanatory letter, trembles on the very brink of pantheism: 'Now this *tertium aliquid* can be no other than an interpenetration of the counteracting powers, partaking of both'. Coleridge is here only a step from Schelling's openly pantheistic theses that 'the system of Nature is at the same time the system of our spirit', and that 'one might explain imagination as the power of transposing itself through complete self-activity into complete passivity'.

(*New Perspectives*, 199)

13. There seems to be a new understanding of his own position in Coleridge's rejection of Schelling's system at the end of 1818. On 30 September he tells J. H. Green, 'I was myself *taken in* by it, retrograding from my own prior and better lights, and adopted it in the metaphysical chapters of my Literary Life' (Griggs, iv. 874); and to C. A. Tulk on 24 November he comments:

> his system is extremely plausible and alluring at a first acquaintance. . . . But as a *system*, it is little more than Behmenism, translated from visions into logic and a sort of commanding eloquence: and like Behmen's it is reduced at last to a mere pantheism, or '*gemina Natura quae fit et facit, creat et creatur*' . . . (Griggs, iv, 883)

Exit the primary imagination.

14. *MS WW* was not identified until 1968. It contains fragmentary and often illegible pencil drafts on leaves cut from a tiny note-pad used by Wordsworth for outdoor composition in February-March 1804.

15. Compare Blake's Printing House in Hell, where the workings of creativity are similarly rendered lifeless by receiving form: 'There they were received by men who

occupied the sixth chamber, and took the forms of books and were arranged in libraries' (*Marriage of Heaven and Hell,* Plate 15; Erdman, 39).

16. Among other Alpine travellers, Francis Towne (see Frontispiece) catches beautifully the stillness and the sculpted planes of the landscape, while Shelley in *Mont Blanc*, 100–2, invests it with movement and strange menace:

> The glaciers creep
> Like snakes that watch their prey, from their far fountains
> Slow rolling on . . .

Coleridge had of course called upon the 'Motionless torrents' and 'silent cataracts' to 'echo GOD!' (*Hymn Before Sunrise in the Vale of Chamouni*, 1802).

17. 'I see in Wordsworth the natural man rising up against the spiritual man continually, and then he is no poet but a heathen philosopher at enmity against all true poetry or inspiration' (Erdman, 654).

18. The two poets of course differ in very many ways, notably in their attitude to the Bible, which was for Wordsworth at all times secondary. Crabb Robinson records in 1825:

> Wordsworth, [Blake] thinks, is no Christian, but a Platonist. He asked me: 'Does he believe in the Scriptures?' On my answering in the affirmative he said he had been much pained by reading the introduction to *The Excursion*——it brought on a fit of illness. The passage was produced and read:
>
> Jehovah—— with his thunder and the choir
> Of shouting angels and the empyreal thrones—
> I pass them unalarmed.
>
> This '*pass them unalarmed*' greatly offended Blake. 'Does Mr Wordsworth think his mind can surpass Jehovah?' I tried to twist this passage into a sense corresponding with Blake's own theories, but failed, and Wordsworth was finally set down as pagan, but still with great praise as the greatest poet of the age.

(Morley, i. 327; Robinson's italics.)

19. See, for instance, *The Darkling Thrush*, 9–10:

> The land's sharp features seemed to be
> The Century's corpse outleant . . .

20. See *1805*, vi 572n.; the lines were probably inserted in January 1807.

21. Wordsworth had been reading Burnet's *Sacred Theory of the Earth* when in February 1798 he wrote in *The Pedlar* of the peak

> Familiar with forgotten years, which shews
> Inscribed as with the silence of the thought
> Upon its bleak and visionary sides
> The history of many a winter storm,
> Or obscure records of the path of fire.

and drafted in the margin of *MS B* the further magnificent apocalyptic lines:

> Or of the day of vengeance when the sea
> Rose like a giant from his sleep and smote
> The hills, and when the firmament of Heaven
> Rained darkness which the race of men beheld—
> Yea, all the men that lived—and had no hope
>
> (Butler, 166–7)

For Wordsworth's apocalyptic geology, see Abrams, *Natural Supernaturalism*, 99–101, and Paul Sheats, *The Making of Wordsworth's Poetry, 1785–1798* (Cambridge, Mass., 1973), 64–5.

22. It is significant that Coleridge had drawn on Milton's line in *Destiny of Nations*, 15–17 ('him first, him last, to view/Through meaner powers and secondary things/Elfulgent'), just before making his famous Berkleyan statement: 'all that meets the bodily sense I deem/Symbolical, one mighty alphabet/For infant minds'.

23. *Wordsworth's Poetry 1787–1814*, 230.

24. Wordsworth had translated the *Manciple's* and *Prioress's Tales*, and some lines from *Troilus and Criseyde*, in December 1801, and no doubt read more widely at the time. For an echo of the *Knight's Tale* in 1802, see p. 165 above.

25. For a further discussion of these questions in terms of Wordsworth's use of language, see Chapter 7.

26. From the draft conclusion written for *The Ruined Cottage* at the beginning of March 1798 (Butler, 268–71). The scheme for *The Recluse* was announced on the sixth (*EY* 212), and *The Ruined Cottage* was certainly part of it—as indeed it was finally, when it became *Excursion*, Book I; see Epilogue.

27. Quoted from *MS W*, see *1805*, xi. 344n.; for the structural importance of the lines in context of the five-Book *Prelude*, see Chapter 8.

28. See Chapter 5, note 21, above.

CHAPTER 7: AS WITH THE SILENCE OF THE THOUGHT

1. February 1804.

2. For an alternative view, see Jonathan Bishop's conclusion in 'Wordsworth and the "Spots of Time"':

> We may now paraphrase the dream as follows: 'If you choose poetry as a way of life, as you have done and are bound to do, you run the severe risk of being overwhelmed by the unconscious forces from which your poetry must derive its vital inspiration, and the significant portion of its subject matter; if you lose your nerve, you will find yourself "burying" your talent to escape the emotional turmoil it brings upon you' (*Casebook*, 153).

3. *Prose Works*, i. 152 and 139; the first quotation is from the Preface to *Lyrical Ballads*, 1800, the second from an 1802 addition.

4. *Observations*, i. 83; Hartley's views of the millenarian tendency of association and language are discussed in Chapter 4.

5. *UTQ* xlii, no. 2 (winter 1973), 164.

6. The passage has notably provided Frances Ferguson with her title, *Wordsworth: Language as Counter-Spirit* (New Haven and London, 1977), and more recently it has been referred to by Mary Jacobus in her claim that Wordsworth is subject not only to a Bloomian anxiety of influence, but also to 'a larger and more inescapable anxiety: that our texts have all been written before . . . that in submitting to textuality, we put on inherited garments' ('Wordsworth and the Language of the Dream', *ELH* xlvi [1979], 641). In each case the interest of the critic is much more theoretical than mine—much less concerned with the ways in which the poet *uses* language, both in his critical pronouncements and elsewhere.

7. The metaphor of the body as clothing, or containing, the soul, is implied for instance in the images of shrine and casket with which the Quixote dream begins and ends.

8. Masson, x. 229–30; the passage is quoted in large part in *Prose Works*, ii. 114–15, and is from the later section of the essay on *Style* that is not included in Jordan.

9. *UTQ* xlii, no. 2, 160.

10. The image, from *Julius Caesar*, II. i. 285–6, has a special appropriateness as Wordsworth had been in London at the time.

11. 'The Stone and the Shell: The Problem of Poetic Form in Wordsworth's Dream of the Arab', *Mouvements premiers: Etudes critiques offertes à Georges Poulet* (Paris, 1972), 126.

12. Jordan, 270; compare Wordsworth's own statement in the *Guide to the Lakes*:

> Power awakens the sublime . . . when it arouses us to a sympathetic energy and calls upon the mind to grasp at something towards which it can make approaches, but which it is incapable of attaining—yet so that it participates [the] force which is acting upon it.
>
> (*Prose Works*, ii. 354)

13. Frances Ferguson seems to me much more pessimistic than the poet is himself. 'Wordsworth', she writes, 'posits the ideal of language as an incarnation rather than a mere garb to thought, only to suggest that the incarnation may (*and most certainly will*) become not an expression of the spirit but a "counter-spirit"' (*Language as Counter-Spirit*, 3–4).

14. Which to judge from frequent borrowings in *The Vale of Esthwaite* was not strictly true.

15. Wordsworth was writing the Preface aided by Coleridge's notes, and for the moment it seemed to represent their joint views of poetry (Griggs, i. 627). It is difficult to know what to make of Wordsworth's repeated later claims that it had been written solely to please Coleridge, but it is not likely that he included any material without modifying it according to his own experience. With the addition of a second volume containing no Coleridge poems, and the disgraceful playing down of *The Ancienl Mariner*, the collection had come to seem very much his own work; and where before it had been anonymous, it was now to appear with his name (alone) on the title-page.

16. The fragments are entered by Wordsworth in fair copy on two facing pages of *Peter Bell MS 2* (Norton *Prelude*, 495–6).

17. According to Hazlitt, in *The Spirit of the Age*, Wordsworth regarded himself as sharing with Rembrandt the ability to transform the world of common experience:

> In the way in which that artist works something out of nothing, and transforms the stump of a tree, a common figure into an *ideal* object, by the gorgeous light and shade thrown upon it, he perceives an analogy to his own mode of investing the minute details of Nature with an atmosphere of sentiment; and in pronouncing Rembrandt to be a man of genius, feels that he strengthens his own claim to the title.
>
> (Howe, xi.93)

18. Wordsworth for the moment accepts the conventional metaphor of language as the clothing of thought, which he will later reject.

19. The third fragment, with its account of 'after loathings, damps of discontent/ Returning ever like the obstinate pains/Of an uneasy spirit', is in fact highly impressive too.

20. Compare the 'Conclusion' to the *Duddon Sonnets*:

> Still glides the stream, and shall for ever glide;
> The form remains, *the function never dies* . . .
>
> (xxxiii, 5–6)

At 1805, xii. 378 Wordsworth revises 'The excellence, *pure spirit* and best power' to 1850 'pure function'.

21. Coleridge's definition is found in fragmentary lecture-notes published after his death by his son-in-law. There is for once a passing reference to Schlegel ('a continental critic'), as Coleridge begins his discussion of 'the confounding mechanical regularity with organic form':

> The form is mechanic when on any given material we impress a pre-determined form, not necessarily arising out of the properties of the material, as when to a mass of wet clay we give whatever shape we wish it to retain when hardened. The organic form, on the other hand, is innate; it shapes as it develops itself from within, and the fulness of its development is one and the same with the perfection of its outward form. Such is the life, such is the form.
>
> (Raysor, i. 224)

Schlegel's *Lectures* were published in Germany in 1809–10, and had been delivered in 1808. It is difficult to quarrel with Norman Fruman's account of this particular piece of plagiarism (*Damaged Archangel*, 141–61).

22. See Chapter 3, pp. 83–6, above. It could be argued that even before the publication of Schlegel's *Lectures*, Germany was a better place than England to hear discussion of organic form (or something like it). It is significant, for instance, that as Abrams points out, 'German thought was much more receptive than English' to Young's *Conjectures on Original Composition* (1759), which makes persistent if unsystematic use of organic metaphor. 'An original', Young writes, in a passage that clearly anticipates Romantic definitions, 'may be said to be of a vegetable nature; it rises spontaneously from the vital root of genius; it grows, it is not made. Imitations are often a sort of manufacture wrought up by those mechanics, art and labour, out of pre-existent materials not their own' (*Mirror and The Lamp*, 199).

23. Organic metaphors are bound to crop up, of course. The letter to Godwin quoted above p. 218, goes so far as to regard individual words as 'germinations of the plant' (Griggs, i. 625), but does not speculate as to the form of larger units. The assumption that Coleridge's first course of Shakespeare Lectures, in 1808, that preceded his reading of Schlegel, contained any reference to organic form is shown by Fruman (*Damaged Archangel*, 152 and 486–7) to have no solid basis.

24. For Coleridge's surely deliberate obtuseness over the child of *Intimations*, see Chapter 3, above; and for his scathing remarks on rustics and 'the best part of language', see *BL* xvii, 197–8. It is interesting that as early as May-June 1800, Coleridge had noted, 'Farmers talk always of their own occupations' (*Notebooks*, i, no 735).

25. From the fragment, *In storm and tempest*, quoted at length pp. 15–16, above. The lines were written in the third person about the Pedlar of *The Ruined Cottage* early in February 1798, and adapted for *The Prelude* (by a simple change of pronoun, 'he' to 'I') in autumn 1799.

26. In Coleridge's terms, which Wordsworth must surely have in mind, the veil is 'A light, a glory, and a luminous cloud/Enveloping the earth' (*Dejection*, 303–4).

27. See the unused *Michael* drafts quoted in Chapter 4, p. 134, above.

28. At times of course the active poet will choose to evoke the silent poetry of the mind that is merely the half-way stage in a fully creative process. Wordsworth does so beautifully in the *Michael* drafts, again using the image of the blind man's special sensitivity:

> If, looking round, I have perchance perceived
> Some vestiges of human hands, some stir
> Of human passion, they to me are sweet
> As lightest sunbreak, or the sudden sound
> Of music to a blind man's ear who sits
> Alone and silent in the summer shade.
> (*Oxford Wordsworth*, ii. 480).

29. To put it all in Coleridge's more theoretical, more pompous terms, words must become 'symbols, harmonious in themselves, and consubstantial with the truths, of which they are the *conductors*' (*CC* vi. 29). For the implications of the lines quoted from *Home at Grasmere* in their original context, see Chapter 4, above.

CHAPTER 8: VERSIONS OF THE FALL

1. For evidence, see Chapter 9, pp. 246–7.

2. The river-imagery of *The Prelude* is discussed in Chapter 10.

3. As M. H. Abrams has put it, *The Prelude* 'presents the growth of the poet's mind as an interaction with the natural milieu by which it is fostered, from which it is tragically alienated, and to which in the resolution it is restored, with a difference attributable to the intervening experiences . . .' 'Structure and Style in the Greater Romantic Lyric', *From Sensibility to Romanticism*, ed. Frederick W. Hilles and Harold Bloom (New York, 1965), 530.

4. For convenience I refer to *1805*, x. 1–566 as Xa, and 567-end as Xb. Though amalgamated in the text of *1805*, they seem originally to have been separate Books, as in *1850*.

5. Originally *Pedlar*, 350–3.

6. For a detailed reconstruction of this intermediate *Prelude*, see Jonathan Wordsworth, 'The Five-Book *Prelude* of Early Spring 1804', JEGP lxxvi (Jan. 1977), 1–25; a more general account of the content of Books IV and V is offered in note 10, below.

7. 'I am anxious to hear how far you are satisfied with yourself at Oxford; and, above all, that you have not been seduced into unworthy pleasures or pursuits.' He believes moral standards at both Universities to have improved very much since his day, when 'The manners of the young men were very frantic and dissolute', but goes on all the same, 'I need not say to you that there is no true dignity but in virtue and temperance, and, let me add, chastity . . . ' (*EY* 453–4).

8. 'Caverns there were within my mind which sun/Could never penetrate' (iii. 246–7); 'Hushed meanwhile/Was the under-soul' (iii. 539–40).

9. For Wordsworth's prose account of the floating island, see *Guide to the Lakes* (*Prose Works*, ii. 184). Catherine Drucker points out to me that a literary precedent for moralizing the island's instability is provided by Spenser's wandering islands of *Faerie Queene*, II. xii. 87ff.

10. The original Book IV was completed at the end of February 1804 in 650 lines. It consisted of two clearly defined sections, the first concerned with the poet's experiences at Hawkshead in summer 1789, the second with education and the beneficial influence of books. *1805*, IV and V were created in a matter of days when *c.* 10 March Wordsworth decided to reorganize his poem, and it seems that all he had to do was divide his existing Book into its component halves, and work up an opening section for each from material at least partly written the previous month. The one major sequence of *1805*, IV and V that was almost certainly not present in the five-Book poem (though it had been composed in February) is the Quixote dream.

11. Wordsworth almost certainly has in mind the near life-sized clock-work model of a tiger savaging a white man that was housed at the East India Company when Lamb was showing him and Dorothy round London in 1802. (W. J. B. Owen, 'Tipu's Tiger', *NQ*, ccxv [1970], 379–80). The model had been made for the tyrant Tipu Sultan, and captured at the fall of Seringapatam. It is now at the Victoria and Albert Museum.

12. As J. C. Maxwell pointed out in the Penguin *Prelude* (1971).

13. Wallace Stevens, conclusion of *Esthétique du mal*.

14. Quoted from *MS W*, see *1805*, xi. 344n.

15. Quoted from *MS W;* see *1805*, xi. 256n.

16. De Quincey's numinous, nebulous goddess, Levana, is very much the equivalent of

the personified Nature who in *1805*, Book I, prompts the child to take the shepherd's boat on Ullswater.

17. 'Years that were far asunder', he writes in the *Confessions*, 'were bound together by subtle links of suffering derived from a common root' (Ward, 57).

18. A year later, in the very different circumstances under which the material from the five-Book poem was revised for *1805*, Book XI, he was to add the sad, self-knowing words, 'I see by glimpses now, when age comes on/May scarcely see at all' (xi. 337–8).

19. See Epilogue, pp. 361–3.

20. The evidence for this sequence of composition is in lines quoted at the beginning of Chapter 9.

21. Though its drafts in *MS WW* follow those of the Crossing of the Alps, it cannot be proved that the Cave of Yordas (finally viii. 711–41) was ever in the text of VI. No fair copy of the Book survives from the period of composition.

22. Fellows of colleges had to resign when they got married, and because of the system of ecclesiastical patronage high-ranking undergraduates were at times in a position to bestow livings on their tutors. For an account of the inequalities of university life at this period, see Ben Ross Schneider, Jun., *Wordsworth's Cambridge Education* (Cambridge, 1957), 21–4.

23. The pathetic episode of the dying woman and her babes in *An Evening Walk*—'Thy breast their death-bed, coffined in thine arms'—owed far more to literary tradition than to personal sympathy; see *Music of Humanity*, 50–5.

24. See *1805*, ix. 296n.

25. See Chapter 7, pp. 204–6, above.

26. McCracken, 138; behind both Godwin and Wordworth, of course, lies *Macbeth*, II. ii. 35–6, 41:

> Methought I heard a voice cry 'Sleep no more;
> Macbeth doth murder sleep . . .'
> Still it cried 'Sleep no more' to all the house . . .

27. As well as Robespierre himself, 107 of his associates were executed, but the Terror ceased at once.

28. See *1805*. x. 103n.; Robespierre in fact achieved supreme power nine months later. Louvet was not as isolated as Wordsworth believed (and as has often been suggested), but Robespierre asked time to prepare his defence, and his strength was finally increased as a result of resisting the challenge; see Lefebvre, 269–70.

29. Compare *PL* i. 392–3, 'First Moloch, horrid king besmeared with blood/Of human sacrifice, and parents' tears . . .'

30. Appropriately the Miltonic echo in this case comes from the poet's lament for the loss of sight:

> Thus with the year
> Seasons return, but not to me returns
> Day, or the sweet approach of even or morn . . .

(*PL* iii. 40–2)

31. Early version of *1805*, xi. 29–34.

32. *Oxford Wordsworth*, i. 302–6; the work was to have been written in collaboration with Francis Wrangham. Only fragments survive.

33. Wordsworth had met Southey with Coleridge the previous October, and at the time

had in fact reproached Mathews for thinking him a coxcomb (*EY* 153–4). It was the inflated Preface to *Joan of Arc* that changed his mind.

34. Crabb Robinson recalls that he had been 'in some measure prepared' for *Political Justice* by an acquaintance with Holcroft's novels' (Sadler, i. 31), and must in fact have in mind *Anna St Ives* (1792); see, for instance, Faulkner, 172, quoted as an epigraph, p. 340, where the heroine sounds exactly as if she has just been reading Godwin. Holcroft is even, in a not very philosophical way, necessitarian at times; see Faulkner, 294–5, quoted in the Epilogue, p. 346, in connection with Godwin and *The Recluse*.

35. See *Prose Works*, i. 20–4, for a discussion both of dating and of background influence.

36. No text of the 1795 *Adventures on Salisbury Plain* has survived, but a rough approximation of it can be obtained by replacing ll. 244–558 of Stephen Gill's text of the poem as it stood in 1799 (Gill, 130–46) by ll. 181–396 of *Salisbury Plain*, 1793 (Gill, 27–34).

37. Such a view was to be the basis of his millenarian thinking in *Home at Grasmere* (1800); see Chapter 4, pp. 000–0, above.

38. The French Constitution of May 1790 had formally renounced all conquest of foreign territory. Motives for an aggressive policy were largely financial, and with a disastrous, and worsening, economic situation it was not likely that Robespierre's death would bring about a return to high principles. During the latter part of 1794 the British army, under the grand old Duke of York, was swept back through the Netherlands and into Germany, returning beaten and demoralized to England in March 1795; for Wordsworth's conflicting feelings over their defeat, see *1805*, x. 258–74.

39. It is interesting that Coleridge should have used the law-court image before Wordsworth, and should have seen in himself a need to prevent 'the passions from turning the reason into an hired advocate' (Griggs, i. 398; March 1798).

40. In addition to reacting against the suppression of feeling, Wordsworth could well have been moving towards his position in *The Borderers* (begun in the autumn), where he is frightened that the human educability in which he continues with Godwin to believe need not, as Godwin asserts, be inevitably a force for good.

41. As, very probably, was the river image at the opening of Book IX; see p. 232, above.

42. See Norton *Prelude*, 520.

43. Godwin's position is further discussed in the Epilogue.

44. 'There comes a time' Wordsworth writes,

> When reason – not the grand
> And simple reason, but that humbler power
> Which carries on its no inglorious work
> By logic and minute analysis—
> Is of all idols that which pleases most
> The growing mind. (xi. 123–8)

Coleridge had been reading Kant since spring 1801, and 'the grand/And simple reason' (*Vernunft*) reappears at xiii. 170 equated with imagination (as it will later be in *Biographia*) as 'reason in her most exalted mood'. Wordsworth is being on this occasion scrupulously fair to the 'humbler power' (*Verstand*; 'understanding' in *Biographia*), which has its place but must not be allowed to become an idol.

45. xi. 198–22; in the five-Book *Prelude* the lines had referred to the summer of 1787, spent with Mary and Dorothy at Penrith.

46. At Goslar during the composition of *1799*, Part I; that is to say, well after the period covered by the *Prelude* narrative.

47. For the probable slackening of belief see Chapter 1, above. Blurring is surely to be

seen in *Tintern Abbey*, 66–76, where Wordsworth attempts to show his former visit to the Wye in terms both of his horrified reaction to political circumstances ('more like a man/ Flying from something that he dreads'), and of a total commitment to Nature. Clarity is not helped by the poet bounding like a roe though 'The coarser pleasures of [his] boyish days/And their glad animal movements [had] all gone by' (ll. 74–5).

48. Compare the earlier confidence of *Tintern Abbey*, when the poet had stood before the landscape of the Wye Valley

> not only with the sense
> Of present pleasure, but with pleasing thoughts
> That in this moment there is life and food
> For future years.

(ll. 63–6)

CHAPTER 9: IF UPON MANKIND HE LOOKS (*1805*, Books VIII and VII)

1. *EY* 508; 10 October 1804. The poem was almost certainly *Yardley Oak*, first published in May 1804 in Hayley's *Life and Posthumous Writing of William Cowper*, iii. 409–16. Dorothy's letter also mentions that she and her brother had seen the aged yew at Lorton on 24 September, and the inference must be that, inspired by Cowper, Wordsworth first wrote *Yew-trees*, then went back to *The Prelude*.

2. It could well be that Wordsworth's opening line, in its echo of *Tintern Abbey's* 'Five years have passed', had for him a talismanic force, as he sought once more to gain inspiration from a review of the past, and willed himself to write as spontaneously as before.

3. The passage opens with vii. 49–50, concludes with xiii. 334–7; the italicized lines do not appear in *1805*.

4. As Robert Young points out to me, there is a parallel here with *Paradise Lost*, in which Books VII and VIII are taken up with the conversation of Raphael and Adam, and VIII in particular takes the narrative back to Adam's creation—'now hear me relate/My story, which perhaps thou hast not heard' (*PL* viii. 204–5)—as *Prelude*, VIII, goes back to Wordsworth's childhood. In each case this is of course a lull before the Fall (for the linking of the two Book IX openings, see pp. 232–3, above).

5. Reminding one, for instance, of the beautifully numinous lines in *Michael*:

> he had been alone
> Amid the heart of many thousand mists
> That came to him and left him on the heights.

(ll. 58–60)

6. *Letters of John Keats*, ed. Maurice Buxton Forman (3rd edn., revised; Oxford, 1947), 272.

7. *Pedlar*, 217–18 (with 'He' for 'I'); incorporated in *The Prelude* as *1799*, ii. 459–60.

8. A claim that Wordsworth goes on to repeat in the closing line of *1805*, where the mind is 'Of substance and of fabric more divine'; in 1798, of course, the life-force had been perceived equally in man and his surroundings.

9. 'Unutterable love' is used only here and at *Pedlar*, 101; the artificer eying his child on the low wall curiously recalls the Cumberland Beggar on his 'low structure of rude masonry' scanning his scraps, and 'the fresher air' that he has come out to seek links back to the poet's 'catch[ing] the motion of the cooler air' at *Ruined Cottage*, 66. Mainly, though, the resemblances are of feeling, style, treatment.

10. From the purely Wordsworthian fragment in the *Christabel Notebook*, belonging probably to summer 1800, a few months only before the discussion of creativity in the Preface to *Lyrical Ballads* (quoted, p. 294):

> There is creation in the eye,
> Nor less in all the other senses; powers
> They are that colour, model, and combine
> The things perceived with such an absolute
> Essential energy that we may say
> That these most godlike faculties of ours
> At one and the same moment are the mind
> And the mind's ministers. In many a walk
> At evening, or by moonlight, or reclined
> At midday upon beds of forest moss,
> Have we to Nature and her [?impulses]
> Of our whole being made free gift, and when
> Our trance had left us, oft have we, by aid
> Of the impressions which it left behind,
> Looked inward on ourselves, and learned perhaps
> Something of what we are. Nor in those hours
> Did we destroy [ ]
> The original impression of delight,
> But by such retrospect it was recalled
> To yet a second and second life . . .

(*Oxford Wordsworth*, v. 343–4)

11. 'Aut videt, aut vidisse putat' (*Aeneid*, vi. 454).

12. Compare ll. 5–6 of Surrey's *A Complaint by the Lover not Beloved*, which Wordsworth could well have come upon in his copy of Anderson's *Poets of Great Britain (i. 598)*:

> Calme is the sea, the waves worke lesse and lesse.
> So am not I, whome Love alas doth wring . . .

13. Wordsworth's prejudice is seen at its worst in the moment in *Michael* when Luke goes to the bad—

> Meanwhile Luke began
> To slacken in his duty, and at length
> He in the dissolute city gave himself
> To evil courses . . .

(ll. 451–4)

—and it is interesting that it is overspill verse from *Michael* that he is drawing on when at the end of VII he suddenly changes his tone; see pp. 304–5, and note 20 below.

14. Panoramas came into vogue in the 1790s. Girtin's, an immense circular view taken from a rooftop near the southern end of Blackfriars Bridge, is thought to have been 9 feet high and 216 feet in circumference. It was on exhibition when Lamb was showing the sights of London to Wordsworth and Dorothy in September 1802, and as the *Prelude* description of Bartholomew Fair (vii. 649–95) draws on a visit made at this time (as, probably, does the 'pageant plaything' of iv. 302–4; see Chapter 8, note 11, above), it seems a fair guess that the poet saw the *Eidometropolis* too, and had it in mind as he was writing Book VII. Lines 244–80 especially show him unusually conscious of parallels between his own position and that of the visual artist.

15. Ford T. Swetnam, 'Satiric Voices of *The Prelude*' (*Bicentenary Studies*, 102) points to a link in Wordsworth's use of the word 'type' at vii. 696 and vi. 571.

16. The showman's platform may well recall *Volpone*, II. ii. Resemblances between Wordsworth's lines and *Bartholomew Fair* are very general, but he can hardly not have Jonson in mind.

17. Wordsworth didn't see *The Beauty of Buttermere* himself, but it was described (very amusingly) in a letter from Mary Lamb to Dorothy of 9 July 1803 (Marrs, ii. 117). Hatfield, the 'bold, bad man', was hanged at Carlisle in September 1803. Though the last of his articles had been printed the previous January, Coleridge had since then been planning, perhaps a comic epic (Griggs, ii. 919), certainly a novel (*Notebooks*, i, no. 1395), about Hatfield, and in August he arranged that the Scottish tour he was making with Wordsworth and Dorothy should take them to Carlisle for the final day of the trial. After Hatfield had been condemned he visited him in prison, but could make nothing of him (*Notebooks*, i, no. 1432). Three of the *Morning Post* articles were reprinted in *Essays on his Own Times by S. T. Coleridge* (1850), and all are to be found, with fascinating additional footnote material, in *CC* iii.

18. Donald P. Sewell informs me that she married a local farmer on 8 March 1808. Her infant's death is not recorded in the Lorton Parish Register, but Daniel Stuart reports her pregnancy on 18 December 1802, and if it was stillborn (as vii. 355–6 seem to imply) perhaps it was buried outside the churchyard.

19. See the Lake District tradition of spectral horsemen on the fells recorded in *An Evening Walk*, 179–90.

20. See *1805*, vii. 701n.; the lines had presumably been written in an attempt to rationalize the behaviour of Luke.

CHAPTER 10: THE IMAGE OF A MIGHTY MIND (1805, Book XIII)

1. James Beattie, *The Minstrel*, Book the First (1771), 12.

2. See Z. S. Fink, *The Early Wordsworthian Milieu* (Oxford, 1958), 45–8.

3. *Survey of the Lakes*, 73.

4. Revising *Descriptive Sketches* in 1836 with the Climbing of Snowdon in mind, Wordsworth gave a new importance and mysteriousness to the cloud-rift:

> A single chasm, a gulf of gloomy blue,
> Gapes in the centre of the sea—and through
> That dark mysterious gulf ascending, sound
> Innumerable streams with roar profound.
>
> (*Oxford Wordsworth*, i. 73, ll. 413–16)

5. *Bicentenary Studies*, 431, ll. 1–16.

6. *New Perspectives*, 24; K. J. 's italics.

7. Professor Johnston rightly points out (*New Perspectives*, 20) that in *Bicentenary Studies* (1970) I overstated the ordinariness of the experience that takes place, or is implied, in *A Night-Piece*.

8. The fusion may in fact go beyond the mere use of one faithful memory to lead up to another: it could be that the light by which Wordsworth originally saw the mist in 1791 was not the moon, but the sun. He sets off after all in line 3 of the *Prelude* account ' to see the sun/Rise from the top of Snowdon', and the passage quoted from *Descriptive Sketches* begins: '—'Tis morn: with gold the verdant mountain glows'. Alternatively perhaps he replaced the moon by the sun in *Descriptive Sketches* because the scene would more appropriately be viewed in daylight by the 'pastoral Swiss', and returned to what he had actually seen when writing the Climbing of Snowdon.

9. See especially *Simon Lee*, 69–76 and *Idiot Boy*, 322–56.

10. Wordsworth's identification with the moon is more important, and unexpectedly different, in the *1850* text; see pp. 328–31.

11. William Bartram, *Travels Through North and South Carolina* (2nd edn., London, 1794) and John Barrow, *Travels in China* (1804) are among the many travel books that *The Prelude* draws upon in passing. It was a kind of reading, exciting and yet leaving all to the imagination, that Wordsworth and Coleridge both particularly enjoyed.

12. For the alternative view, see Robert Langbaum's bold statement that in *The Prelude* 'the words *soul* and "imagination" are used interchangeably' ('The Evolution of Soul in Wordsworth's Poetry', *PMLA* lxxxii [1967]; reprinted *Casebook*, 218–35).

13. Found on the verso of the Pierpont Morgan *Description of a Beggar* manuscript, apparently of *c.* May 1797:

> Yet once again do I behold the forms
> Of these huge mountains, and yet once again,
> Standing beneath these elms, I hear thy voice,
> Beloved Derwent, that peculiar voice
> Heard in the stillness of the evening air,
> *Half heard and half created.*
>
> (*Oxford Wordsworth*, v. 340)

14. *On Wordsworth's 'Prelude'* (Princeton, 1963), 91–2.

15. Wordsworth's image of usurpation, which appears first in the Climbing of Snowdon, and is discussed in Chapter 6, above, seems also to be Miltonic: the moon in *Comus*, 331ff., is 'dammed up/With black usurping mists'. It is interesting that she should in the same passage be invoked to stoop down her face 'And disinherit Chaos'.

16. From a draft conclusion to *The Ruined Cottage* of spring 1798; Butler, 274–5. For a discussion of the imaginative process implied, see Chapter 6, above.

17. The 'spots of time', of course, attach themselves to their involutes, and achieve their power to nourish and invisibly repair the poet's mind and imagination, *before* they are submitted to the Word, re-created (or incarnated) as poetry.

18. 'It is apparent, then, that in Wordsworth's sustained myth of mind in its interchange with nature, the imagination plays a role equivalent to that of the Redeemer in Milton's providential plot. For in Milton's theodicy it is the birth, death, and return of the risen Christ to save mankind and to restore a lost paradise which serves to demonstrate the "goodness infinite . . ./That all this good of evil shall produce,/And evil turn to good"' (*Natural Supernaturalism*, 119).

19. The spirit-world of *1799*, Part I, though perhaps no more credible, had at least had a purpose.

20. Compare the sad transformation of the end of Waiting for the Horses, where the seven taut lines of *1805*, xi. 382–8 are replaced by twelve flaccid ones (*1850*, xii. 324–35 in order to blurr the claims that had originally been made.

21. In the opening lines, for instance, Cambridge is an eddy that sucks the poet in.

22. See Mary Jacobus' elegant and detailed account, *Tradition and Experiment*, 111–16.

23. Wordsworth does of course use the river as a connective image in the *Duddon Sonnets* of 1820, but, as he points out in the Postscript, the subject in this case is particular rather than general. Despite this he is, or pretends to be, concerned at encroaching upon Coleridge's plans for *The Brook*. There is surely a little mischief in his comment: 'There is a sympathy in streams, "one calleth to another"; and I would gladly believe that *The Brook* will ere long murmur in concert with *The Duddon*' (*Oxford Wordsworth*, iii. 503–4).

24. The 'pensive Sara' of *The Eolian Harp*, whose eye at a convenient moment darts 'a mild reproof', bidding the poet to stop speculating and 'walk humbly with [his] God' (ll. 49–52); Lamb in *This Lime-Tree Bower*, the truest Londoner of them all, who has allegedly 'pined/And hungered after Nature, many a year/In the great city pent' (ll. 28–30); the cradled Hartley of *Frost at Midnight*; the unresponding Wordsworth of *The Nightingale*; Dorothy in *Tintern Abbey*.

25. *Intimations*, 180–1, in the text of 1807—the original reading had been 'What though it be past the hour . . .'.

26. 'The organic form . . . is innate; it shapes as it develops itself from within, and the fulness of its development is one and the same with the perfection of its outward form. Such is the life, such the form' (Raysor, i. 224).

EPILOGUE: THE LIGHT THAT NEVER WAS (The Recluse)

1. George Ticknor, *Life, Letters and Journals* (2 vols., Boston, 1876), ii. 167.

2. Creation was computed at 4004 B.C.

3. Joseph Priestley, *Institutes of Natural and Revealed Religion* (2 vols., 1772), 2nd edn., 1782, ii. 416; Priestley's italics. The passage was pointed out to me originally by Jonathan Nevitt, to whom I am also grateful for information about the early writings of Godwin.

4. *Observations on Man*, ii. 379–80. 'For my own part', Priestley wrote, 'I do not hesitate to rank *Hartley's Observations on Man* among the greatest efforts of human genius; and, considering the great importance of the object of it, I am clearly of opinion, *that it is, without exception, the most valuable production of the mind of man*' (*Institutes*, ii. 161).

5. As a scientist, Priestley is known chiefly for his work on electricity (which had an obvious bearing on his view that God is present in the material universe as energy), and for his discovery, in 1774, of oxygen.

6. Joseph Priestley, *An Essay on the First Principles of Government; and on the Nature of Political, Civil, and Religious Liberty* (1768), 8. 'Extravagant as some may suppose these views to be', he continues, 'I think I could show them to be fairly suggested by the true theory of human nature . . .'. He is writing with Hartley very much in mind. It is associationism that offers 'the true theory of human nature', and which 'has a tendency to reduce the state of those who have eaten of the tree of the knowledge of good and evil, back again to a paradisiacal one (*Observations on Man*, i. 83); see Chapter 4, pp. 128–9, above.

7. Richard Price, *Observations on the Importance of the American Revolution, and the Means of Making it a Benefit to the World* (1785), 6. Price, like Priestley, lays very great stress on 'the progressive course of human improvement'. The United States will, he trusts, become 'the seat of liberty, science [i.e. knowledge] and virtue . . . whence there is reason to hope these sacred blessings will spread till they become universal' (p. 3). For Price's reaction to the French Revolution, and an admirable assessment of Burke's attack on his Sermon, see D. O. Thomas, *The Honest Mind: The Thought and Work of Richard Price* (Oxford, 1977), 294–342.

8. Edmund Burke, *Reflections on the Revolution in France, and on the Proceedings in Certain Societies in London Relative to that Event* (1790), 96–7; Burke's italics.

9. Joseph Priestley, *Letters to the Right Honourable Edmund Burke Occasioned by his Reflections on the Revolution in France* (1791), 147.

10. *A Letter from Earl Stanhope to the Right Honourable Edmund Burke* (1790), 34. As Chairman of the Revolution Society (set up in 1788 to commemorate the English

'Glorious Revolution' of 1688), Stanhope had conveyed to the French National Assembly a congratulatory address which had been moved by Price on the day of his sermon at the Old Jewry, and which particularly upset Burke; see Richard Price, *A Discourse on the Love of our Country* (1789), Additions to the Appendix, 3–4.

11. *A Vindication of the Rights of Men in a Letter to the Right Honourable Edmund Burke* (published anonymously, 1790), 72, 139; author's italics.

12. Thomas Paine, *Rights of Man: Part the Second, Combining Principle and Practice* (1792), 167.

13. *Correspondence of Robert Southey with Caroline Bowles*, ed. Edward Dowden (Dublin, 1881), 52. The passage is quoted—as are a number of others cited or discussed in this chapter—in M. H. Abrams's invaluable essay, 'English Romanticism: The Spirit of the Age', *Romanticism Reconsidered*, ed. Northrop Frye (New York, 1963), 26–72.

14. See Lefebvre, 145–76 and 206–41, and Chapter 8, above.

15. Faulkner, 294–5.

16. Godwin of course knew Holcroft (they met first in 1787), and acknowledged his influence, and it cannot be denied that Holcroft was the first into print with the standard Godwinian views; see e.g. Faulkner, 172 (quoted above, p. 340). Differences of background and preoccupation are crucial, however. Holcroft is an actor turned playwright, with no formal education, and no cause to be establishing in detail a philosophical system; Godwin, by contrast, was born into a dissenter's family, educated at a dissenting academy, and spent almost the first thirty years of his life as a member of dissenting congregations. His thinking may be confused, but it is at all times moral, philosophical, above all determinist: 'The assassin cannot help the murder he commits any more than the dagger' (*PJ* ii. 690).

17. *Political Justice* (2nd edn., 2 vols., 1796) i. 94; it has to be said that this passage is not in the first edition, but it merely puts more succinctly the central Godwinian position. For a comparable statement in 1793, see *PJ* ii. 593: 'The legitimate instrument of effecting political reformation is truth. Let truth be incessantly studied, illustrated and propagated, and the effect is inevitable.'

18. See David V. Erdman, 'Coleridge, Wordsworth and the Wedgwood Fund: Part I, Tom Wedgwood's "Master Stroke"', *BNYPL* lx (Sept 1956), 430.

19. In 1797 Coleridge added a footnote to the quoted lines: 'This paragraph is intelligible to those, who, like the author, believe and feel the sublime system of Berkley [*sic*]; and the doctrine of the final happiness of all men.' Berkeley's idealism is brought to the service of Hartley's (and Priestley's) millenarian optimism.

20. *Institutes*, ii. 161, quoted note 4, above.

21. Though no reference to the scheme of *The Recluse* survives before early March 1798, it is not impossible that *The Pedlar* had been written and inserted into *The Ruined Cottage* in February with the intention of adapting the bare narrative of the previous summer to be part of the newly conceived philosophical poem.

22. *Specimens of the Table Talk of the Late Samuel Taylor Coleridge*, ed. Henry Nelson Coleridge (2 vols., 1835), ii. 70–1.

23. Like Peacock in *Melincourt, or Sir Oran Haut-ton* (1817), Coleridge has in mind the Scottish anthropologist Lord Monboddo, who had claimed that his flute-playing orang-outang was an example of 'the infantine state of our species'.

24. 'I have cautiously discriminated the terms, the *reason* and the *understanding*, encouraged and confirmed by the authority of our genuine divines and philosophers before the revolution:

both life and sense,
Fansie and understanding, whence the soule
Reason receives, and reason is her being,
Discursive or intuitive; discourse
Is oftest yours, the latter most is ours,
Differing but in degree, of kind the same.'

(*BL* x. 92–3)

The revolution referred to is of course that of 1688, not 1789.

25. Griggs, i. 632 (see also ii. 671); the period between these two letters interestingly straddles the composition of the Preface to *Lyrical Ballads*, later described by Coleridge as half the child of his own brain (Griggs, ii. 830). What is implied is not that Coleridge was from the first aware of theoretical differences between himself and Wordsworth, but that his scheme was altogether, and typically, more ambitious.

26. *Immanuel Kant in England, 1793–1838* (Princeton, 1931), 67.

27. In fact of course the wings of the butterfly form within the dormant chrysalis, not in the active caterpillar stage, which might alter Coleridge's symbolism a bit.

28. *Religious Musings*, 414 and *Frost at Midnight*, 59–60.

29. See Chapter 3, pp. 86–7, above.

30. The passage from *Biographia* describing *The Brook* is quoted in Chapter 10, pp. 333–4, above.

31. Compare the prayer with which the Prospectus concludes: 'let my life/Express the image of a better time' (ll. 73–4).

32. In Wordsworth's private and domestic joy the re-echoed cry of 'Worthy the Lamb' becomes Joanna's laugh that is tossed from one Cumbrian mountain to the next (*To Joanna*, 52ff.).

33. The 'awful voice of thunder' in Bürger's *Chase* (an influence on *The Ancient Mariner* as well as the source of *Hart-leap Well*) had of course intervened to punish the cruelty of Earl Walter (see Chapter 4, above), but such crudities had no place in the poetry of the One Life at Alfoxden, or indeed in the work of Goslar. Nor does *Hart-leap Well* contain a personal God.

34. It is significant that in the letter of *c.* 10 March 1798 where Coleridge quotes for his brother Wordsworth's recent lines on the social effects of the One Life—'The joy of that pure principle of love'—he also cites from Cowper a passage (*Task*, v. 496–508) in which knowledge and love are singled out for their power to establish public virtue (Griggs, i. 396–8). The letter shows Coleridge carefully toning down his Unitarianism, trying to make it acceptable to George (who was eight years older, and a father-figure as well as Anglican parson), but it is nonetheless a valuable statement of the views and influences he shared with Wordsworth at the moment when *The Recluse* was first projected.

35. Lines 859–74, looking forward to the first visits of Coleridge and the Hutchinson sisters to Dove Cottage, though placed late in *MS B*, are not found in the drafts of *MS R*, and must therefore have been written before ll. 469–859.

36. On 10 June 1803 Coleridge believed Wordsworth to have *The Recluse* 'sub malleo ardentem', and on 14 October he was still more optimistic: 'I rejoice . . . with a deep and true joy that he has at length yielded to my urgent and repeated—almost unremitting—requests and remonstrances, and will go on with *The Recluse* exclusively' (Griggs, ii. 950, 1013). Nothing seems actually to have been achieved at this period (see Dorothy's sisterly

comments, *EY* 421, 423). If anything at all was written for *The Recluse* in the years 1800–6, it was probably in a brief moment during spring 1801; see Ketcham, 110.

37. Coleridge did in fact claim in May 1805 to have written notes on *The Recluse* and sent them from Malta with a certain Major Adye, who died from plague *en route* (Griggs, ii. 1169). It is not a very convincing story.

38. See Jonathan Wordsworth, 'On Man, on Nature, and on Human Life', *RES* New Series xxxi, no. 121 (Feb. 1980), 17–29, and Appendix above.

39. *EY* 518; the terms of Wordsworth's early references to *The Excursion* in fact vary considerably, the oddest allusion being that of 3 June 1805, to writing in addition to *The Recluse* 'a narrative poem of the epic kind' (*EY* 594). My reasons for thinking that the poet's intention should not be taken at face-value are put forward in 'That Wordsworth Epic', *WC* (winter 1980), 34–5.

40. The Solitary's story was revised, reordered, and expanded to form *Excursion*, II-IV at Allan Bank in the winter of 1809–10 (see *MY* i. 392). On the basis of surviving MSS it is not possible to be certain either how much of the final text existed in 1806, or what was then the shape of the narrative. *Prelude, MS X*, however, preserves a version of Book II (lacking the details of the Solitary's marriage, ll. 185–210, and the account of the finding of the old shepherd, ll. 730–904), and fair copy material in *D.C.MSS 69, 70*, and *73* may also derive from the early period.

41. Quotations from *The Tuft of Primroses* are drawn from *D. C. MS 65*, and line-references given for convenience to Helen Darbishire's text in *Oxford Wordsworth*, v, Appendix C.

42. James Butler, in the one critical essay that has given a full seriousness to *The Tuft of Primroses*, points to 'the odor of death and decay in the diction' of the poem. 'Time after time', he writes, 'the diction suggests what is happening to the earthly paradise and to the speaker's repose' ('Wordsworth's *Tuft of Primroses*: "An Unrelenting Doom"', *SIR* xiv [summer 1975], 243).

43. The biblical reference is composite. See on the one hand the 'faithful and wise steward' of Luke, 12: 42 and Paul's statement 'it is required in stewards that a man be found faithful' (1 Cor. 4:2), and on the other, the parables of the unjust steward (Luke, 16) and of the talents (Matthew, 25). In this last case, the two servants who have made good use of their talents (Wordsworth could hardly be unaware of the pun) are praised and rewarded, but the 'unprofitable servant' (verse 30) is cast into outer darkness. It is noticeable that both Luke, 12 and Matthew, 25 concern readiness for the Second Coming of Christ.

44. After finishing the thirteen-Book *Prelude* in May 1805, Wordsworth revised it during the copying of *MSS A* and *B* (Nov. 1805–Feb. 1806), and was said by Joseph Farington to be working on it again in November 1806; he then read the poem to Coleridge in January 1807, and, as a result of his suggestions, carried out the first of the extensive revisions that can be identified in the manuscripts (see Norton *Prelude*, 520–1). How often in this process his eyes would have lighted on a particular passage there is no means of knowing, but, given his memory for blank verse, it is probable that he in fact knew a great deal of the poem by heart.

45. The echo that one should be hearing is *Solitary Reaper*, 23–4,

> Some natural sorrow, loss, or pain,
> That has been and may be again.

46. Professor Butler claims that 'Wordsworth's inability to sustain in [*The Tuft of*

Primroses] the symbolic patterns created in *The Prelude* and *Home at Grasmere* explains why the poet could not complete what he took to be his life's work' (*SIR* xiv. 237–8). I am sure he is right in all that he says about the weakening of the vale as a symbol for Wordsworth, but see it as the effect of a cause that goes far deeper.

47. The fact that St. Basil in his retreat from the world was encouraged by an only sister offers a touching parallel, but fourth-century Christianity cannot be, and isn't, presented as an ideal for *The Recluse*. The account of the sacking of the Grande Chartreuse, cribbed from *Descriptive Sketches*, has no forward-looking implications at all, being clearly suggested by fear that solitude and contemplation may be broken in upon.

48. See *Prose Works*, i. 196ff., for evidence that his indignation was very widely shared.

49. Twenty-seven numbers of *The Friend*, edited, and very largely written, by Coleridge, appeared June 1809–March 1810.

50. It is a further extraordinary fact that Wordsworth's account of *The Recluse* in the *Excursion* Preface actually doubles the amount of work still to be done. In March 1804 he had described his aims to De Quincey as consisting of a moral and philosophical poem, a narrative one, and, least important, a 'tributary' account of his own early life (*EY* 454). On completion of the 1805 *Prelude* a year later, the same threefold scheme, of the central *Recluse*, *Excursion* and *Prelude*, is described to Sir George Beaumont (*EY* 594–5). Suddenly in 1814, however, a new section is added. Developing his famous simile, Wordsworth describes *The Prelude* as the ante-chapel to the Gothic church of the *Recluse*, and goes on to say that the church itself is to consist of *The Excursion*, flanked *on both sides* by 'meditations in the author's own person'. The unwritten, and unwriteable, philosophical centre of *The Recluse* has split in two. Why it should have done so we cannot know, but George Ticknor's conversation with Wordsworth in 1838 shows that the scheme in this triple form—quadruple if one includes *The Prelude*—long continued to have an existence in the poet's mind, and to increase the pressures he felt to be upon him.

51. Professor Darlington (p. 25) regards 1812–14 as the probable date of Mary Wordsworth's transcription of the first part of *MS D*, and the brief resumption of work on *Home at Grasmere* that it implies. I think myself that 1815–16, after the publication of *The Excursion* and the Prospectus, is very much more likely.

52. For an account of the last three *Prelude* manuscripts (*MSS C, D* and *E*, respectively of 1816–19, 1832, and 1839), see Norton *Prelude*, 521–2.

53. In addition to producing the first major *Prelude* revisions, the years following *The Excursion* are responsible for publication of *The White Doe of Rylstone* (1815), *Thanksgiving Ode* (1816), *Peter Bell* and *The Waggoner* (1819), two editions of the *Collected Poems* (1815 and 1820), and three sonnet-sequences (*Duddon*, 1820, *Ecclesiastical Sketches* and *Memorials of a Tour on the Continent*, 1822)—most of them being either composed or substantially revised during the period. There were also significant prose works.

54. 'We all think there is a grandeur in this poem', Dora writes to her future husband, Edward Quillinan, 'but it ought to have been in *The Recluse*, and Mother on that account but half enjoys it.' A month later her complaint is that until the new collection, *Poems* 1828, is in print her father's 'great work will never be touched'. 'Every day', she continues, 'he finds something to alter, or new stanzas to add, or a fresh sonnet—or a fresh poem growing out of one just finished, which he always promises shall be his last' (D. C. Papers, quoted Darlington, 27).

55. Dora reports on 3 December 1831 that 'Father has taken up *The Recluse* with good earnest' (Vincent, 94–5), and six days later the news is confirmed by an unpublished Dorothy *Journal* (quoted, Darlington, 28). *Home at Grasmere* at this moment is

substantially revised, and Mary's transcription of *MS D*, begun fifteen years before, is completed; but the poem in its corrected form is no more a basis than it had originally been for leading on into the central philosophical sections of *The Recluse*.

56. D. C. Papers; quoted Darlington, 30.

57. *Life, Letters and Journals*, ii. 167.

Bibliography

1. Manuscripts Cited
2. Texts of Wordsworth and his Circle
3. Other Relevant Literary Texts
4. Background Material:
   (a) Philosophical, Intellectual, and Political
       i. Pre-1800, ii. More Recent Studies
   (b) Local History, Travel, Memoirs, etc.
       i. Pre-1900, ii. Modern Studies
5. Literary Criticism and Scholarship:
   (a) General Studies and Collections
   (b) More Detailed Critical and Scholarly Work

For convenience, Section 1 tabulates the MSS that have been cited, according to their catalogue numbers at the Wordsworth Library, Grasmere. In Sections 2–4 modern editions, where they exist and are broadly reliable, have been listed in preference to early printed material. Where several editions of a given work or writer have been cited, those chiefly used in this book are marked with an asterisk. An effort has been made in Section 5 to categorize recent scholarly and critical material, but there will certainly be cases where distinctions are misleading. Occasionally it has seemed useful to indicate the content or purpose of a work, but no attempt has been made to do so consistently.

1. MANUSCRIPTS CITED

MSS are listed under the poems they contain, and arranged in the order of their composition. The second column provides the *name* under which they have been cited, and the third, their number in the catalogue at the Wordsworth Library.

The Pedlar	*MS 18A*	*D.C. MS 16*
	MS E	*D.C. MS 37*
The Two-Part *Prelude* (1799)	*MS JJ*	*D.C. MS 19*

	MS RV	*D.C. MS 21*
	MS V	*D.C. MS 22*
	MS U	*D.C. MS 23*
Fragments	*Peter Bell MS 2*	*D.C. MS 33*
The Prospectus	*MS 1*	*D.C. MS 45*
Home at Grasmere	*MS R*	*D.C. MS 28*
	MS A	*D.C. MS 58*
	MS B	*D.C. MS 59*
	MS D	*D.C. MS 76*
Fragments	*Christabel Notebook*	*D.C. MS 15*
Michael	*MS 1*	*D.C. MS 30*
	MS 2	*D.C. MS 31*
The Barberry-Tree	*MS in the Library at Christ Church, Oxford*	
The Five-Book *Prelude* (1804)	*MS WW*	*D.C. MS 38A*
	MS W	*D.C. MS 38*
The 1805 *Prelude*	*MS X*	*D.C. MS 47*
	MS Y	*D.C. MS 48*
	MS Z	*D.C. MS 49*
	MS A	*D.C. MS 52*
	MS B	*D.C. MS 53*
The Excursion, Books I-IV	*Prelude, MS X*	*D.C. MS 47*
	MS 69	*D.C. MS 69*
	MS 70	*D.C. MS 70*
	MS 73	*D.C. MS 73*
The Tuft of Primroses		*D.C. MS 65*
The 1850 *Prelude*	*MS C*	*D.C. MS 82*
	MS D	*D.C. MS 124*
	MS E	*D.C. MS 145*

2. TEXTS OF WORDSWORTH AND HIS CIRCLE: POEMS, JOURNALS, LETTERS, ETC.

COLERIDGE, SAMUEL TAYLOR, *Poems on Various Subjects* (1796).
——, *Poems*, 2nd edn., *To which are now added Poems by Charles Lamb and Charles Lloyd* (Bristol and London, 1797).
——, *Fears in Solitude, France an Ode, and Frost at Midnight* (1798).
——, *Poetical Works*, ed. E. H. Coleridge (2 vols., Oxford, 1912).
——, * *Poems*, selected and ed. John Beer, Everyman's Library, revised edn. (1973).

COLERIDGE, SAMUEL TAYLOR (contd.), *Collected Coleridge*, Bollingen Series lxxv (Princeton, N. J.).
i. *Lectures 1795 on Politics and Religion*, ed. Lewis Patton and Peter Mann (1971).
ii. *The Watchman*, ed. Lewis Patton (1970).
iii. *Essays on His Times*, ed. David V. Erdman (3 vols., 1978).
iv. *The Friend*, ed. Barbara Rooke (2 vols., 1969).
vi. *Lay Sermons*, ed. R. J. White (1972).
——, *Biographia Literaria*, ed. J. Shawcross (2 vols., Oxford, 1907).
——, **Biographia Literaria*, ed. George Watson, Everyman's Library (1965).
——, *Specimens of the Table Talk of the Late Samuel Taylor Coleridge*, ed. Henry Nelson Coleridge (2 vols., 1835).
——, *Anima Poetae*, ed. E. H. Coleridge (1895).
——, *Shakespearean Criticism*, ed. Thomas Middleton Raysor (2 vols., 1933).
——, *Miscellaneous Criticism*, ed. Thomas Middleton Raysor (1936).
——, *Notebooks*, ed. Kathleen Coburn (New York, 1957–).
——, *Letters*, ed. E. L. Griggs (6 vols., Oxford, 1956–71).
DE QUINCEY, THOMAS, **Confessions of An English Opium-Eater and Other Writings*, ed. Aileen Ward, Signet Classics (New York, Toronto, London, 1966).
——, *Recollections of the Lakes and the Lake Poets*, ed. David Wright, Penguin (1970).
——, **De Quincey as Critic*, ed. John E. Jordan (1973).
——, *Collected Writings*, new and enlarged edn., David Masson (14 vols., Edinburgh, 1889–90).
HUTCHINSON, SARA, *Letters*, ed. Kathleen Coburn (1954).
LAMB, CHARLES, *Works*, ed. E. V. Lucas (7 vols., 1903–4).
——, *Lamb as Critic*, ed. Roy Park (1980).
LAMB, CHARLES AND MARY ANNE, *Letters*, ed. Edwin J. Marrs (Ithaca, N. Y., 1975–).
LLOYD, CHARLES, *Poems* (Carlisle, 1795).
——, *See* Coleridge, *Poems*, 2nd edn. (1797).
——, and Lamb, Charles, *Blank Verse* (1798).
——, *Edmund Oliver* (2 vols., Bristol, 1798).
——, *Poems* (1823).
LOVELL, ROBERT, AND SOUTHEY, ROBERT, *Poems* (1795).
ROBINSON, HENRY CRABB, *Books and their Writers*, ed. E. J. Morley (3 vols., 1938).
——, *Diary, Reminiscences and Correspondence of Henry Crabb Robinson*, ed. Thomas Sadler (3 vols., 1869).
——, *Correspondence of Henry Crabb Robinson with the Wordsworth Circle*, ed. E. J. Morley (2 vols., Oxford, 1927).

SOUTHEY, ROBERT, *see* Lovell, Robert, above.

——, *Joan of Arc: An Epic Poem* [including the original version of Coleridge's *Destiny of Nations*], 1796.

——, *Poems* (Bristol, 1797); Vol. II (Bristol, 1799).

——, *Thalaba the Destroyer* (2 vols., 1801).

——, *Madoc* (2 vols., 1805).

——, *Wat Tyler: A Dramatic Poem in Three Acts* (pirated 1817).

——, *Poetical Works* (10 vols., 1837–8).

——, and Coleridge, Samuel Taylor (Anon.), *Omniana or Horae Otiosiores* (2 vols., 1810).

——, *Southey's Common-place Book*, ed. John Wood Warter (4 vols., 1849).

——, *Selections from the Letters of Robert Southey*, ed. John Wood Warter (4 vols., 1856).

——, *The Correspondence of Robert Southey with Caroline Bowles*, ed. Edward Dowden (Dublin, 1881).

——, *New Letters of Robert Southey*, ed. Kenneth Curry (2 vols., New York and London, 1965).

WORDSWORTH, DORA, *Letters*, ed. Howard P. Vincent (Chicago, 1944).

WORDSWORTH, DOROTHY, *Journals*, ed. E. de Selincourt (2 vols., 1951).

——, **Journals*, Oxford Paperbacks, ed. Mary Moorman (London, Oxford, New York, 1971).

WORDSWORTH, JOHN, *Letters*, ed. Carl H. Ketcham (Ithaca, N. Y., 1969).

WORDSWORTH, MARY, *Letters*, ed. Mary E. Burton (Oxford, 1958).

WORDSWORTH, WILLIAM, *'The Salisbury Plain Poems'*, ed. Stephen Gill, Cornell Wordsworth Series (Ithaca, N. Y., 1975).

——, *The Borderers*, ed. Robert Osborn, Cornell Wordsworth Series (Ithaca, N. Y., 1982).

——, *'The Ruined Cottage' and 'The Pedlar'*, ed. James Butler, Cornell Wordsworth Series (Ithaca, N.Y., 1979).

——, 'Two Early Texts' [*A Night-Piece* and *The Discharged Soldier*], ed. Beth Darlington, *Bicentenary Wordsworth Studies*, ed. Jonathan Wordsworth (Ithaca, N. Y., 1970), 425–48.

——, *Lyrical Ballads 1798*, ed. W. J. B. Owen (Oxford, 1967).

——, *'The Prelude' 1798–99*, ed. Stephen Parrish, Cornell Wordsworth Series (Ithaca, N. Y., 1977).

——, *'Home at Grasmere'*, ed. Beth Darlington, Cornell Wordsworth Series (Ithaca, N. Y., 1977).

——, **Lyrical Ballads 1798, 1800*, ed. R. L. Brett and A. R. Jones (1963).

——, *The Prelude*, ed. E. de Selincourt, 2nd edn., revised Helen Darbishire (Oxford, 1959).

——, *The Prelude*, ed. James Maxwell, Penguin (1971).

——, **'The Prelude', 1799, 1805, 1850*, ed. Jonathan Wordsworth, M. H.

Abrams, and Stephen Gill, Norton Critical Edition (New York, 1979).
——, *Poems in Two Volumes 1807*, ed. Helen Darbishire (Oxford, 1914).
——, *The Excursion* (1814).
——, *Poetical Works*, ed. E. de Selincourt and Helen Darbishire (5 vols., Oxford, 1940–9).
——, *Prose Works*, ed. A. B. Grosart (3 vols., 1876); still required for Fenwick Notes.
——, **Prose Works*, ed. W. J. B. Owen and Jane Worthington Smyser (3 vols., Oxford, 1974).
——, *Letters of William and Dorothy Wordsworth*, ed. E. de Selincourt, *The Early Years, 1787–1805*, revised Chester L. Shaver (Oxford, 1967); *The Middle Years, 1806–11*, revised Mary Moorman and Alan Hill (Oxford, 1970); *The Later Years, 1821–28*, revised Alan Hill (Oxford, 1978); *1829–34* revised Alan Hill (Oxford, 1979); *1835–39* revised Alan Hill (Oxford, 1982); 1840–50 not yet revised.
——, *The Love Letters of William and Mary Wordsworth*, ed. Beth Darlington (Ithaca, N. Y., 1981).

3. OTHER RELEVANT LITERARY TEXTS

AKENSIDE, MARK, *The Pleasures of Imagination: A Poem in Three Books* (1744).
——, **Poems* (1772); including the revised but incomplete four-Book *Pleasures of The Imagination.*
——, *The Pleasures of Imagination*, ed., with a Critical Essay, by Mrs Barbauld (1795).
ANDERSON, ROBERT, ED., *The Works of the British Poets* (13 vols., 1795).
BEATTIE, JAMES, *The Minstrel*, Book I (1771), Book II (1774).
BLAKE, WILLIAM, *Poetry and Prose*, ed. David V. Erdman, Commentary by Harold Bloom (New York, 1965).
BOWLES, WILLIAM LISLE, *Poetical Works*, ed. George Gilfillan (2 vols., Edinburgh, 1855).
BUNYAN, JOHN, *The Pilgrim's Progress*, ed. James Blanton Wharey, 2nd edn., Roger Sharrock (Oxford, 1960).
BÜRGER, GOTTFRIED, *The Lass of Fair Wone*, anon. trans. [by William Taylor] of *Des Pfarrers Tochter von Taubenhain, Monthly Magazine* iii (Apr. 1796), 223–4.
——, *The Chase and William and Helen*, anon. trans. [by Walter Scott] of *Der Wilde Jäger* and *Lenore* (Edinburgh, 1796).
BURNS, ROBERT, *Poems and Songs*, ed. James Kingsley (3 vols., Oxford, 1968).
BYRON, GEORGE GORDON, LORD, *English Bards and Scotch Reviewers: A Satire* (1809).
CHATTERTON, THOMAS, *Poems Supposed to have been Written at Bristol, by*

Thomas Rowley, and Others, in the Fifteenth Century, ed. Lancelot Sharpe (Cambridge, 1794).

CHAUCER, GEOFFREY, *Poetical Works*, ed. F. N. Robinson (1957).

COLERIDGE, SAMUEL TAYLOR, ED., *Sonnets from Various Authors*, ed. Paul M. Zall (Glendale, Calif., 1968).

COLLINS, WILLIAM, *see* Gray, Thomas, *below*.

COWPER, WILLIAM, *Poems* (2 vols., 1786).

——, *Poetical Works*, ed. H. S. Milford, 4th edn. with Corrections and Additions by Norma Russell, Oxford Standard Authors (1971).

CROWE, WILLIAM (ANON.), *Lewesdon Hill* (Oxford, 1788).

DARWIN, ERASMUS, *The Botanic Garden*, Part I, 'The Economy of Vegetables' (1791), Part II, 'The Loves of the Plants' (1789).

DRYDEN, JOHN, *Essays*, ed. W. P. Ker (2 vols., Oxford, 1900).

——, *Poems*, ed. James Kingsley (4 vols., Oxford, 1958).

FAWCETT, JOSEPH, *The Art of War: A Poem* (1795).

——, *Poems* (1798).

GODWIN, WILLIAM, *Caleb Williams*, ed. David McCracken, Oxford English Novels (1970).

GOLDSMITH, OLIVER, *see* Gray, Thomas, *below*.

GRAY, THOMAS, *Poems of Gray, Collins and Goldsmith*, ed. Roger Lonsdale, Longman Annotated English Poets (1969).

——, *Correspondence*, ed. P. Toynbee and L. Whibley (3 vols., Oxford, 1935).

HAZLITT, WILLIAM, *Works*, ed. P. P. Howe (21 vols., 1930–4).

——, *Letters*, ed. Herschel Moreland Sikes (1979).

HERBERT, GEORGE, *Works*, ed. F. E. Hutchinson (Oxford, 1941).

HOLCROFT, THOMAS, *Anna St Ives*, ed. Peter Faulkner, Oxford English Novels (1970).

——, *Memoirs* [completed by Hazlitt], *Complete Works of William Hazlitt*, ed. P. P. Howe (21 vols., 1930–4), iii. 1–305.

HUNT, LEIGH, *The Feast of the Poets* (1814).

JOHNSON, SAMUEL, *Lives of the Most Eminent English Poets*, ed. G. B. Hill (3 vols., Oxford, 1905).

JONSON, BEN, ED. C. H. Herford and Percy Simpson (11 vols., Oxford, 1925–52).

KEATS, JOHN, *Poems*, ed. Miriam Allott, Longman Annotated English Poets (1970).

——, *Letters*, ed. Maurice Buxton Forman, 3rd edn. revised (Oxford, 1947).

——, *The Keats Circle: Letters and Papers, 1816–1878*, ed. Hyder Edward Rollins (2 vols., Cambridge, Mass., 1948).

KNOX, VICESIMUS (ANON.) *Extracts, Elegant, Instructive, and Entertaining, in Poetry, from the Most Approved Authors* (2 vols., 1791).

——, *Extracts, Elegant, Instructive, and Entertaining, in Prose, Selected from the Best Modern Authors* (2 vols., 1791).

KNOX, VICESIMUS (ANON.) (contd.), *Epistles, Elegant, Familiar, and Instructive, Selected from the Best Writers, Ancient as well as Modern* (2 vols., 1791).

MACPHERSON, JAMES ('OSSIAN'), *Fingal: An Ancient Epic Poem in Six Books*, 'Translated from the Galic Language' (1762).

——, *Temora: An Ancient Epic Poem in Eight Books*, 'Translated from the Galic Language' (1763).

MARVELL, ANDREW, *Works, with a New Life of the Author*, ed. Edward Thompson (3 vols., 1776).

——, *Poems and Letters*, ed. H. M. Margoliouth (2 vols., Oxford, 1927).

MILTON, JOHN, *Poems*, ed. John Carey and Alistair Fowler, Longman Annotated English Poets (1968).

——, *Complete Prose Works*, ed. Don. M. Wolfe *et. al.* (7 vols., New Haven, Conn., and London, 1953–74).

PEACOCK, THOMAS LOVE, *Novels*, ed. D. Garnett (2 vols., 1963).

PERCY, THOMAS, *Reliques of Ancient English Poetry*, ed. T. Percy [nephew], 3 vols., 1794.

POPE, ALEXANDER, Twickenhan Edition, ed. John Butt *et al.* (9 vols., 1961–7).

ROGERS, SAMUEL, *The Pleasures of Memory* (1792).

——, *Poems* (1812).

SCHILLER, FREDERICK, *The Robbers*, anon. English translation (1792).

——, *Wallenstein, A Drama,* trans. S. T. Coleridge (1800).

——, *The Death of Wallenstein, A Tragedy*, trans. S. T. Coleridge (1800).

SCOTT, SIR WALTER, *Minstrelsy of the Scottish Border* (2 vols., Kelso, 1802).

——, *The Lay of the Last Minstrel* (1805).

——, *Poetical Works*, ed. J. L. Robertson (Oxford, 1894).

SEWARD, ANNA, *Letters, 1784-1807* (6 vols., London and Edinburgh, 1811).

SHAKESPEARE, WILLIAM, *Complete Works*, ed. Peter Alexander (London and Glasgow, 1951).

SHELLEY, PERCY BYSSHE, *Poetical Works*, ed. Thomas Hutchinson (Oxford, 1907).

——, *Complete Poetical Works*, ed. Neville Rogers, Vol. I, 1802–13 (1972); Vol. II, 1814–17 (1975); not yet completed.

——, *Prose*, ed. David Lee Clark (Albuquerque, New Mexico, 1954).

——, *Letters*, ed. Frederick L. Jones (2 vols., Oxford, 1904).

SMITH, CHARLOTTE, *Elegiac Sonnets, with Additional Sonnets and Other Poems* (1789).

SOUTHEY, ROBERT, ED., *The Annual Anthology*, Vol. I (1799), Vol. II (1800).

SPENSER, EDMUND, *The Faerie Queene*, ed. A. C. Hamilton, Longman Annotated English Poets (1977).

THELWALL, JOHN, *The Peripatetic, or Sketches of the Heart, of Nature and Society* (3 vols., 1793).
——, *Poems Written in Close Confinement in the Tower* (1795).
——, *Poems Written Chiefly in Retirement* (Hereford, 1801).
THOMSON, JAMES, *The Seasons* (1730).
——, *The Seasons* (1746); with final revisions.
——, *The Castle of Indolence* (1748).
——, *Poetical Works*, ed. J. Logie Robinson, Oxford Standard Authors (Oxford, 1908).
TRAHERNE, THOMAS, *Poems, Centuries and Three Thanks-Givings*, ed. A. Ridler, Oxford Standard Authors (1966).
VAUGHAN, HENRY, *Works*, ed. L. C. Martin (2 vols., Oxford, 1914).
WILLIAMS, HELEN MARIA, *Poems* (2 vols., 1786).
YOUNG, EDWARD, *Night Thoughts* (1750).

4. BACKGROUND MATERIAL

(*a*) *Philosophical, Intellectual, and Political*

i. Pre-1800

ADDISON, JOSEPH, 'The Pleasures of the Imagination', *Spectator* ccccxi-xii, *see Eighteenth Century Critical Essays*, ed. Scott Elledge.
BERKELEY, GEORGE, *Works*, ed. A. A. Luce and T. E. Jessop (9 vols., London and New York, 1948–57).
BLAIR, HUGH, 'Dissertation Concerning the Poems of Ossian', *Works of Ossian* (2 vols., 1765).
——, *Lectures on Rhetoric and Belles Lettres* (2 vols., 1783).
BURKE, EDMUND, *A Philosophical Enquiry into the Origin of our Ideas of the Sublime and Beautiful*, ed. J. T. Boulton (Oxford, 1958).
——, *Reflections on the Revolution in France, and on the Proceedings in Certain Societies in London Relative to that Event* (1790).
BURNET, THOMAS, *The Sacred Theory of the Earth* (1684).
CUDWORTH, RALPH, *The True Intellectual System of the Universe* (1678).
DARWIN, ERASMUS, *Zoonomia, Or the Laws of Organic Life* (2 vols., 1794–6).
EDGEWORTH, MARIA, *The Parent's Assistant* (3 vols., 1796).
——, AND EDGEWORTH, RICHARD LOVELL, *Practical Education* (2 vols., 1798).
Eighteenth Century Critical Essays, ed. Scott Elledge (2 vols., Ithaca, N. Y., 1961).
Encyclopaedia Britannica, 3rd edn. (18 vols., Edinburgh, 1797).
GODWIN, WILLIAM, *An Enquiry Concerning Political Justice* (2 vols., 1793); 2nd edn., revised (2 vols., 1796).

HARTLEY, DAVID, *Observations on Man, His Frame, His Duty, and His Expectations* (2 vols., 1749).

——, *Hartley's Theory of the Human Mind on the Principle of the Association of Ideas*, ed. Joseph Priestley (1775).

——, *Observations on Man*, reissued with Notes by H. Pistorius (3 vols., 1791).

JOHNSON, SAMUEL, *A Dictionary of the English Language*, 4th edn., revised (2 vols., 1773).

KANT, IMMANUEL, *Critique of Pure Reason*, trans. N. Kemp Smith (1929).

——, *Critique of Aesthetic Judgement*, trans. J. C. Meredith (Oxford, 1911).

LOCKE, JOHN, *Educational Writings*, ed. James L. Axtell (Cambridge, 1968).

LOWTH, ROBERT, *Lectures on the Sacred Poetry of the Hebrews*, trans. G. Gregory (2 vols., 1787).

MACKINTOSH, JAMES, *Vindiciae Gallicae* (1791).

PAINE, THOMAS, *Rights of Man, Being an Answer to Mr Burke's Attack on the French Revolution*, Part I (1791).

——, *Rights of Man: Part the Second, Combining Principles and Practice* (1792).

PRICE, RICHARD, *Observations on the Importance of the American Revolution, and the Means of Making it a Benefit to the World* (1785).

——, *A Discourse on the Love of Our Country* (1789).

PRIESTLEY, JOSEPH, *An Essay on the First Principles of Government and on the Nature of Political, Civil, and Religious Liberty* (1768).

——, *Institutes of Natural and Revealed Religion*, 2nd edn. (2 vols., Birmingham, 1782).

——, ed., *Hartley's Theory of the Human Mind, on the Principles of the Association of Ideas (1775)*.

——, *Disquisitions Relating to Matter and Spirit* (2 vols., 1777).

——, *Letters to the Right Honourable Edmund Burke Occasioned by his Reflections on the Revolution in France* (1791).

——, *The Present State of Europe Compared with Antient Prophecies: A Sermon Preached at the Gravel Pit Meeting in Hackney, February 28, 1794*.

ROUSSEAU, JEAN-JACQUES, *Oeuvres Complètes*, ed. Bernard Gagnebin and Marcel Raymond (Paris, 1959–69).

SCHLEGEL, WILLIAM AUGUSTUS, *Lectures on Dramatic Art and Literature*, trans. John Black (2 vols., 1815).

SHAFTESBURY, ANTHONY ASHLEY COOPER, EARL OF, *Characteristics of Men, Manners, Opinions, Times*, ed. John M. Robinson (3 vols., 1900).

STANHOPE, CHARLES, *A Letter from Earl Stanhope to the Right Honourable Edmund Burke* (1790).

WILLIAMS, HELEN MARIA, *Letters written in France in the Summer of 1790* (1790).

WILLIAMS, HELEN MARIA (contd.), *Letters on the French Revolution* (1970).

——, *Letters Containing a Sketch of the Politics of France from May 1793 till July 1794* (2 vols., Dublin, 1794).

WOLLSTONECRAFT, MARY (ANON.), *A Vindication of the Rights of Men in a Letter to the Right Honourable Edmund Burke* (1790).

——, *A Vindication of the Rights of Women*, Vol. I (1792).

YOUNG, EDWARD, *Conjectures on Original Composition*, ed. Edith Morley (Manchester, 1918).

ii. Modern Studies

ABRAMS, M. H., 'English Romanticism: The Spirit of the Age', *Romanticism Reconsidered*, ed. Northrop Frye (New York, 1963), 26–72.

AULARD, A., *Histoire politique de la Revolution* (Paris, 1901).

BENNETT, JONATHAN, *Locke, Berkeley, Hume* (1971).

BUSSIERE, GEORGES AND LEGOUIS, EMILE, *Le Général Michel Beaupuy* (Paris, 1891).

ERDMAN, DAVID V., *Blake: Prophet Against Empire: A Poet's Interpretation of the History of His Own Times* (Princeton, N. J., 1954).

GIRTIN, THOMAS AND LOSHAK, DAVID, *The Art of Thomas Girtin (1954)*.

GOODWIN, ALBERT, *The Friends of Liberty: The English Democratic Reform Movement in the Age of the French Revolution* (1979).

LEFEBVRE, GEORGES, *The French Revolution*, (i) *From its Origins to 1793*, trans. Elizabeth Moss Evanson (London and New York, 1962); (ii) *From 1793 to 1799*, trans. John Hall Stewart and James Friguglietti (London and New York, 1964).

LLOYD, HUMPHREY, *The Quaker Lloyds in the Industrial Revolution* (1975).

MADELIN, LOUIS, *The French Revolution*, English edn. (1916).

NUTTALL, A. D., *Philosophy and the Literary Imagination* (1974).

O'GORMAN, F., *The Whig Party and the French Revolution* (1967).

THOMAS, D. O., *The Honest Mind: The Thought and Work of Richard Price* (Oxford, 1977).

THOMIS, MALCOLM I., AND HOLT, PETER, *Threats of Revolution in Britain, 1789–1848* (1977).

THOMPSON, E. P., *The Making of the English Working Class* (1963).

——, 'Disenchantment or Default? A Lay Sermon', *Power and Consciousness*, ed. Conor Cruise O' Brien and William Dean Vanech (London and New York, 1969), 150–81.

WATSON, J. STEVEN, *The Reign of George III, 1760–1815* (Oxford, 1960).

WELLEK, RÉNÉ, *Immanuel Kant in England, 1793–1838* (Princeton, 1931).

WILLEY, BASIL, *The Eighteenth Century Background* (1940).

(*b*) *Local History, Travel, Memoirs, etc.:*

i. Pre–1900

ABERGAVENNY, THE EARL OF, *Correct Statement of the Loss of the Earl of Abergavenny, East Indiaman, John Wordsworth, Commander, Which was Driven Furiously on the Rocks off the Bill of Portland, February 5 1805* (Anon.)

——, *An Authentic Narrative of the Loss of the Earl of Abergavenny, East Indiaman, Captain John Wordsworth, Off Portland,* by a Gentleman of the East-India House [Wordsworth's 'right' pamphlet].

ALLSOP, THOMAS, (ANON.) *Letters, Conversations and Recollections of S. T. Coleridge* (2 vols., 1836).

BARROW, JOHN, *Travels in China* (1804).

BARTRAM, WILLIAM, *Travels Through North and South Carolina,* 2nd edn. (1794).

BUDWORTH, JOSEPH, *A Fortnight's Ramble to the Lakes in Westmoreland, Lancashire, and Cumberland* (1792).

CARLYLE, THOMAS, *Reminiscences,* ed. James Anthony Froude (1881).

CLARKE, JAMES, *A Survey of the Lakes of Cumberland, Westmorland and Lancashire* (1787).

COLERIDGE, SARA, *Memoir and Letters,* ed. Sara Coleridge Jr. (2 vols., 1873).

COTTLE, JOSEPH, *Early Recollections; Chiefly Relating to the late Samuel Taylor Coleridge* (2 vols., 1837).

COXE, WILLIAM, *Lettres de M. William Coxe à M. W. Melmoth, sur l'état politique, civil, et naturel de la Suisse; traduite de L'Anglois* [by Raymond de Carbonnières], 2nd edn. (2 vols., Paris, 1782); the edition owned by Wordsworth.

FARINGTON, JOSEPH R. A., *Diary,* ed. Kenneth Garlick and Angus Macintyre (New Haven, Conn., 1978–).

FIELD, BARRON, *Memoirs of Wordsworth,* ed. Geoffrey Little (Sydney, 1975).

GILLMAN, JAMES, *The Life of Samuel Taylor Coleridge* (1838).

GILPIN, WILLIAM, *Observations on the River Wye* (1782).

——, *Observations, relative chiefly to Picturesque Beauty, made in the year 1772, in several parts of England; particularly the Mountains and Lakes of Cumberland and Westmoreland* (2 vols., 1786).

——, *Three Essays: on Picturesque Beauty; on Picturesque Travel; and on Sketching Landscape* (1792).

HAYDON, BENJAMIN ROBERT, *Diary,* ed. Willard Bissell Pope (2 vols., Cambridge, Mass., 1960).

HAYLEY, WILLIAM, *The Life and Posthumous Writings of William Cowper* (Chichester, 1803).

HUTCHINSON, W., *The History and Antiquities of Cumberland* (2 vols., 1794).

NICHOLS, REVD WILLIAM LUKE, *The Quantocks and their Associations* (1891).

NICHOLSON, JOSEPH AND BURN, RICHARD, *The History and Antiquities of the Counties of Westmorland and Cumberland* (2 vols., 1777).

PAUL, C. KEGAN, *William Godwin: His Friends and Contemporaries* (2 vols., 1876).

PENNANT, THOMAS, *Tour of Scotland in 1772* (Chester, 1774).

Penrith, History of, Anon. (Penrith, 1858).

RAWNSLEY, HARDWICKE DRUMMOND, *Reminiscences of Wordsworth among the Peasantry of Westmoreland* (1882; reprinted 1968).

ROGERS, SAMUEL, *Reminiscences and Table Talk*, collected C. H. Powell (1903).

SANDFORD, MRS HENRY, *Thomas Poole and His Friends* (2 vols., 1888).

SOTHEBY, W. *A Tour through Parts of Wales: Sonnets, Odes and other Poems* (1794).

STODDART, JOHN, *Remarks on Local Scenery and Manners in Scotland* (2 vols., 1801).

TAYLOR, HENRY, *Notes from Books, in Four Essays* (1849).

——, *Autobiography* (2 vols., 1885).

TICKNOR, GEORGE, *Life, Letters and Journals* (2 vols., Boston, 1876).

WEST, THOMAS (ANON.), *The Antiquities of Furness* (1774).

——, *Guide to the Lakes*, 3rd edn. revised and enlarged (1784).

WILKINSON, JOSEPH, *Select Views in Cumberland, Westmoreland, and Lancashire* (1810); contains first version of Wordsworth's *Guide to the Lakes*.

WILKINSON, THOMAS, *Tours to the British Mountains* (1824).

WILSON, JOHN, *The Recreations of Christopher North* (3 vols., Edinburgh and London, 1842).

WORDSWORTH, CHRISTOPHER, *Memoirs of William Wordsworth* (2 vols., 1851).

ii Modern Studies

BARKER, FELIX AND JACKSON, PETER, *Two Thousand Years of London* (1974).

COLLINGWOOD, W. G., *Lake District History* (Kendal, 1925).

FERGUSON, R. S., *A History of Cumberland* (1890).

——, *A History of Westmorland* (1894).

GEORGE, M. DOROTHY, *London Life in the Eighteenth Century* (1925; Peregrine Books, 1965).

HOWE, H. W., *Greta Hall*, revised Robert Woof (Stoke Ferry, Norfolk, 1977).

JAY, EILEEN, *Wordsworth at Colthouse* (Kendal, 1970).

RUDÉ, GEORGE, *Hanoverian London, 1714–1808* (1971).

THOMPSON, T. W., *Wordsworth's Hawkshead*, ed. Robert Woof (Oxford, 1970).

WILDI, MAX, 'Wordsworth and the Simplon Pass', *Swiss Studies in English*, lxxxviii (1976), 176–208.

5. LITERARY CRITICISM AND SCHOLARSHIP

(*a*) *General Studies and Collections*

ABRAMS, M. H., *The Mirror and the Lamp: Romantic Literary Theory and the Critical Tradition* (New York, 1953).

——, *Natural Supernaturalism: Tradition and Revolution in Romantic Literature* (New York, 1971).

——, ed., *English Romantic Poets: Modern Essays in Criticism* (New York, 1960); 2nd edn. enlarged (London, Oxford, New York, 1975).

——, ed., *Wordsworth: A Collection of Critical Essays, Twentieth Century Critical Views* (Englewood Cliffs, N. J., 1972).

APPLEYARD, J. A., *Coleridge's Philosophy of Literature* (Cambridge, Mass., 1965).

BATE, WALTER JACKSON, *Coleridge* (1968).

——, *The Burden of the Past and the English Poet* (Toronto, 1971).

BATESON, F. W., *Wordsworth: A Reinterpretation* (1954).

BEER, JOHN, *Wordsworth and the Human Heart* (1978).

——, *Wordsworth in Time* (London and Boston, 1979).

BLOOM, HAROLD, *The Visionary Company* (1961).

——, ed., *Romanticism and Consciousness: Essays in Criticism* (New York, 1960).

——, *The Anxiety of Influence* (New York, 1973).

——, *A Map of Misreading* (New York, 1975).

——, *Poetry and Repression* (1976).

BOSTETTER, EDWARD, *The Romantic Ventriloquists* (Seattle, 1963).

BRADLEY, A. C., *Oxford Lectures on Poetry (1909).*

BRISMAN, LESLIE, *Milton's Poetry of Choice and Its Romantic Heirs* (Ithaca, N. Y., and London, 1973).

——, *Romantic Origins* (Ithaca, N. Y., 1978).

BYRD, MAX, *London Transformed: Images of the City in the Eighteenth Century* (New Haven, Conn., and London, 1978).

CLARKE, C. C., *Romantic Paradox: An Essay on the Poetry of Wordsworth* (1787).

CORNWELL, JOHN, *Coleridge, Poet and Revolutionary 1772–1804* (1973).

DANBY, JOHN F., *The Simple Wordsworth: Studies in the Poems, 1797–1807* (1960).

Dekker, George, *Coleridge and the Literature of Sensibility* (1978).

De Selincourt, Ernest, *Dorothy Wordsworth: A Biography* (Oxford, 1933).

Ferry, David, *The Limits of Mortality* (Middletown, Conn., 1959).

Fruman, Norman, *Coleridge, The Damaged Archangel* (New York, London, 1971).

Frye, Northrop, ed., *Romanticism Reconsidered* (New York, 1963).

Grob, Alan, *The Philosophic Mind: A Study of Wordsworth's Poetry and Thought 1795–1805* (Columbus, Ohio, 1973).

Hartman, Geoffrey H., *The Unmediated Vision: An Interpretation of Wordsworth, Hopkins, Rilke, and Valéry* (New Haven, Conn., 1954).

——, *Wordsworth's Poetry 1787–1814* (New Haven, Conn., and London, 1964).

——, *Beyond Formalism: Literary Essays, 1958–1970* (New Haven, Conn., and London, 1970).

——, ed., *New Perspectives on Coleridge and Wordsworth: Selected Papers from the English Institute* (New York, 1972).

——, *The Fate of Reading and Other Essays* (Chicago and London, 1975).

Harvey, W. J. and Gravil, Richard, eds., *Wordsworth, 'The Prelude': A Casebook* (1972).

Havens, Raymond Dexter, *The Mind of a Poet: A Study of Wordsworth's Thought* (2 vols., Baltimore, 1941).

Hayden, John O., ed., *Romantic Bards and British Reviewers: A Selected Edition of the Contemporary Reviews* (1971).

——, *The Romantic Reviewers, 1802–1824* (1969).

Hilles, Frederick W. and Bloom, Harold, eds., *From Sensibility to Romanticism* (New York, 1965).

Hirsch, E. D., Jr., *Wordsworth and Schelling: A Typological Study of Romanticism* (New Haven, Conn., 1960).

Jack, Ian, *English Literature, 1815–1832* (Oxford, 1967).

Jackson, J. R. de J., ed., *Coleridge: The Critical Heritage* (1970).

Jones, Alun R. and Tydeman, William, eds., *Wordsworth, 'Lyrical Ballads': A Casebook* (1972).

Jones, John, *The Egotistical Sublime: A History of Wordsworth's Imagination* (London, 1954).

King, Alec, *Wordsworth and the Artist's Vision* (1966).

Leavis, F. R., *Revaluation: Tradition and Development in English Poetry* (1936).

McFarland, Thomas, *Coleridge and the Pantheist Tradition* (Oxford, 1969).

McMaster, Graham, ed., *William Wordsworth: A Critical Anthology*, Penguin Critical Anthologies (1972).

Moorman, Mary, *William Wordsworth: A Biography; The Early Years* (Oxford, 1957), *The Later Years* (Oxford, 1967).

ONORATO, RICHARD J., *The Character of the Poet: Wordsworth in 'The Prelude'* (Princeton, 1971).

PARKER, REEVE, *Coleridge's Meditative Art* (Ithaca, N. Y., and London, 1975).

PATER, WALTER, *Appreciations, With an Essay on Style* (London and New York, 1889).

PERKINS, DAVID, *The Quest for Permanence: The Symbolism of Wordsworth, Shelley and Keats* (Cambridge, Mass., 1959).

——, *Wordsworth and the Poetry of Sincerity* (Cambridge, Mass., and London, 1964).

PIPER, H. W., *The Active Universe* (London, 1962).

PRICKETT, STEPHEN *Coleridge and Wordsworth: The Poetry of Growth* (Cambridge, 1971).

RENWICK, W. L., *English Literature 1789–1815* (Oxford, 1963).

RICHARDS, I. A., *Coleridge on Imagination* (London, 1934).

SHEATS, PAUL, *The Making of Wordsworth's Poetry, 1785–1798* (Cambridge, Mass., 1973).

SHERRY, CHARLES, *Wordsworth's Poetry of the Imagination* (Oxford, 1980).

SULTANA, DONALD, *Samuel Taylor Coleridge in Malta and Italy* (New York, 1969).

THOMSON, A. W., ED., *Wordsworth's Mind and Art: Essays Old and New* (Edinburgh, 1969).

TODD, F. M., *Politics and the Poet, a Study of Wordsworth* (1957).

WALSH, WILLIAM, *Coleridge: The Work and the Relevance* (1967).

WARNOCK, MARY, *Imagination* (Oxford, 1976).

WESLING, DONALD, *Wordsworth and The Adequacy of Landscape* (1970).

WILLEY, BASIL, *Samuel Taylor Coleridge* (London, 1972).

WLECKE, ALBERT O., *Wordsworth and the Sublime* (Berkeley, Los Angeles, London, 1973).

WORDSWORTH, JONATHAN, ED., *Bicentenary Wordsworth Studies* (Ithaca, N. Y., and London, 1970).

YARLOTT, GEOFFREY, *Coleridge and the Abyssinian Maid* (1967).

(b) *More Detailed Critical and Scholarly Work*

ABRAMS, M. H., 'The Correspondent Breeze: A Romantic Metaphor', *English Romantic Poets*, ed. M. H. Abrams, 2nd edn. (London, Oxford, New York, 1975), 37–54.

——, 'Structure and Style in the Greater Romantic Lyric', *From Sensibility to Romanticism*, ed. Frederick W. Hilles and Harold Bloom (New York, 1965), 527–60.

BATE. W. JACKSON, 'Coleridge on the Function of Art', *Perspectives of Criticism*, xx (Cambridge, Mass., 1950), 125–59.

BERNHARDT-KABISH, ERNEST, 'Wordsworth: The Monumental Poet', *PQ* xliv, no. 4 (Oct. 1965), 503–18.

BISHOP, JONATHAN, 'Wordsworth and the "Spots of Time" ', reprinted in *Wordsworth, 'The Prelude': A Casebook*, ed. W. J. Harvey and Richard Gravil (London, 1972), 134–54.

BUTLER, JAMES A., 'Wordsworth's *Tuft of Primroses:* "An Unrelenting Doom" ', *SIR* xiv (summer 1975), 237–48.

——, 'Wordsworth, Cottle, and the *Lyrical Ballads*: Five Letters, 1797–1800', *JEGP* lxxv, nos. 1, 2 (Jan.–Apr. 1976), 139–53.

CURTIS, JARED R., *Wordsworth's Experiments with Tradition: The Lyric Poems of 1802* (Ithaca, N. Y., and London, 1971).

DAVIES, HUGH SYKES, 'Another New Poem by Wordsworth', *EC* xv (1965), 135–61.

ELTON, F. HENLEY AND STAM, DAVID H., *Wordsworthian Criticism, 1945–1964: An Annotated Bibliography*, revised edn. (New York, 1965).

ERDMAN, DAVID V., 'Coleridge, Wordsworth, and the Wedgwood Fund', *BNYPL* lx (Sept.–Oct. 1956), 425–43, 487–507.

EVEREST, KELVIN, *Coleridge's Secret Ministry: The Context of the Conversation Poems* (1979).

FERGUSON, FRANCES, *Wordsworth: Language as Counter-Spirit* (New Haven, Conn., and London, 1977).

FINCH, JOHN ALBAN, 'Wordsworth's Two-Handed Engine' and 'On the Dating of *Home at Grasmere*: A New Approach', *Bicentenary Wordsworth Studies*, ed. Jonathan Wordsworth (Ithaca, N. Y., 1970), 1–13 and 14–28.

GILL, STEPHEN., 'Wordsworth's "Never Failing Principle of Joy" ', *ELH* xxxiv, no. 2 (June 1967), 208–24.

——, 'Wordsworth's Breeches Pocket: Attitudes to the Didactic Poet', *EC* xix, no. 4 (Oct. 1969), 385–400.

——, 'The Original *Salisbury Plain* ', *Bicentenary Wordsworth Studies*, ed. Jonathan Wordsworth (Ithaca, N. Y., 1970), 142–79.

HAVEN, RICHARD AND JOSEPHINE, AND ADAMS, MAURIANNE, *Samuel Taylor Coleridge: An Annotated Bibliography of Criticism and Scholarship, 1793–1899* (Boston and London, 1976).

HEALEY, GEORGE HARRIS, *The Cornell Wordsworth Collection: A Catalogue of Books and Manuscripts* (Ithaca, N. Y., 1957).

HEATH, WILLIAM, *Wordsworth and Coleridge: A Study of Their Literary Relations in 1801–1802* (Oxford, 1970).

JACOBUS, MARY, 'Southey's Debt to *Lyrical Ballads*', *RES* New Series xxii, no. 85 (1971), 20–36.

——, *Tradition and Experiment in Wordsworth's Lyrical Ballads, 1798* (Oxford, 1976).

——, 'Wordsworth and the Language of the Dream', *ELH* xlvi (1979), 618–44.

JOHNSTON, KENNETH, 'The Idiom of Vision', *New Perspectives on Coleridge and Wordsworth*, ed. Geoffrey H. Hartman (New York and London, 1972), 1–39.

LAND, STEPHEN K., 'The Silent Poet: An Aspect of Wordsworth's Semantic Theory', *UTQ* xlii, no. 2 (winter 1973), 157–69.

LANGBAUM, ROBERT, 'The Evolution of Soul in Wordsworth's Poetry', reprinted in *Wordsworth, 'The Prelude': A Casebook*, ed. W. J. Harvey and Richard Gravil (London, 1972), 218–35.

LEGOUIS, EMILE, *William Wordsworth and Annette Vallon* (London and Toronto, 1922).

LINDENBERGER, HERBERT, *On Wordsworth's 'Prelude'* (Princeton, 1963).

LOGAN, JAMES VENABLE, *Wordsworthian Criticism: A Guide and Bibliography* (Columbus, Ohio, 1947).

MCFARLAND, THOMAS, 'The Origin and Significance of Coleridge's Theory of the Secondary Imagination', *New Perspectives on Coleridge and Wordsworth*, ed. Geoffrey H. Hartman (New York and London, 1972), 195–246.

MACGILLIVRAY, J. R., 'The Three Forms of *The Prelude*, 1798–1805', reprinted in *Wordsworth, 'The Prelude': A Casebook*, ed. W. J. Harvey and Richard Gravil (1972), 99–115.

MILLER, J. HILLIS, 'The Still Heart: Poetic Form in Wordsworth; *NLH* ii, no. 2 (winter 1971), 297–310.

——, 'The Stone and the Shell: The Problem of Poetic Form in Wordsworth's Dream of the Arab', *Mouvements premiers: Études critiques offertes à Georges Poulet* (Paris, 1972), 125–47.

NEWLYN, LUCY, '"In City Pent": Echo and Allusion in Wordsworth, Coleridge and Lamb, 1797–1801', *RES* New Series xxxii, no. 128 (Nov. 1981), 408–28.

OWEN, W. J. B., 'Tipu's Tiger', *NQ* ccxv (1970), 379–80.

——, 'Annotating Wordsworth', *Editing Texts of the Romantic Period*, ed. John D. Baird (Toronto, 1972), 49–71.

PARRISH, STEPHEN MAXFIELD, *The Art of the 'Lyrical Ballads'* (Cambridge, Mass., 1973).

PIRIE, DAVID, 'A Letter to [Asra]', *Bicentenary Wordsworth Studies*, ed. Jonathan Wordsworth (Ithaca, N. Y., 1970), 294–339.

REED, MARK L., 'Wordsworth, Coleridge, and the "Plan" of the *Lyrical Ballads*', *UTQ* xxxiv, no. 3 (Apr. 1965), 238–53.

——, *Wordsworth: The Chronology of the Early Years, 1770–1799* (Cambridge, Mass., 1967)'

——, 'More on the 'Wordsworth Poem' [authentication of *The Barberry-Tree*], *College English* xxviii, no. 1 (Oct. 1967), 60–1.

——, 'The Speaker of *The Prelude*', *Bicentenary Wordsworth Studies*, ed. Jonathan Wordsworth (Ithaca, N. Y., 1970), 276–93.

——, *Wordsworth: The Chronology of the Middle Years, 1800–1815* (Cambridge, Mass., 1975).

RICKS, CHRISTOPHER, 'Wordsworth: "A Pure Organic Pleasure from the Lines"', *EC* xxi, no. 1 (Jan. 1971), 1–32.

SCHNEIDER, BEN ROSS, JR. *Wordsworth's Cambridge Education* (Cambridge, 1957).

SHEPHERD, RICHARD HERNE, *The Bibliography of Coleridge: Published and Privately Printed Writings in Verse and Prose*, Revised, Corrected, and Enlarged, by W. F. Prideaux (1900; reprinted 1970).

SMYSER, JANE WORTHINGTON Wordsworth's Dream of Poetry and Science', *PMLA* lxxi (1956), 269–75.

STAM, DAVID H., *Wordsworthian Criticism, 1964–1973: An Annotated Bibliography* (New York, 1974).

SWETNAM, FORD T., 'Satiric Voices in *The Prelude*', *Bicentenary Wordsworth Studies*, ed. Jonathan Wordsworth (Ithaca, N. Y., 1970), 92–110.

WHALLEY, GEORGE, *Coleridge and Sara Hutchinson and the Asra Poems* (1955).

WILLEY, BASIL, 'Coleridge on Imagination and Fancy', *Proceedings of the British Academy* xxxii (1946).

WOOF, ROBERT, 'Wordsworth's Poetry and Stewart's Newspapers: 1797–1803', *SIB* xv (1962), 149–89.

——, 'A Coleridge–Wordsworth Manuscript and "Sarah Hutchinson's Poets"' *SIB* xix (1966), 226–31.

——, 'John Stoddart, "Michael" and *Lyrical Ballads*', *Ariel* i, no. 2 (Apr. 1970), 7–22.

——, 'Wordsworth and Coleridge: Some Early Matters', *Bicentenary Wordsworth Studies*, ed. Jonathan Wordsworth (Ithaca, N. Y., 1970), 76–91.

WORDSWORTH, JONATHAN, 'The New Wordsworth Poem' [authentication of *The Barberry-Tree*], *College English* xxvii, no. 6 (Mar. 1967), 455–65.

——, *The Music of Humanity: A Critical Study of Wordsworth's 'Ruined Cottage'* (London and York, 1969).

——, and Gill, Stephen, 'The Two-Part *Prelude* of 1798–9', *JEGP* lxxii, no. 4 (Oct. 1973), 503–25.

——, 'Startling the Earthworms' [redating of *Adventures on Salisbury Plain*], *TLS*, 3 Dec. 1976, p. 1524.

——, 'The Five-Book *Prelude* of Early Spring 1804 *JEGP* lxxvi, no. 1 (Jan. 1977), 1–25.

——, 'On Man, on Nature, and on Human Life' [redating of *Home at Grasmere* and the Prospectus], *RES* New Series xxxi, no. 121 (Feb. 1980), 17–29.

——, 'That Wordsworth Epic', *WC* xi, no. 3 (winter 1980), 34–5.

Index